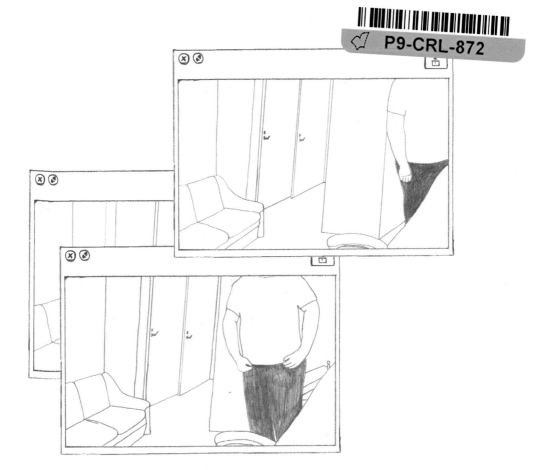

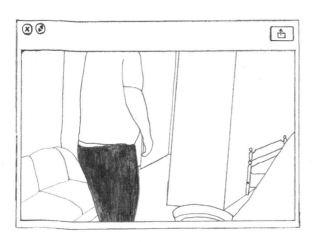

CYBERMAN

AN ON-SCREEN DOCUMENTARY

VERONIKA MUCHITSCH

FIRST PUBLISHED IN 2022 BY
MYRIAD EDITIONS
WWW.MYRIADEDITIONS.COM

MYRIAD EDITIONS
AN IMPRINT OF NEW INTERNATIONALIST PUBLICATIONS
THE OLD MUSIC HALL, 106-108 COWLEY RD,
OXFORD OX4 1JE

FIRST PRINTING
1 3 5 7 9 10 8 6 4 2

A CIP CATALOGUE RECORD FOR THIS BOOK
IS AVAILABLE FROM THE BRITISH LIBRARY

ISBN (PAPERBACK): 978-1-8383860-2-3
ISBN (EBOOK): 978-1-8383860-3-0

PRINTED IN POLAND
WWW.LFBOOKSERVICES.CO.UK

VERONIKA MUCHITSCH AKA LB JEFFERIES

CYBER MAN

AN ON-SCREEN DOCUMENTARY

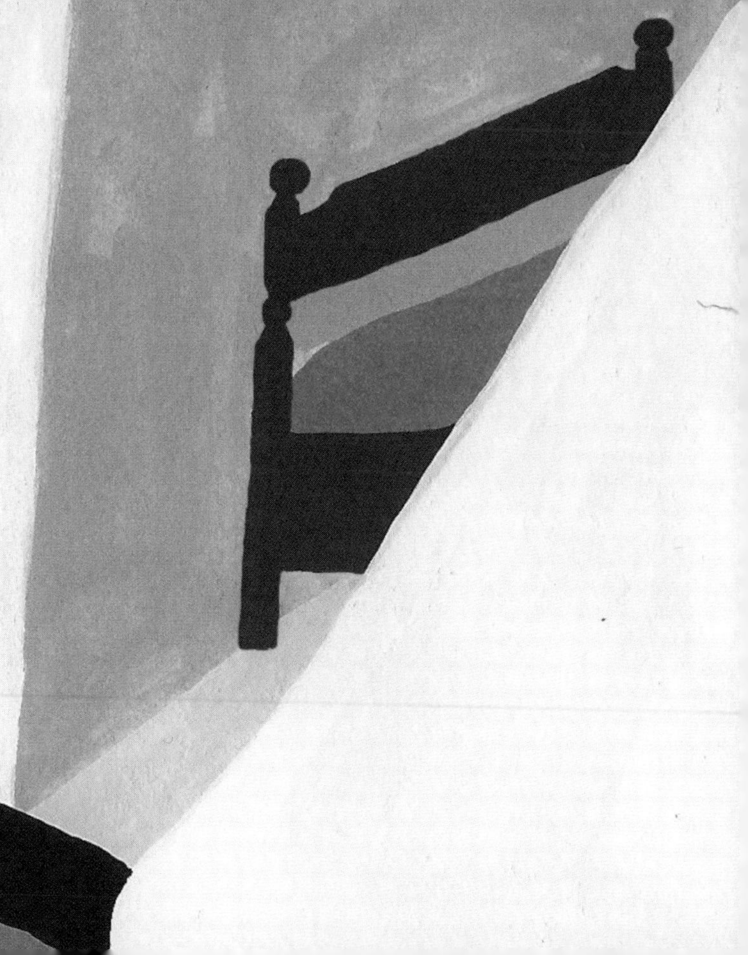

myriad

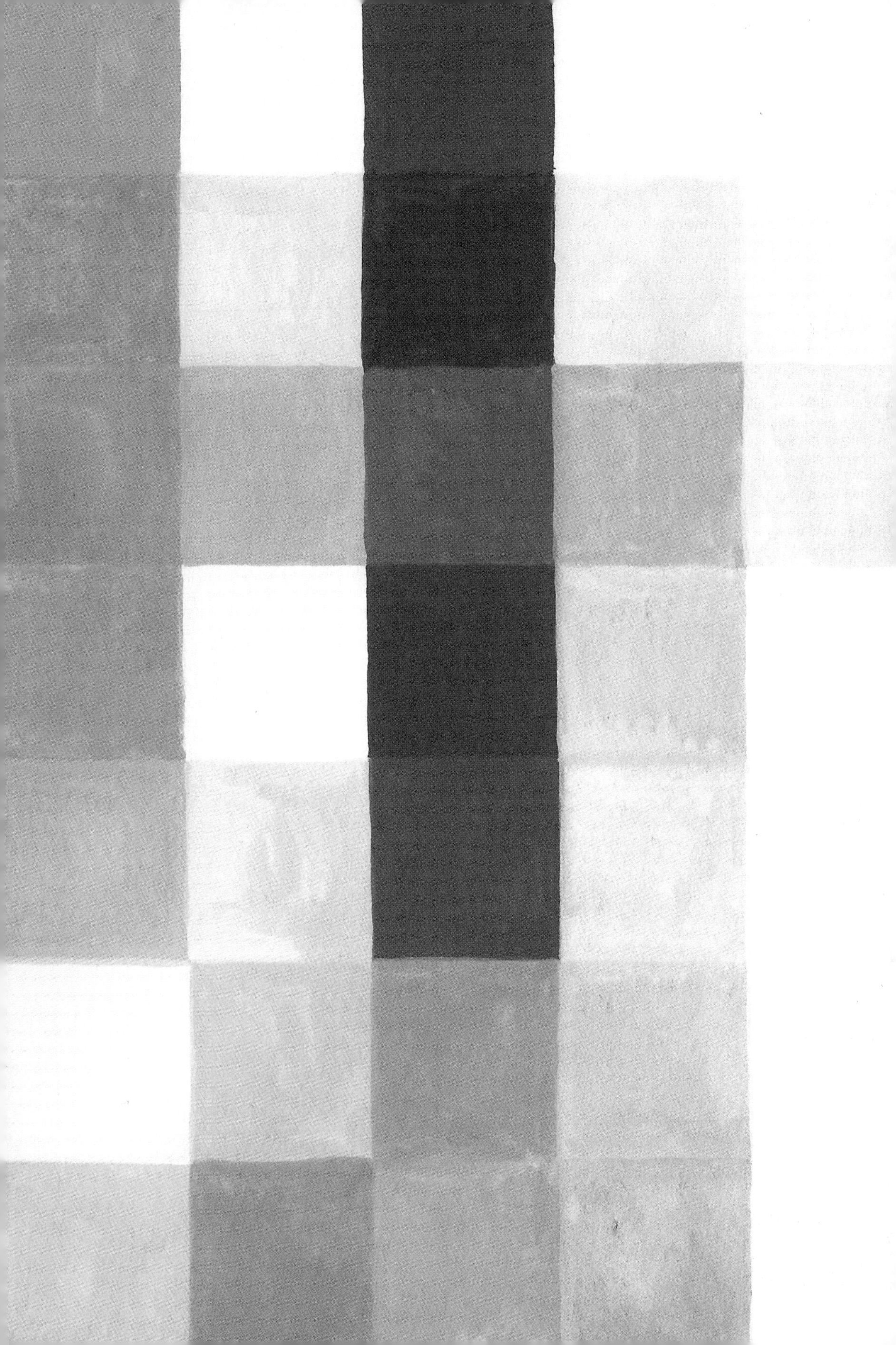

TO ARI, AND TO SOLITUDE

23.03.2016

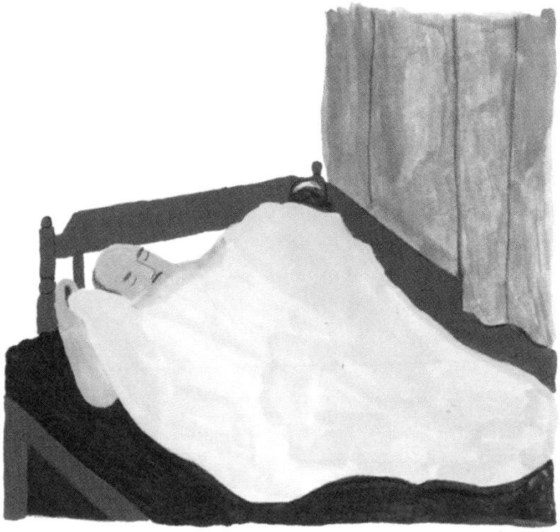

20:11

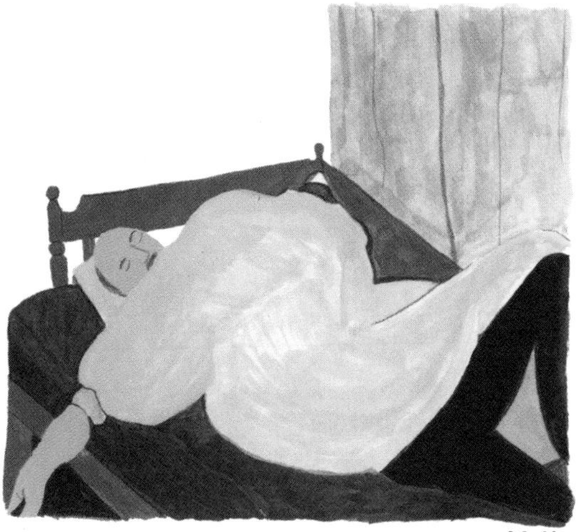

20:14

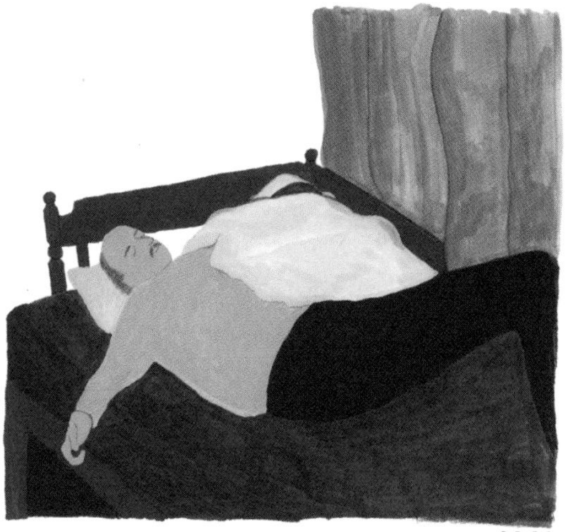

20:21

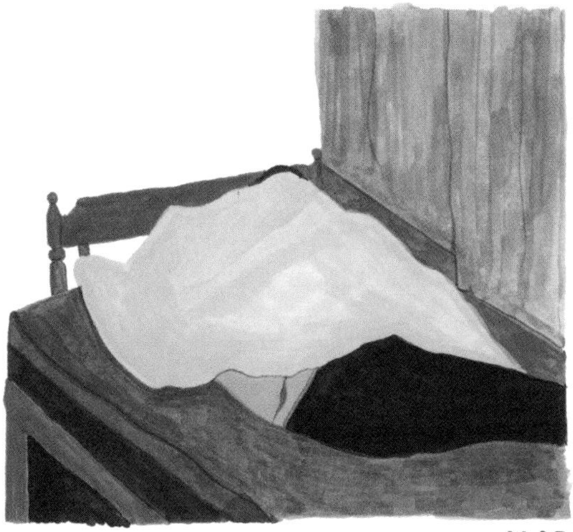

20:35

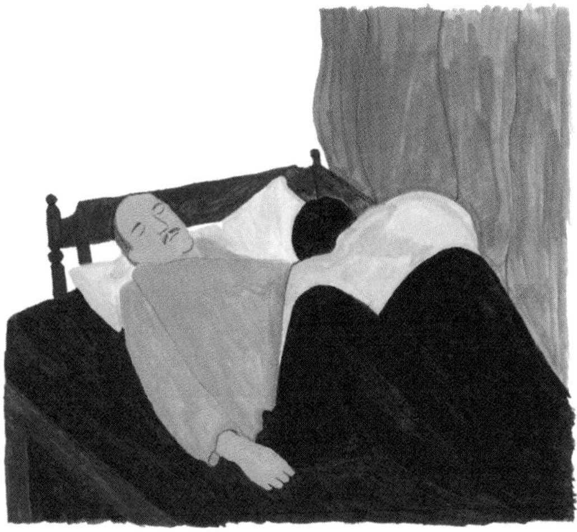

21:00

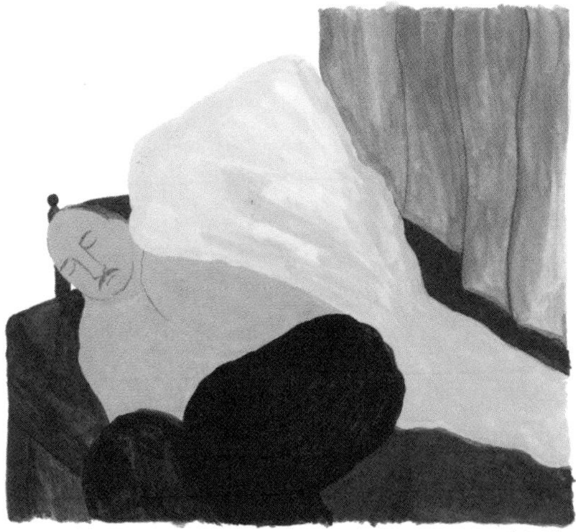

21:00

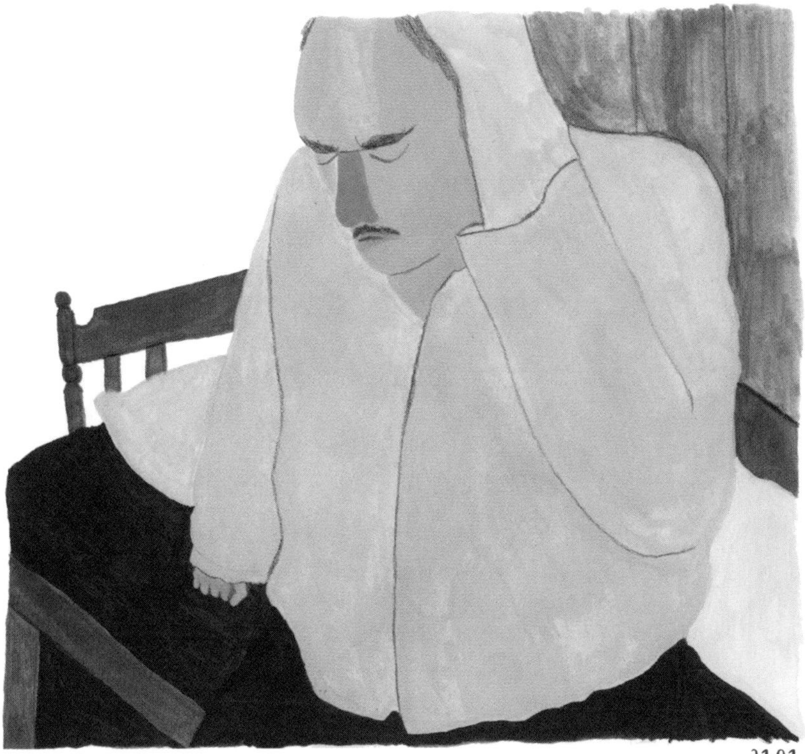

21:01

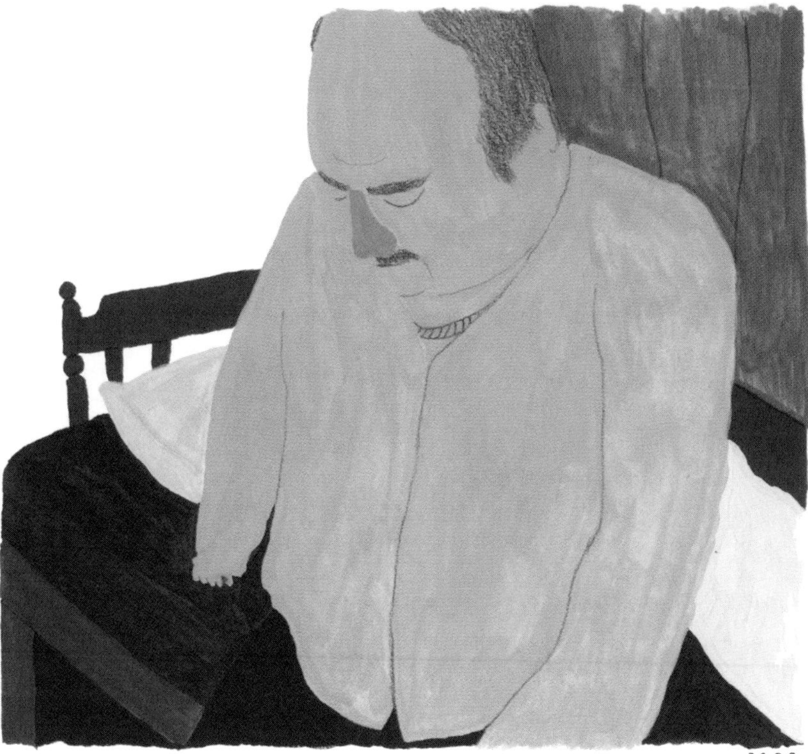

21:06

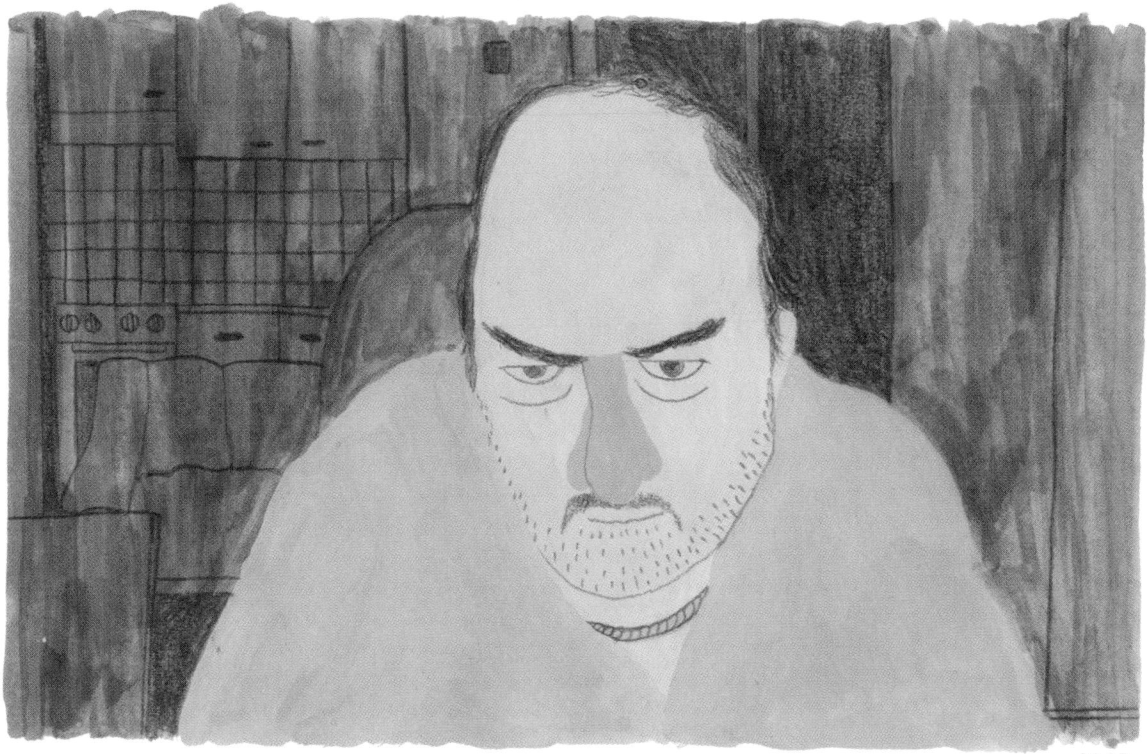

21:07

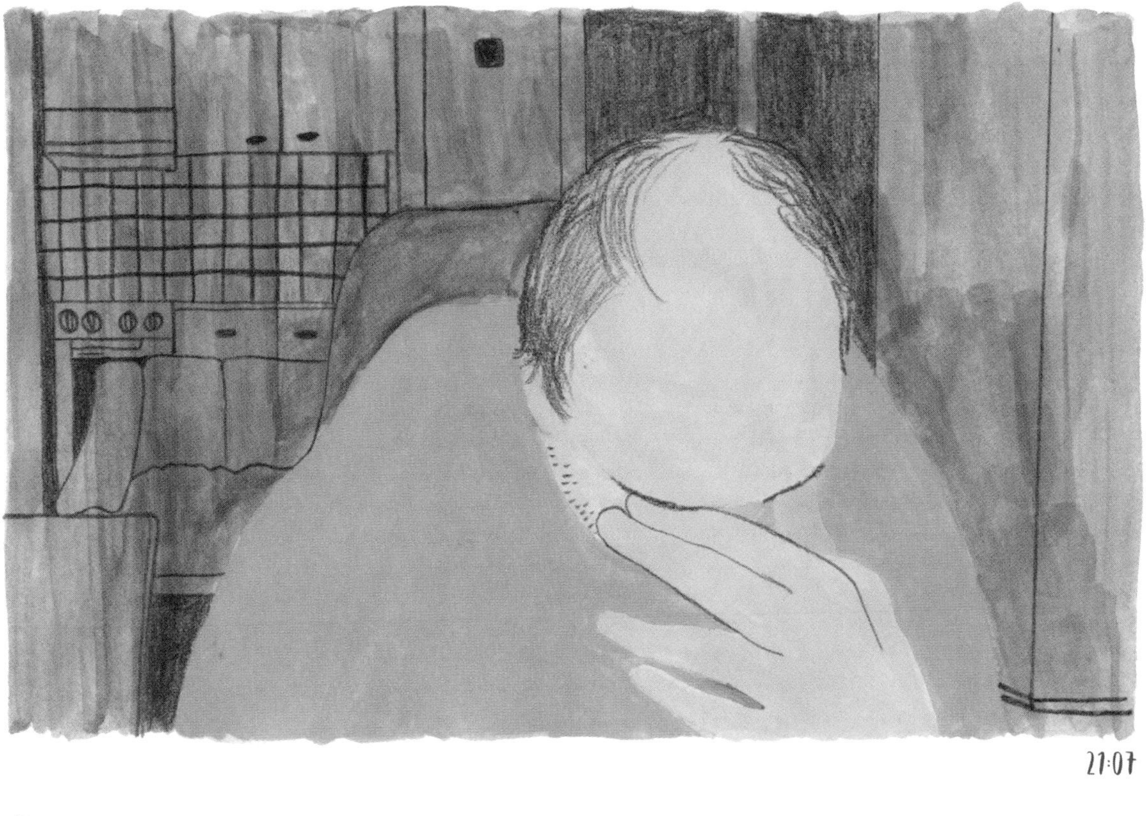

21:07

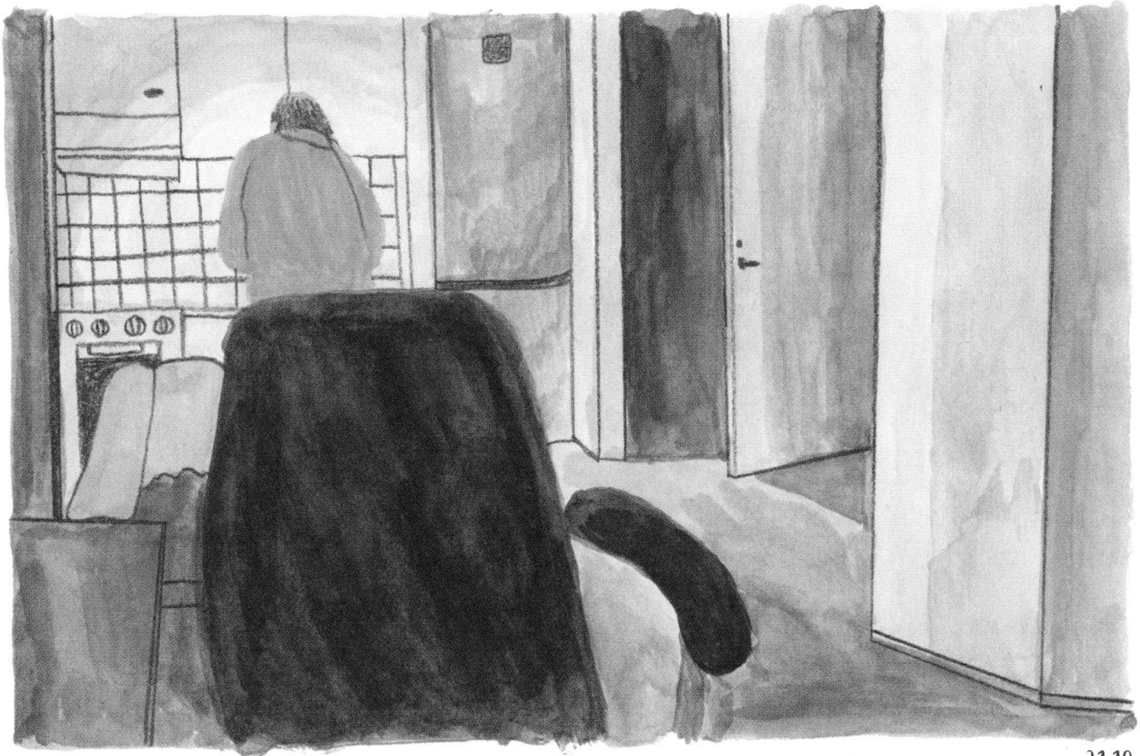

21:10

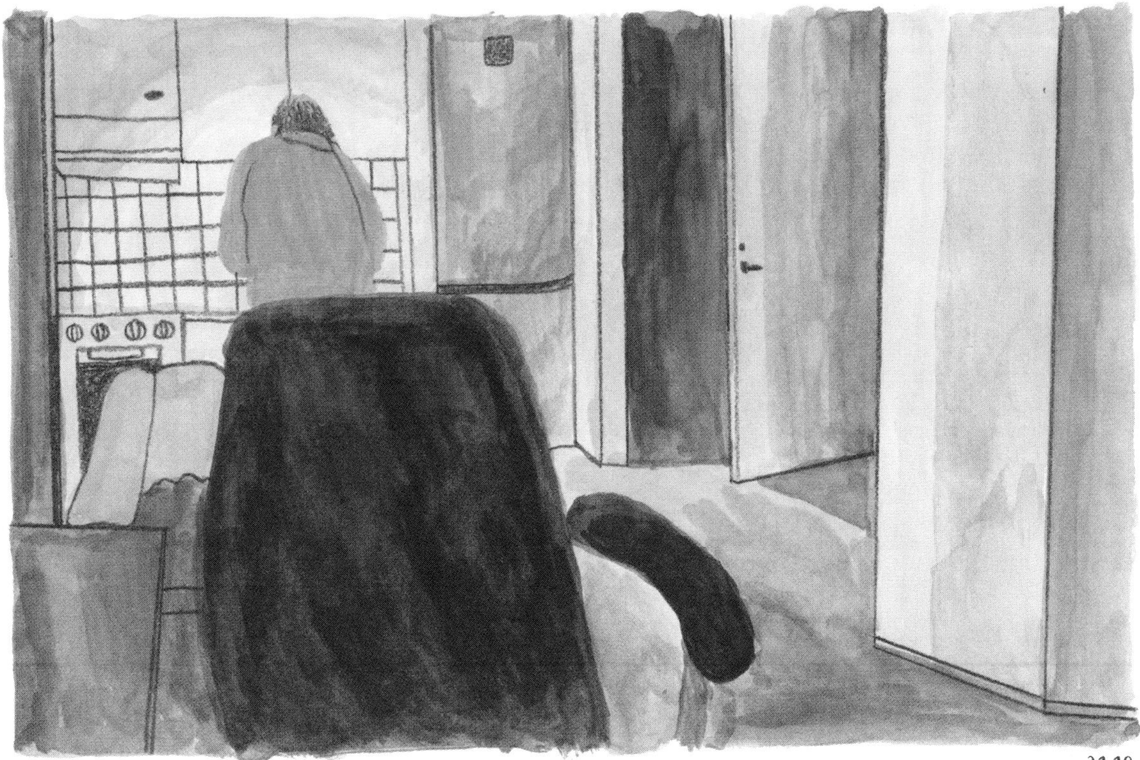

21:10

25.03.2016

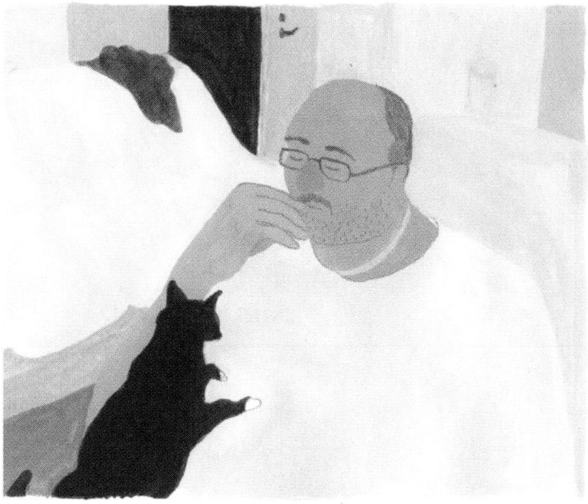

16:25

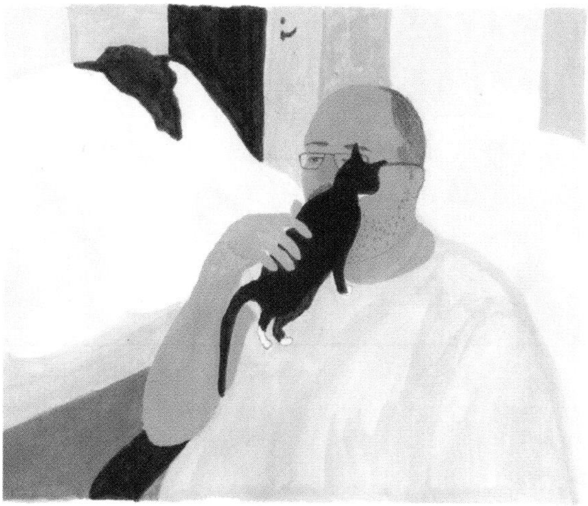

16:25

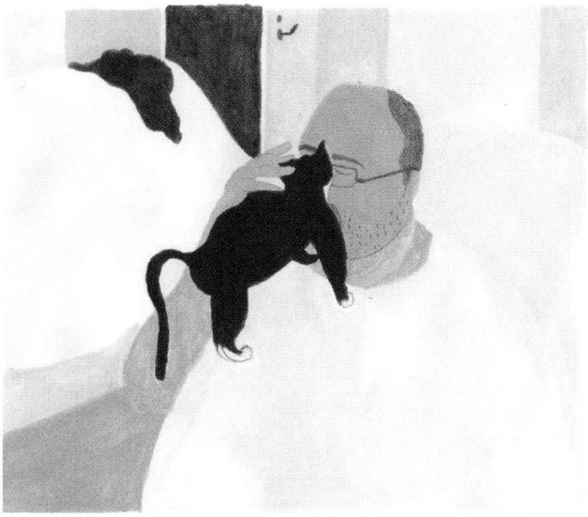

16:25

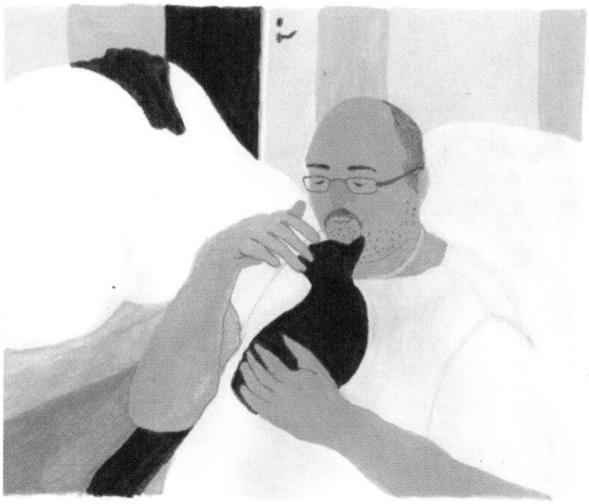

16:25

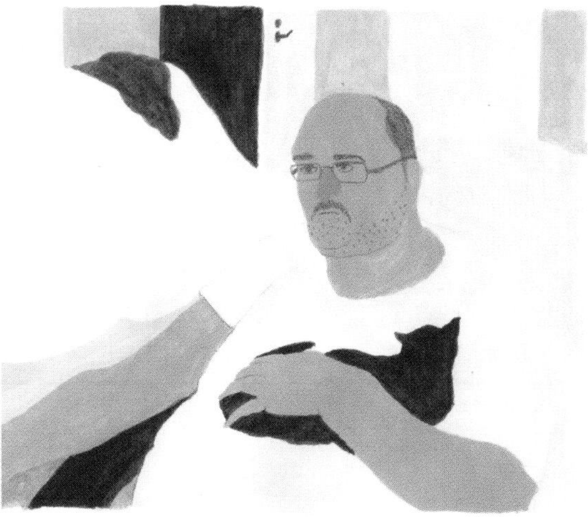

16:28

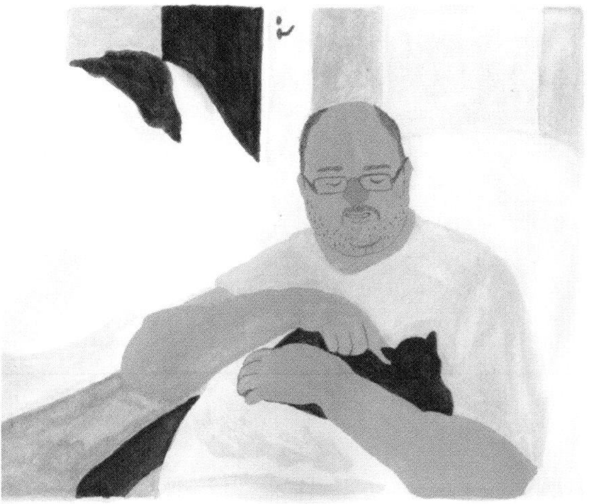

16:28

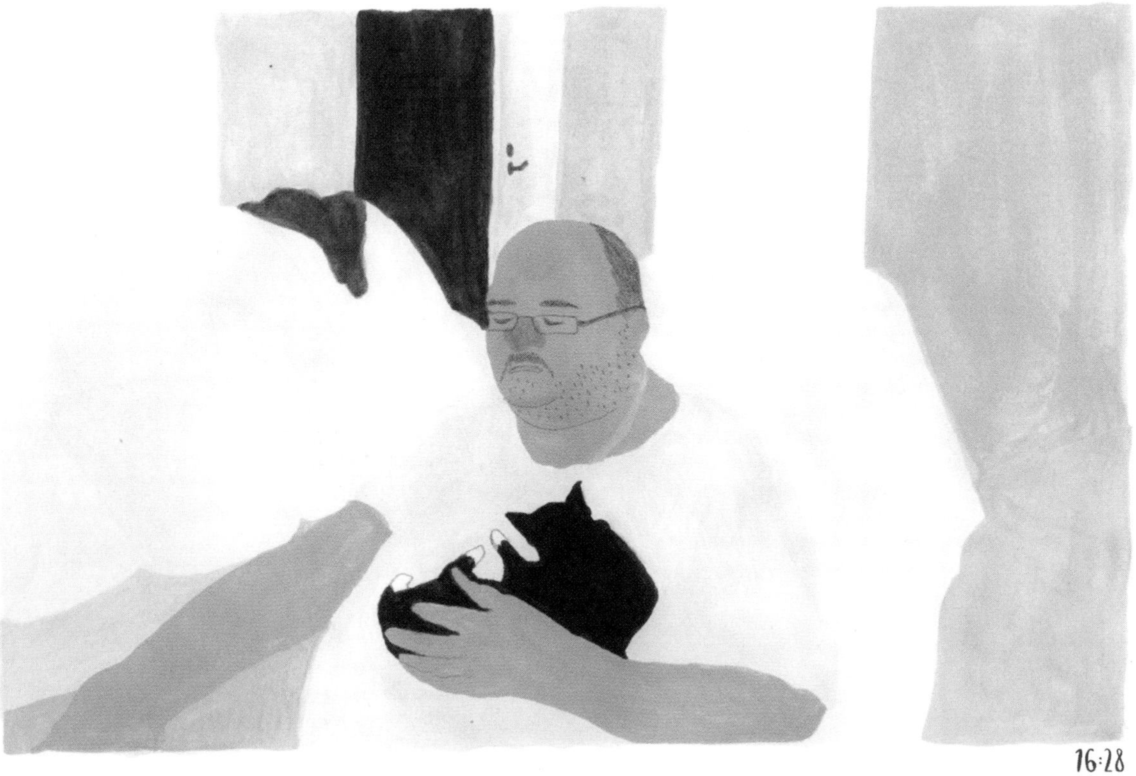

16:28

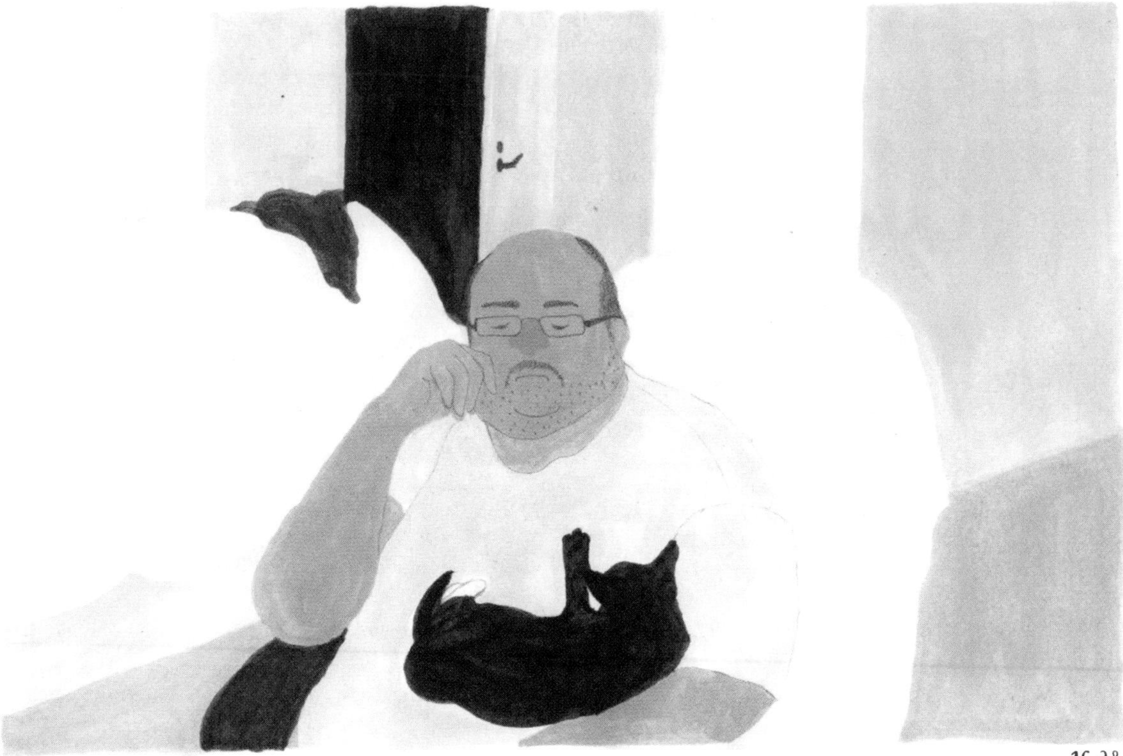

16:28

27.03.2016

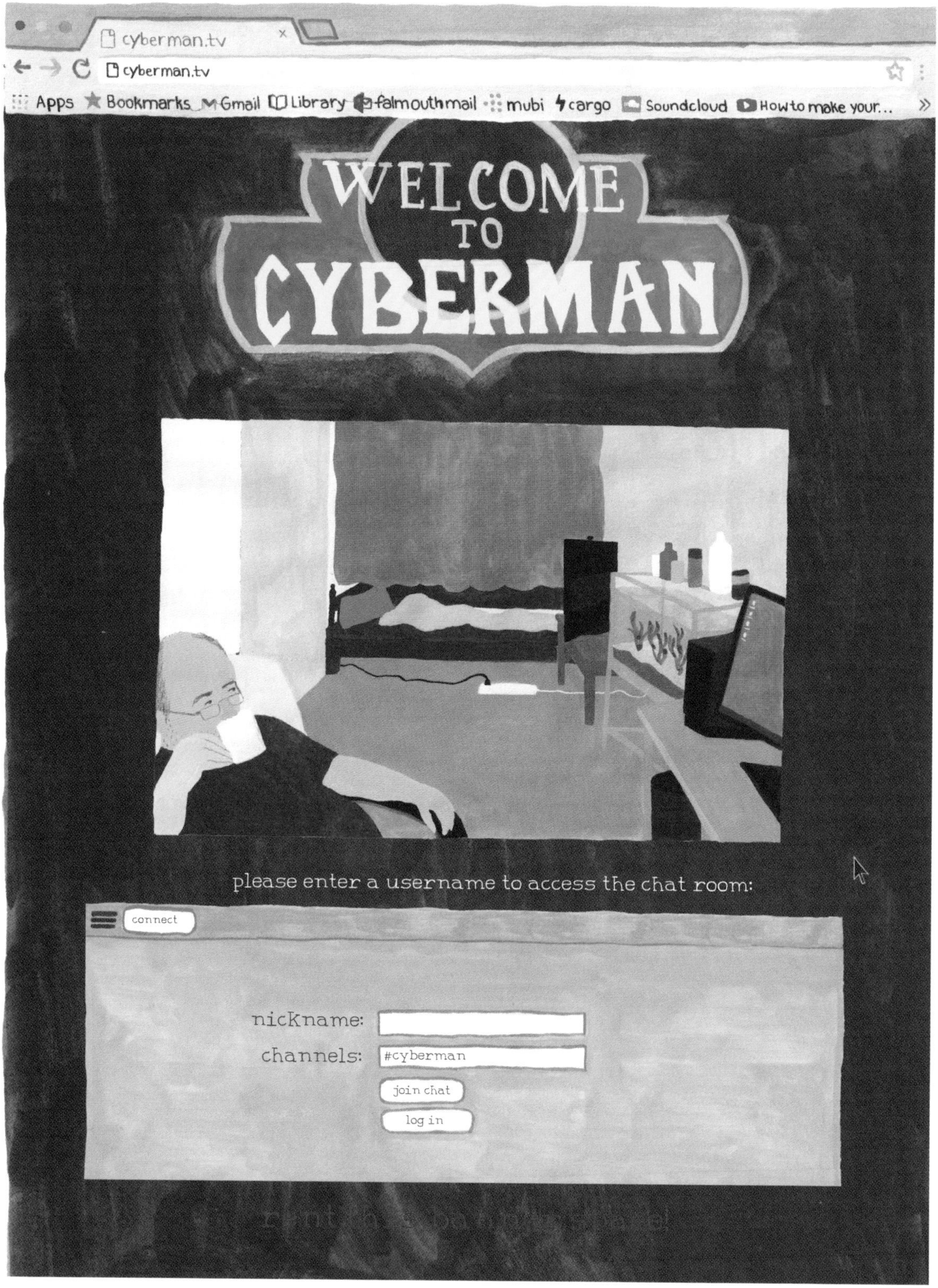

cyberman.tv
cyberman.tv
Apps
Bookmarks
Gmail
Library
falmouthmail
mubi
cargo
Soundcloud
How to make your...
WELCOME TO CYBERMAN
please enter a username to access the chat room:
connect
nickname:
channels:
#cyberman
join chat
log in

18:41

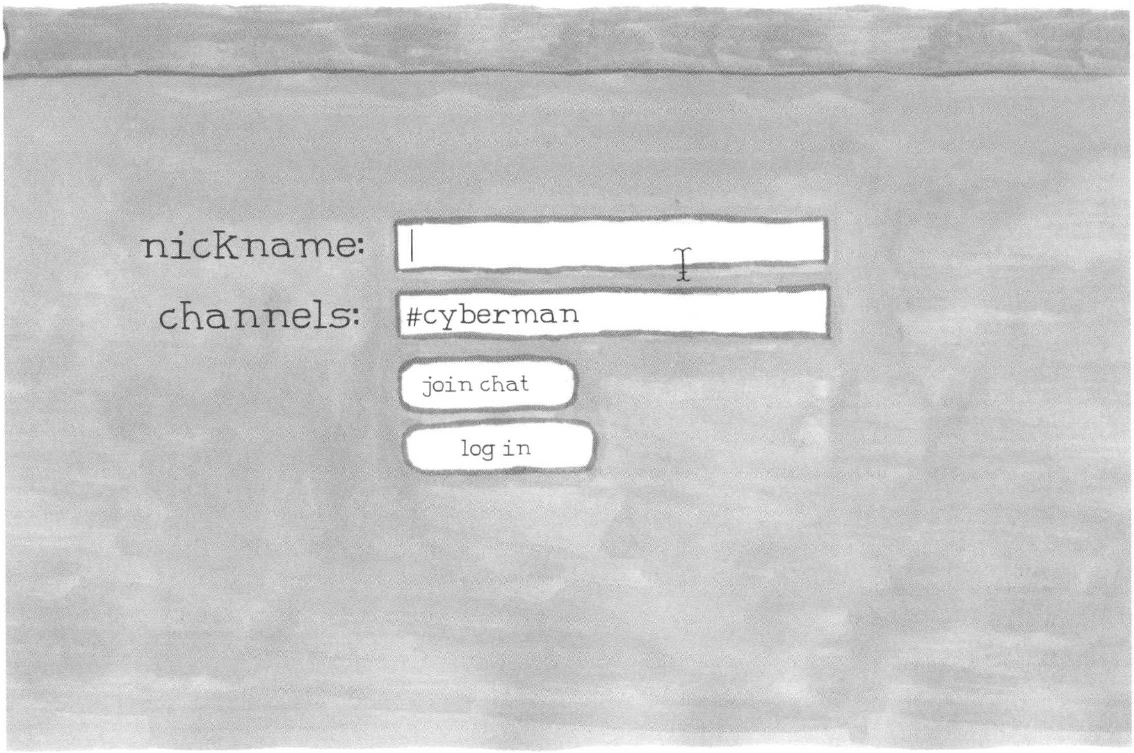
nickname:
channels:
#cyberman
join chat
log in

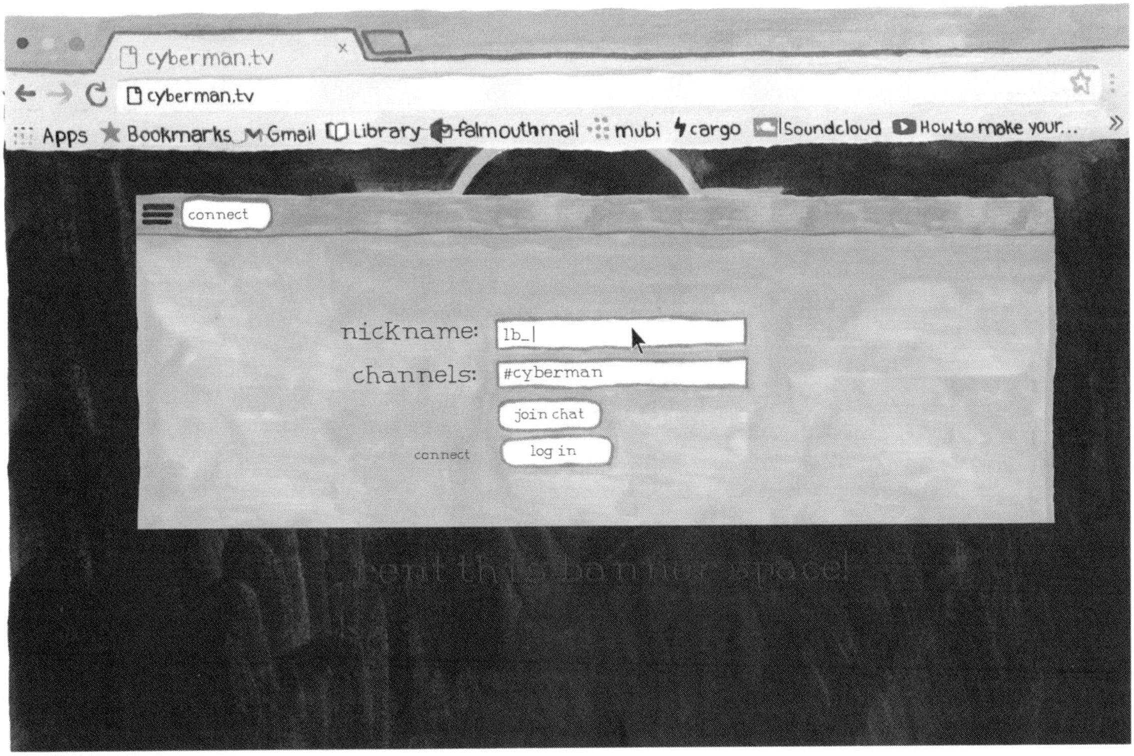
cyberman.tv
cyberman.tv
Apps
Bookmarks
Gmail
Library
falmouthmail
mubi
cargo
Soundcloud
How to make your...
connect
nickname:
lb_
channels:
#cyberman
join chat
connect
log in
rent this banner space!

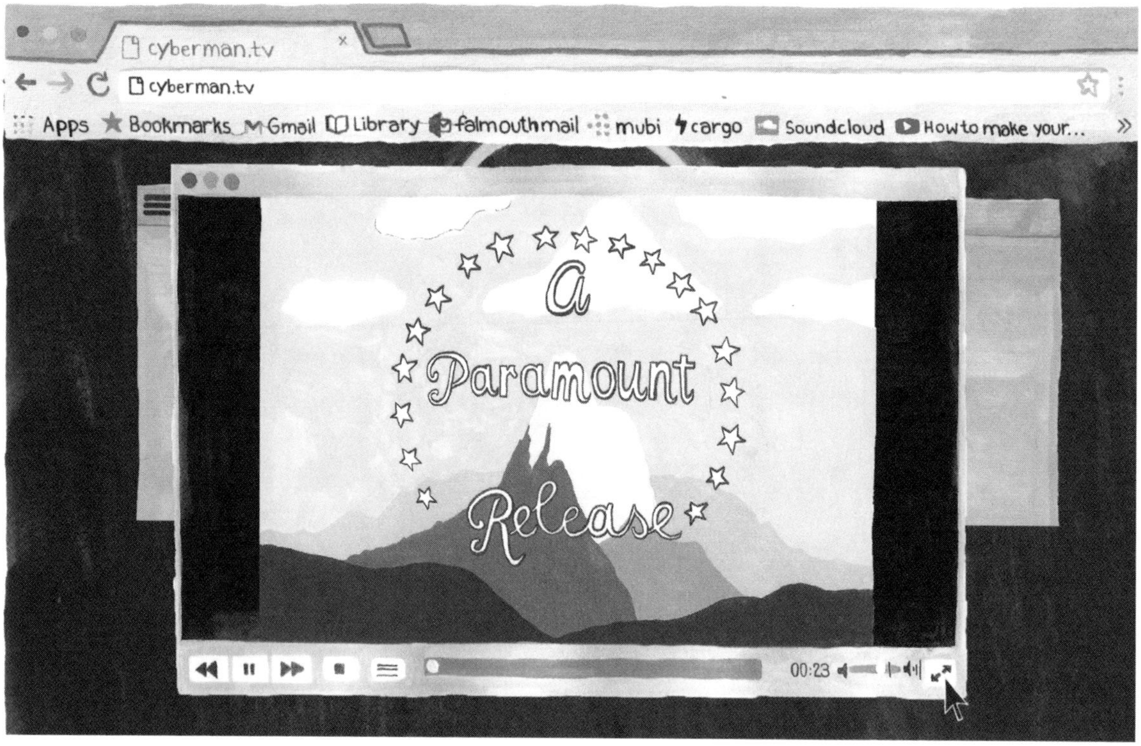
cyberman.tv
cyberman.tv
Apps
Bookmarks
Gmail
Library
falmouthmail
mubi
cargo
Soundcloud
How to make your...
a
Paramount
Release
00:23

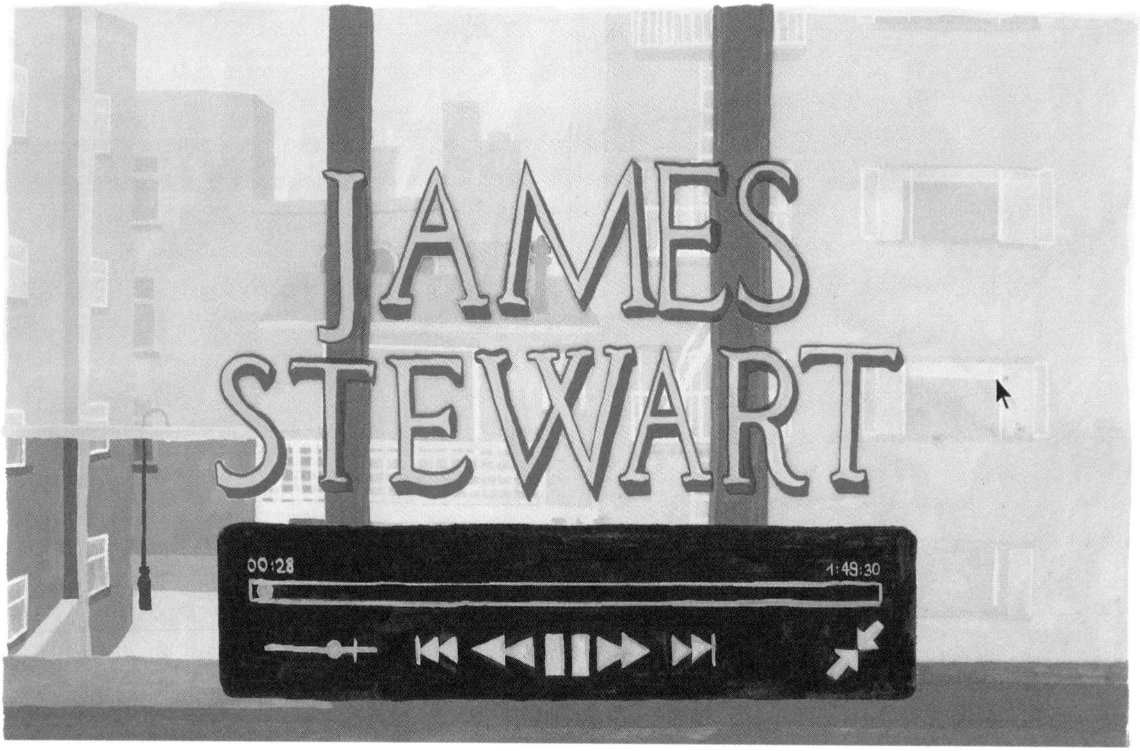
JAMES
STEWART
00:28
1:49:30

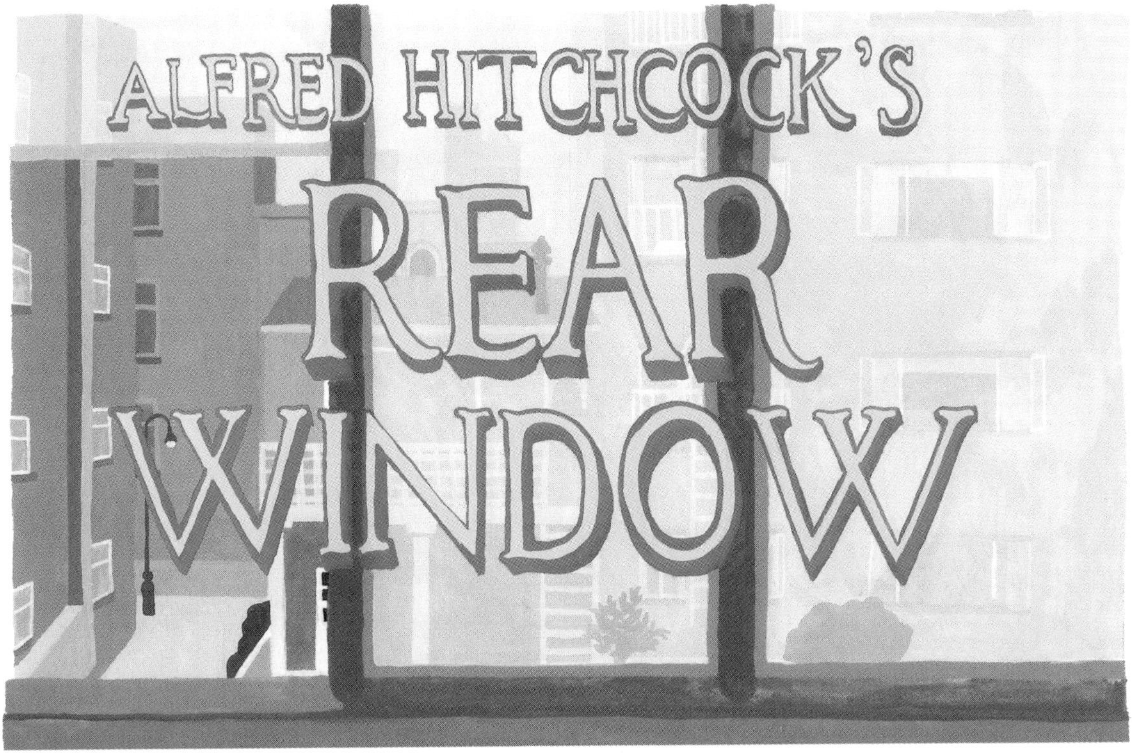
ALFRED HITCHCOCK'S
REAR
WINDOW

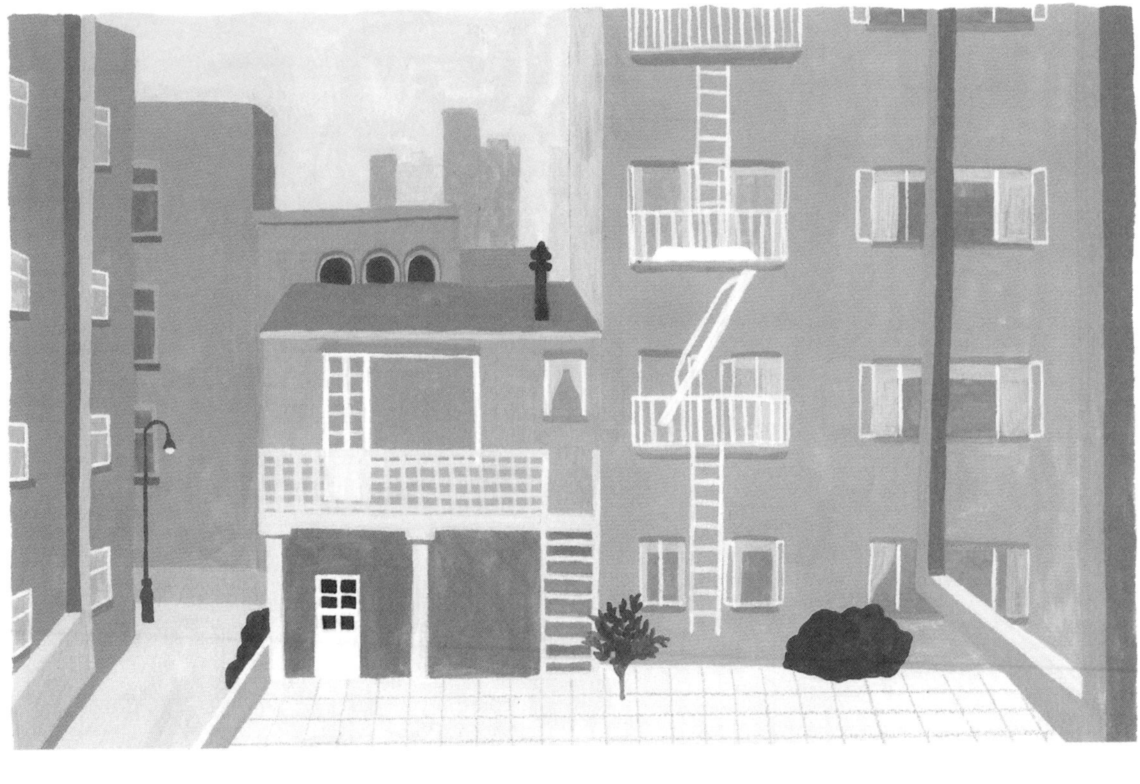

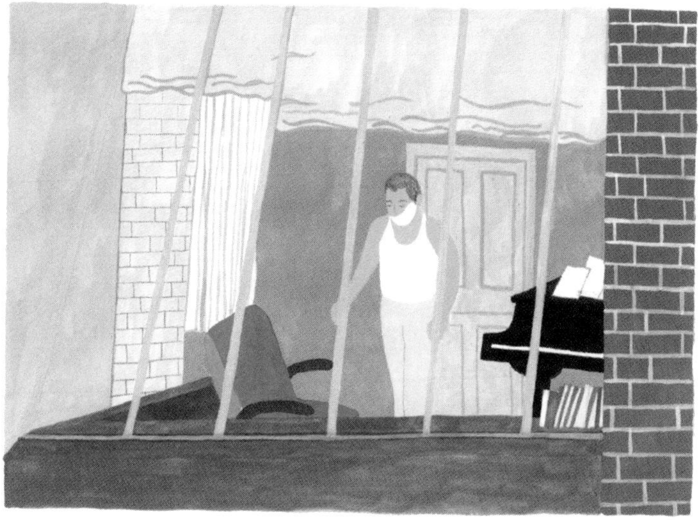

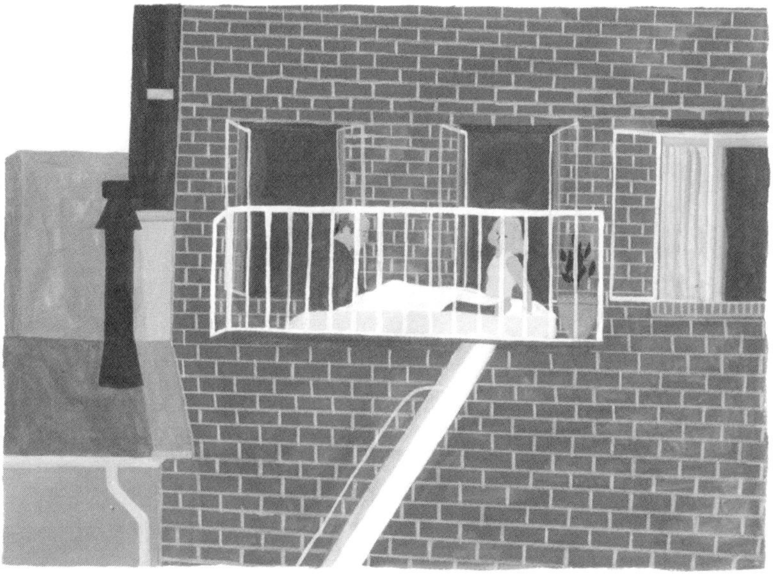

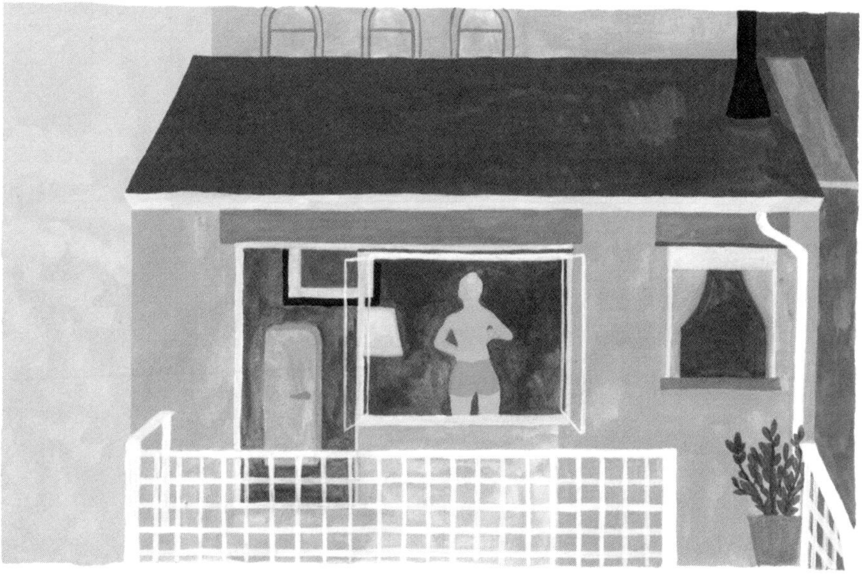

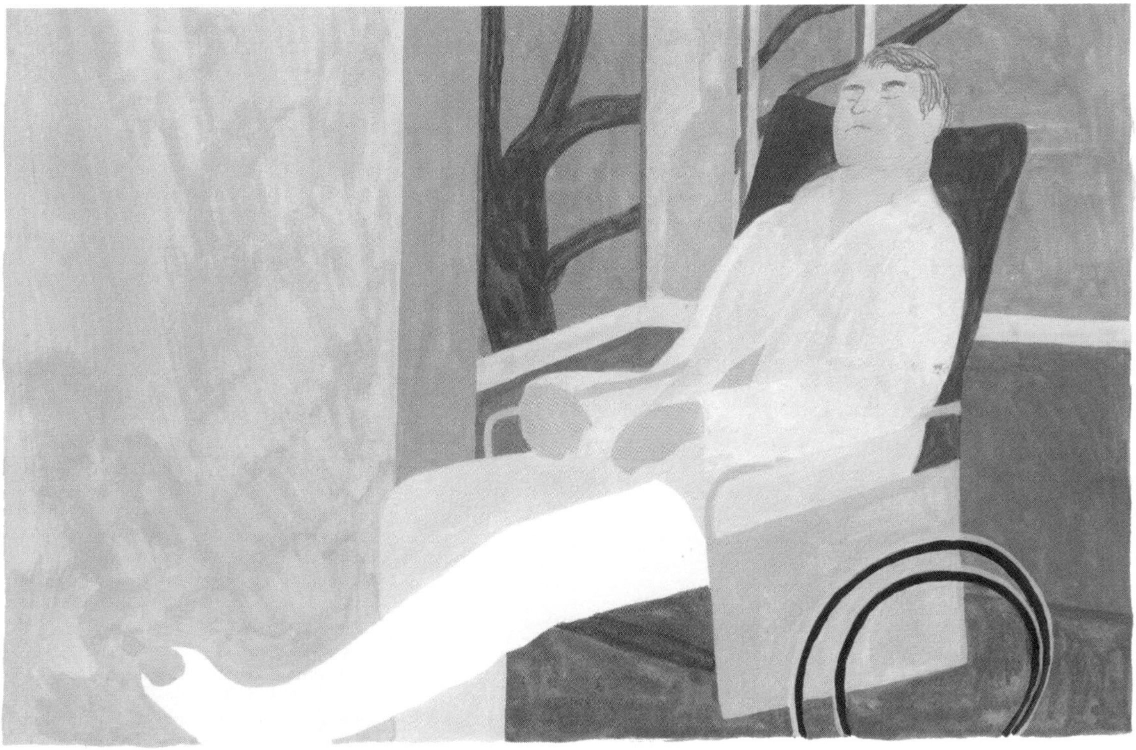

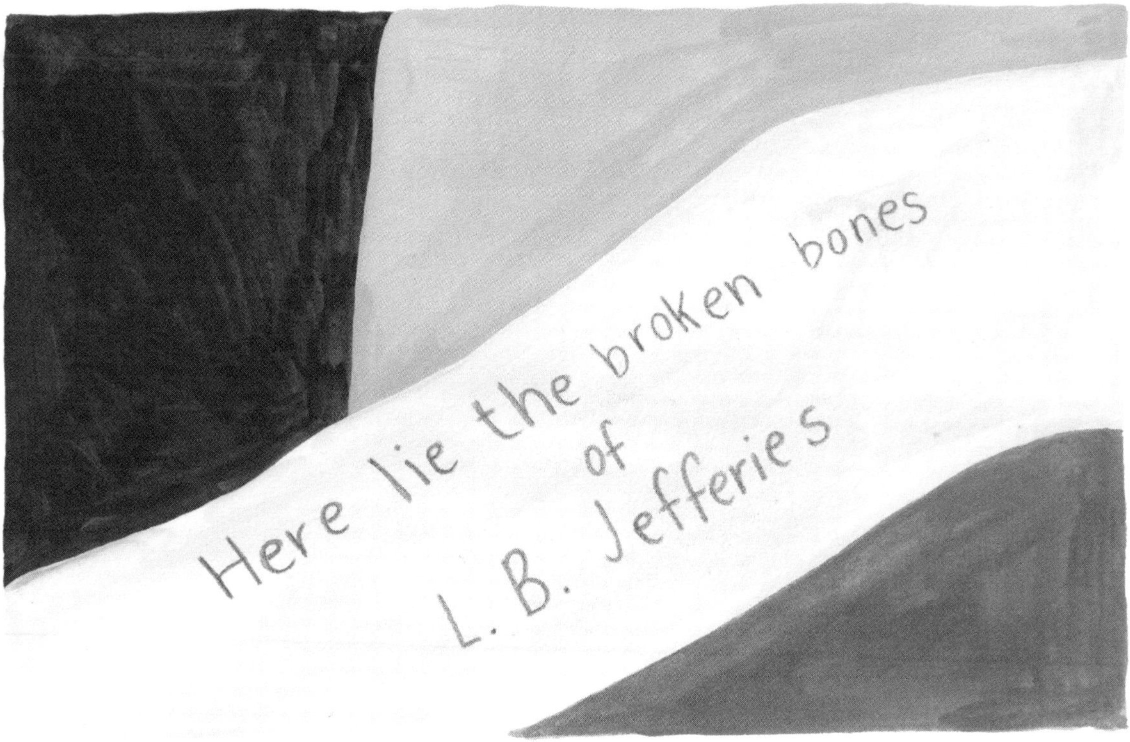
Here lie the broken bones
of
L.B. Jefferies

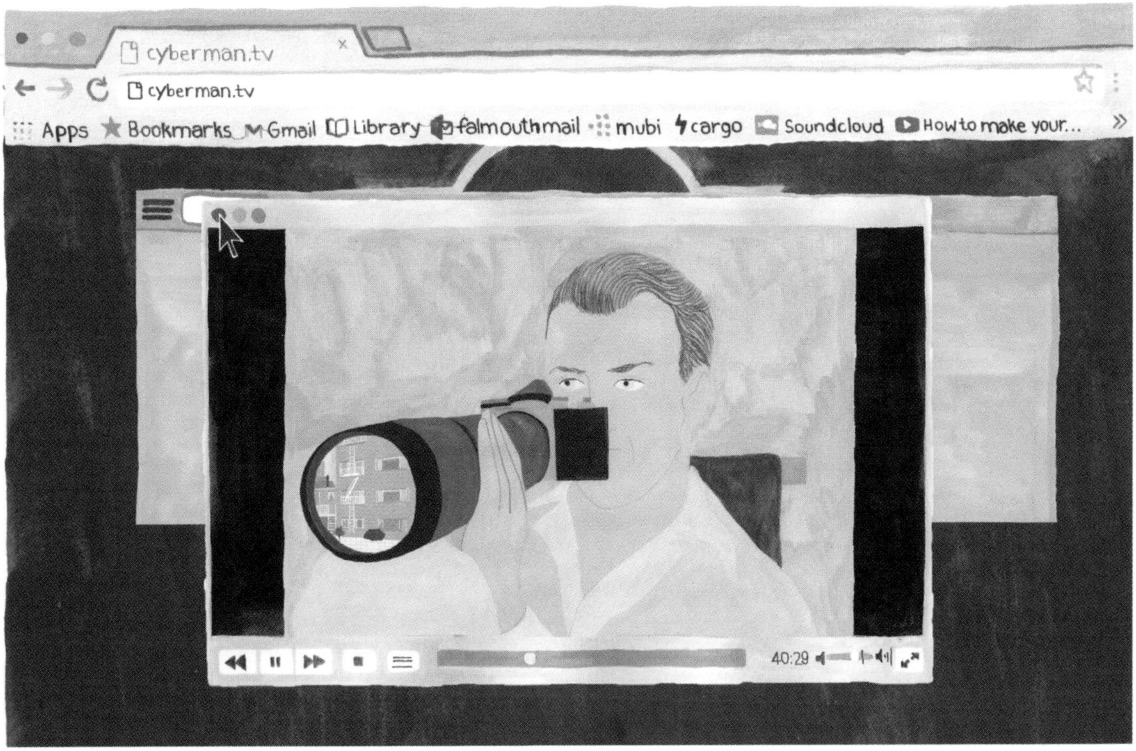
cyberman.tv
cyberman.tv
Apps
Bookmarks
Gmail
Library
falmouthmail
mubi
cargo
Soundcloud
How to make your...
40:29

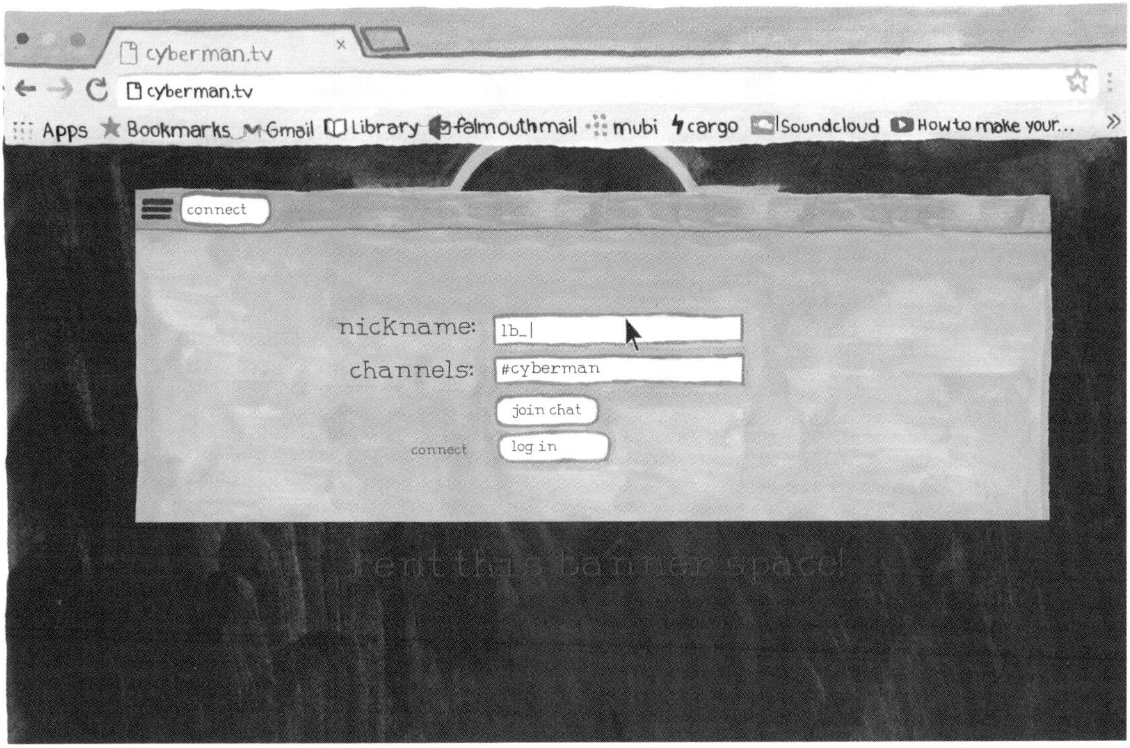
cyberman.tv
cyberman.tv
Apps
Bookmarks
Gmail
Library
falmouthmail
mubi
cargo
Soundcloud
How to make your...
connect
nickname:
lb_|
channels:
#cyberman
join chat
connect
log in
rent this banner space!

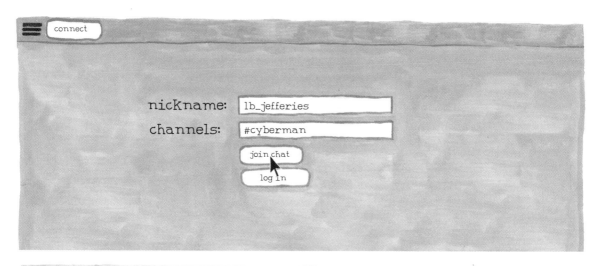

nickname: lb_jefferies

channels: #cyberman

join chat

log in

status   #cyberman

#cyberman: welcome to cyberman

[18:42] == lb_jefferies [webchat@host-95-195-138-143.mobileonline.telia.com] has joined #cyberman
[18:42] <lb_jefferies> hi cyberman
[18:42] <lb_jefferies> how are you doing?
[18:42] == joppe [webchat@c-cf6671d5.58-1-64736c10.custbrdbandsbolaget.se] has quit [quit: page closed]
[18:42] <teuvo_ rantala> ei se Kuulemma

18:42

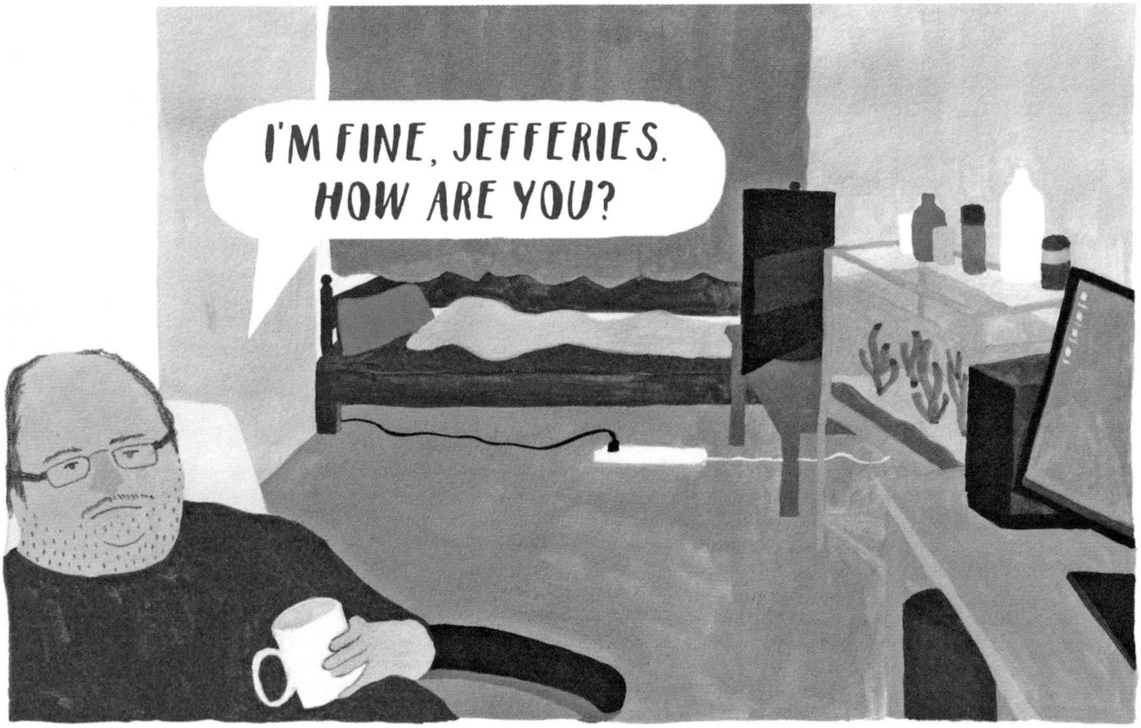
I'M FINE, JEFFERIES.
HOW ARE YOU?

18:42

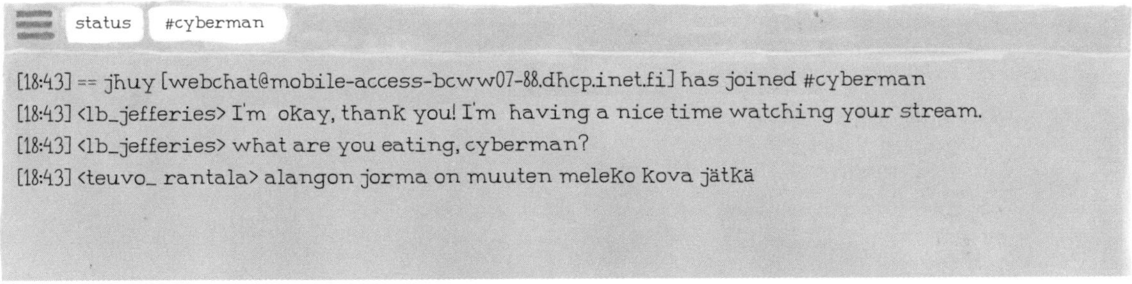
status
#cyberman
[18:43] == jhuy [webchat@mobile-access-bcww07-88.dhcp.inet.fi] has joined #cyberman
[18:43] <lb_jefferies> I'm okay, thank you! I'm having a nice time watching your stream.
[18:43] <lb_jefferies> what are you eating, cyberman?
[18:43] <teuvo_ rantala> alangon jorma on muuten meleko kova jätkä

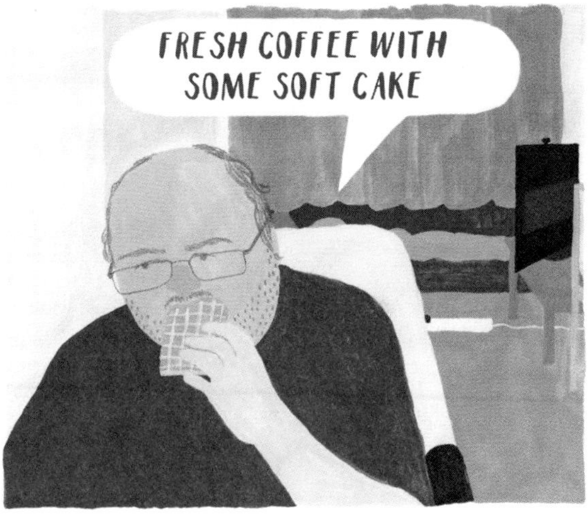
FRESH COFFEE WITH
SOME SOFT CAKE

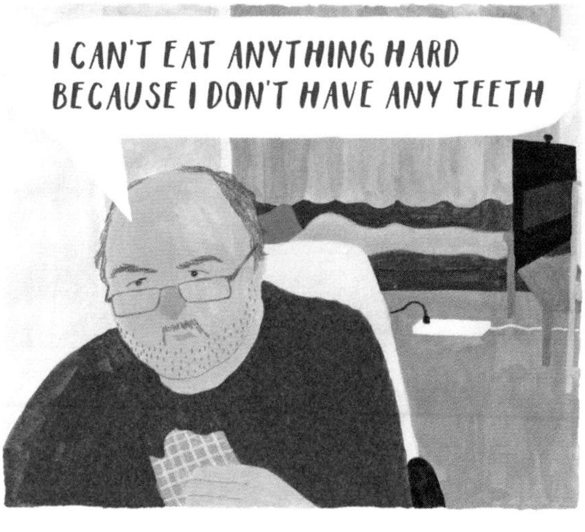
I CAN'T EAT ANYTHING HARD
BECAUSE I DON'T HAVE ANY TEETH

status #cyberman

[18:44] <lb_jefferies> I saw you have a cat. where is she?
[18:45] <daddybear> c==3

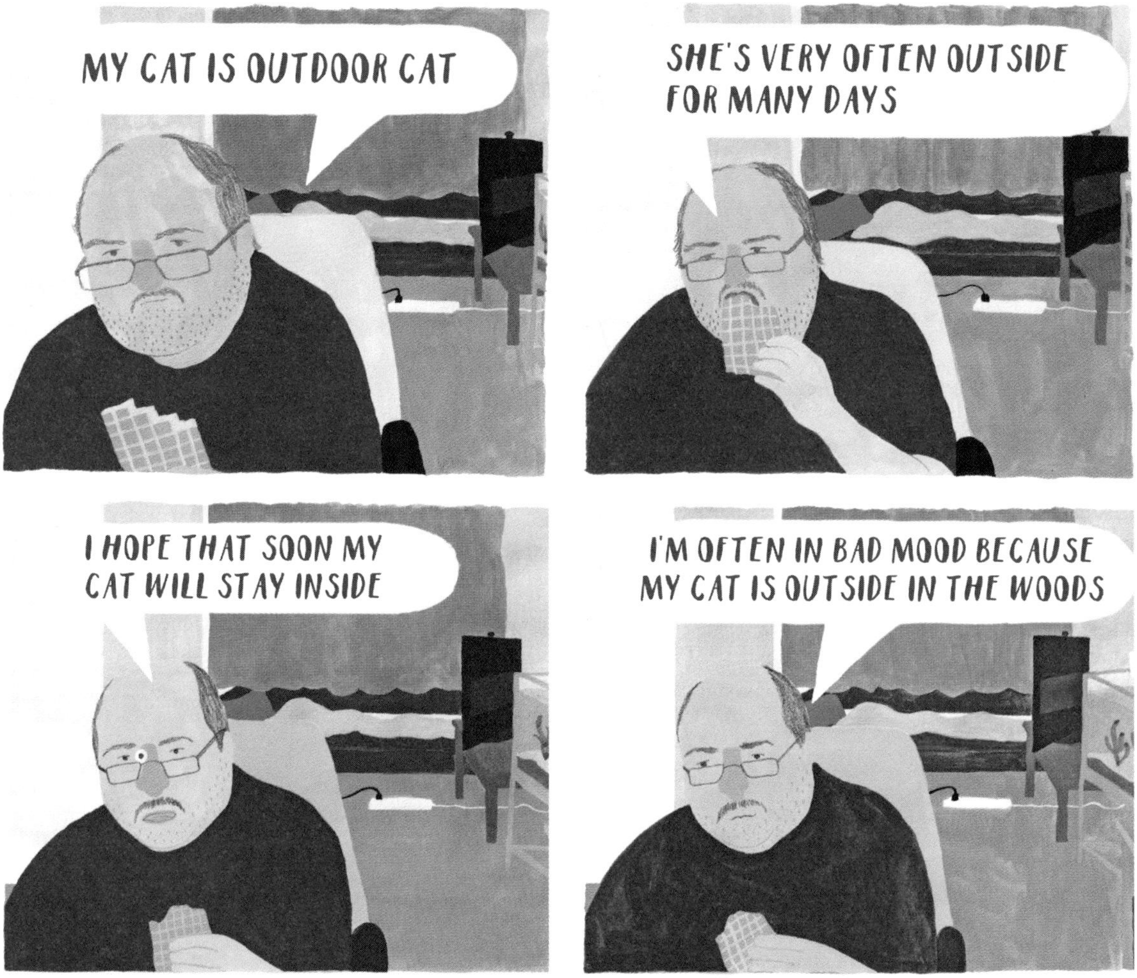
MY CAT IS OUTDOOR CAT
SHE'S VERY OFTEN OUTSIDE FOR MANY DAYS
I HOPE THAT SOON MY CAT WILL STAY INSIDE
I'M OFTEN IN BAD MOOD BECAUSE MY CAT IS OUTSIDE IN THE WOODS

status #cyberman

[18:45] <daddybear> she's running from you
[18:46] <@irsto> se uus kissa kait on jättäny tulematta takas. mut voi se vielä sieltä tulla. kuulemma on tyypillistä kissoile että voivat olla pitkäänkin poissa kota ja ilmestyä sit taas
[18:46] <lb_jefferies> do you go outside sometimes?

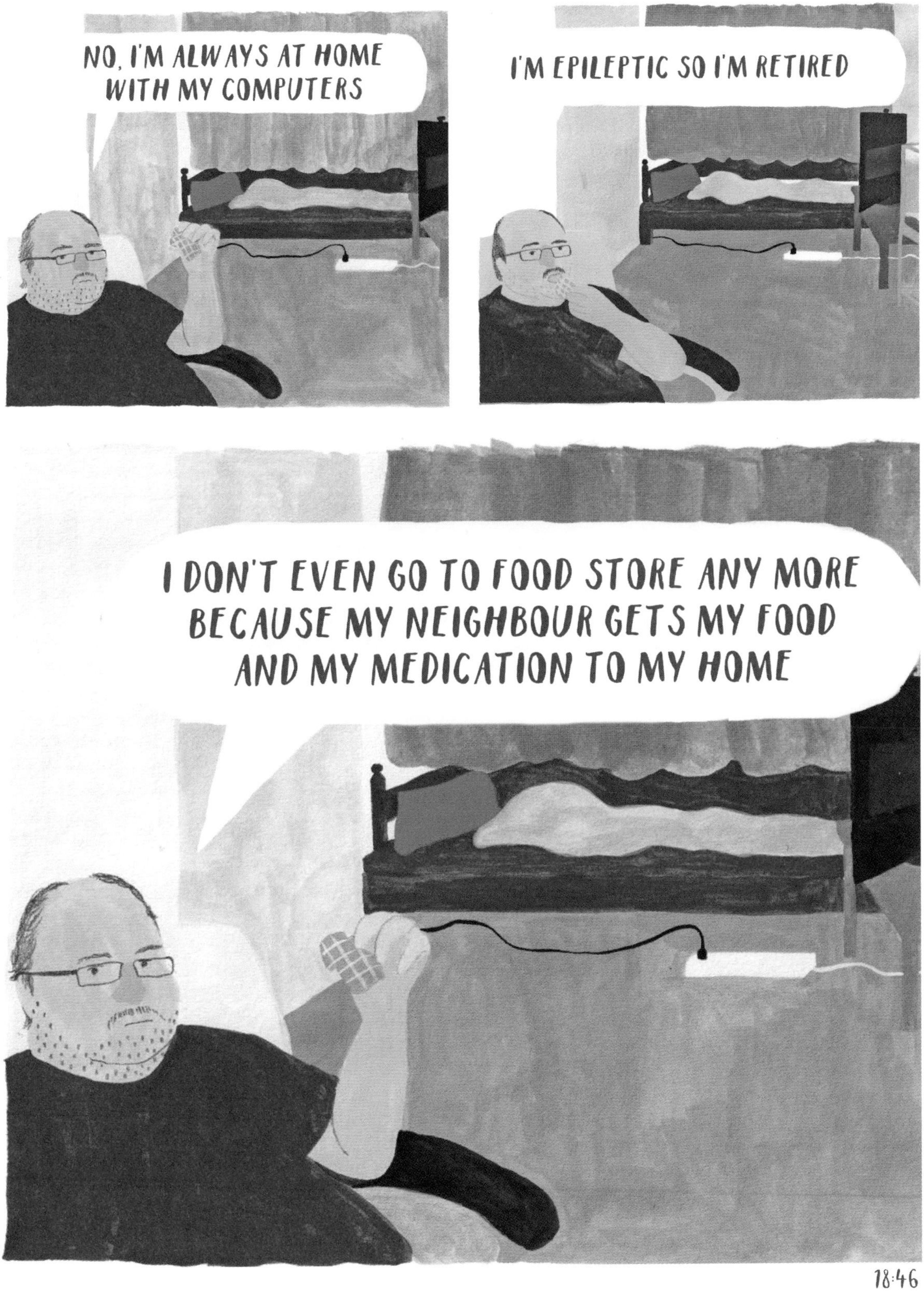
NO, I'M ALWAYS AT HOME WITH MY COMPUTERS
I'M EPILEPTIC SO I'M RETIRED
I DON'T EVEN GO TO FOOD STORE ANY MORE BECAUSE MY NEIGHBOUR GETS MY FOOD AND MY MEDICATION TO MY HOME
18:46

status #cyberman

[18:47] <lb_jefferies> ah oKay.
[18:47] == exorzist [exorzist@exorzistii.users.quaKenet.org] has joined #cyberman
[18:48] <joop> varmaa muKava rinKirunKata pienellä poruKalla ja jeesustella Kun on KaiKKi bannittu ihan turhaan : D
[18:48] <lb_jefferies> and do you spend all your time live-streaming online?

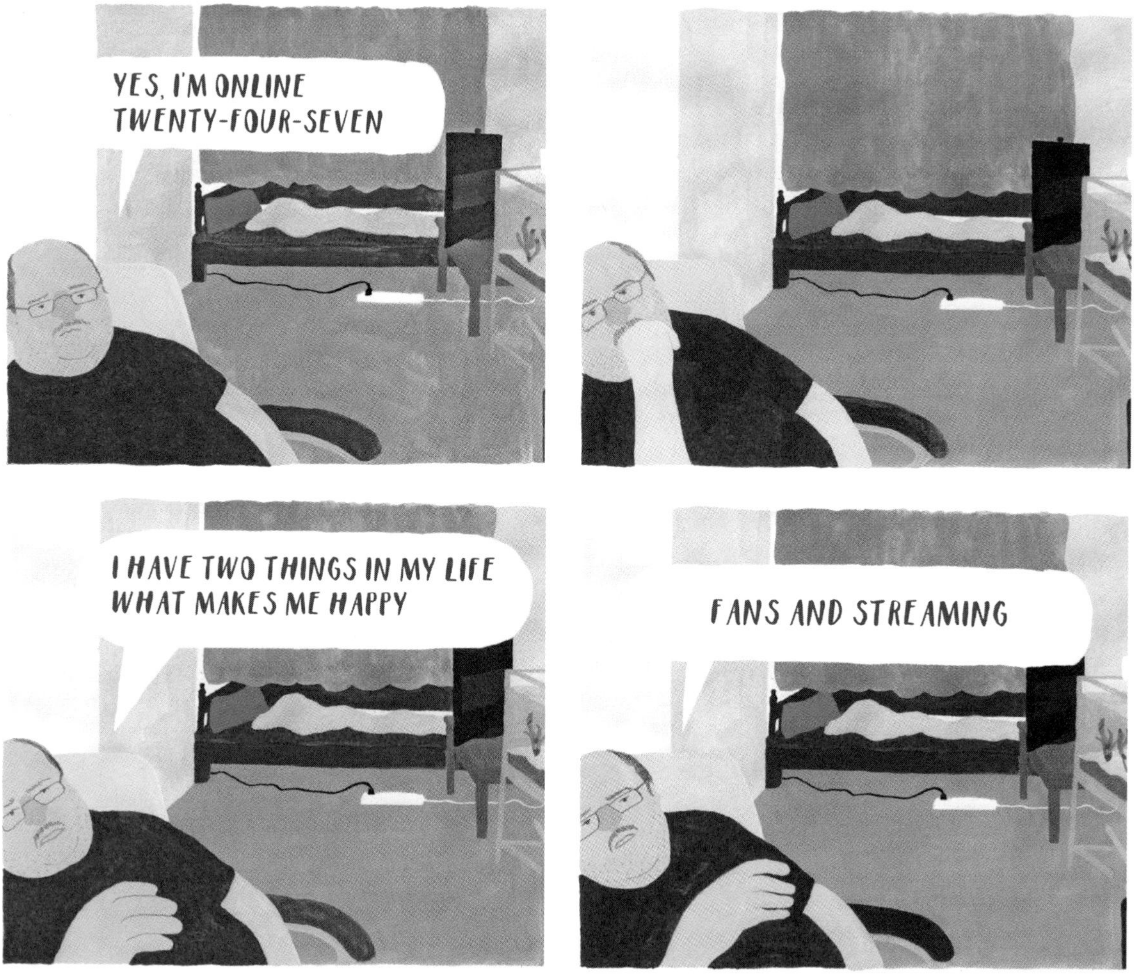

YES, I'M ONLINE TWENTY-FOUR-SEVEN
I HAVE TWO THINGS IN MY LIFE WHAT MAKES ME HAPPY
FANS AND STREAMING

status #cyberman

[18:49] <teuvo_rantala> meleKo Kova jätKä seKi

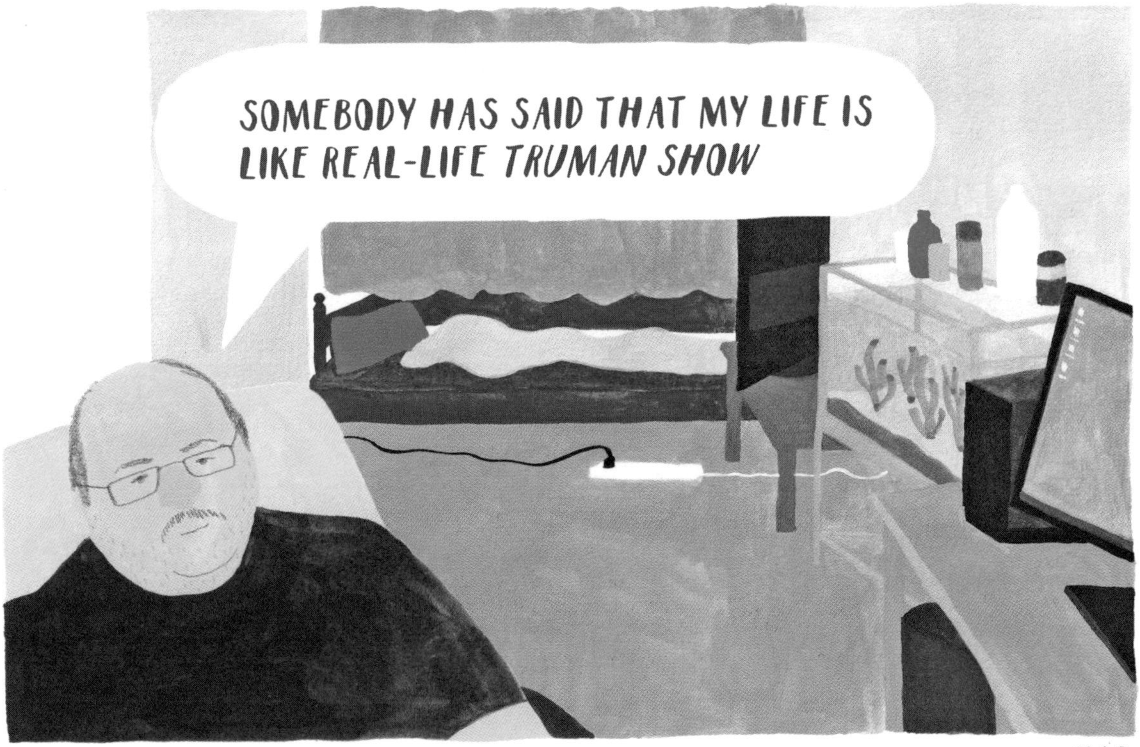
SOMEBODY HAS SAID THAT MY LIFE IS LIKE REAL-LIFE *TRUMAN SHOW*

18:49

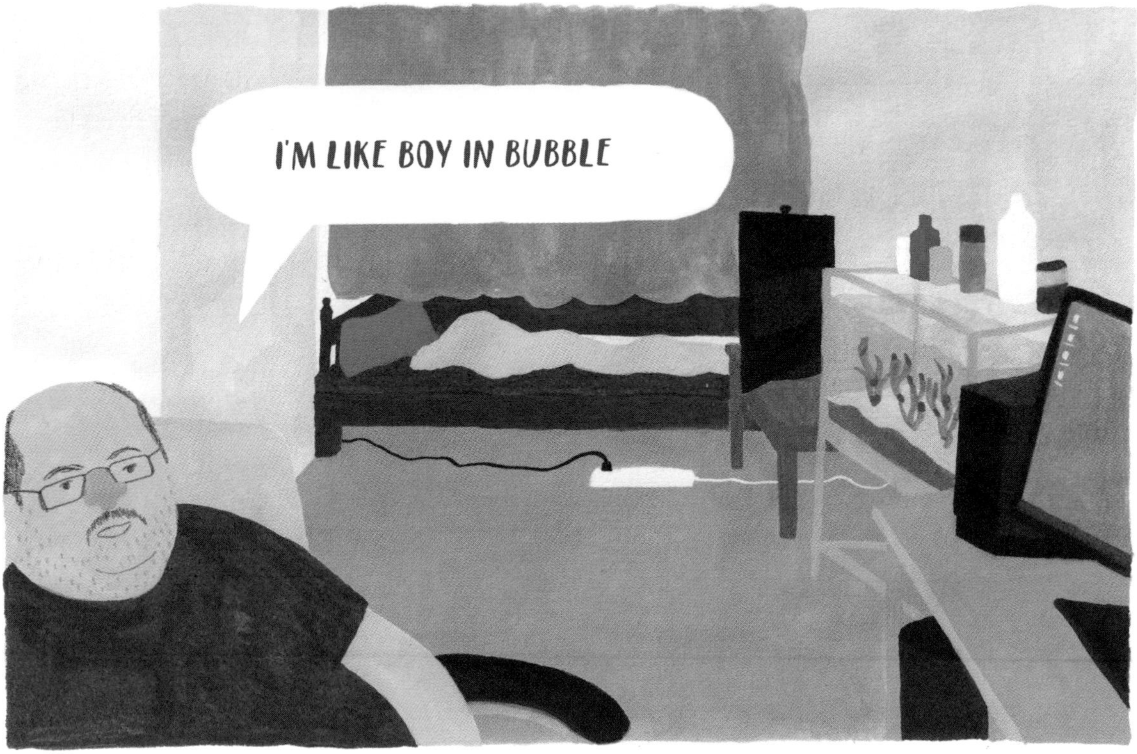
I'M LIKE BOY IN BUBBLE

18:49

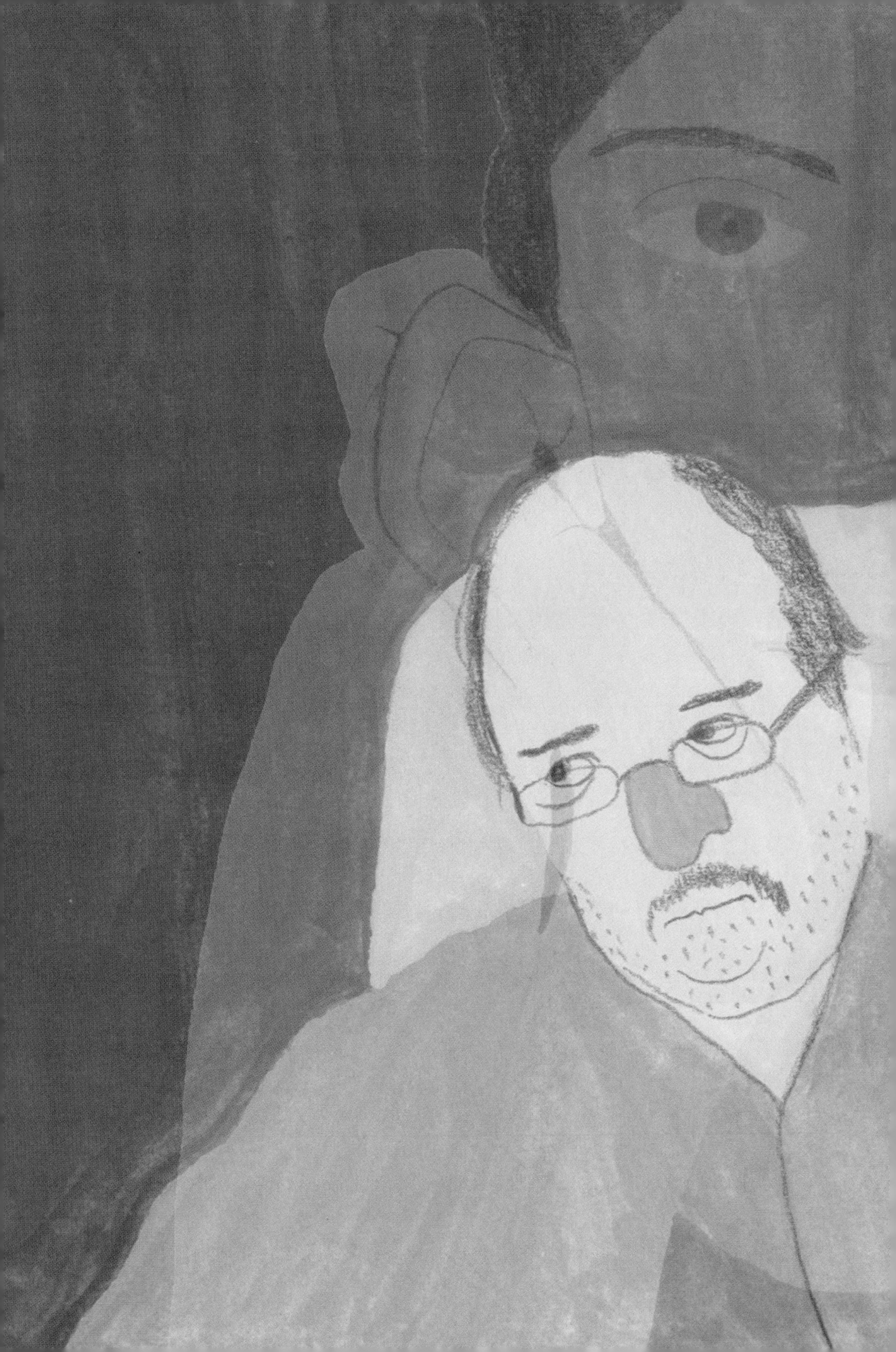

78:50

30.03.2016

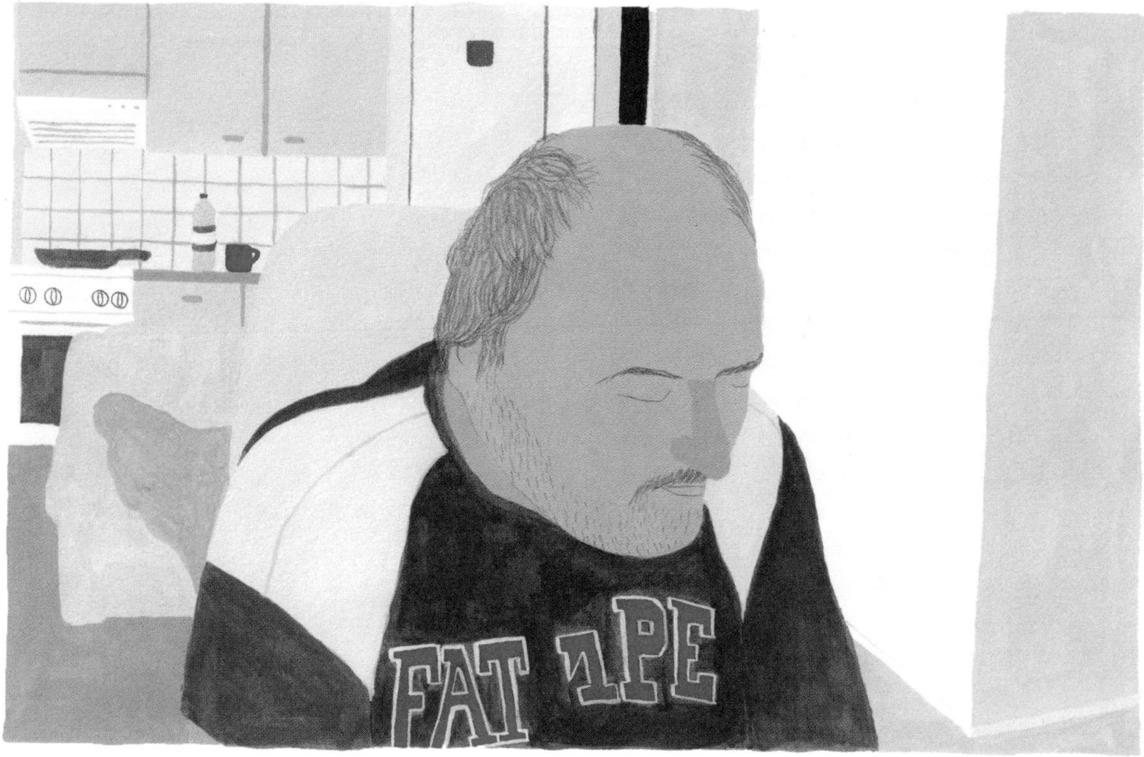
FAT

13:50

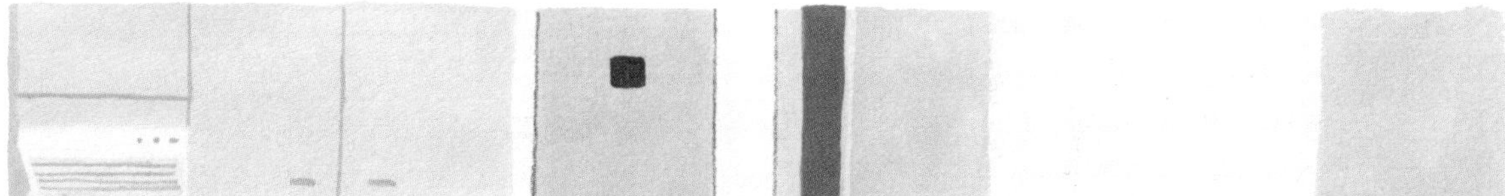
FAT PIPE

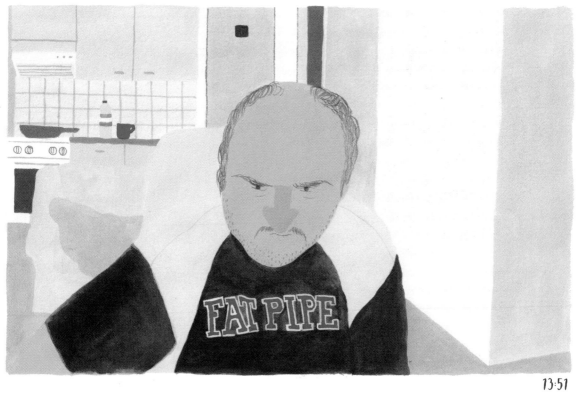

13:51

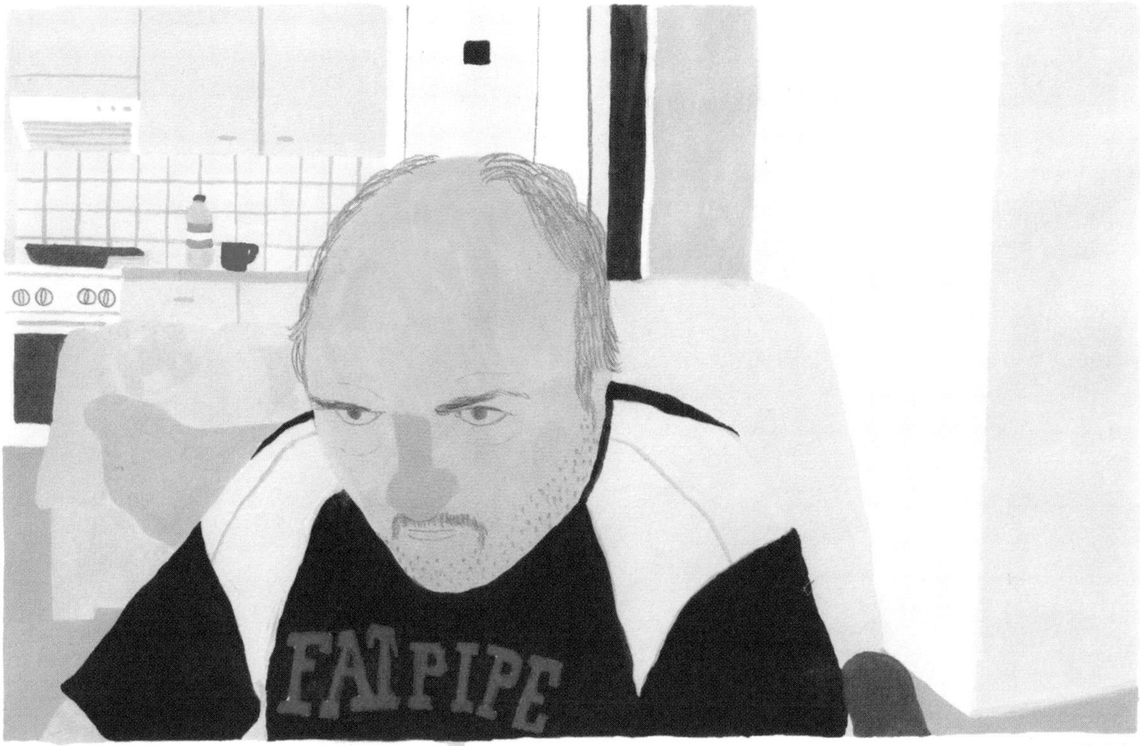
FATPIPE

13:56

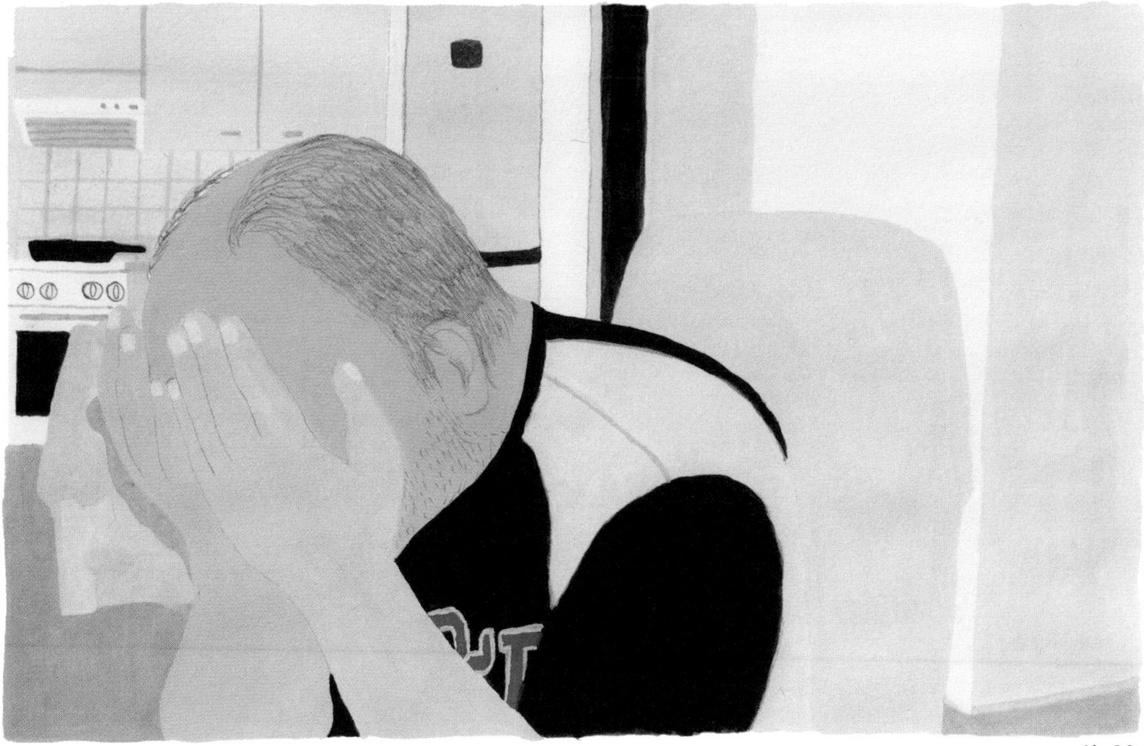

14:00

31.03.2016

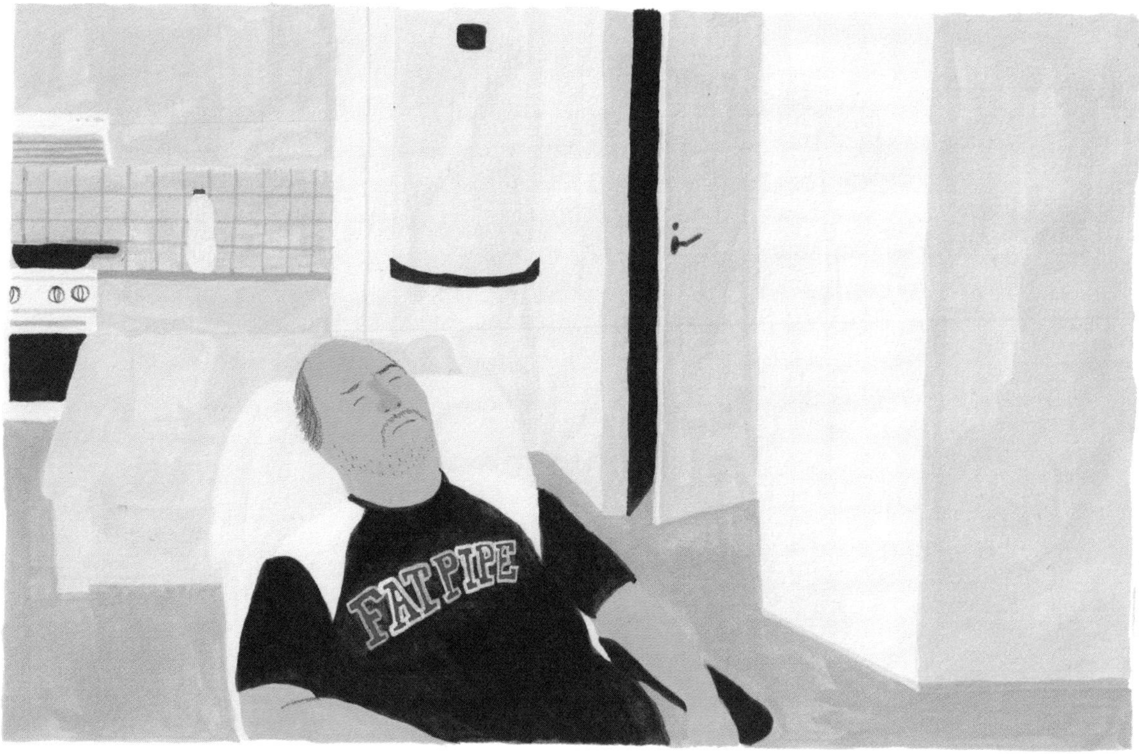
FAT PIPE

15:58

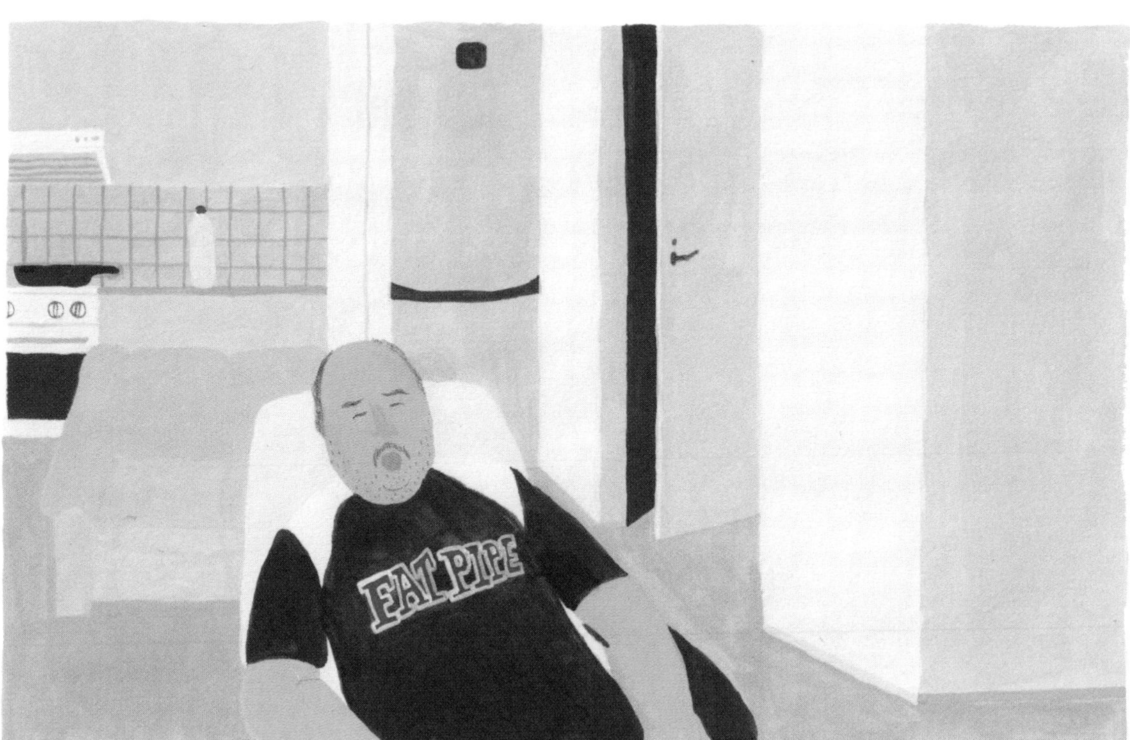
FAT PIPE

15:58

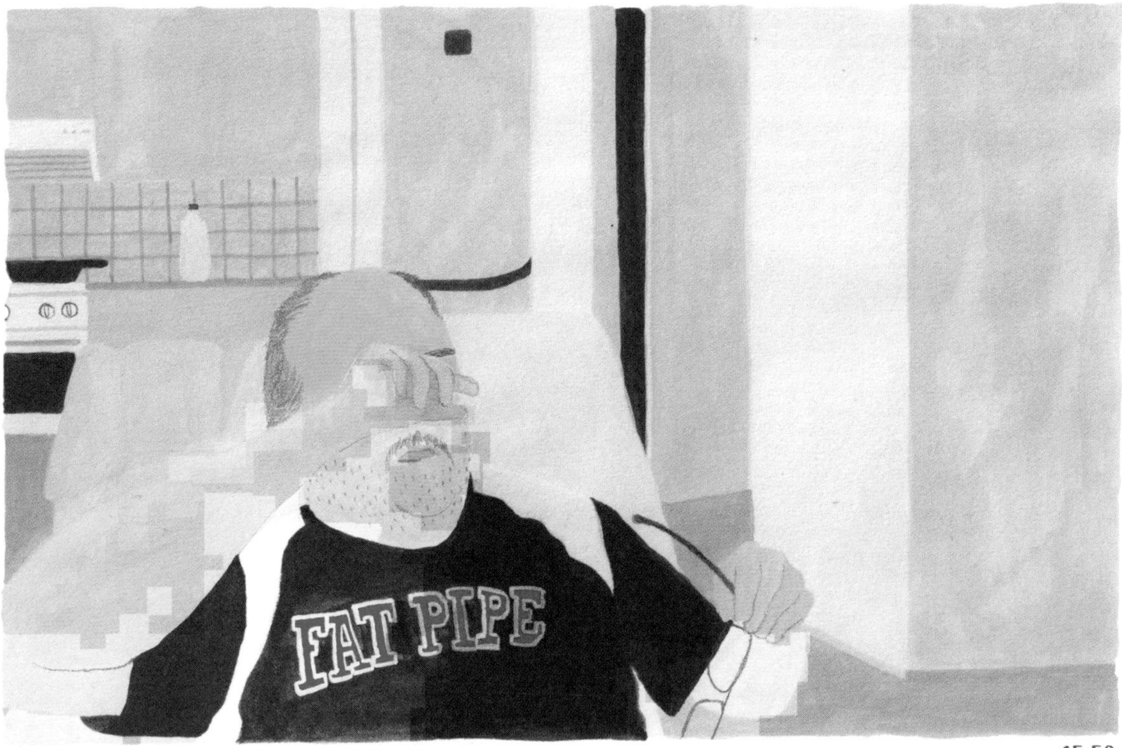
FAT PIPE

15:59

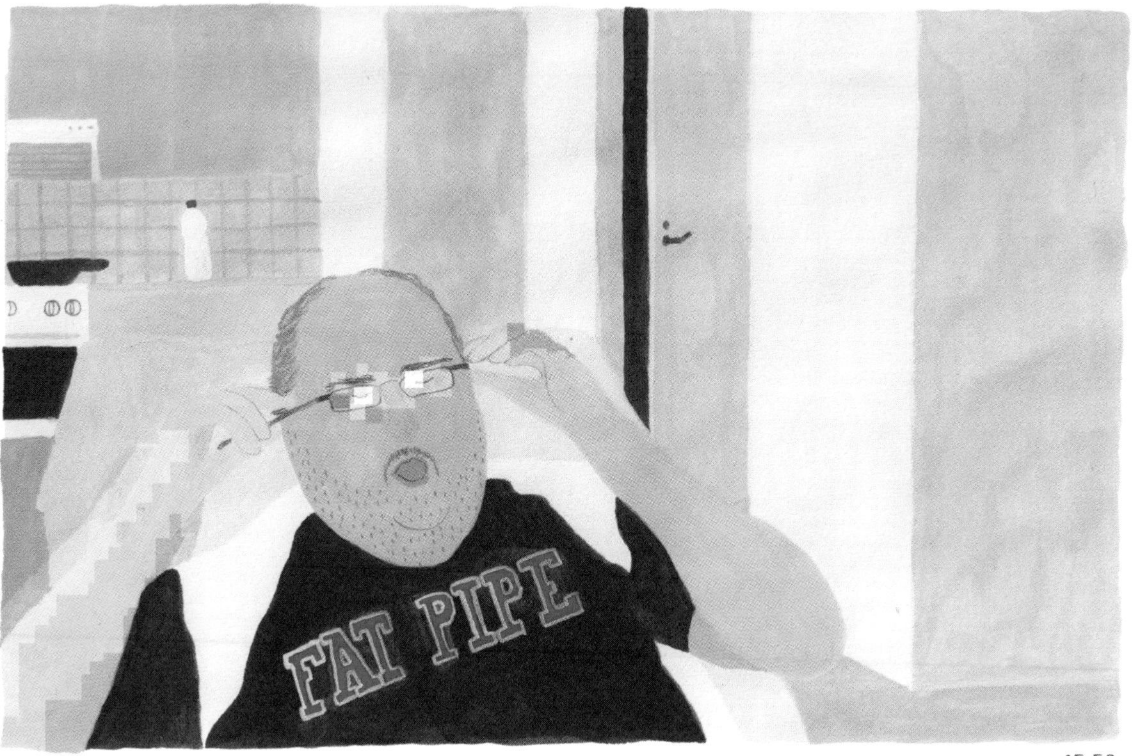
FAT PIPE

15:59

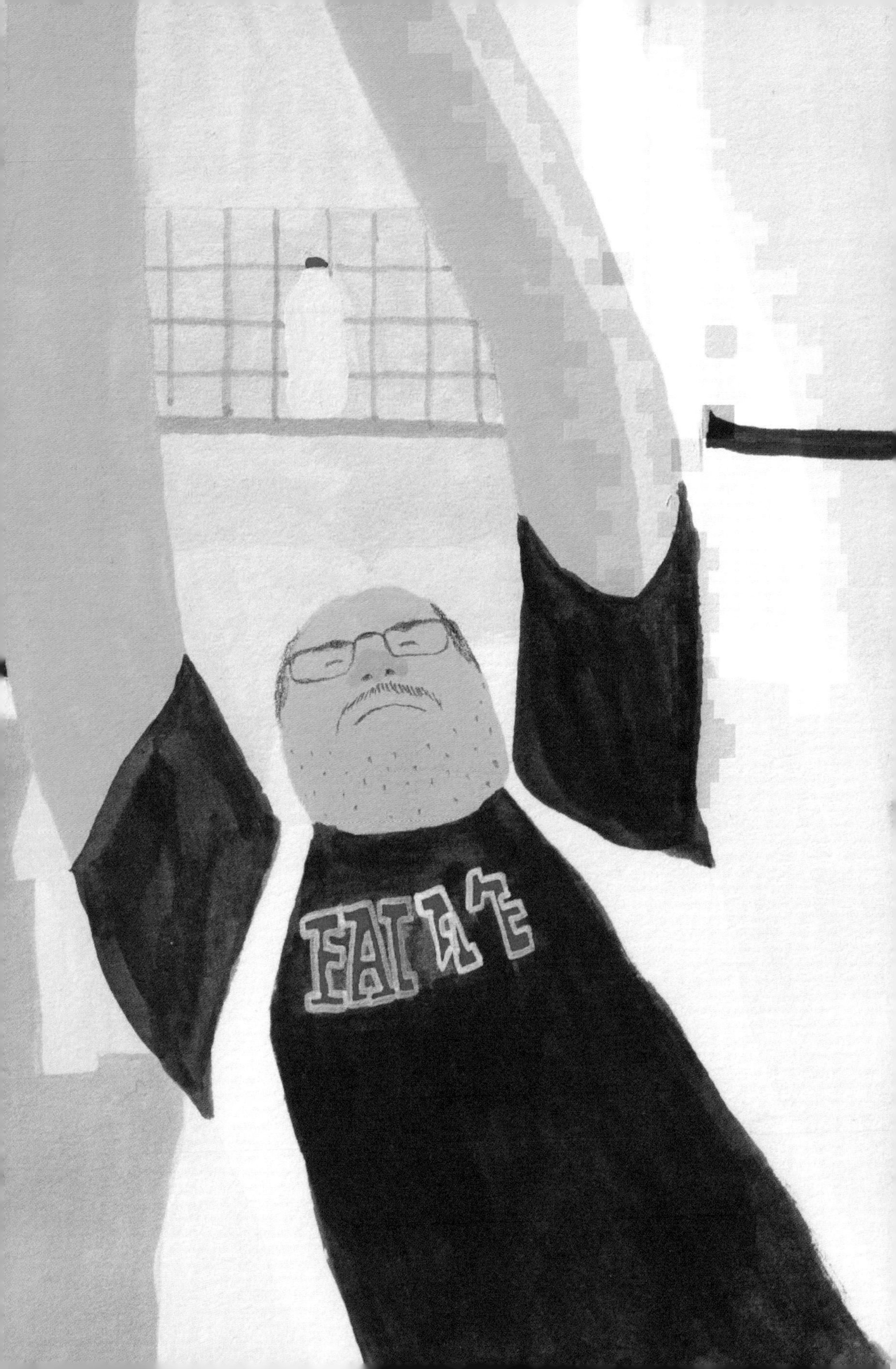

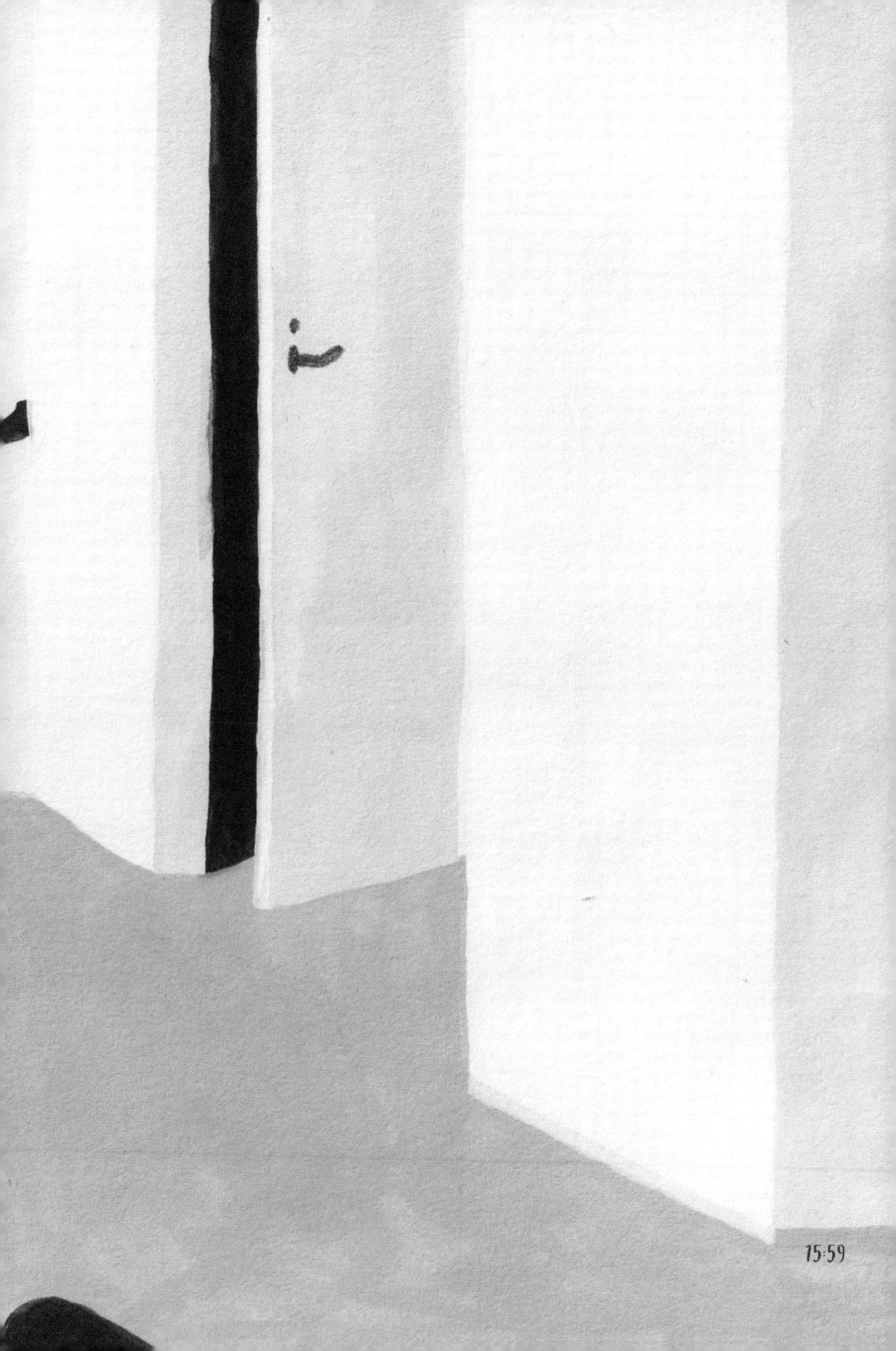
15:59

11.04.2016

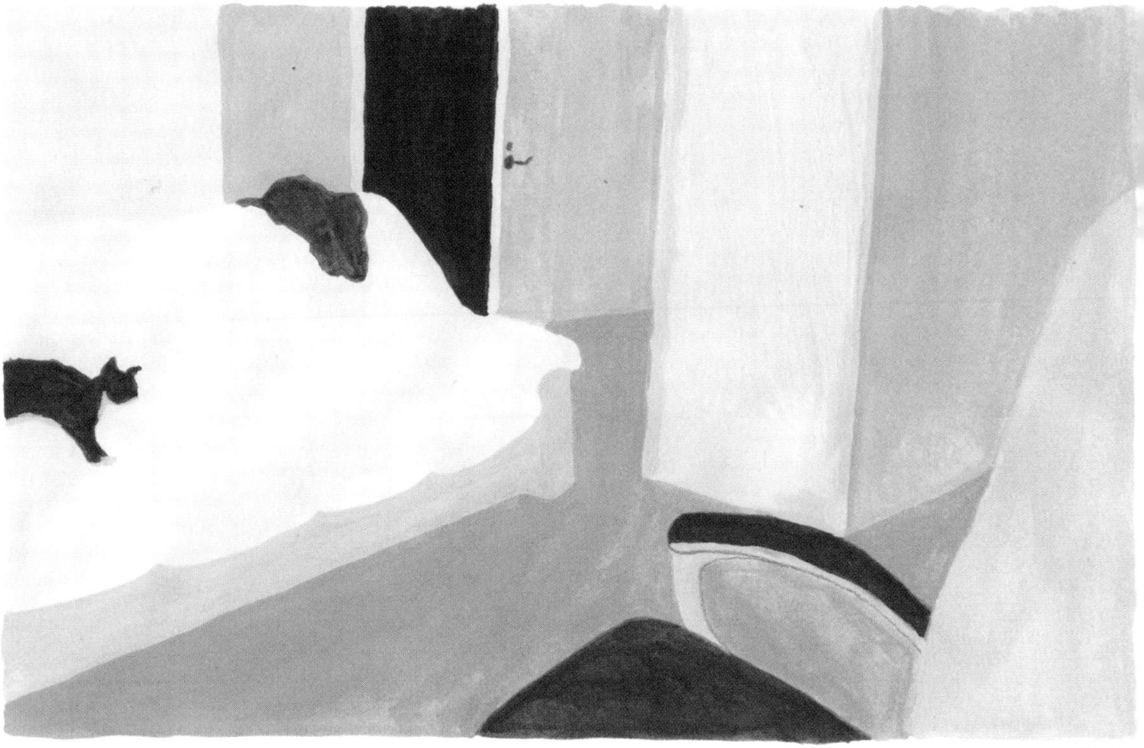

16:38

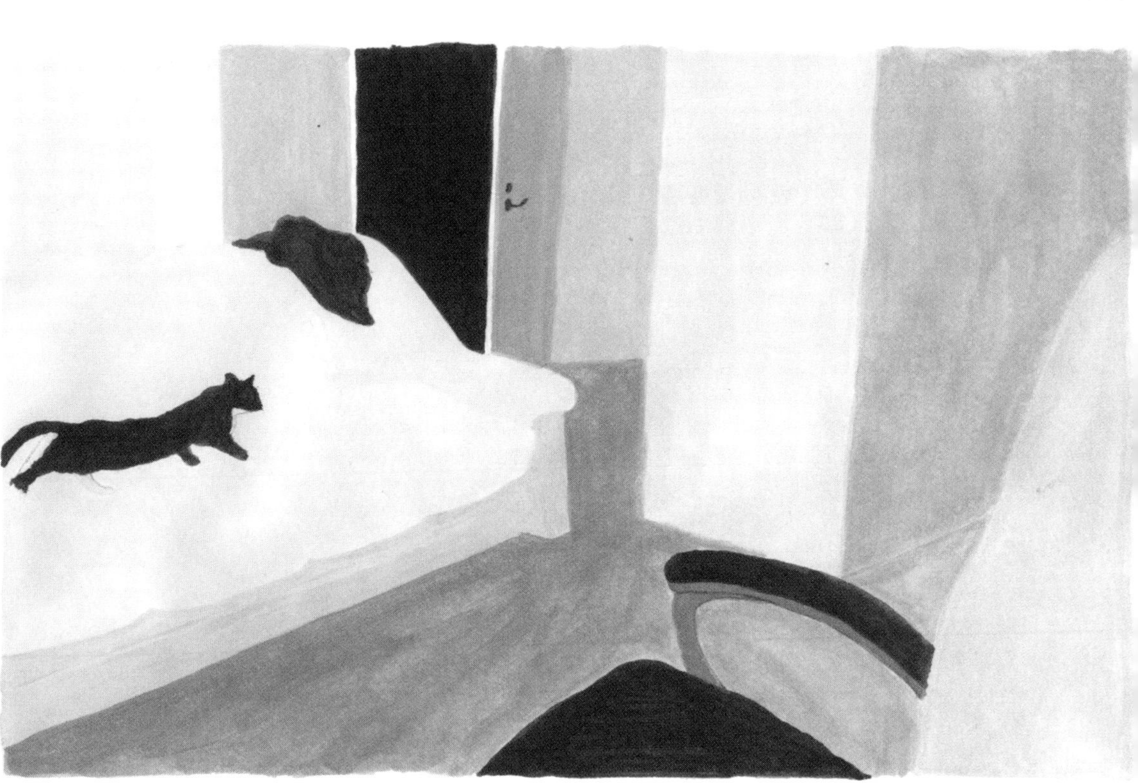

16:38

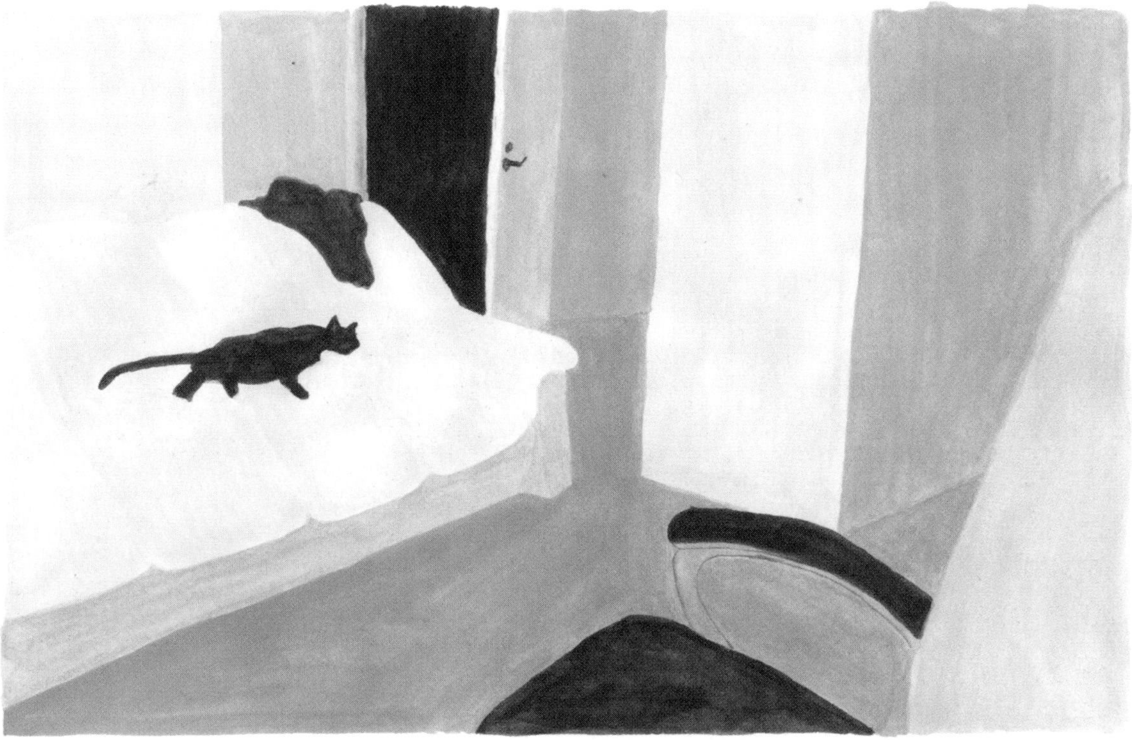

16:38

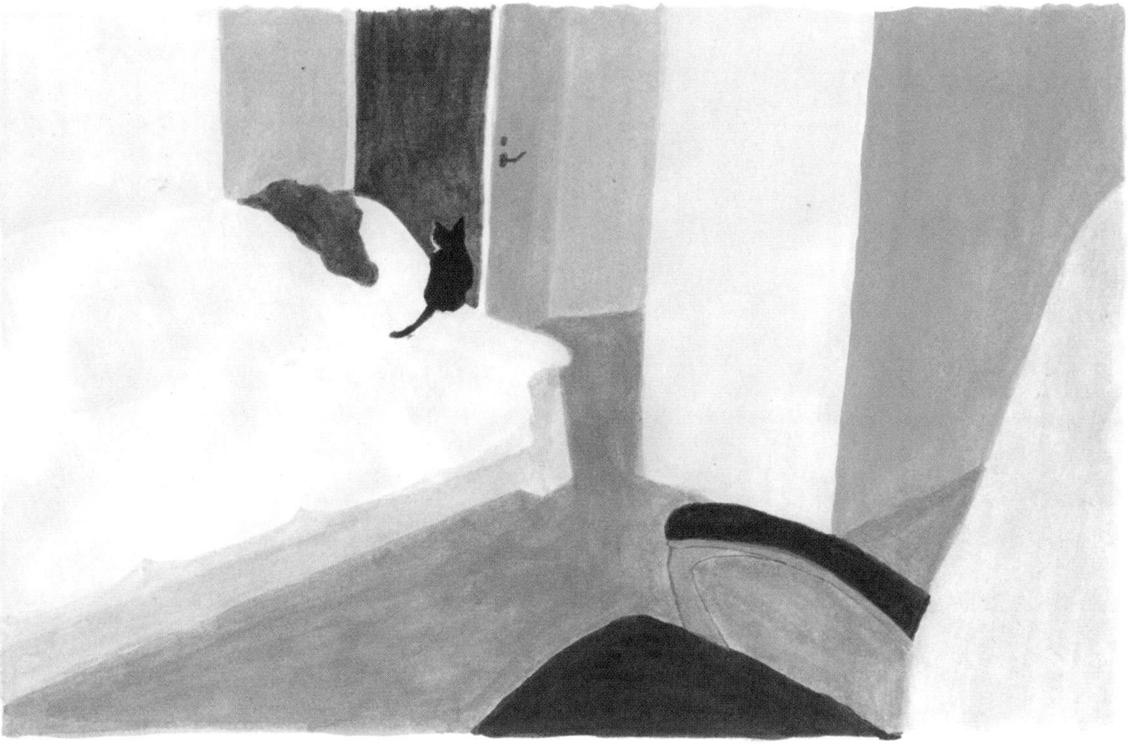

16:38

20.04.2016

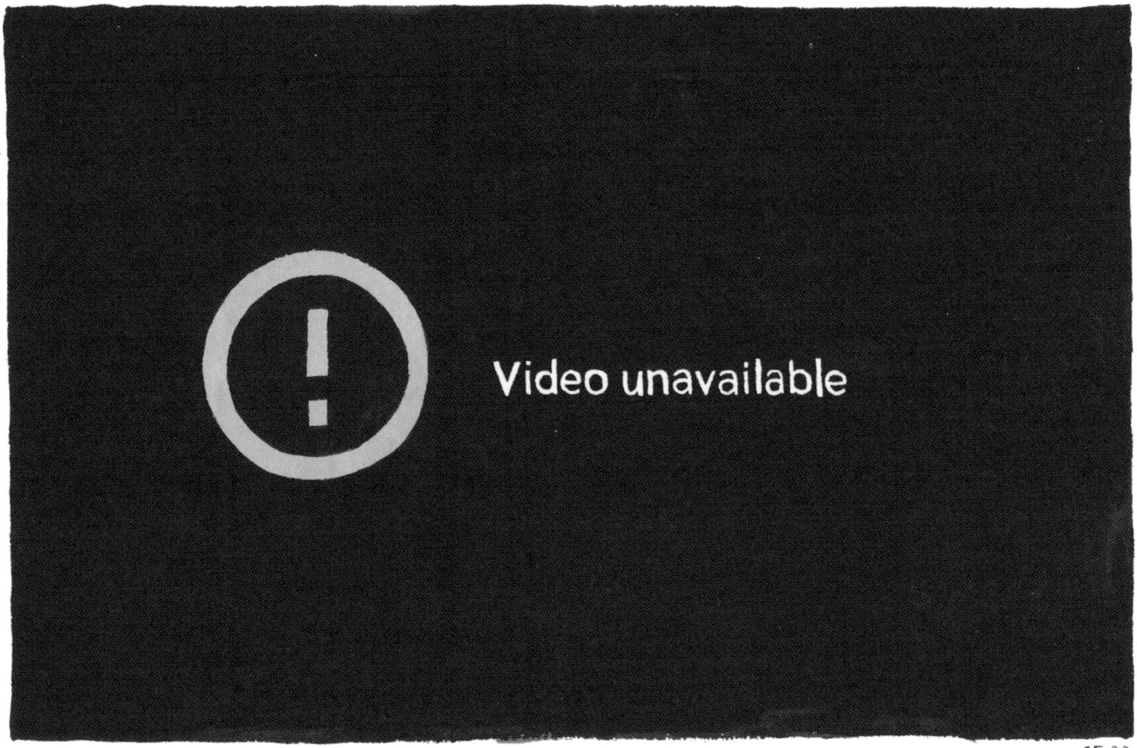
Video unavailable

15:22

21.04.2016

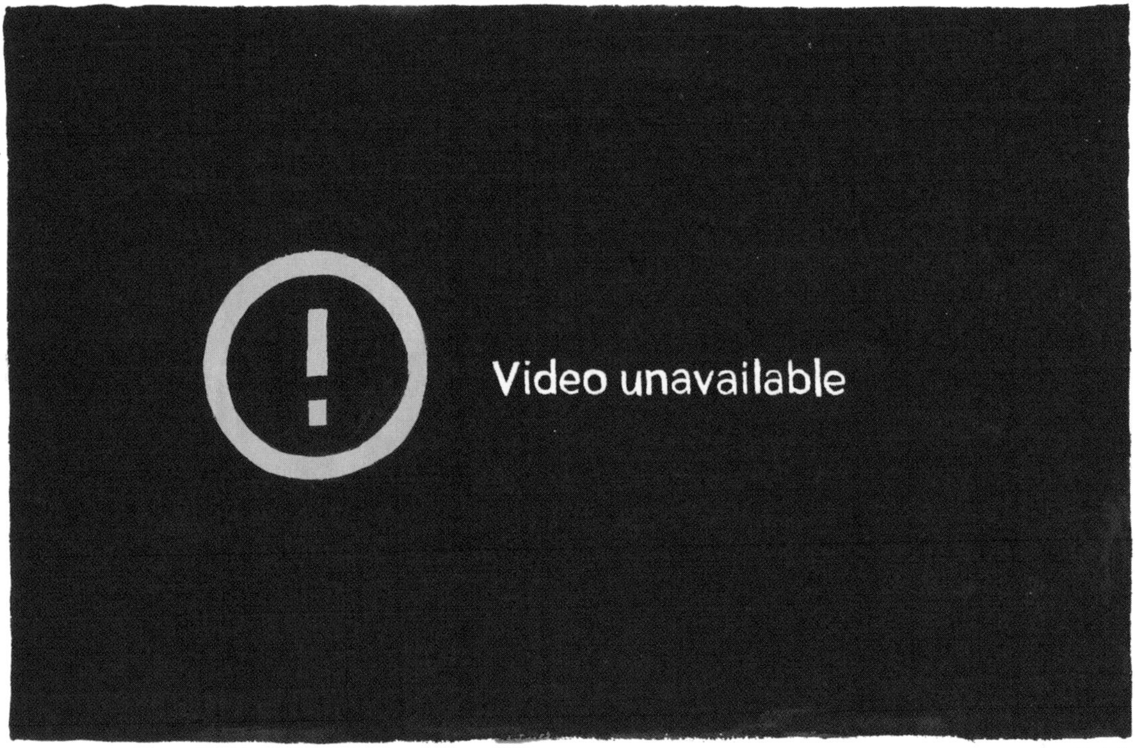
Video unavailable

17:35

25.04.2016

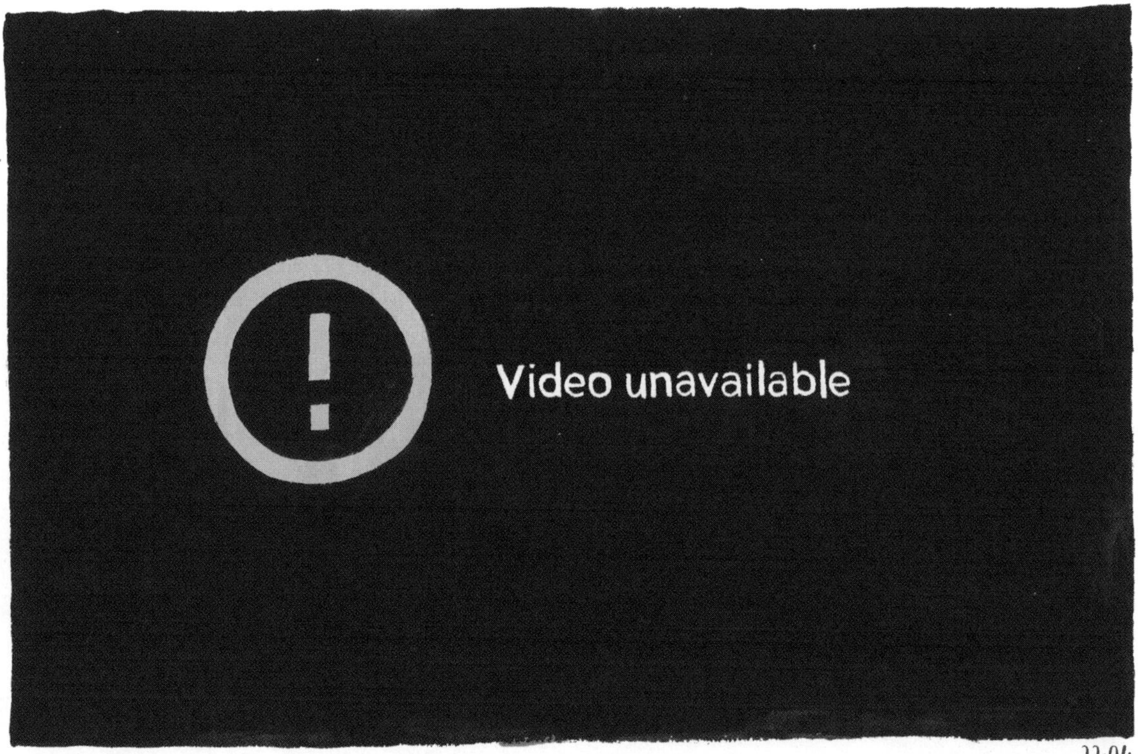
Video unavailable

22:04

27.04.2016

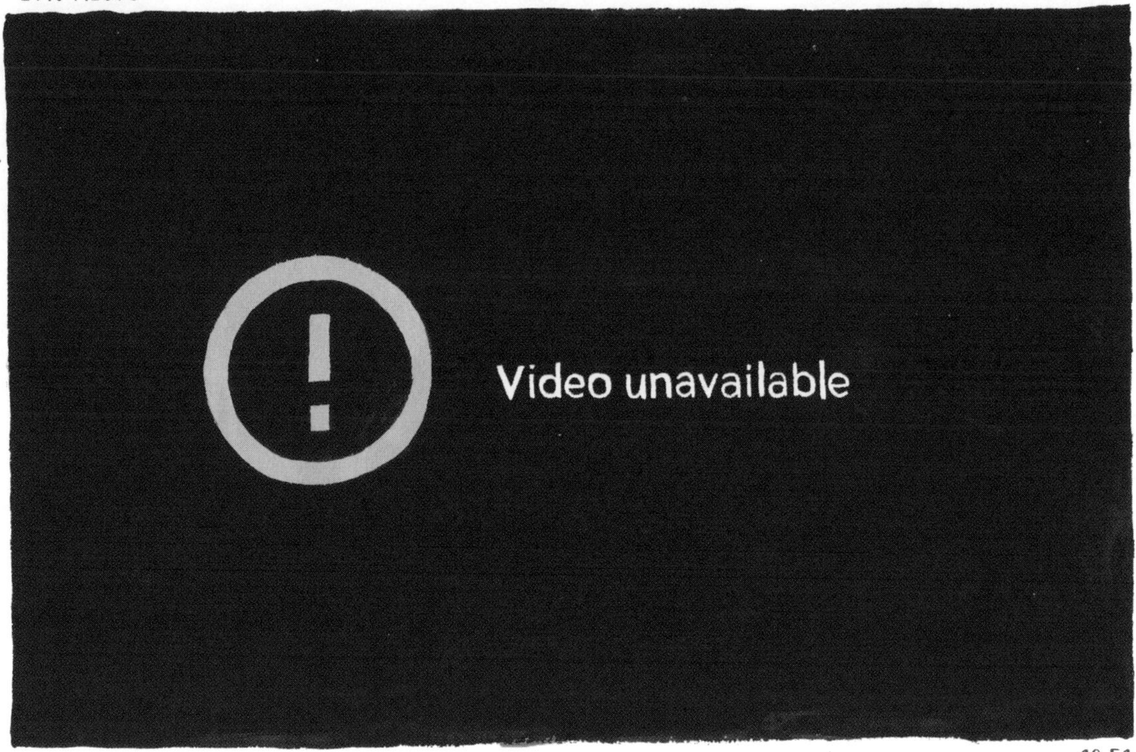
Video unavailable

10:51

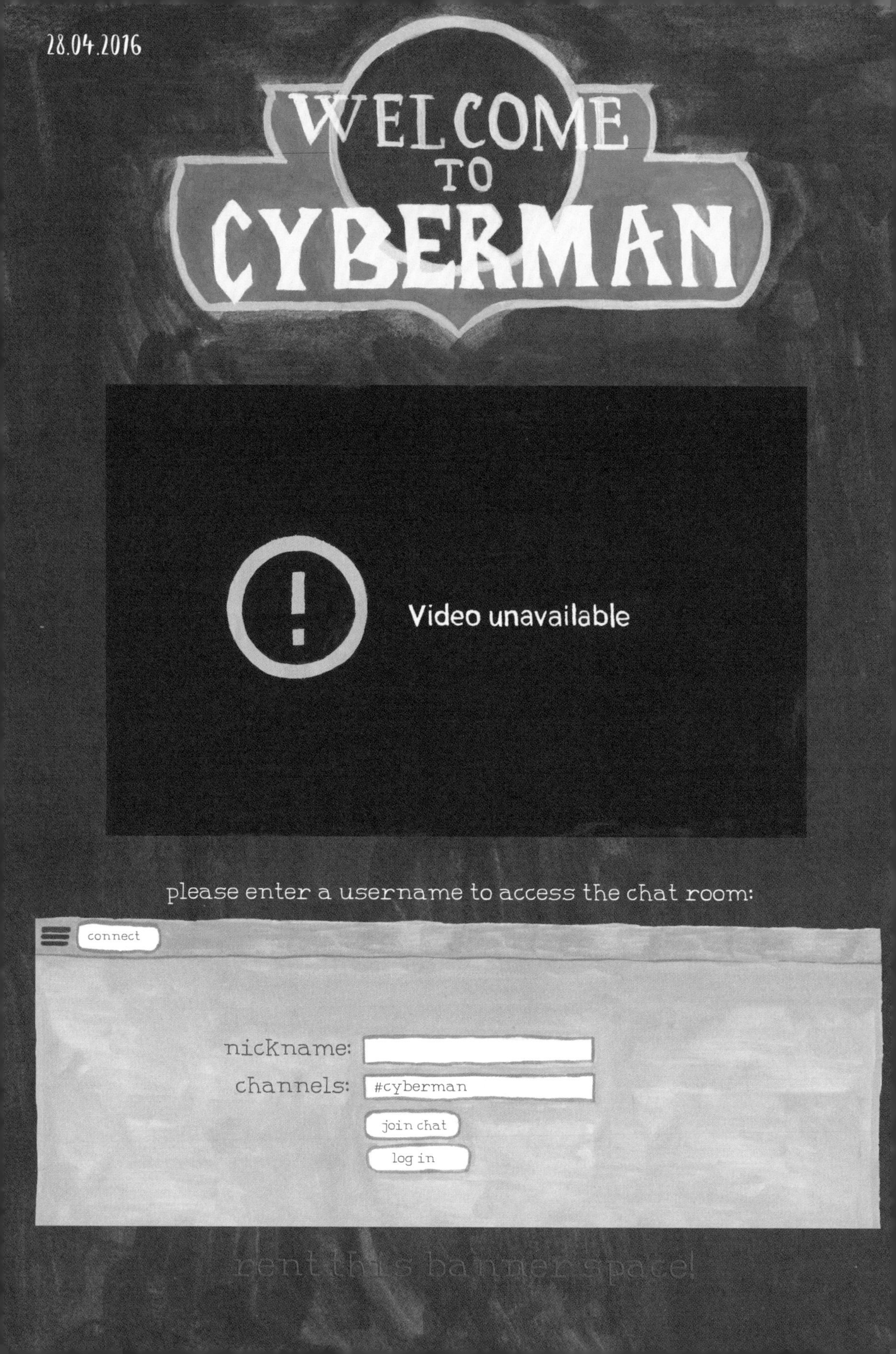
28.04.2016
WELCOME
TO
CYBERMAN
Video unavailable
please enter a username to access the chat room:
connect
nickname:
channels:
#cyberman
join chat
log in
rent this banner space!

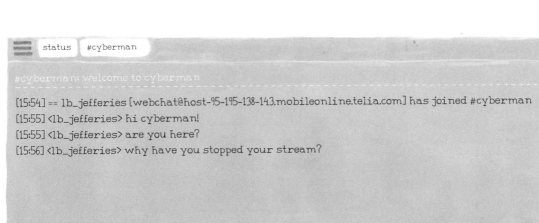

status   #cyberman

#cyberman: welcome to cyberman
- -
[15:54] == lb_jefferies [webchat@host-95-195-138-143.mobileonline.telia.com] has joined #cyberman

[15:55] <lb_jefferies> hi cyberman!

[15:55] <lb_jefferies> are you here?

[15:56] <lb_jefferies> why have you stopped your stream?

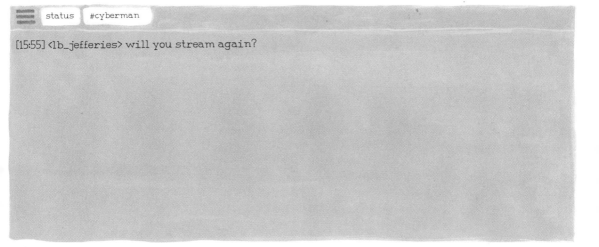

status   #cyberman

[15:55] <lb_jefferies> will you stream again?

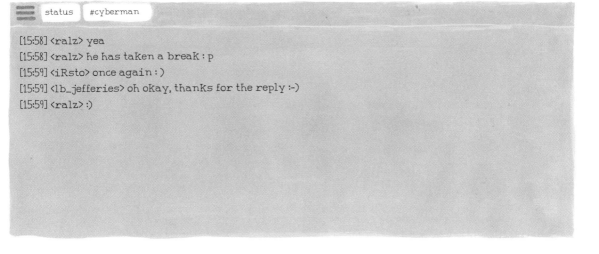

status   #cyberman

[15:58] <ralz> yea

[15:58] <ralz> he has taken a break : p

[15:59] <iRsto> once again :)

[15:59] <lb_jefferies> oh okay, thanks for the reply :-)

[15:59] <ralz> :)

11.06.2016

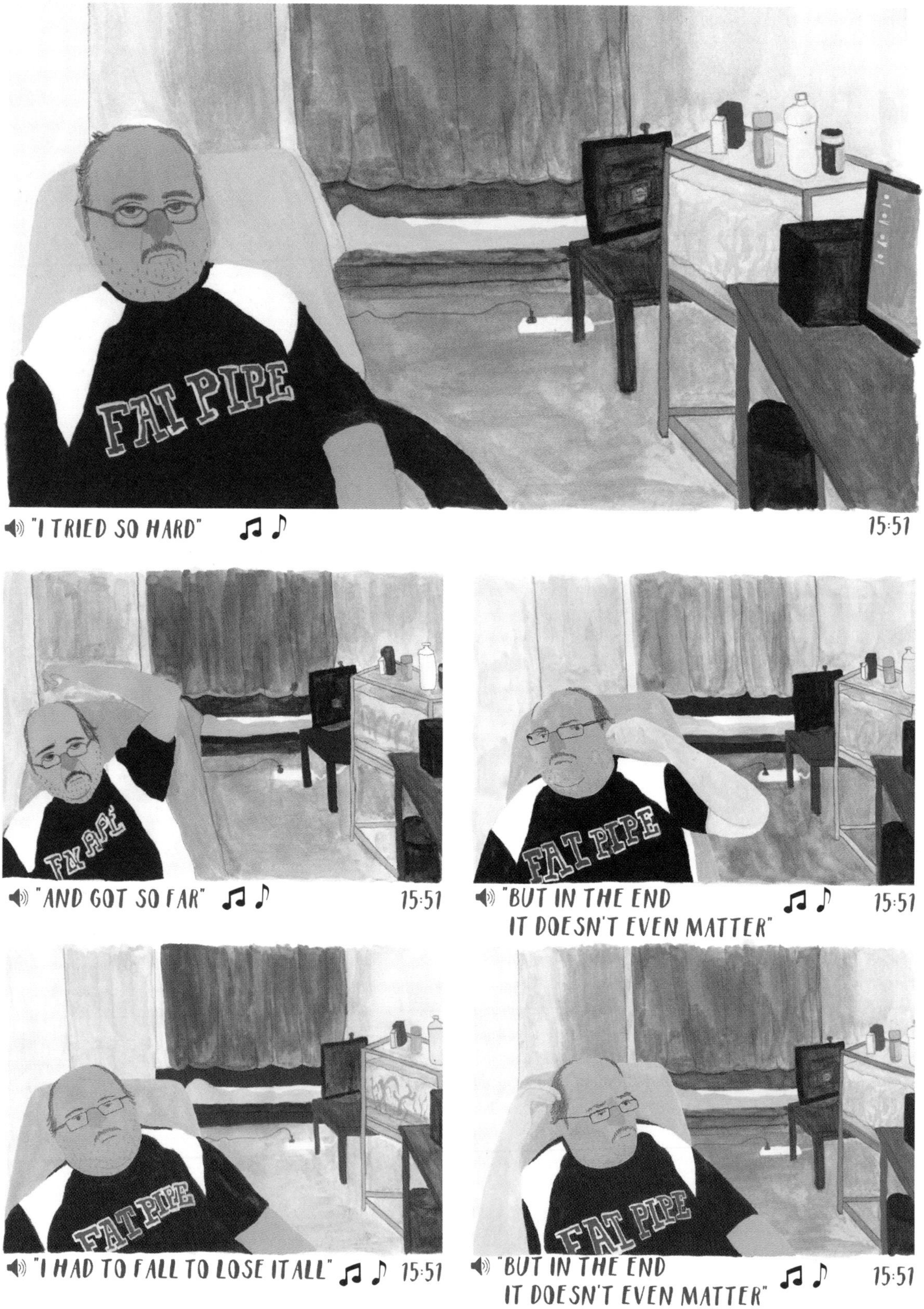
FAT PIPE
"I TRIED SO HARD" ♫ ♪
15:51
"AND GOT SO FAR" ♫ ♪
15:51
FAT PIPE
"BUT IN THE END IT DOESN'T EVEN MATTER" ♫ ♪
15:51
FAT PIPE
"I HAD TO FALL TO LOSE IT ALL" ♫ ♪
15:51
FAT PIPE
"BUT IN THE END IT DOESN'T EVEN MATTER" ♫ ♪
15:51

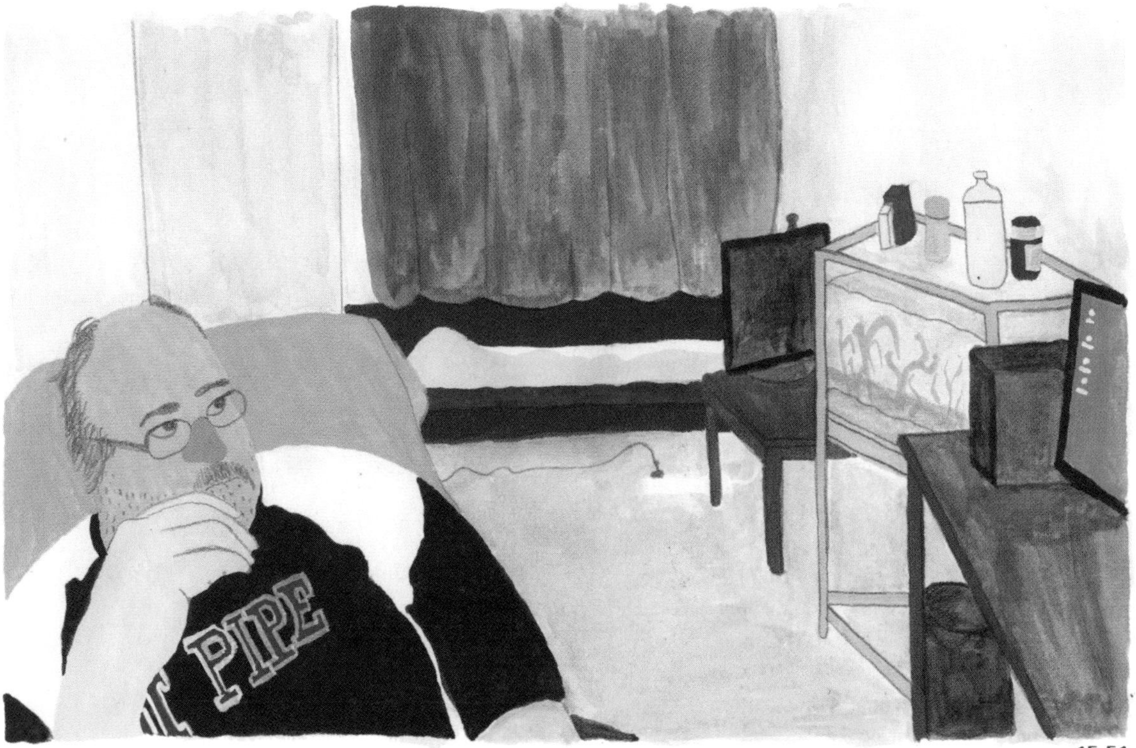
PIPE

. . . ♫♪ 15:51

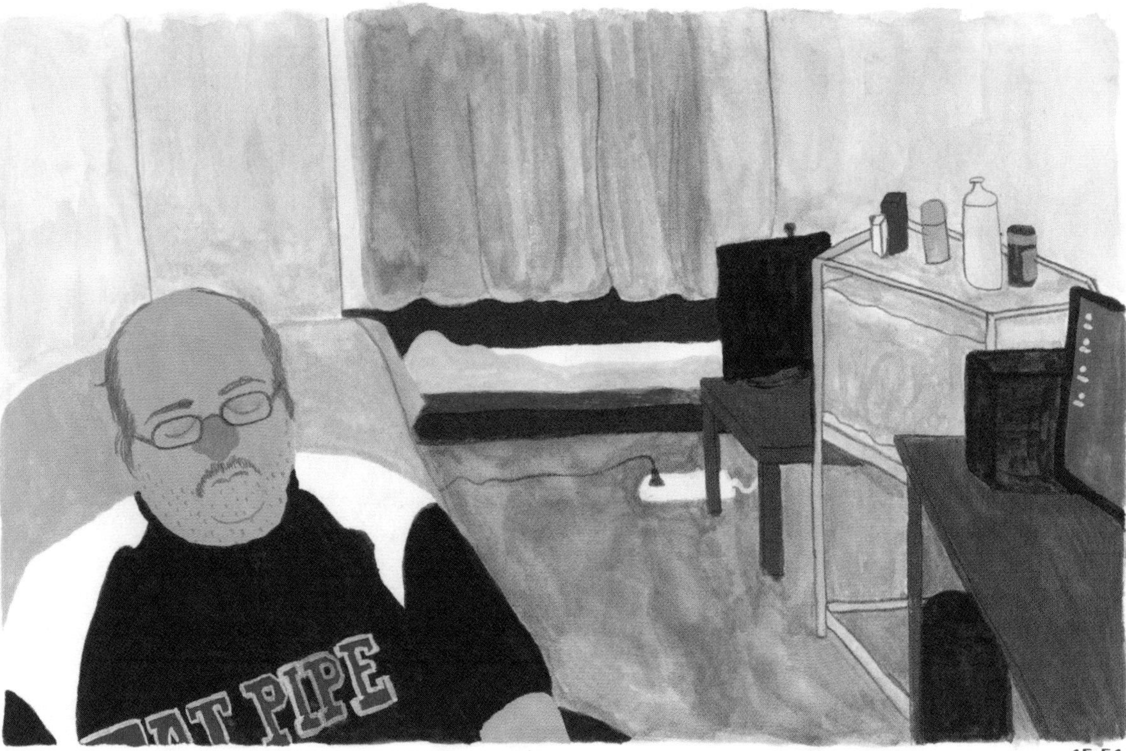
PIPE

"ONE THING, I DON'T KNOW WHY..." ♫♪ 15:51

27.06.2016

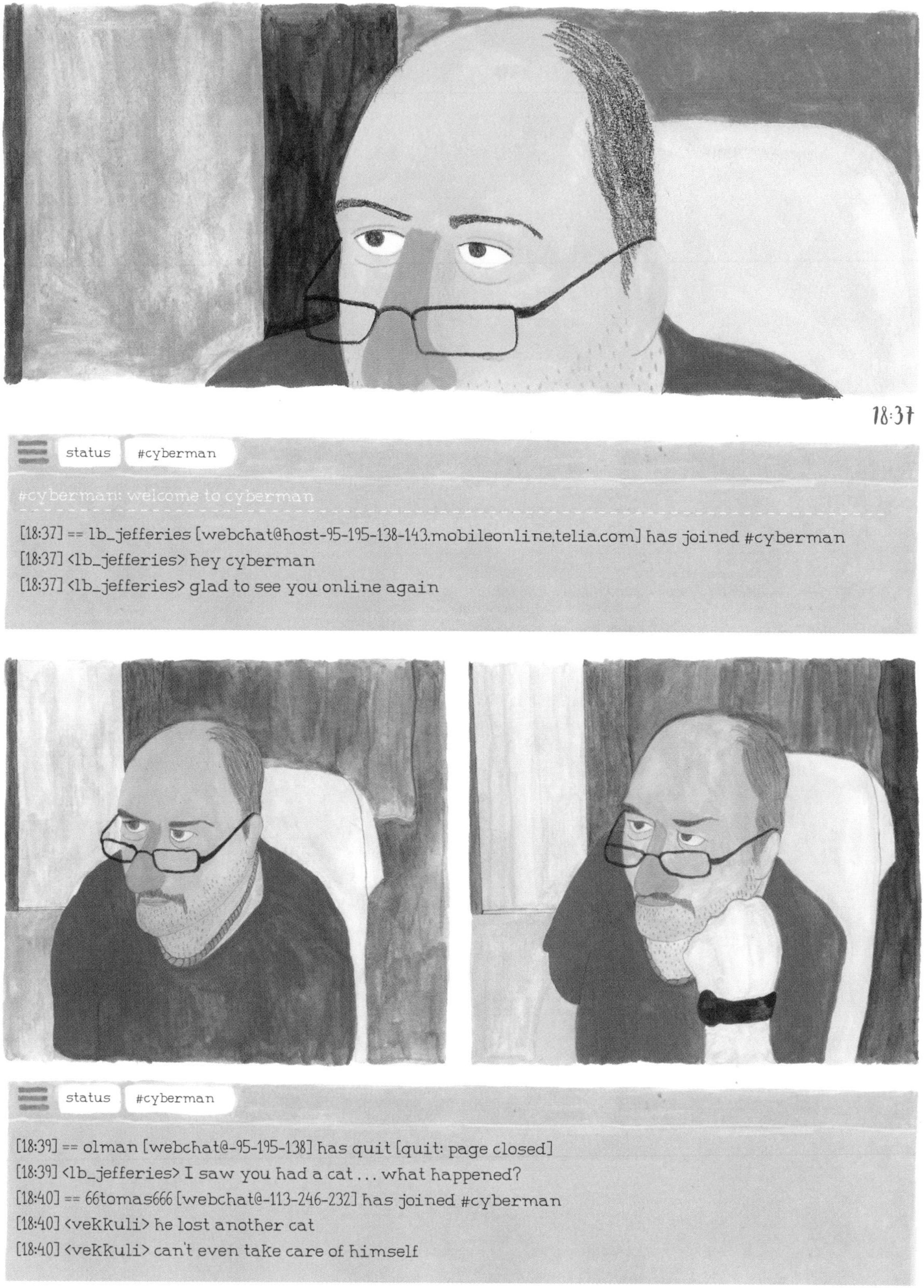
18:37
status
#cyberman
#cyberman: welcome to cyberman
[18:37] == lb_jefferies [webchat@host-95-195-138-143.mobileonline.telia.com] has joined #cyberman
[18:37] <lb_jefferies> hey cyberman
[18:37] <lb_jefferies> glad to see you online again
status
#cyberman
[18:39] == olman [webchat@-95-195-138] has quit [quit: page closed]
[18:39] <lb_jefferies> I saw you had a cat . . . what happened?
[18:40] == 66tomas666 [webchat@-113-246-232] has joined #cyberman
[18:40] <veKKuli> he lost another cat
[18:40] <veKKuli> can't even taKe care of himself

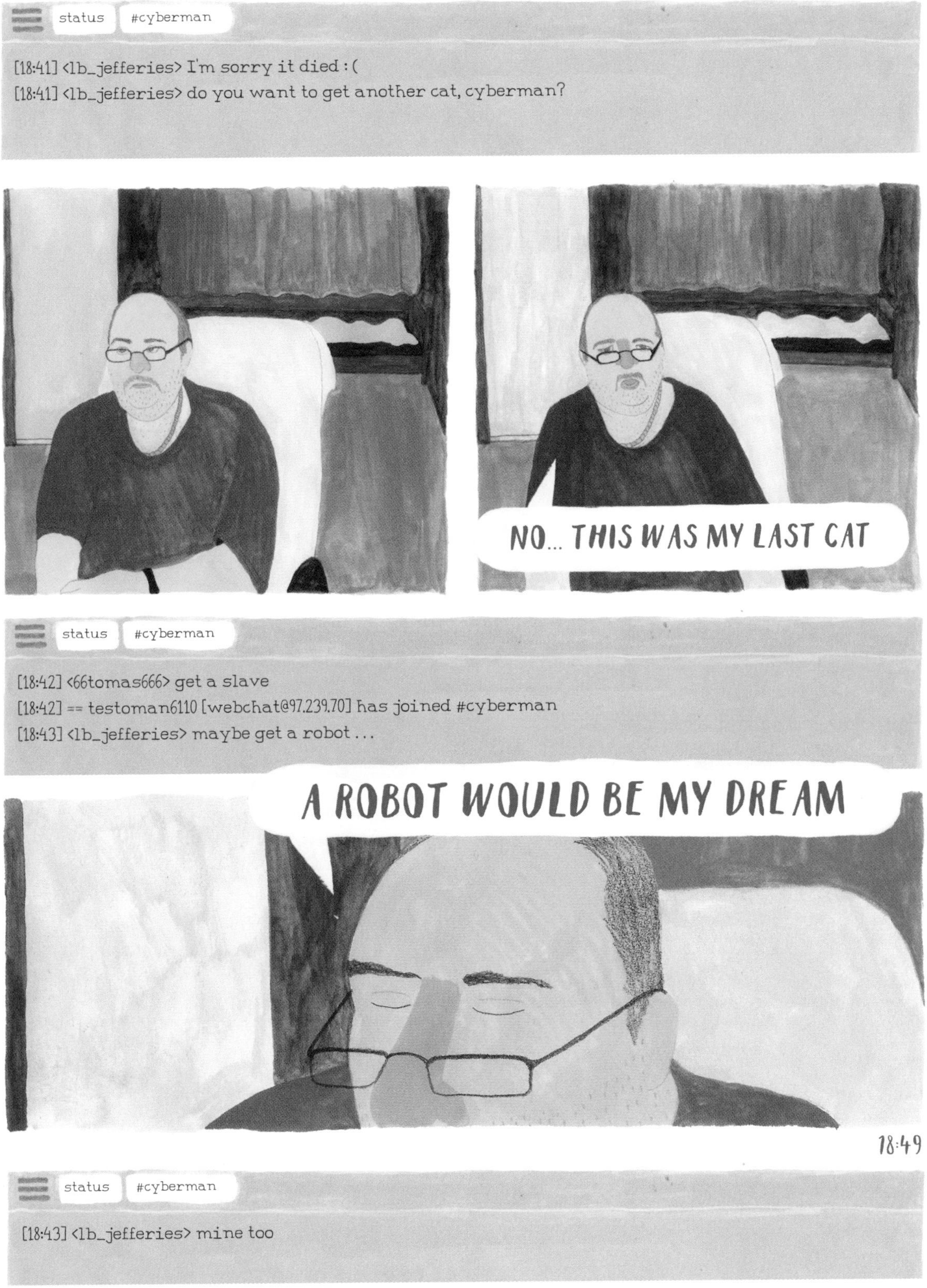
status
#cyberman
[18:41] <lb_jefferies> I'm sorry it died :(
[18:41] <lb_jefferies> do you want to get another cat, cyberman?
NO... THIS WAS MY LAST CAT
status
#cyberman
[18:42] <66tomas666> get a slave
[18:42] == testoman6110 [webchat@97.239.70] has joined #cyberman
[18:43] <lb_jefferies> maybe get a robot...
A ROBOT WOULD BE MY DREAM
18:49
status
#cyberman
[18:43] <lb_jefferies> mine too

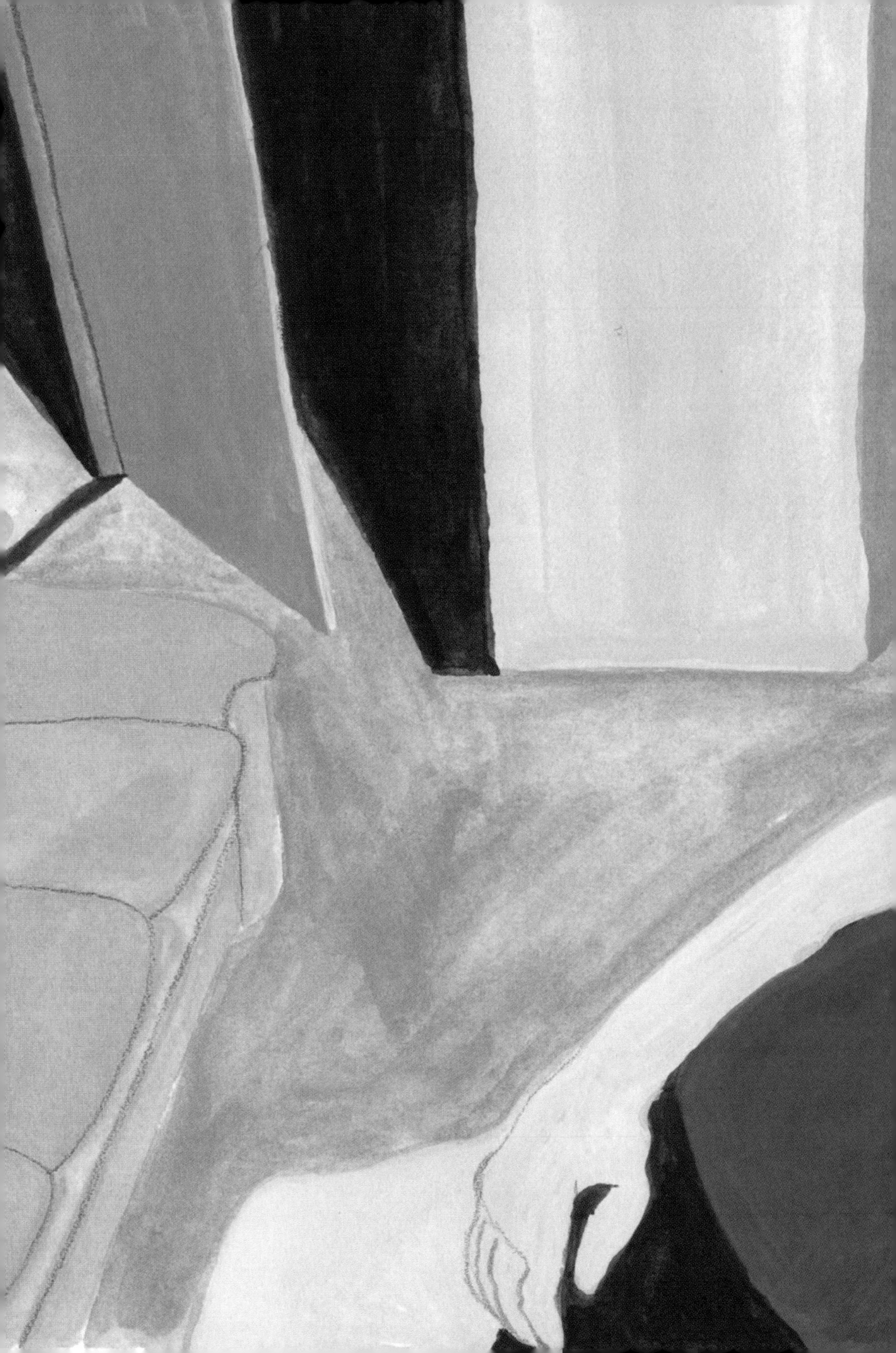

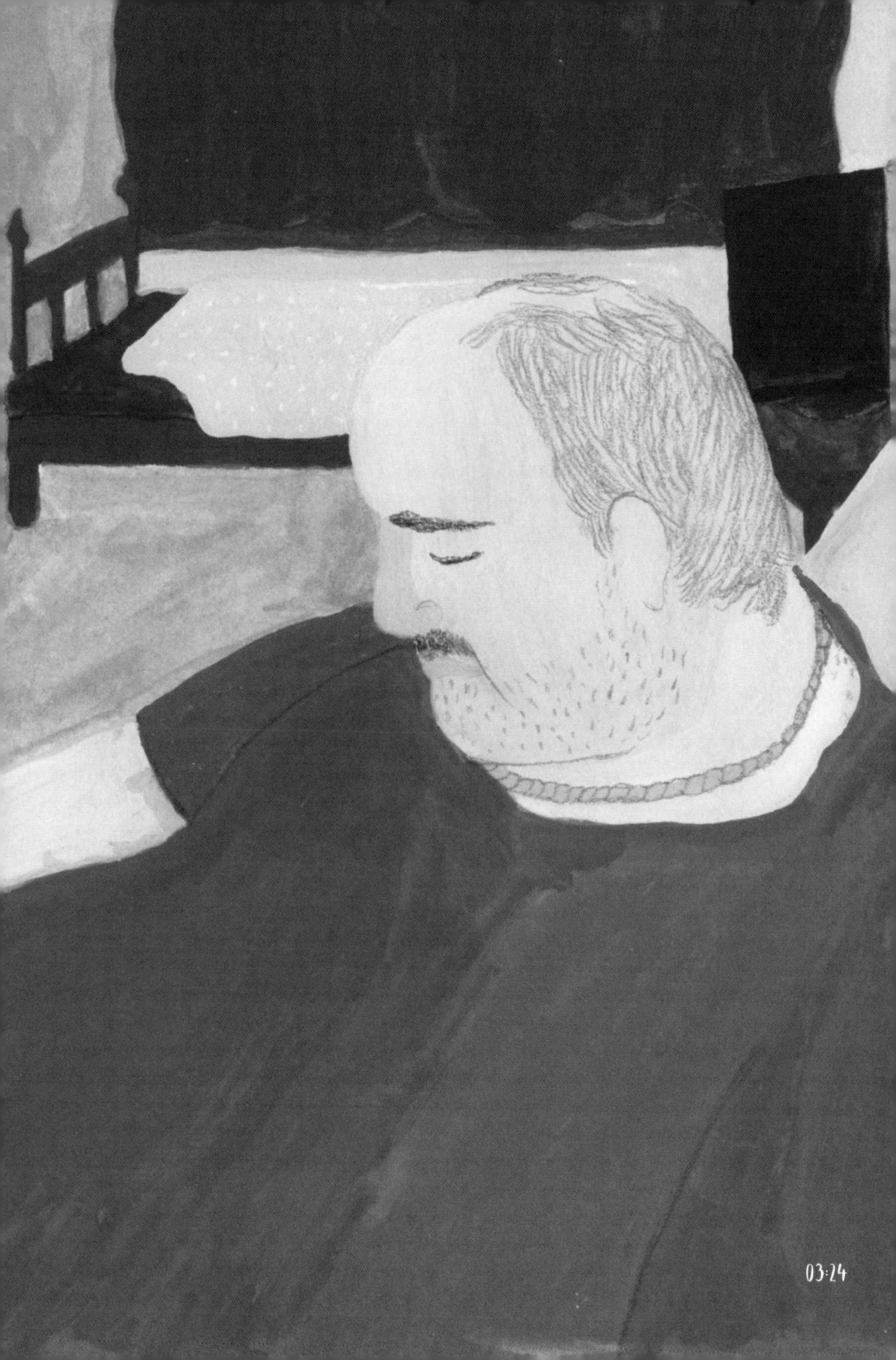
03:24

30.06.2016

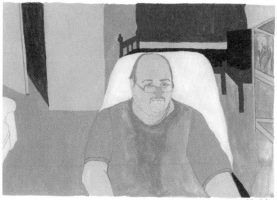
18:04

18:04

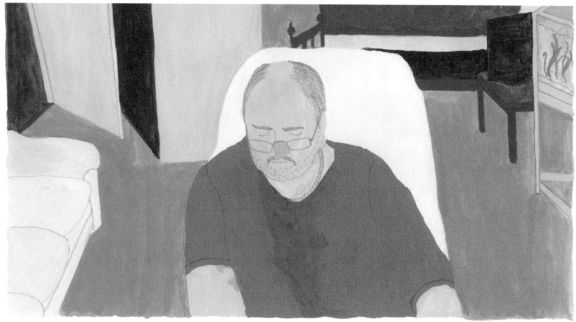
18:06

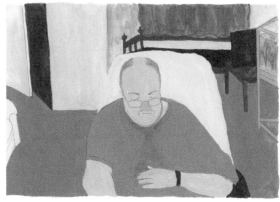
18:09

18:10

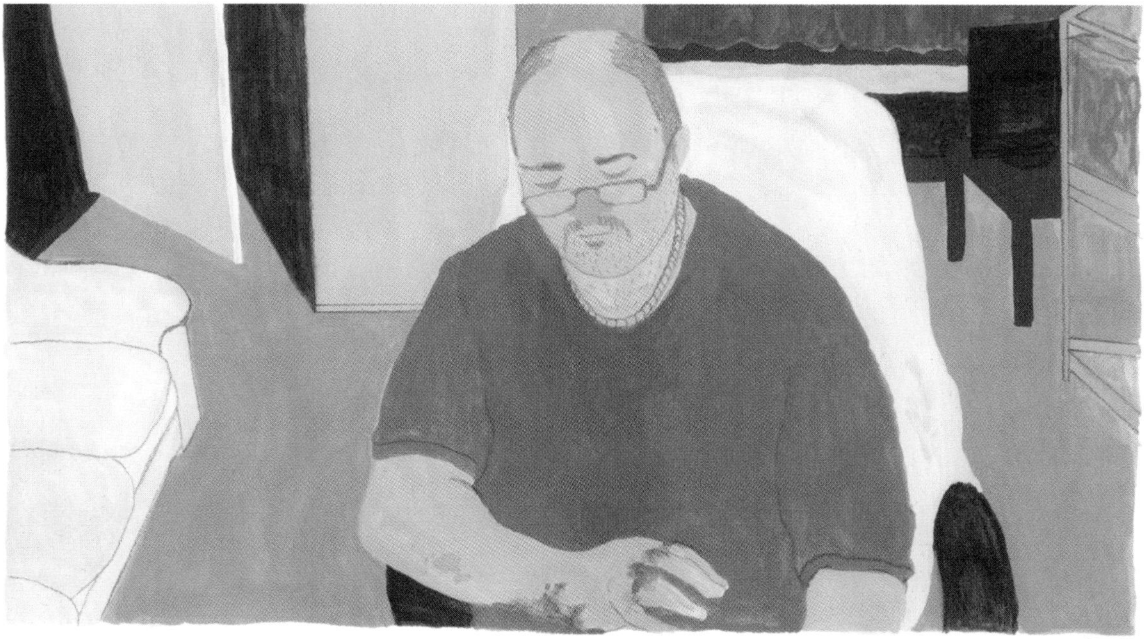

18:13

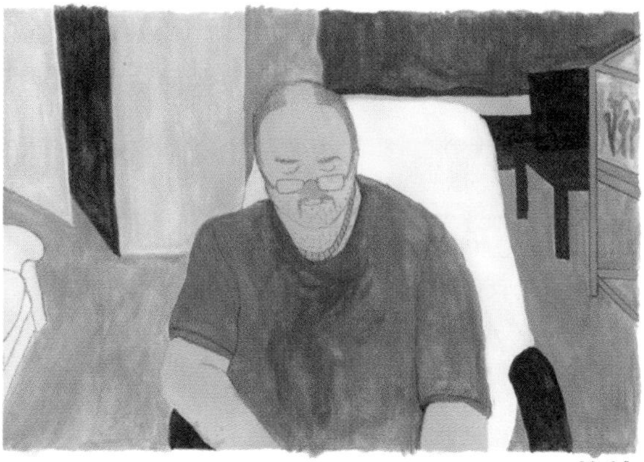

18:16

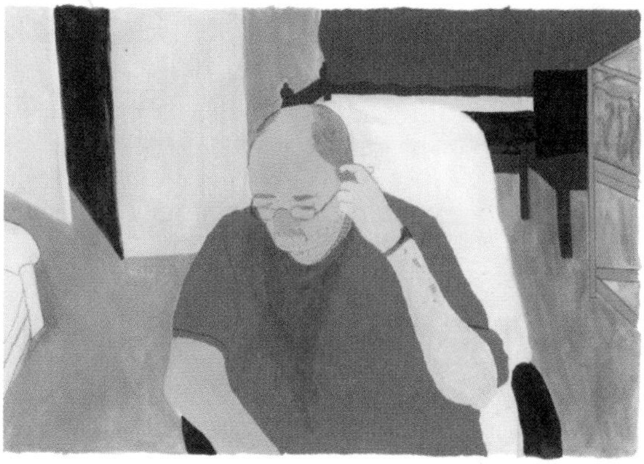

18:16

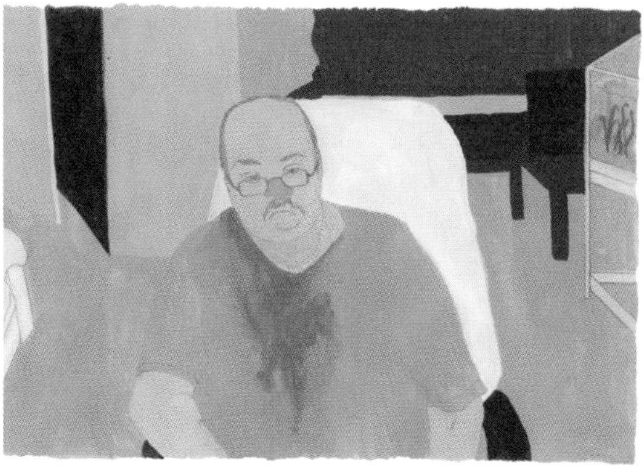

18:17

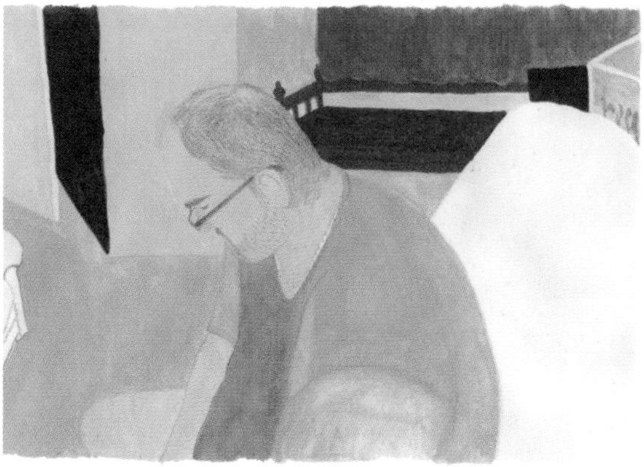

18:21

03.07.2016

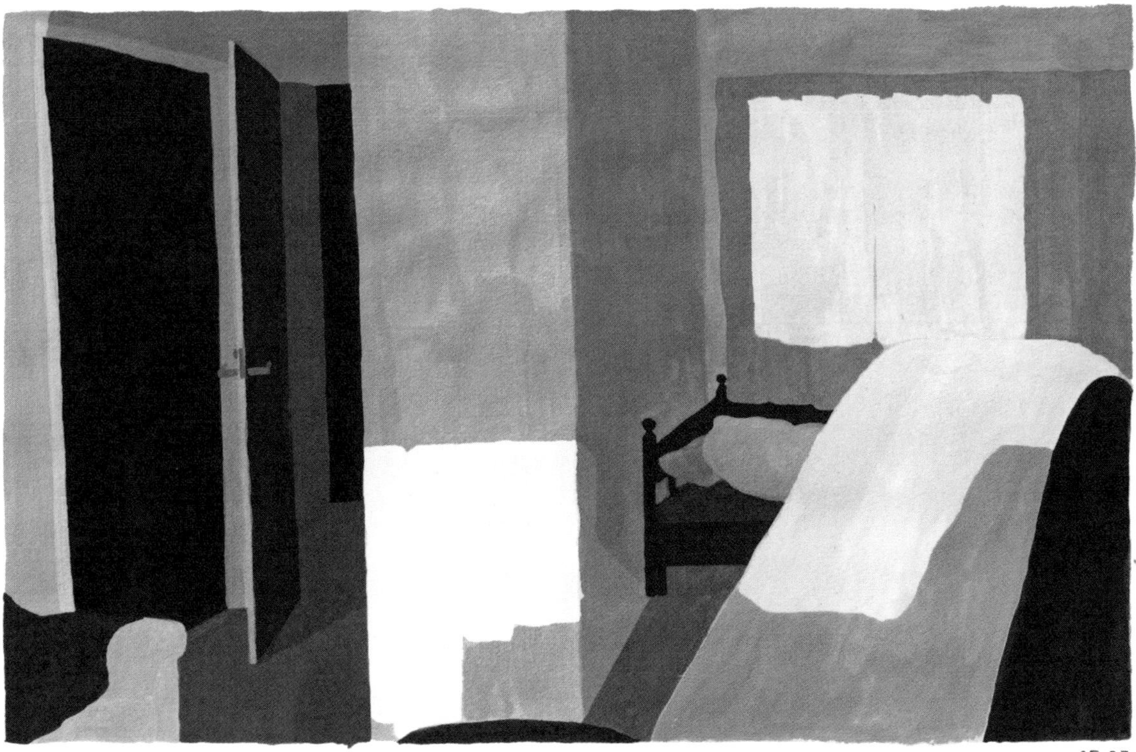

15:07

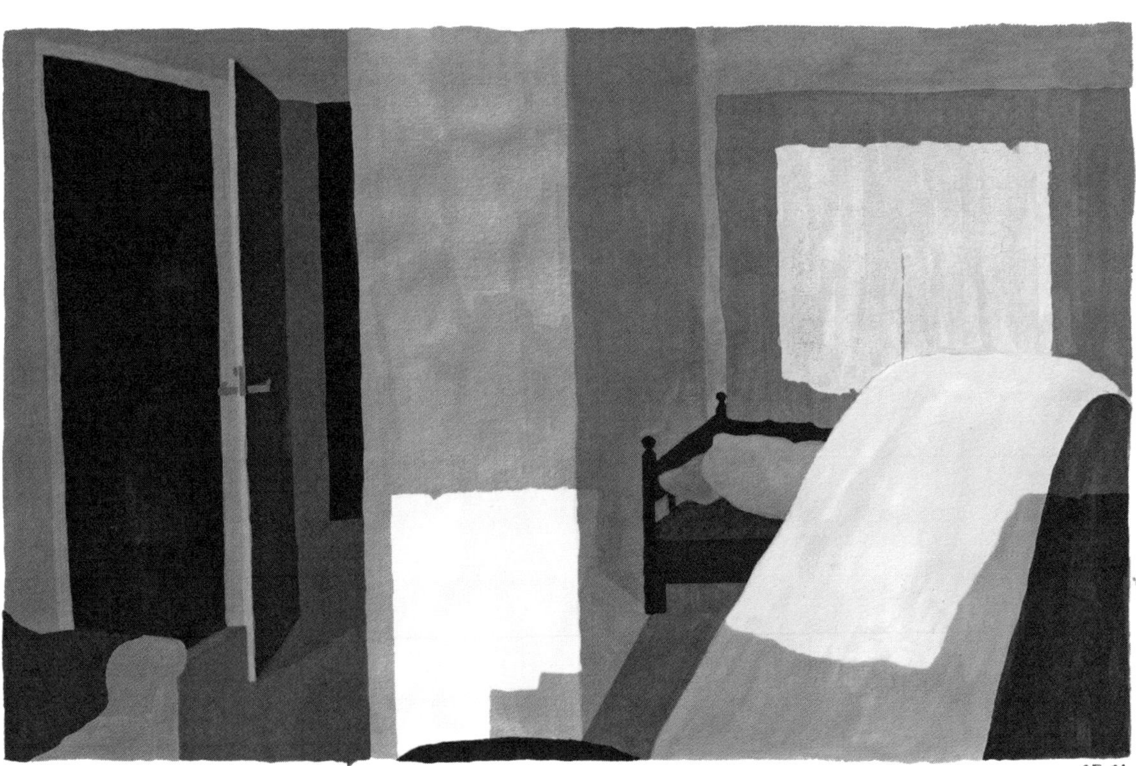

15:14

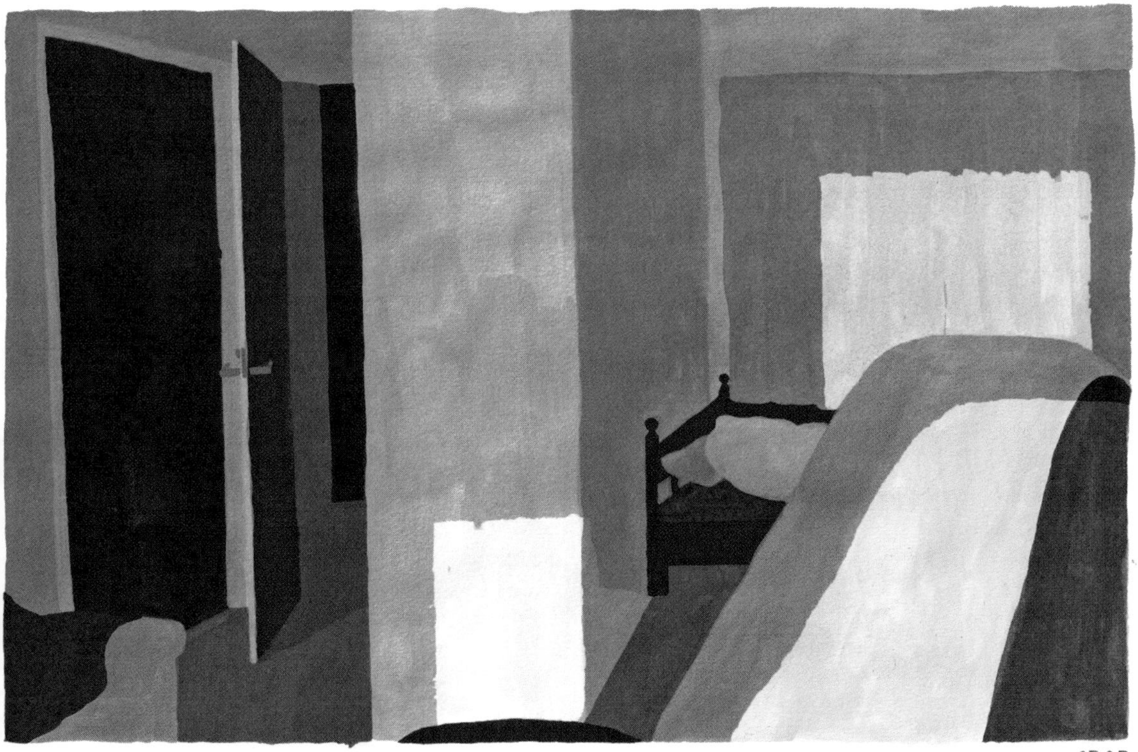

15:25

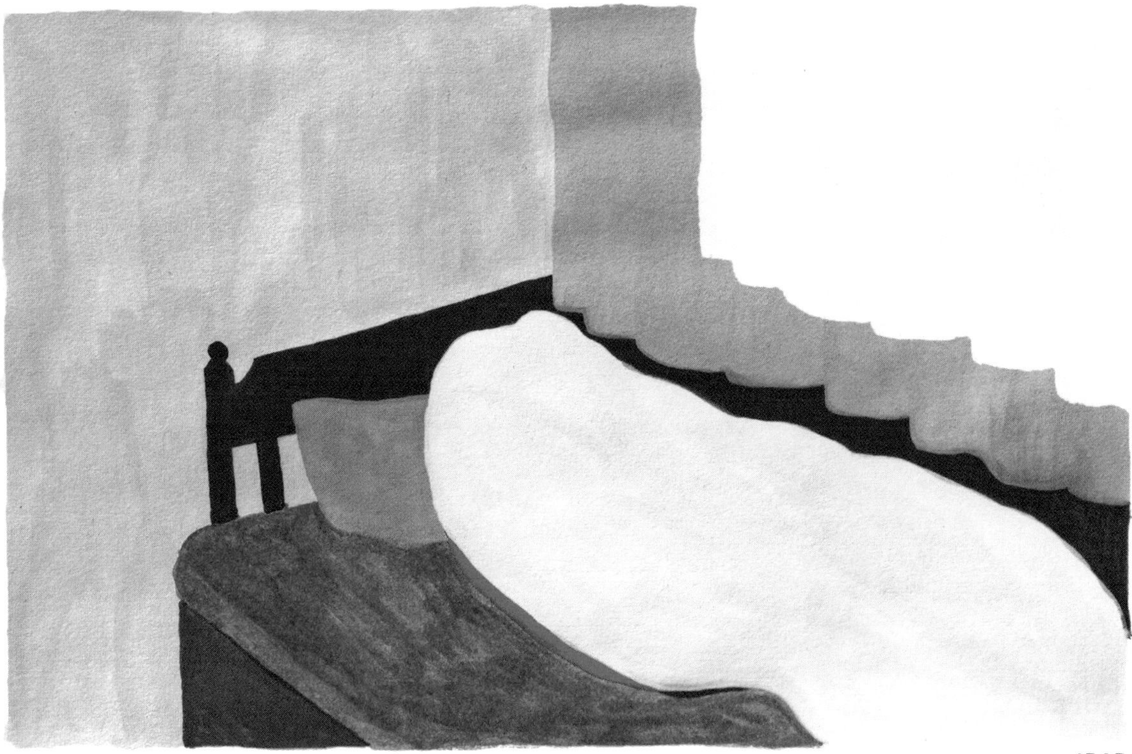

15:25

06.07.2016

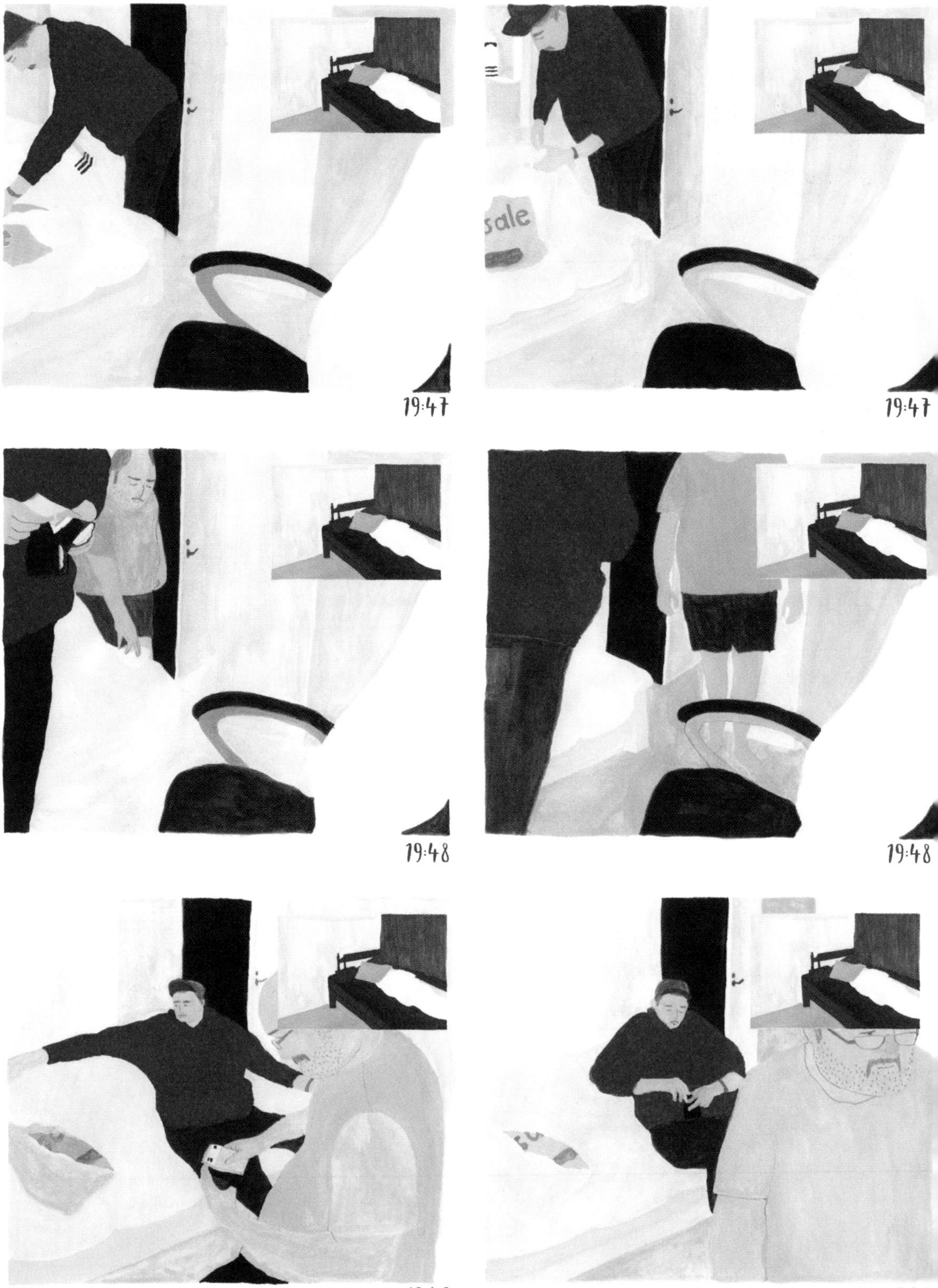
sale
19:47
19:47
19:48
19:48
19:49
19:49

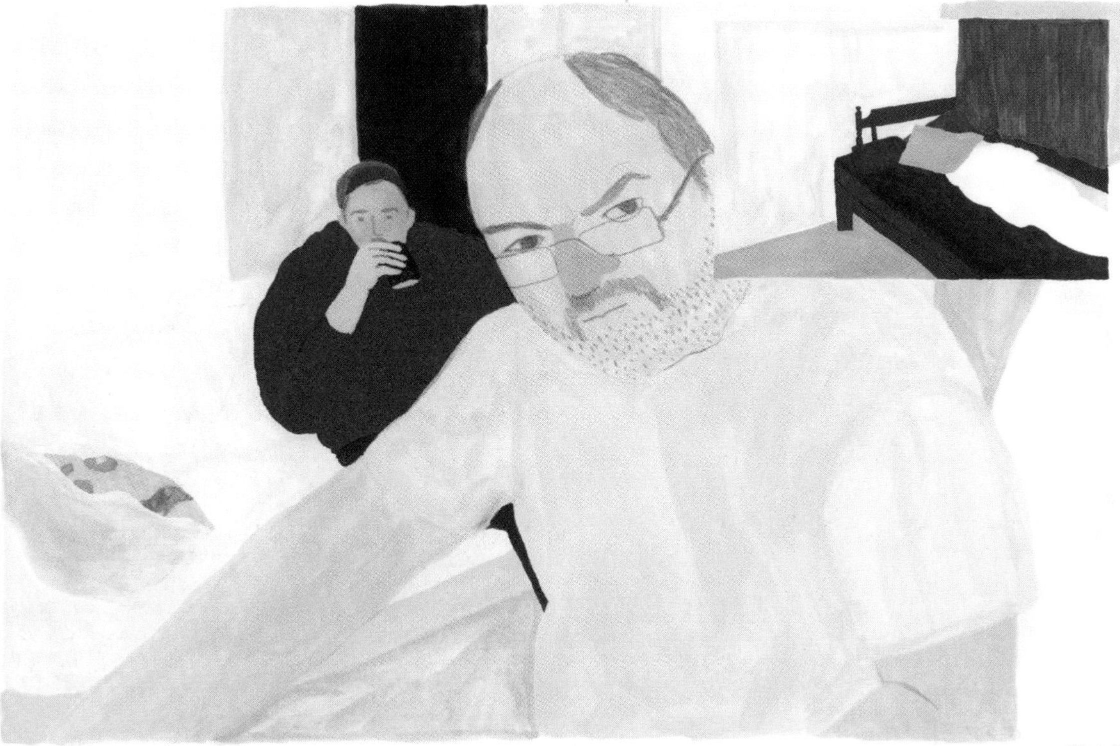

19:49

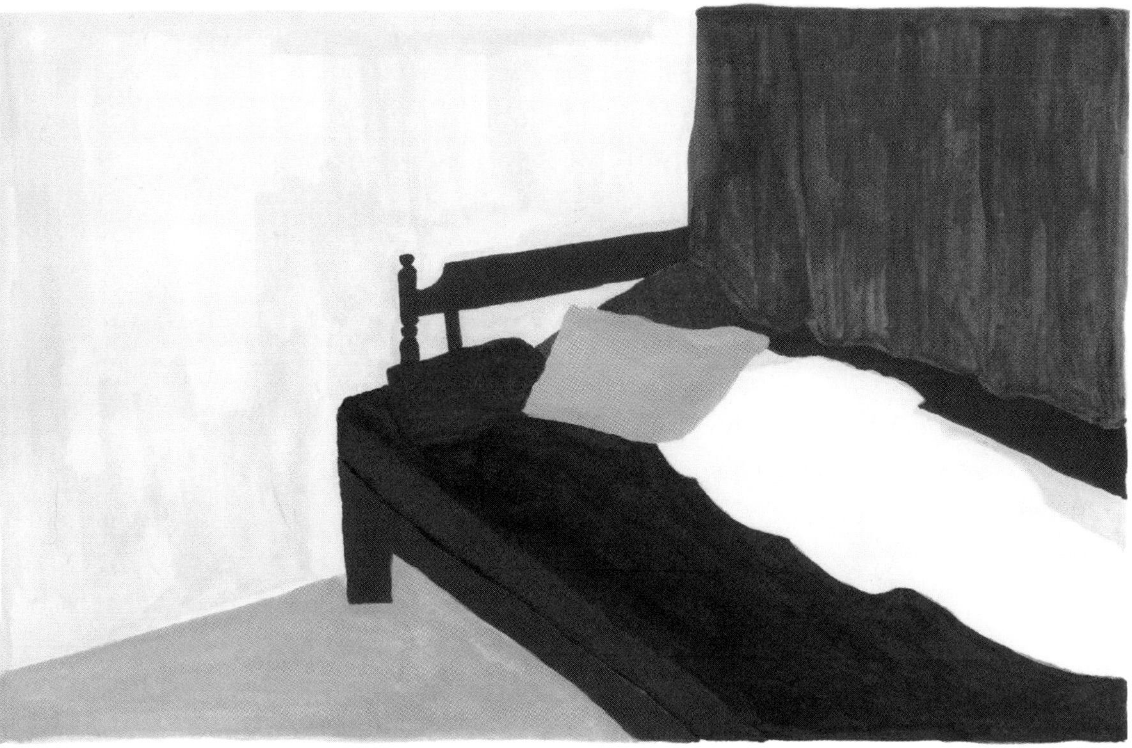

19:49

07.07.2016

status | #cyberman

#cyberman: welcome to cyberman

[22:28] == lb_jefferies [webchat@host-95-195-138-143.mobileonline.telia.com] has joined #cyberman
[22:28] == oldman [webchat@host-95-195-138-143.mobileonline.telia.com] has quit [quit: page closed]
[22:28] <jaKenK> cyberman plz acKnowledge me
[22:29] <_66tomas666> are you watching porn?

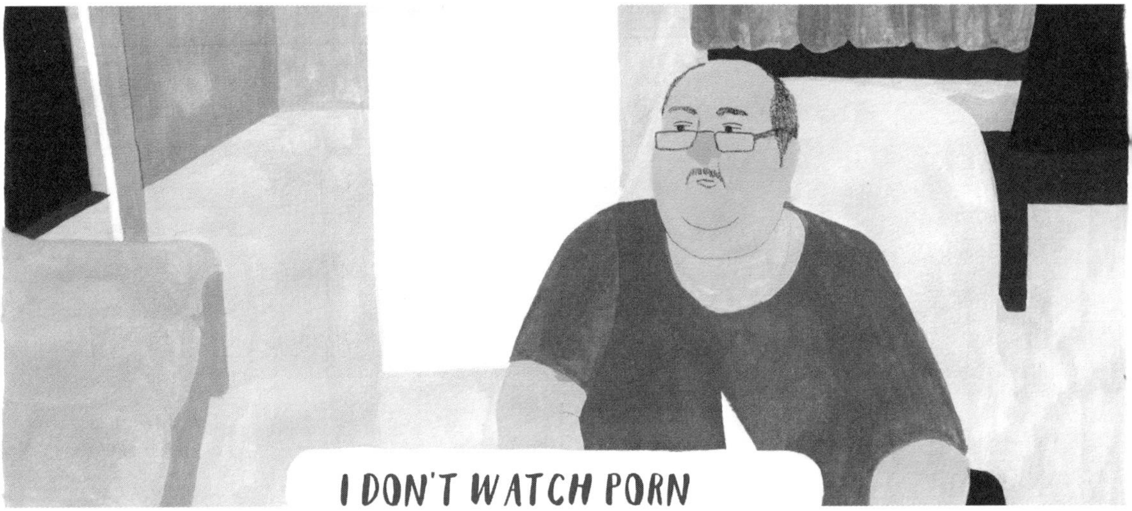
I DON'T WATCH PORN

22:29

status | #cyberman

[22:30] <jaKenK> did you move house?
[22:31] <jaKenK> hello?
[22:31] <jaKenK> I saw you liKe 5 years ago
[22:31] <janKeK> how are you?

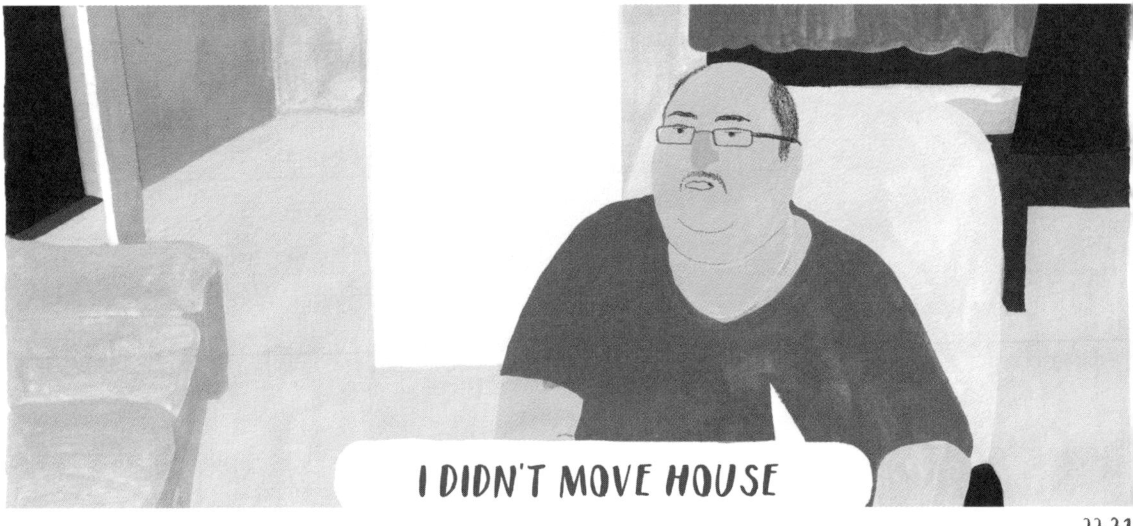
I DIDN'T MOVE HOUSE

22:31

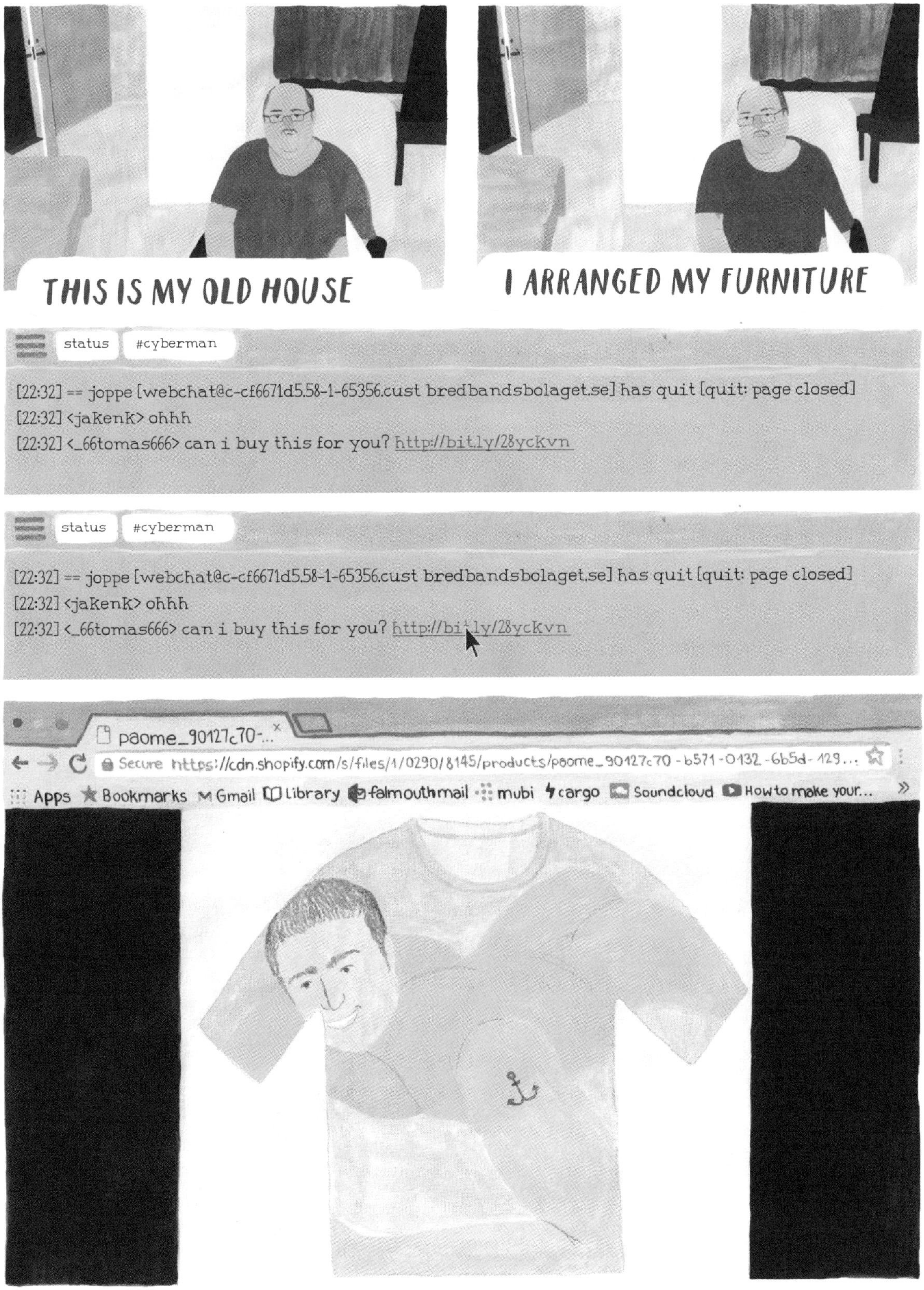
THIS IS MY OLD HOUSE
I ARRANGED MY FURNITURE
status
#cyberman
[22:32] == joppe [webchat@c-cf6671d5.58-1-65356.cust bredbandsbolaget.se] has quit [quit: page closed]
[22:32] <jaKenK> ohhh
[22:32] <_66tomas666> can i buy this for you? http://bit.ly/28ycKvn
status
#cyberman
[22:32] == joppe [webchat@c-cf6671d5.58-1-65356.cust bredbandsbolaget.se] has quit [quit: page closed]
[22:32] <jaKenK> ohhh
[22:32] <_66tomas666> can i buy this for you? http://bit.ly/28ycKvn
paome_90127c70-...
Secure https://cdn.shopify.com/s/files/1/0290/8145/products/paome_90127c70-b571-0132-6b5d-129...
Apps Bookmarks Gmail Library falmouthmail mubi cargo Soundcloud How to make your...

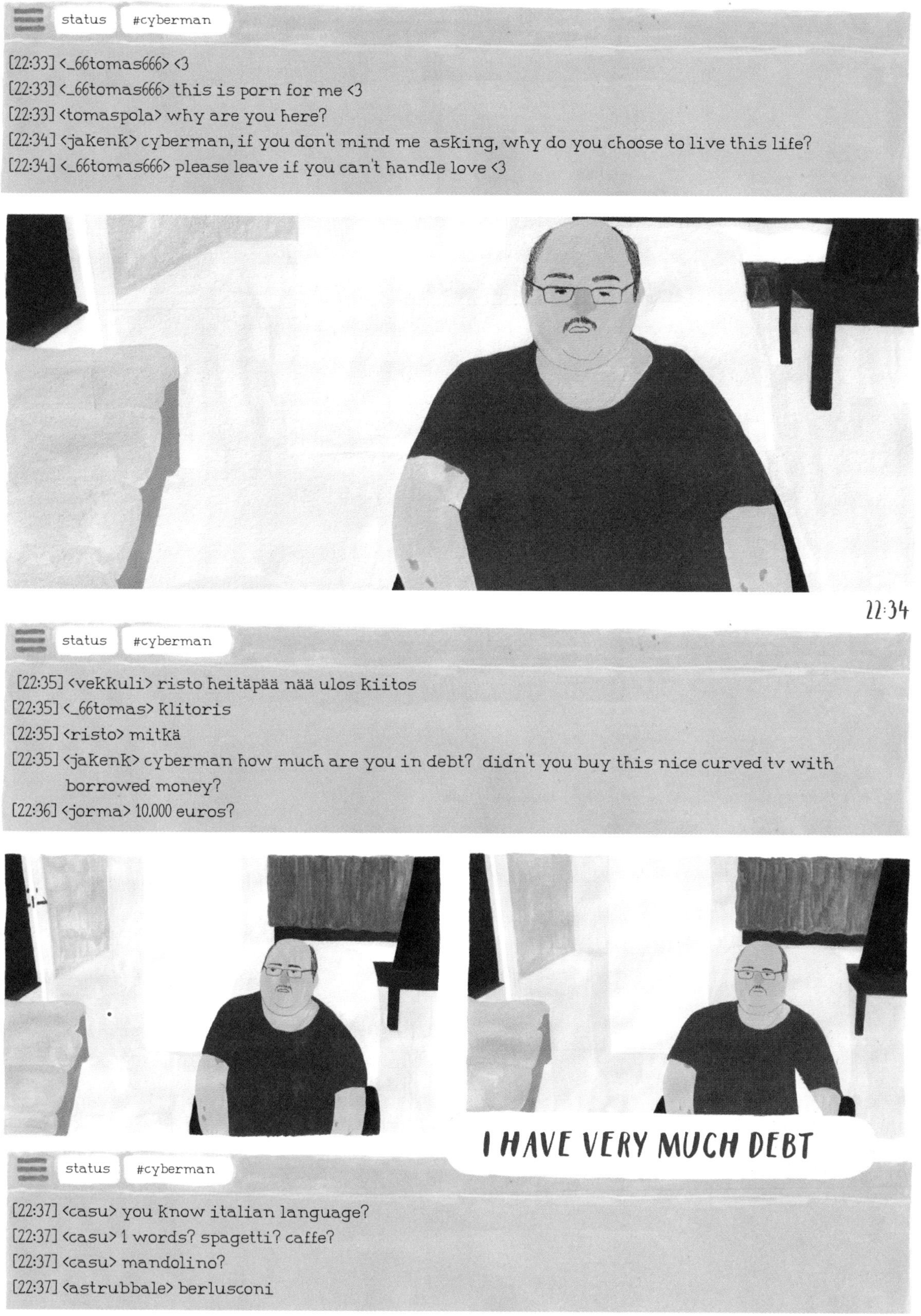
status #cyberman
[22:33] <_66tomas666> <3
[22:33] <_66tomas666> this is porn for me <3
[22:33] <tomaspola> why are you here?
[22:34] <jaKenK> cyberman, if you don't mind me asking, why do you choose to live this life?
[22:34] <_66tomas666> please leave if you can't handle love <3
22:34
status #cyberman
[22:35] <veKKuli> risto heitäpää nää ulos Kiitos
[22:35] <_66tomas> Klitoris
[22:35] <risto> mitKä
[22:35] <jaKenK> cyberman how much are you in debt? didn't you buy this nice curved tv with borrowed money?
[22:36] <jorma> 10.000 euros?
I HAVE VERY MUCH DEBT
status #cyberman
[22:37] <casu> you Know italian language?
[22:37] <casu> 1 words? spagetti? caffe?
[22:37] <casu> mandolino?
[22:37] <astrubbale> berlusconi

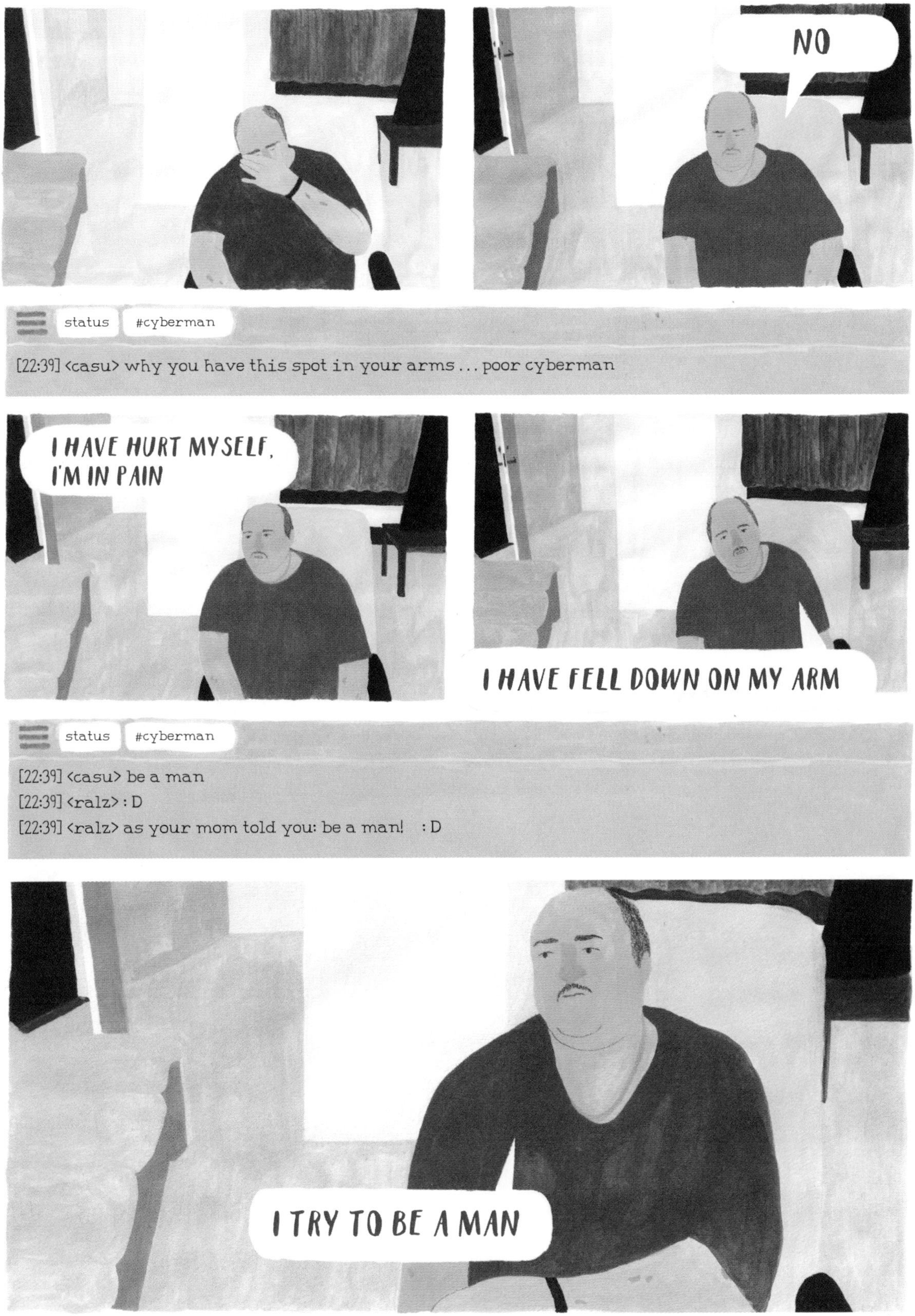
NO
status
#cyberman
[22:39] <casu> why you have this spot in your arms ... poor cyberman
I HAVE HURT MYSELF, I'M IN PAIN
I HAVE FELL DOWN ON MY ARM
status
#cyberman
[22:39] <casu> be a man
[22:39] <ralz> : D
[22:39] <ralz> as your mom told you: be a man! : D
I TRY TO BE A MAN

22:39

09.07.2016

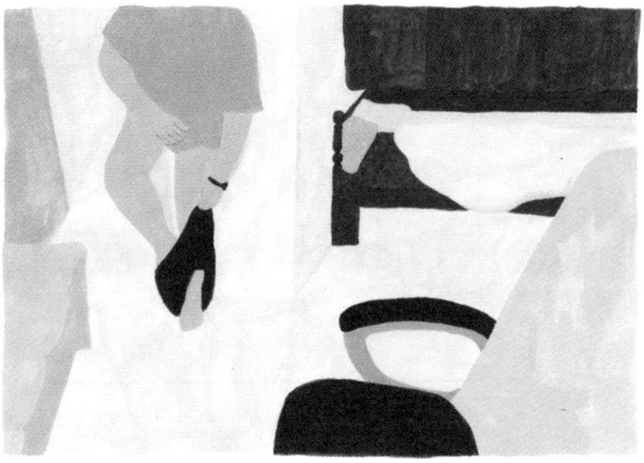

18:49

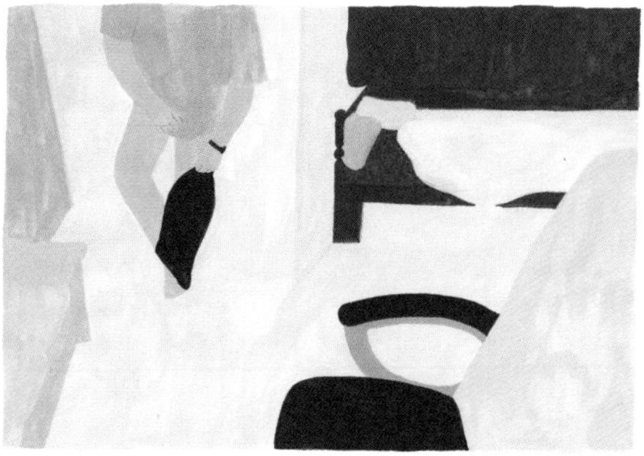

18:49

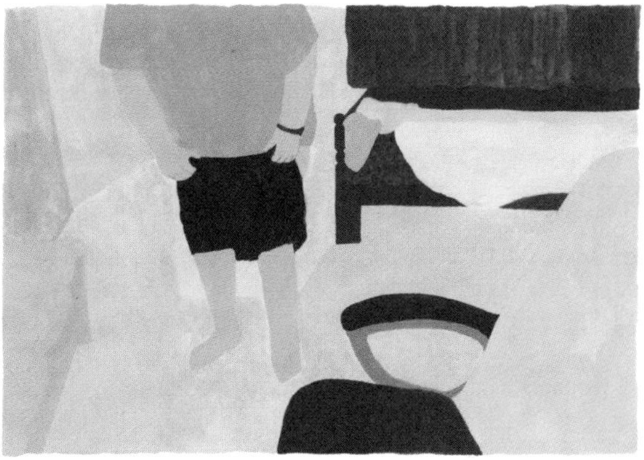

18:49

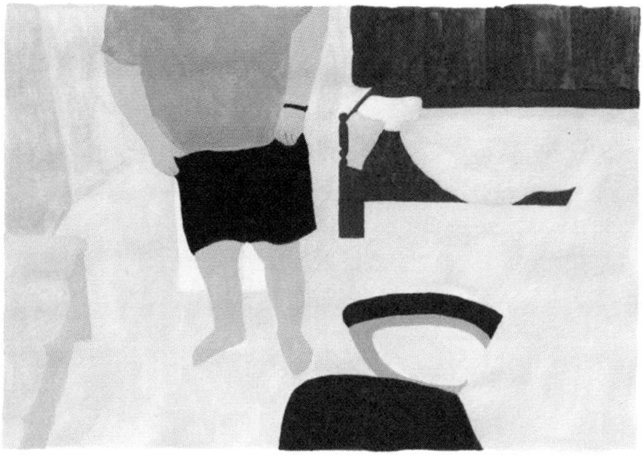

18:49

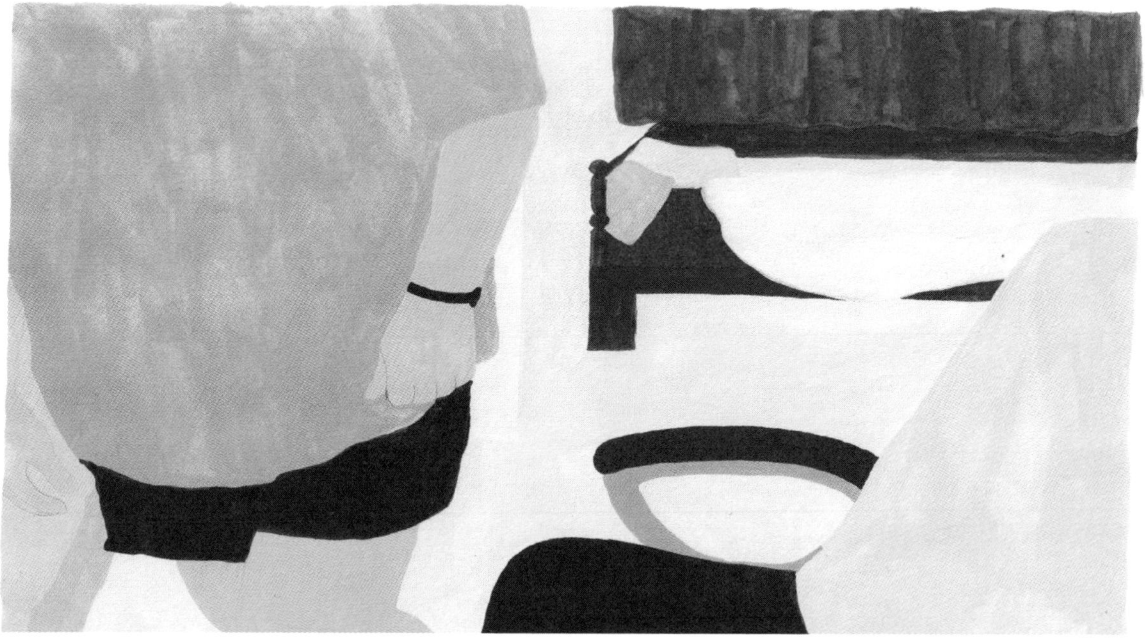

18:50

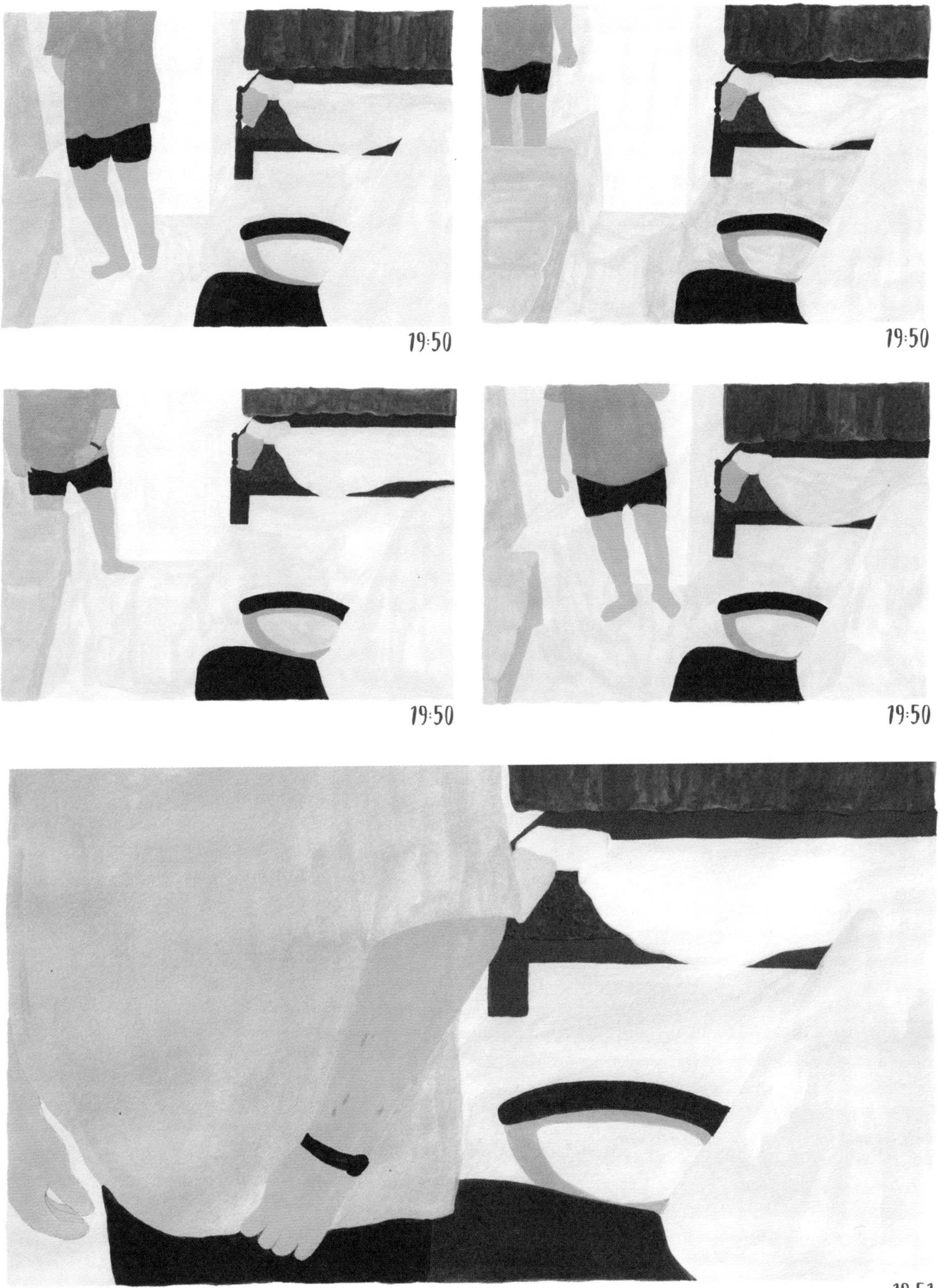
19:50
19:50
19:50
19:50
19:51

10.07.2016

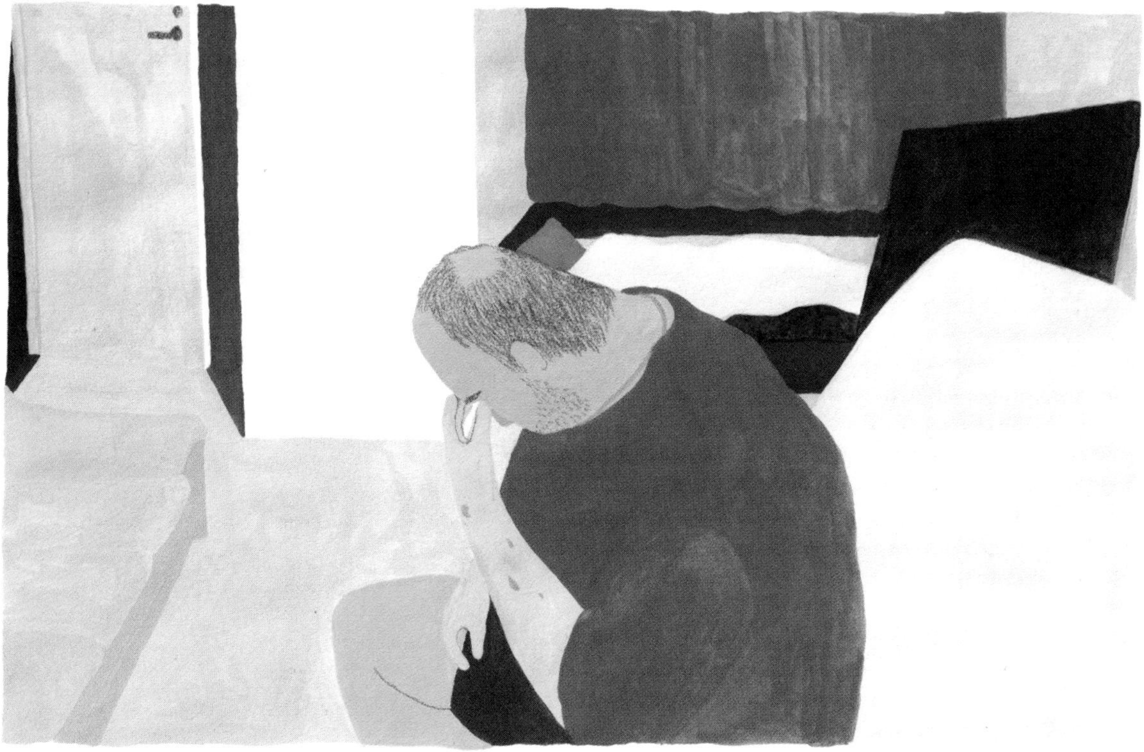

16:05

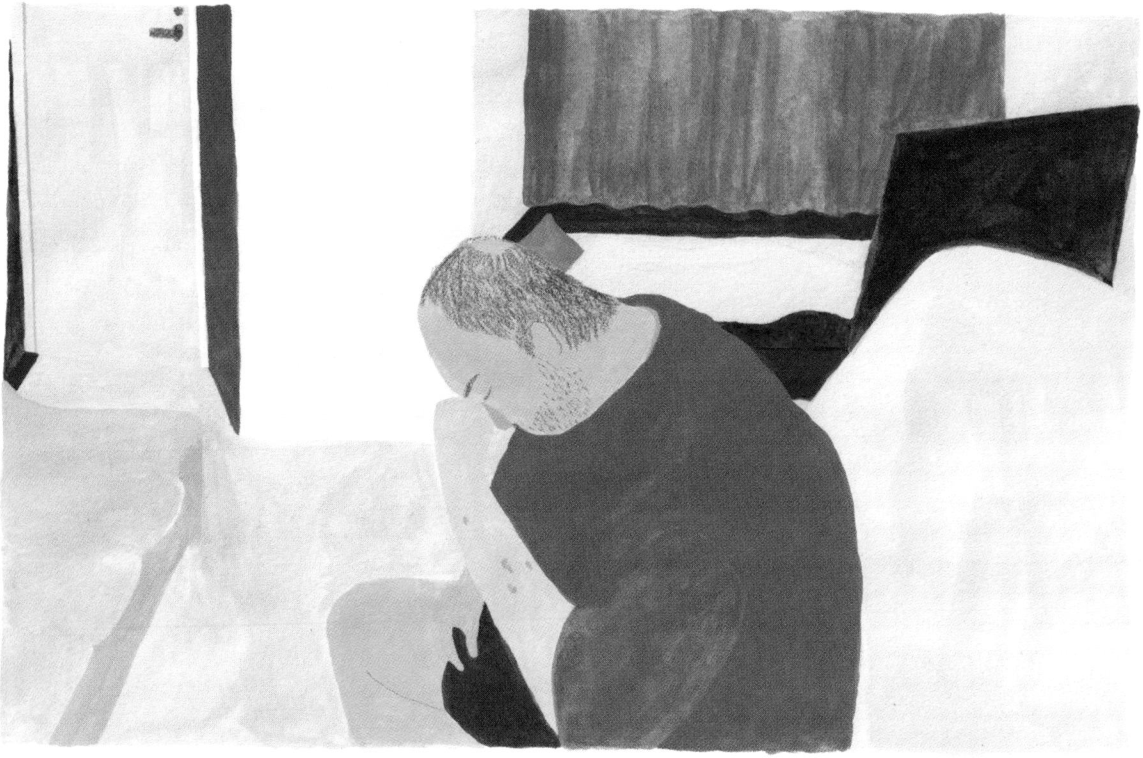

16:05

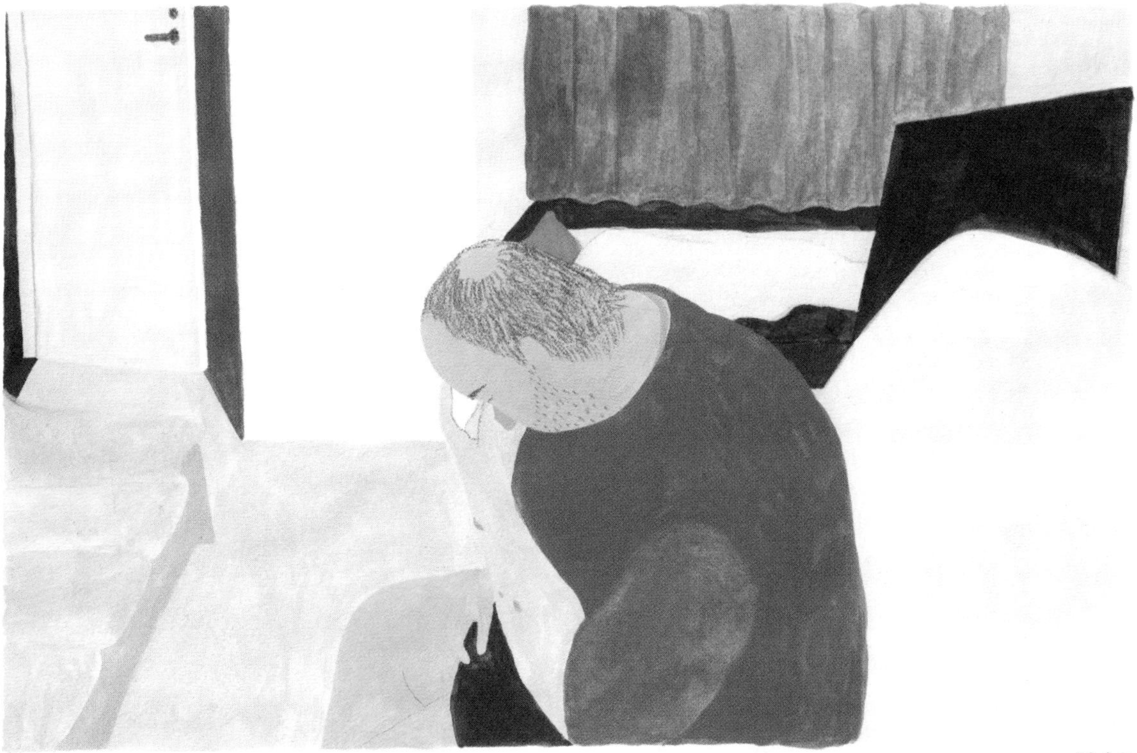

16:41

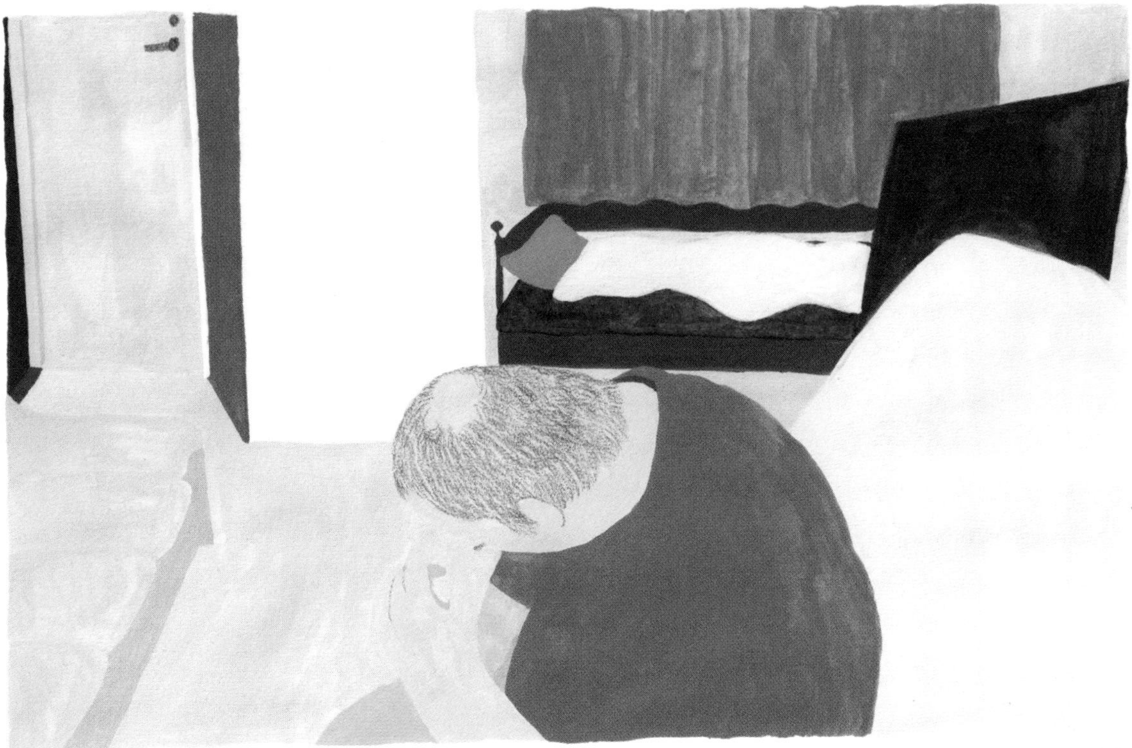

16:43

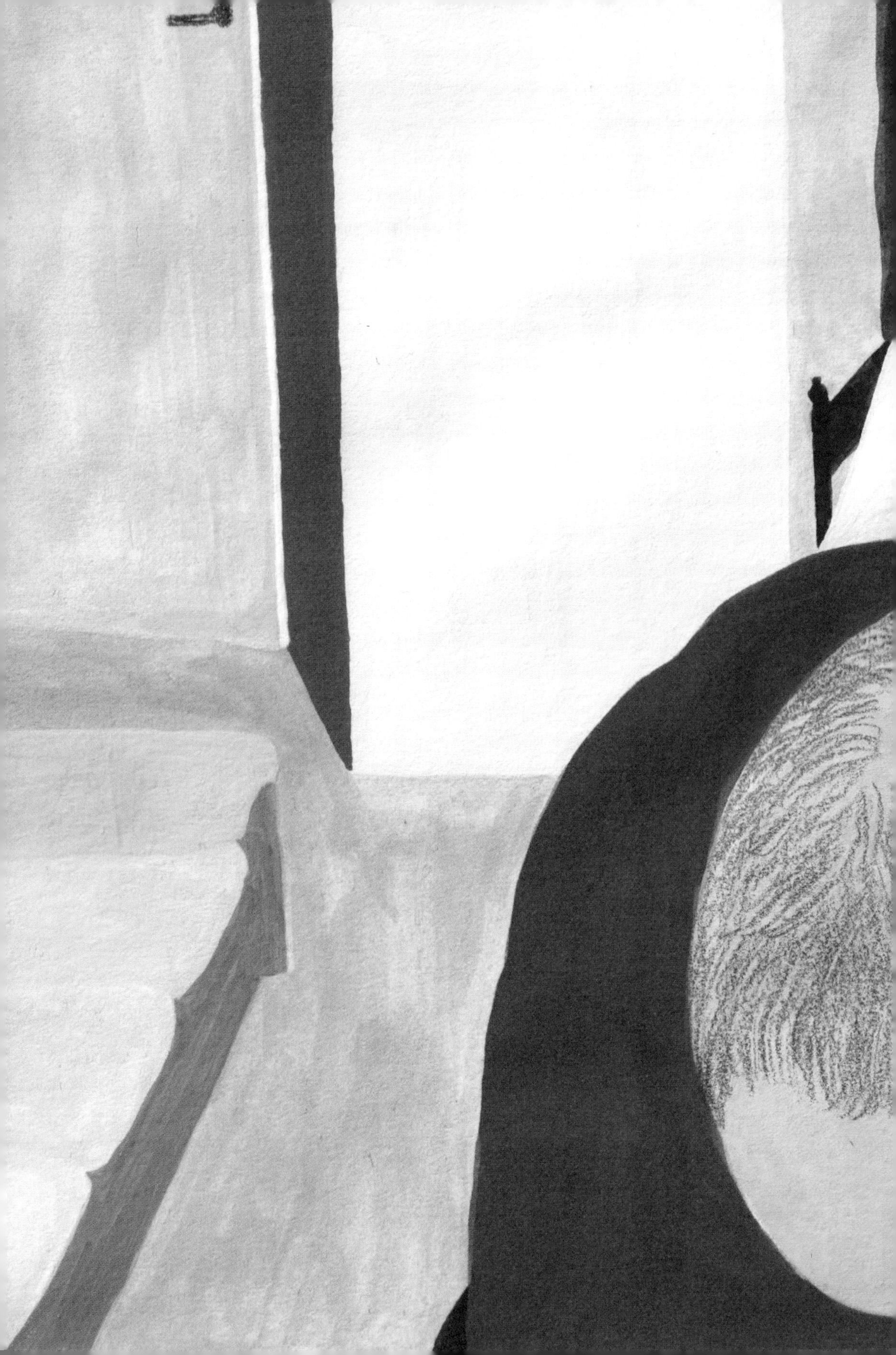

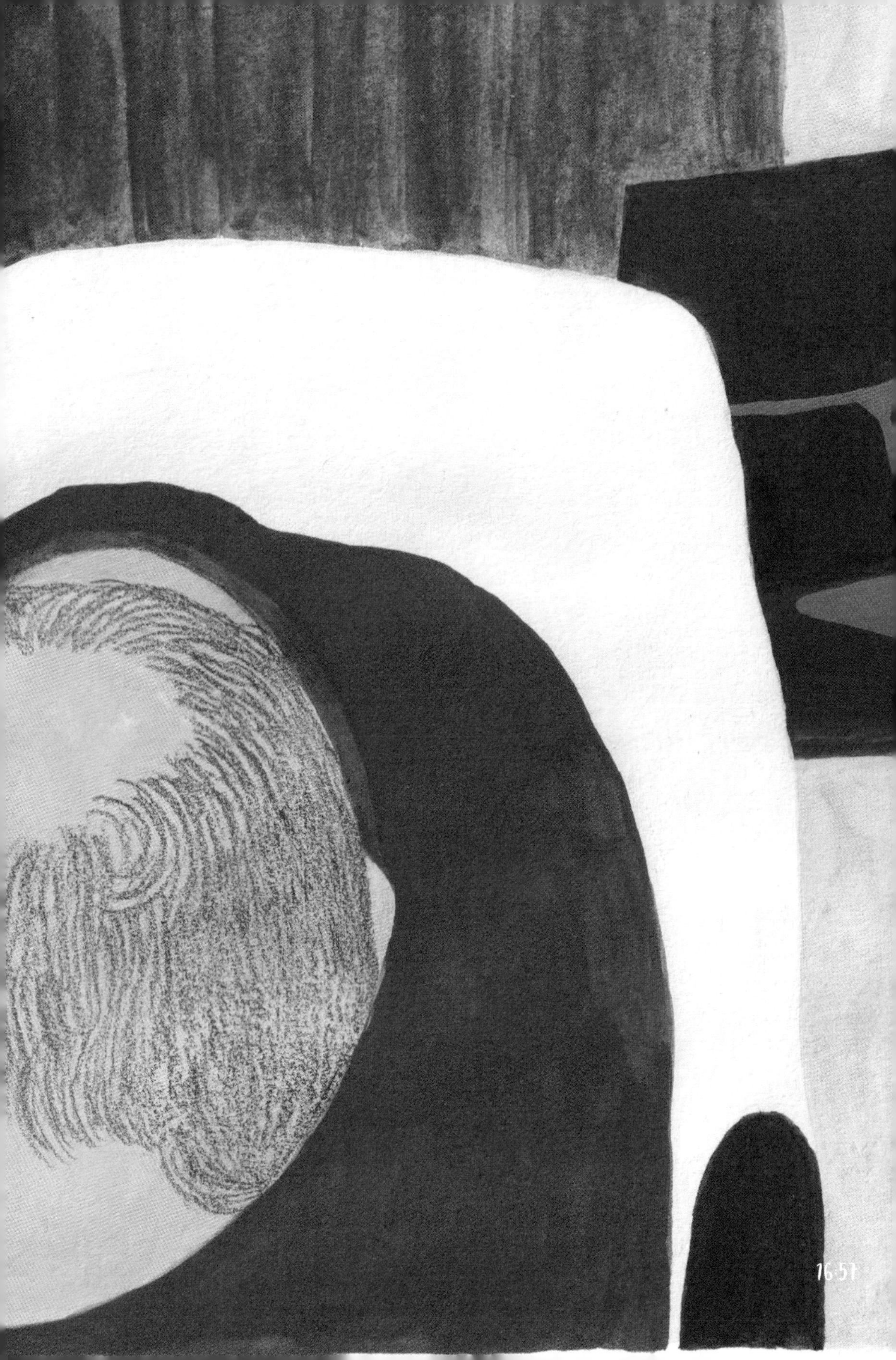

13.07.2016

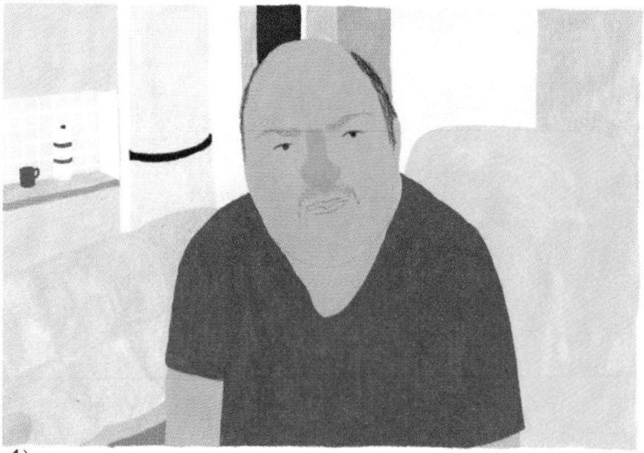

...

15:02

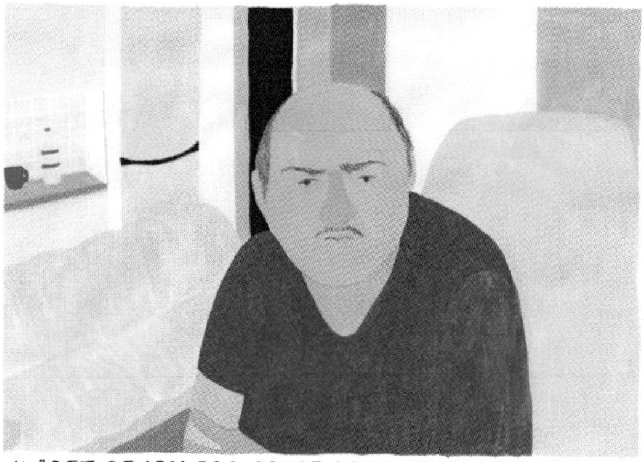

"GET READY FOR SOME GLAM AND GLITTER BECAUSE HERE COMES MILEY."

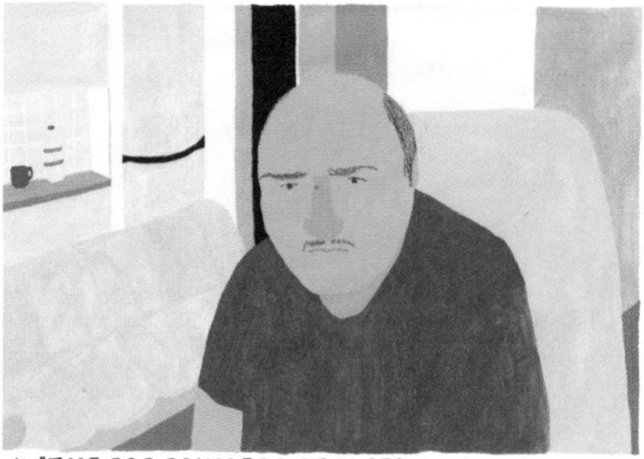

"THE POP PRINCESS STARTED OUT AS DISNEY SWEETHEART HANNAH MONTANA"

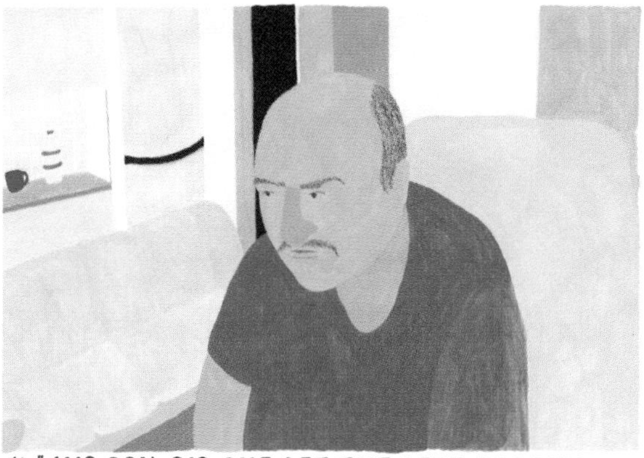

"AND BOY, DID SHE GET THE BEST OF BOTH WORLDS!"

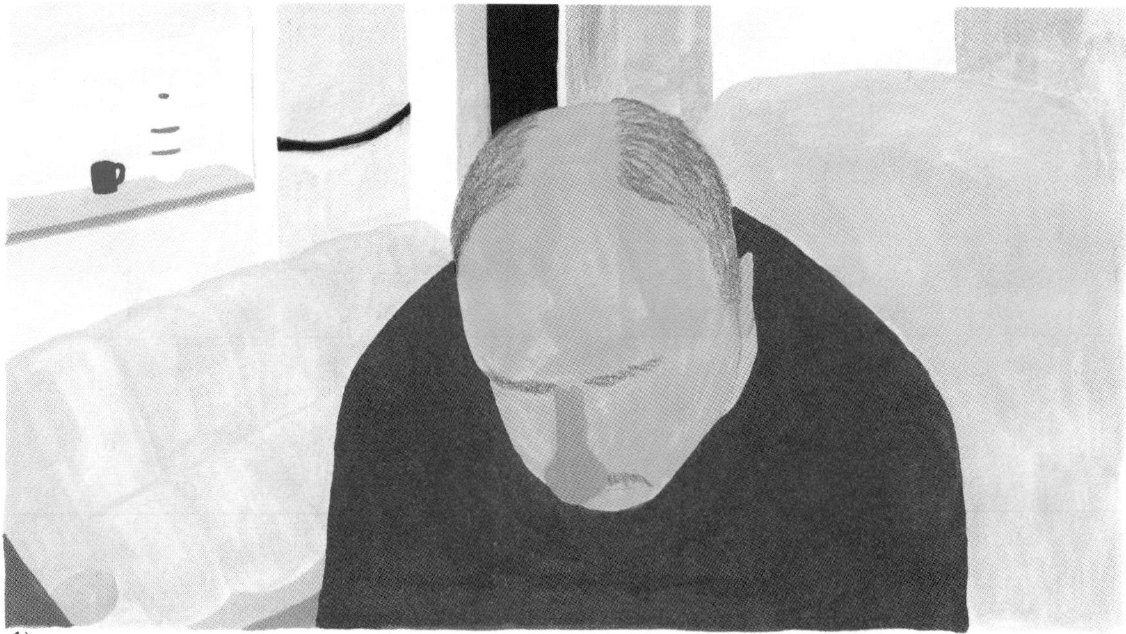

"MILEY TWERKED HER WAY TO THE TOP OF THE INDUSTRY"

15:02

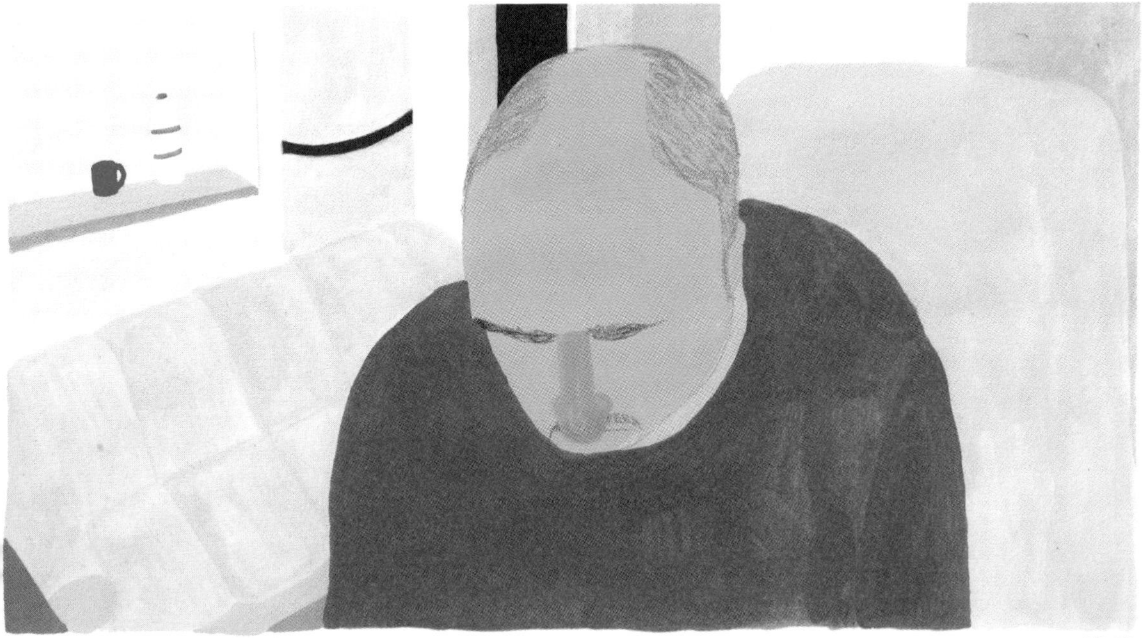

"AND MEGA STARDOM" 15:02

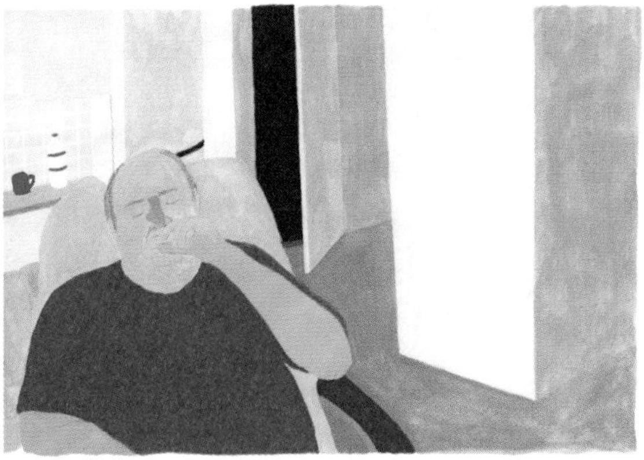

"HER MULTI-MILLION DOLLAR MANSIONS ARE LITERALLY NEXT LEVEL."

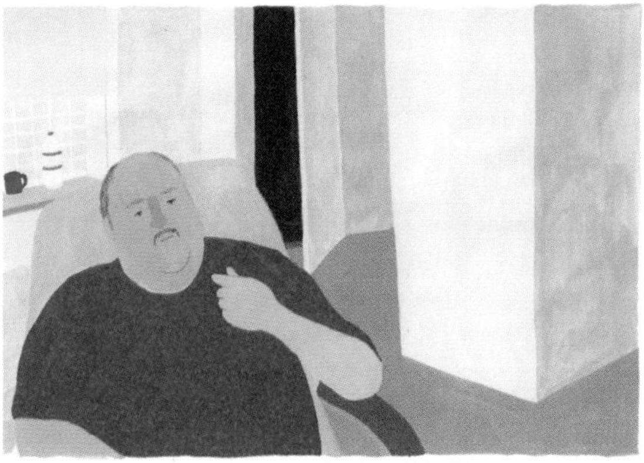

"THERE IS NO DESIGNER LABEL TOO EXPENSIVE,"

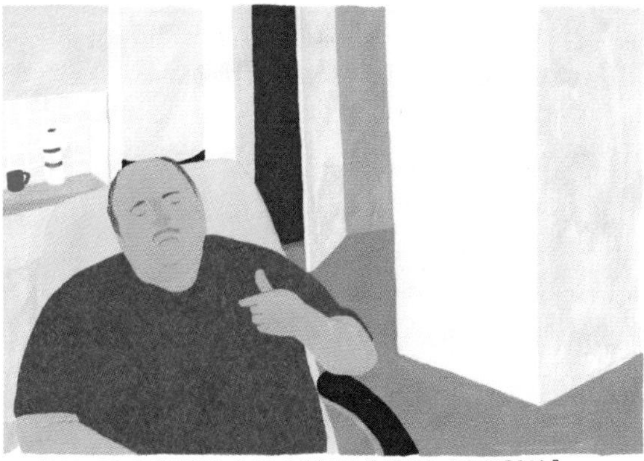

"NO COSMETIC PROCEDURE TOO COSTLY."

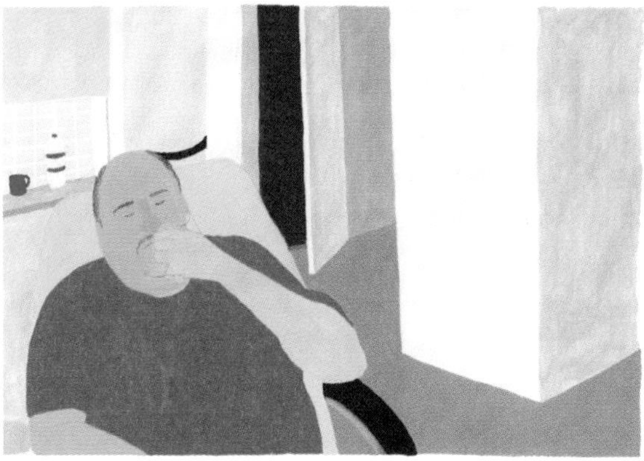

"'CAUSE A FACE LIKE THAT DOESN'T COME CHEAP."

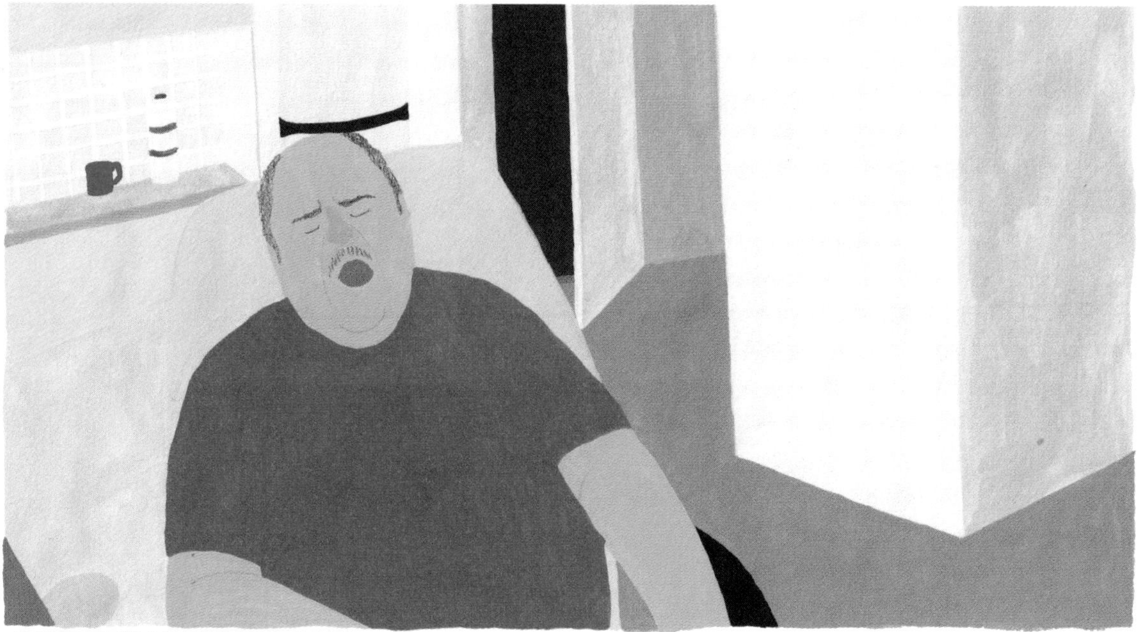

🔊 "STICK IT ON THE BILL, DOC!"

15:02

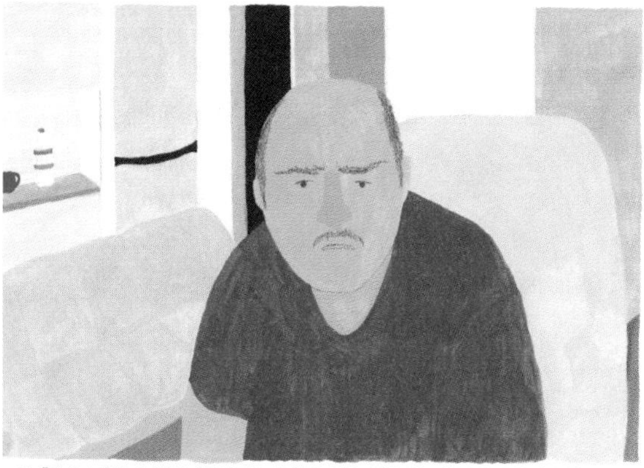

🔊 "DON'T LET ENVY GET TO YOU, AND BRACE YOURSELF FOR SOME HEAVY BLING."

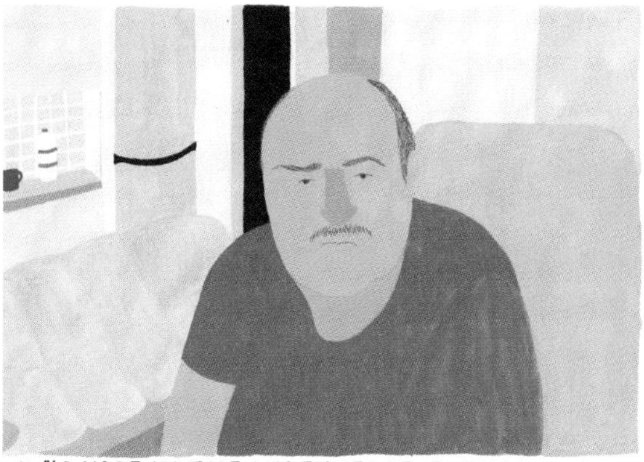

🔊 "'CAUSE IN THE MILEYVERSE, EVERYTHING IS CUSTOMIZED"

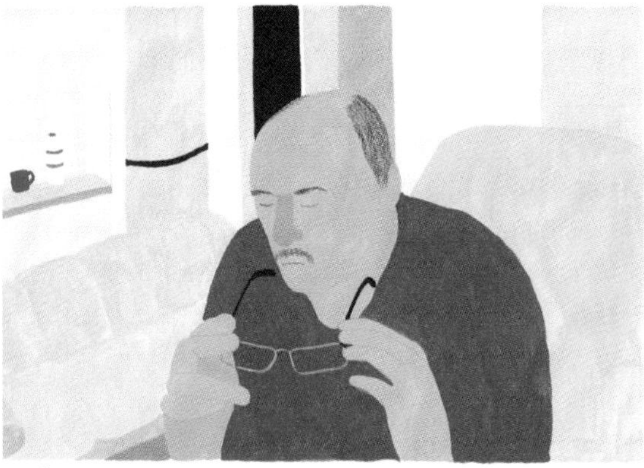

🔊 "AND THERE IS NO NEED TO CHECK THE PRICE"

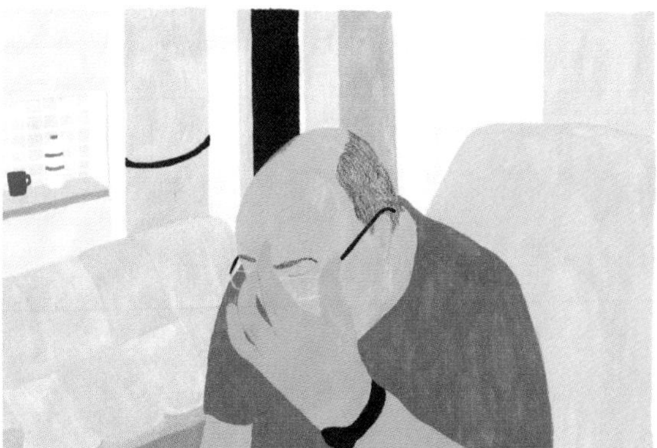

🔊 "FROM TAILORED FUR COATS TO TOILET SEATS TRICKED OUT WITH JEWELS."

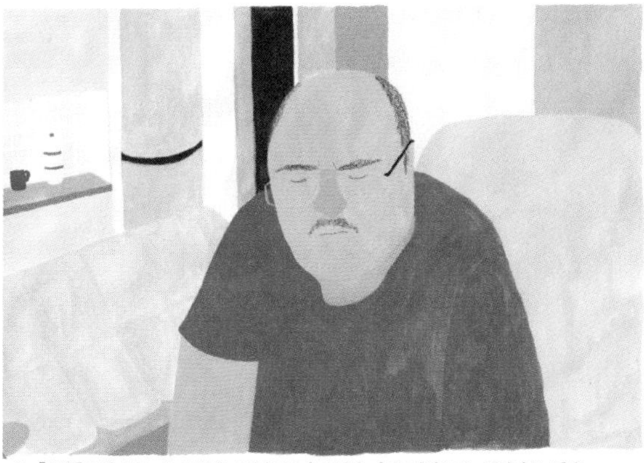

"HERE IS A POP ICON WHO KNOWS HOW TO ROCK HER EMPIRE!"

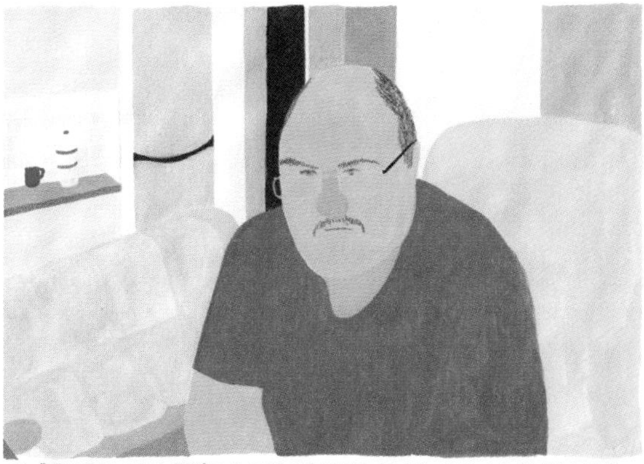

"EVEN MILEY'S ASSISTANT HAS AN ASSISTANT, AND BY THE WAY, THEY HAVE AN ASSISTANT TOO."

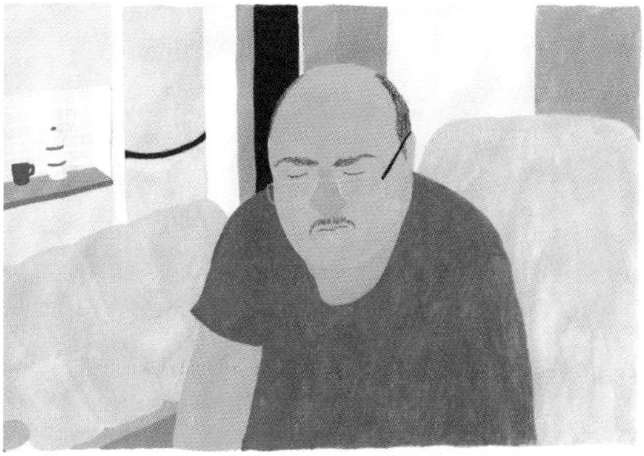

"WATCH OUT FOR THIS WRECKING BALL OF GOLD"

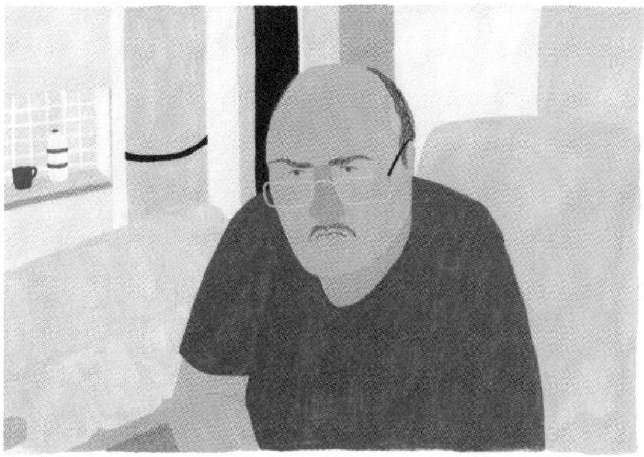

"THIS LIFESTYLE IS GOING TO KNOCK YOU OUT!"

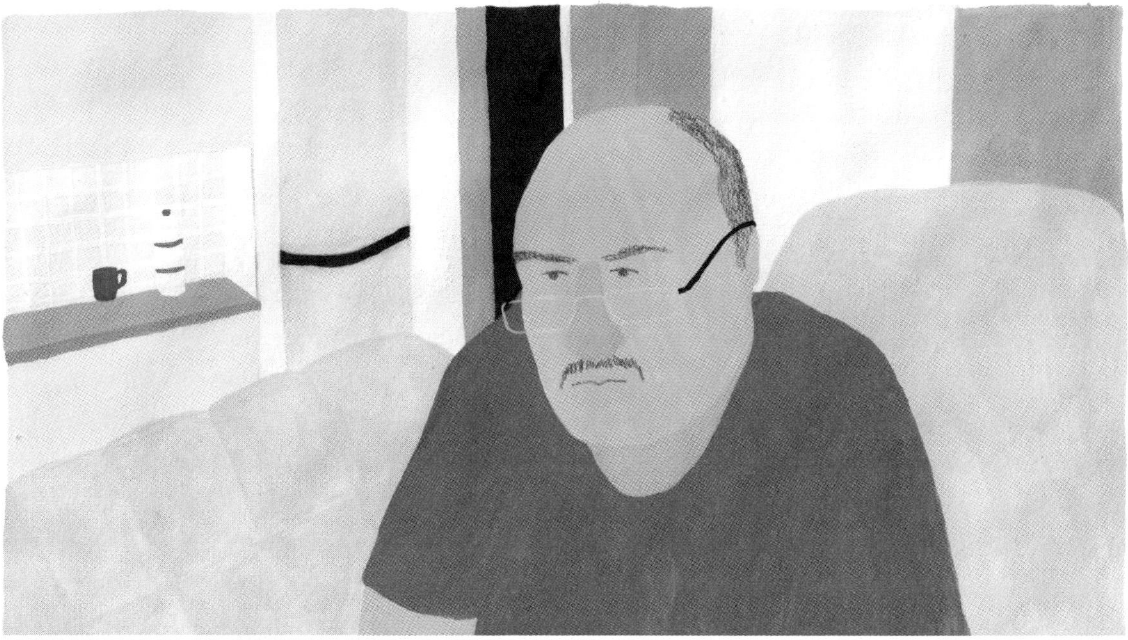

"WELCOME TO LIVE, LAUGH, LUXURY: MILEY CYRUS"

15:03

20.07.2016

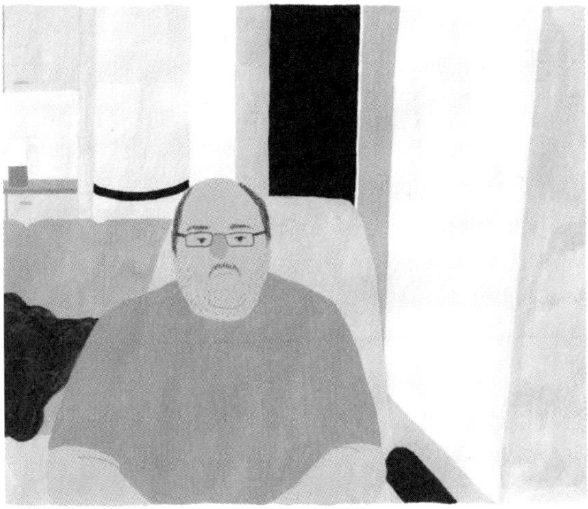

16:20

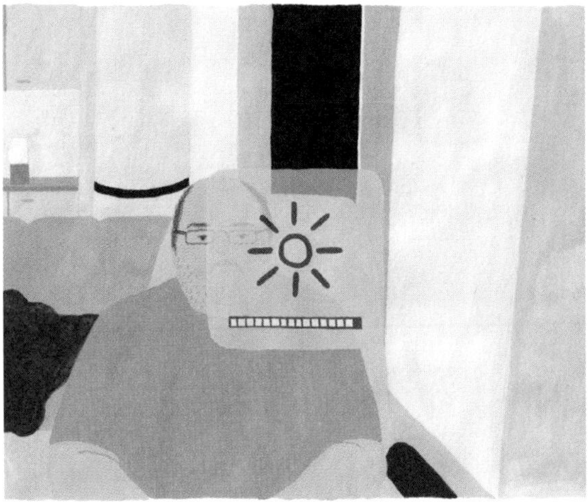

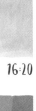

16:20

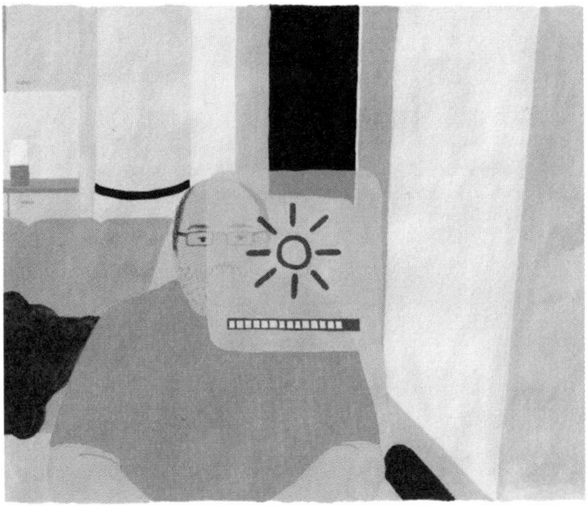

16:20

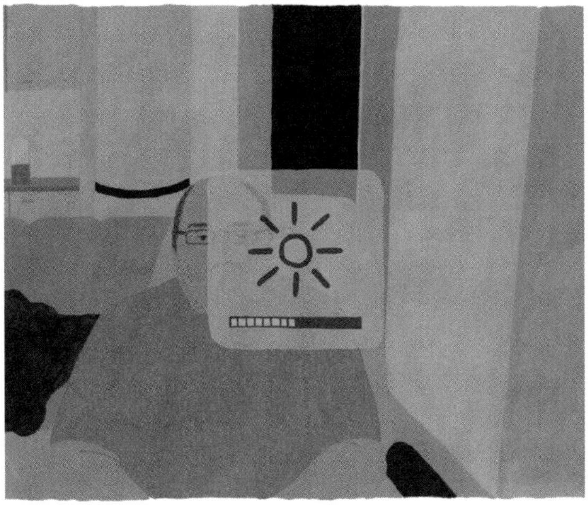

16:20

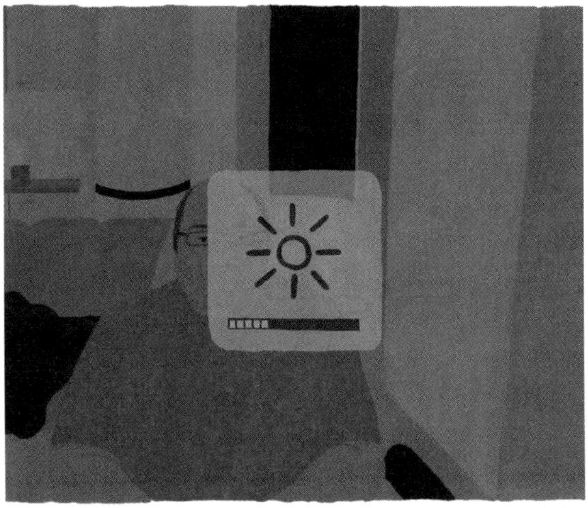

16:20

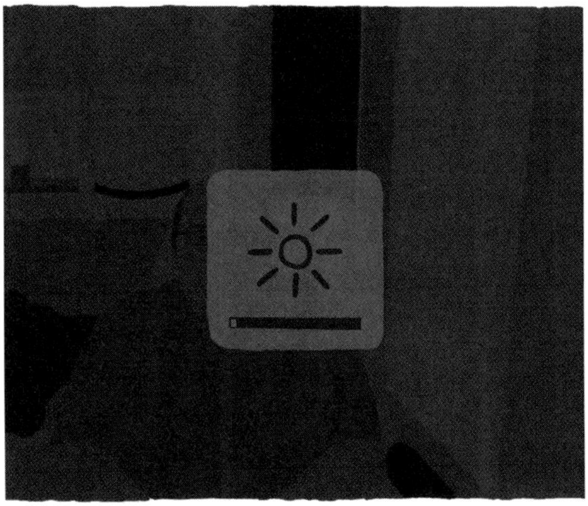

16:20

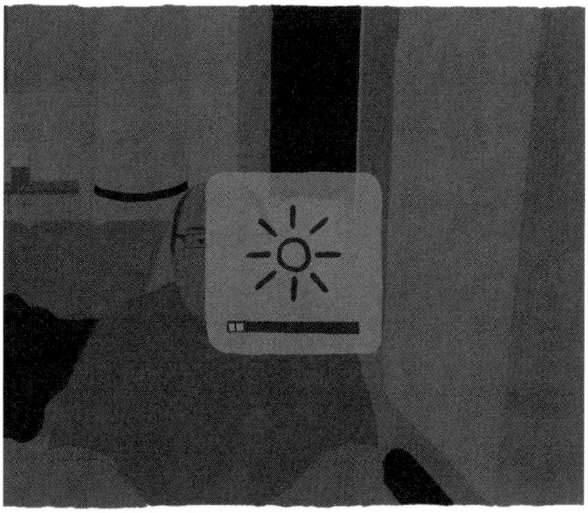

16:20

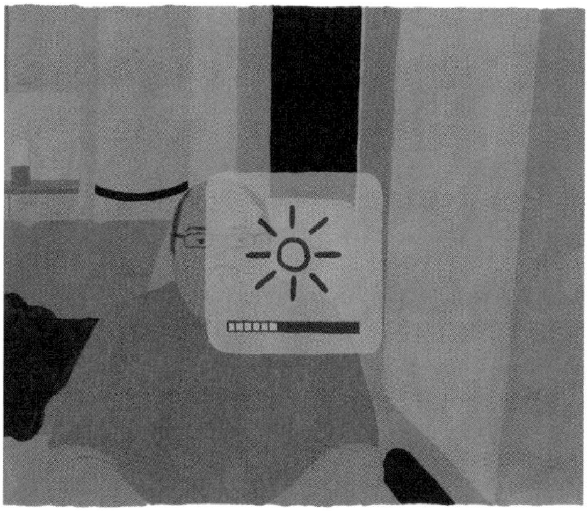

16:20

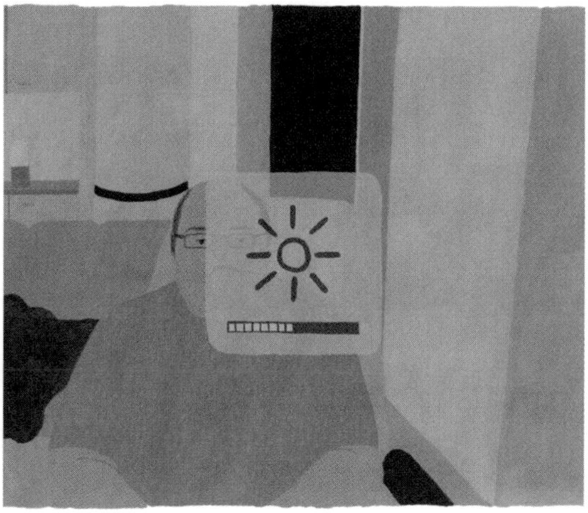

16:20

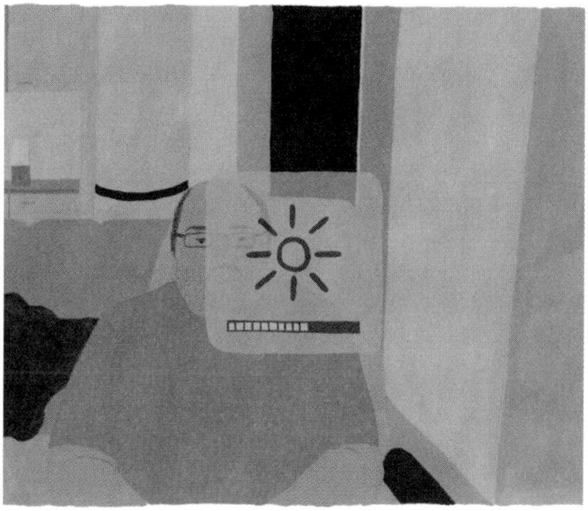

16:20

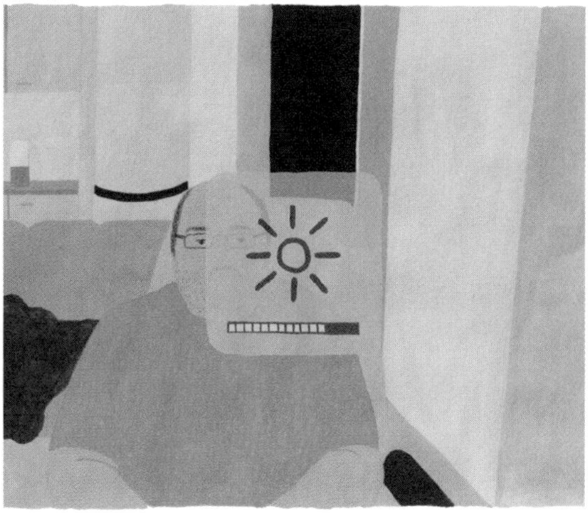

16:20

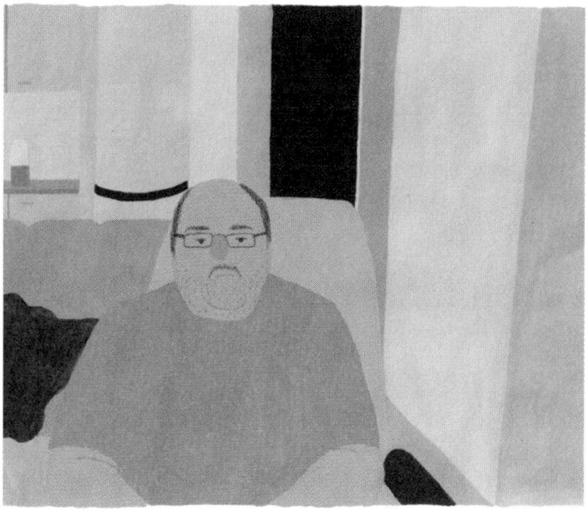

16:20

26.07.2016

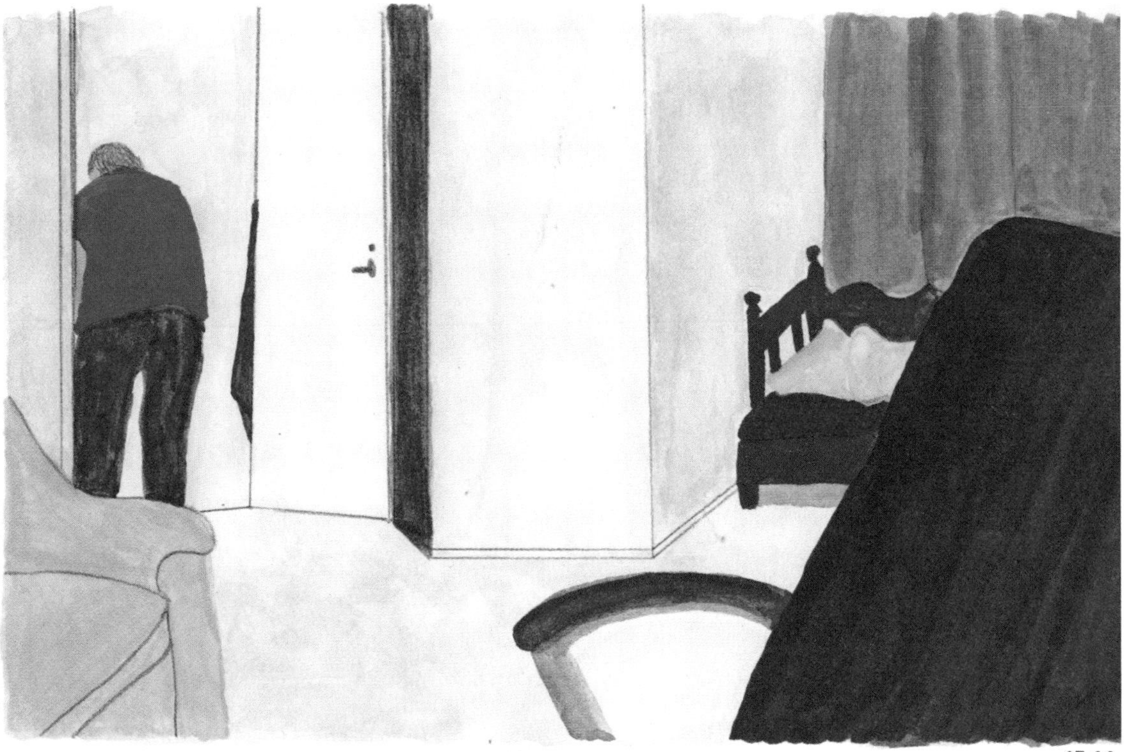

15:00

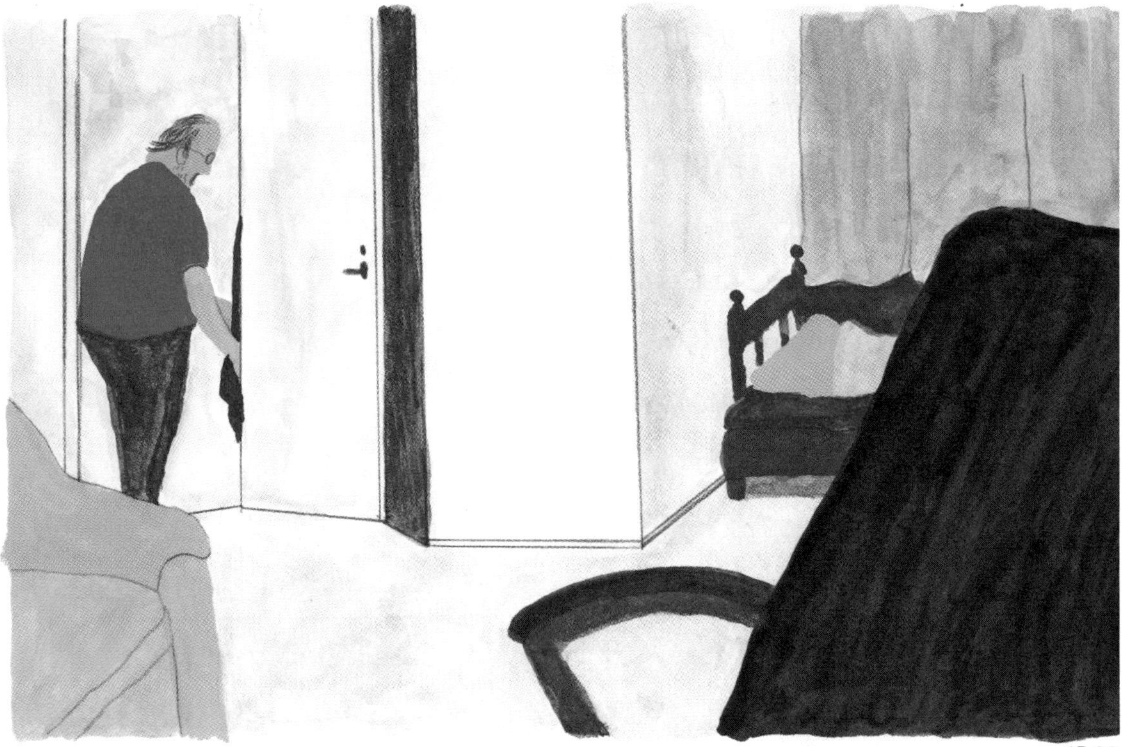

15:01

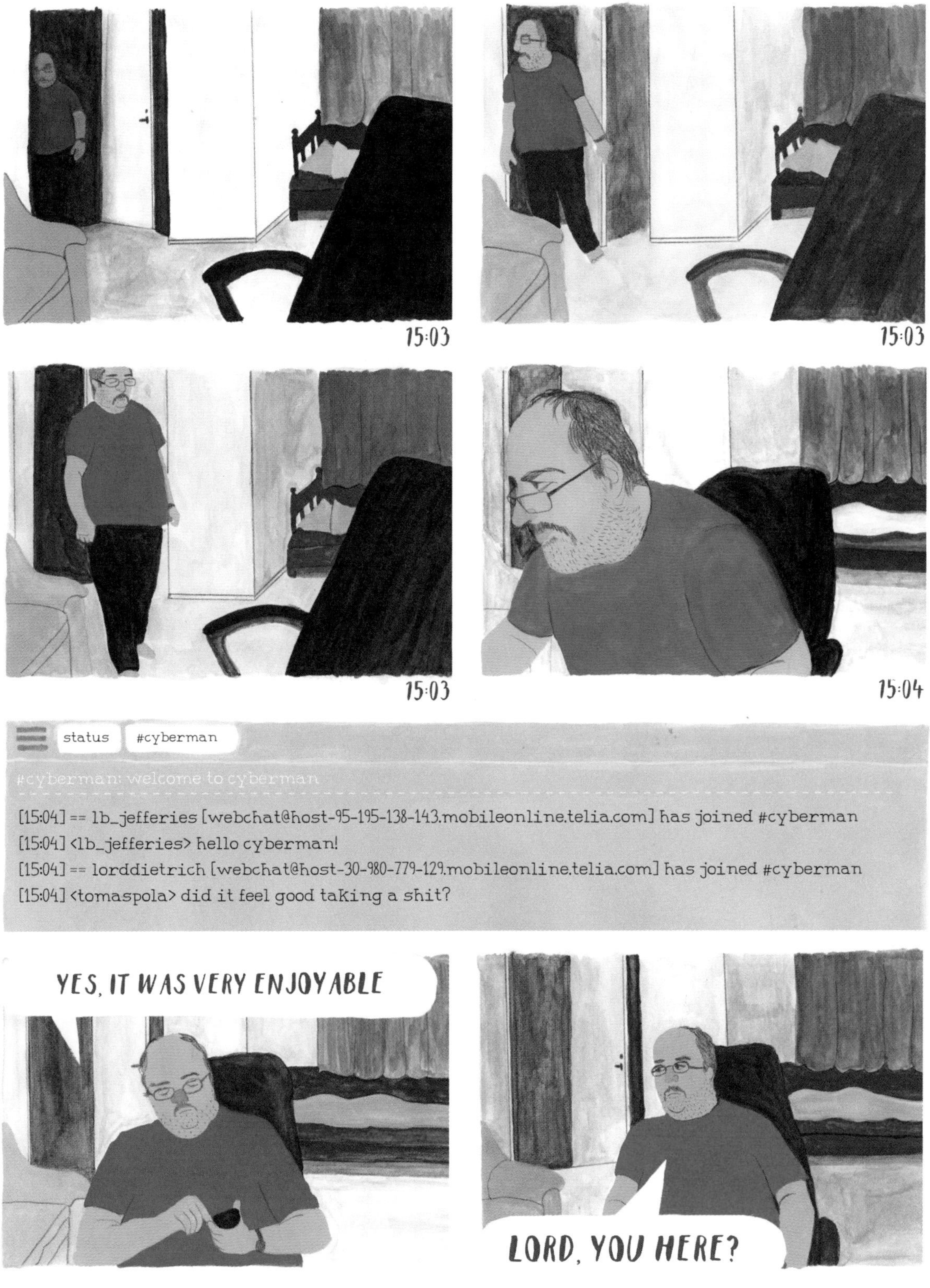
15:03
15:03
15:03
15:04
status
#cyberman
#cyberman: welcome to cyberman
[15:04] == lb_jefferies [webchat@host-95-195-138-143.mobileonline.telia.com] has joined #cyberman
[15:04] <lb_jefferies> hello cyberman!
[15:04] == lorddietrich [webchat@host-30-980-779-129.mobileonline.telia.com] has joined #cyberman
[15:04] <tomaspola> did it feel good taking a shit?
YES, IT WAS VERY ENJOYABLE
LORD, YOU HERE?

status #cyberman

[15:05] <lorddietrich> yo
[15:05] <lorddietrich> how is you and your health doing?

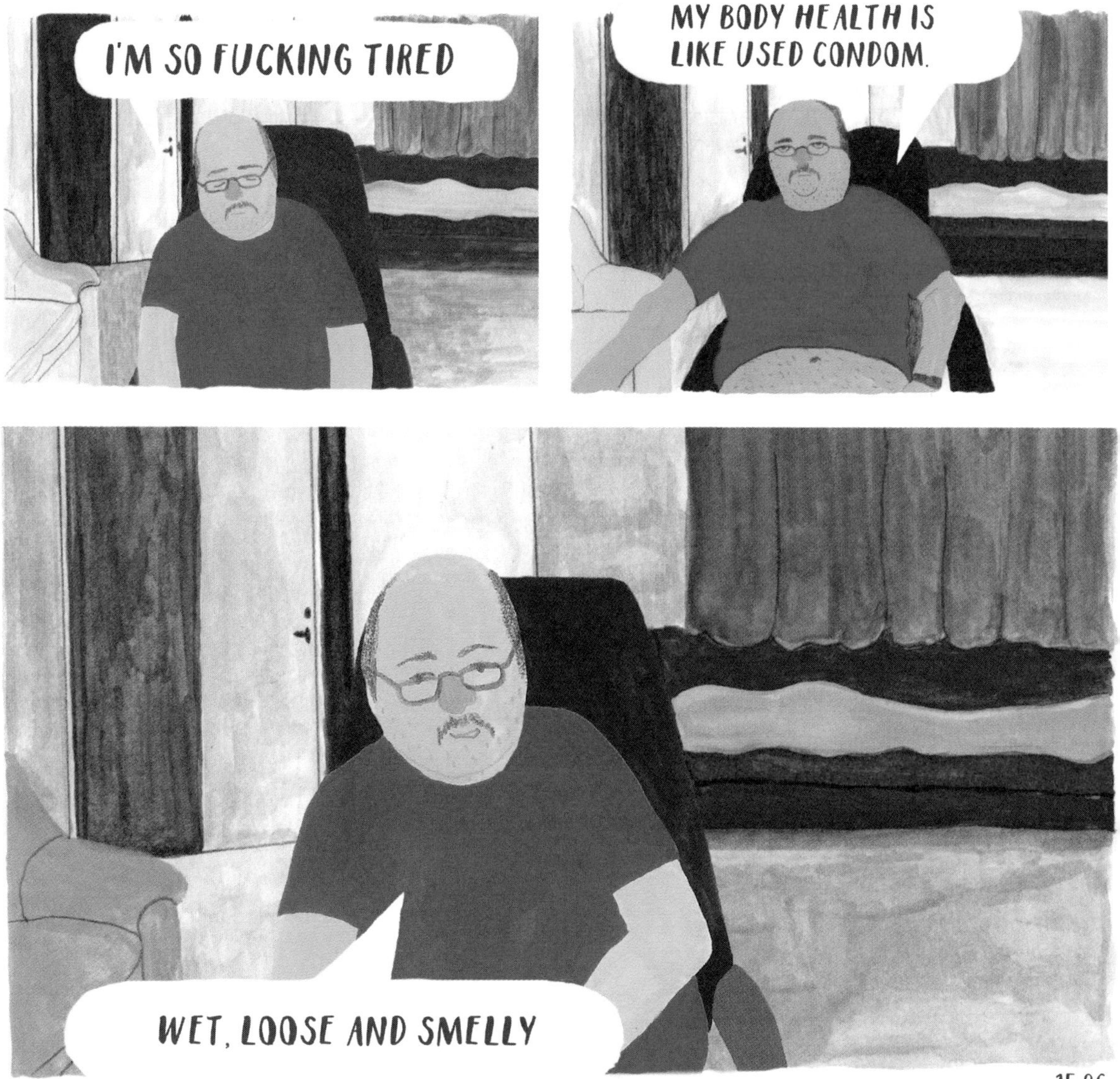
I'M SO FUCKING TIRED
MY BODY HEALTH IS LIKE USED CONDOM.
WET, LOOSE AND SMELLY

15:06

status #cyberman

[15:06] <froggy> yuck
[15:06] <froggy> do you always tell people everything?
[15:07] <trollerama> would you like my pussy?

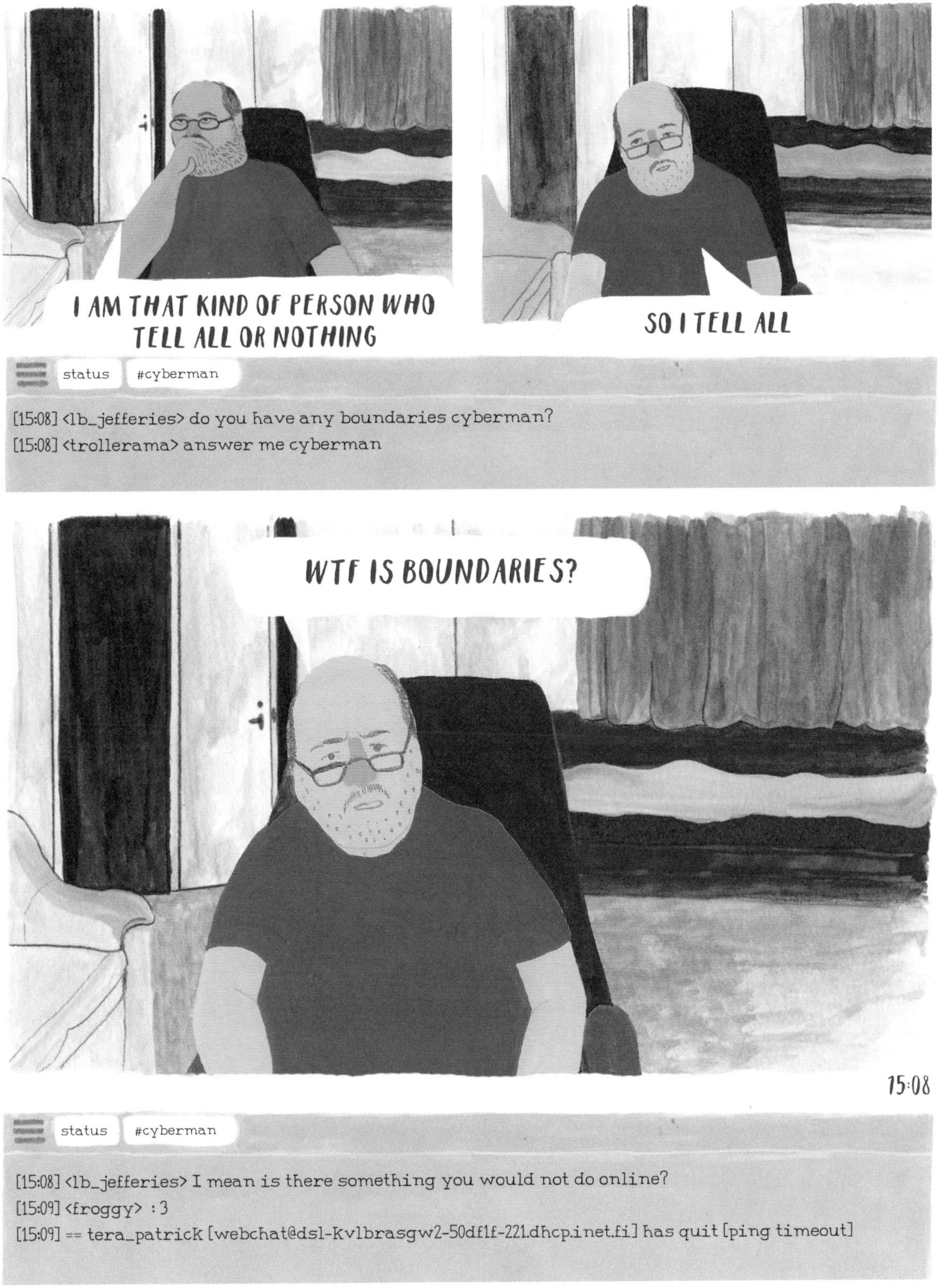
I AM THAT KIND OF PERSON WHO TELL ALL OR NOTHING
SO I TELL ALL
status #cyberman
[15:08] <lb_jefferies> do you have any boundaries cyberman?
[15:08] <trollerama> answer me cyberman
WTF IS BOUNDARIES?
15:08
status #cyberman
[15:08] <lb_jefferies> I mean is there something you would not do online?
[15:09] <froggy> :3
[15:09] == tera_patrick [webchat@dsl-kvlbrasgw2-50df1f-221.dhcp.inet.fi] has quit [ping timeout]

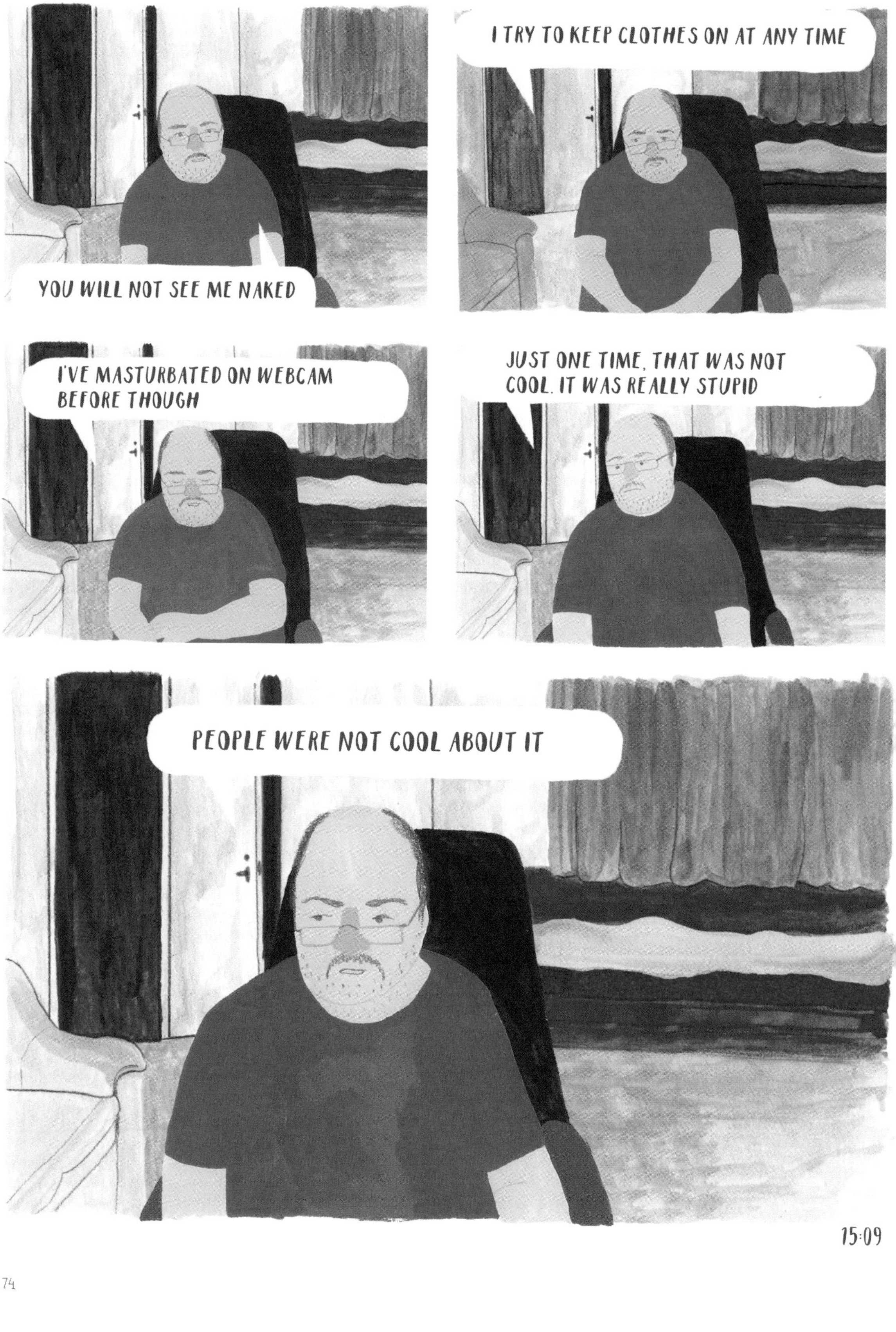
YOU WILL NOT SEE ME NAKED
I TRY TO KEEP CLOTHES ON AT ANY TIME
I'VE MASTURBATED ON WEBCAM BEFORE THOUGH
JUST ONE TIME, THAT WAS NOT COOL. IT WAS REALLY STUPID
PEOPLE WERE NOT COOL ABOUT IT
15:09

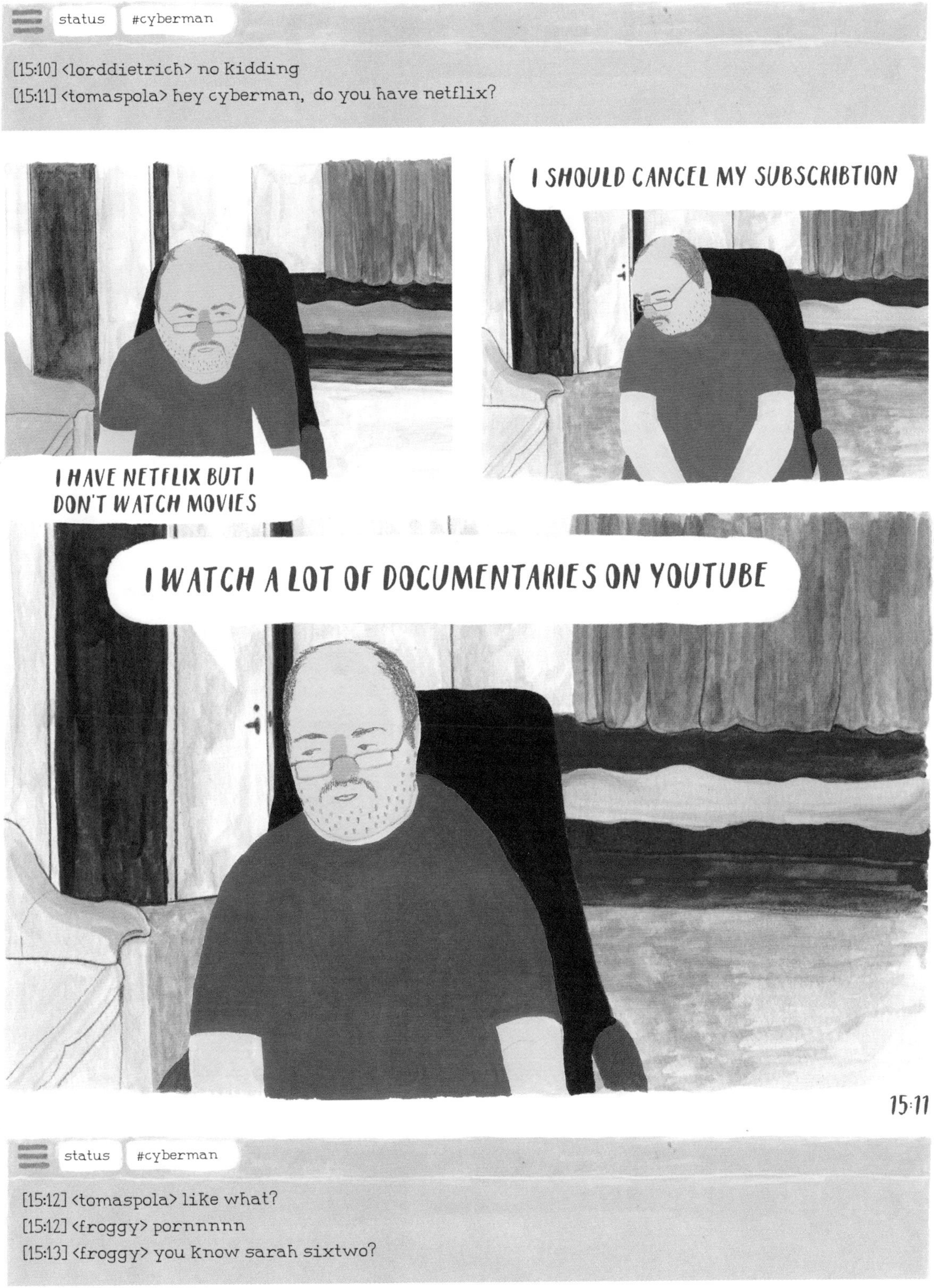
status
#cyberman
[15:10] <lorddietrich> no kidding
[15:11] <tomaspola> hey cyberman, do you have netflix?
I HAVE NETFLIX BUT I DON'T WATCH MOVIES
I SHOULD CANCEL MY SUBSCRIBTION
I WATCH A LOT OF DOCUMENTARIES ON YOUTUBE
15:11
status
#cyberman
[15:12] <tomaspola> like what?
[15:12] <froggy> pornnnnn
[15:13] <froggy> you know sarah sixtwo?

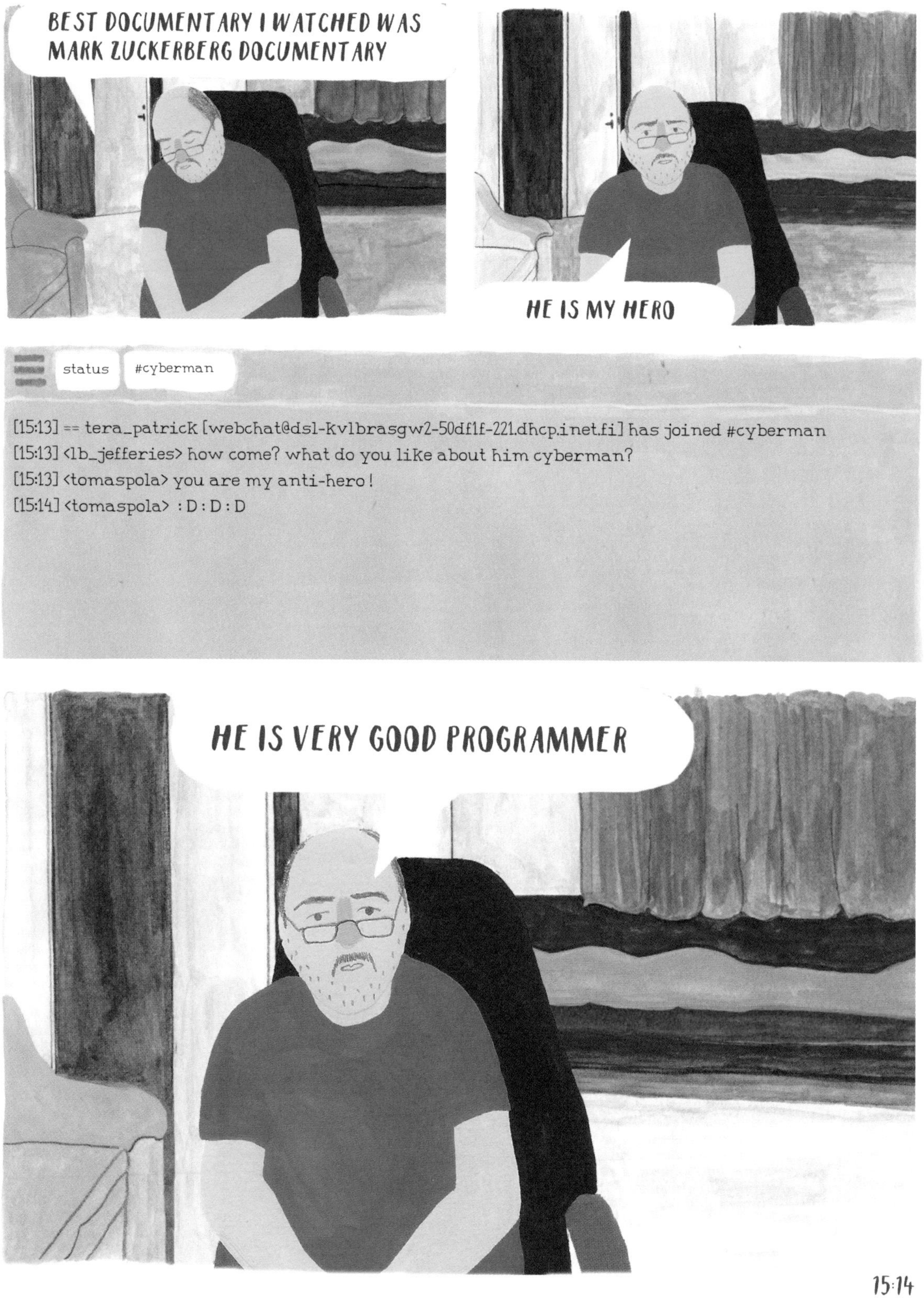
BEST DOCUMENTARY I WATCHED WAS MARK ZUCKERBERG DOCUMENTARY
HE IS MY HERO
status
#cyberman
[15:13] == tera_patrick [webchat@dsl-kvlbrasgw2-50df1f-221.dhcp.inet.fi] has joined #cyberman
[15:13] <lb_jefferies> how come? what do you like about him cyberman?
[15:13] <tomaspola> you are my anti-hero!
[15:14] <tomaspola> :D:D:D
HE IS VERY GOOD PROGRAMMER

15:14

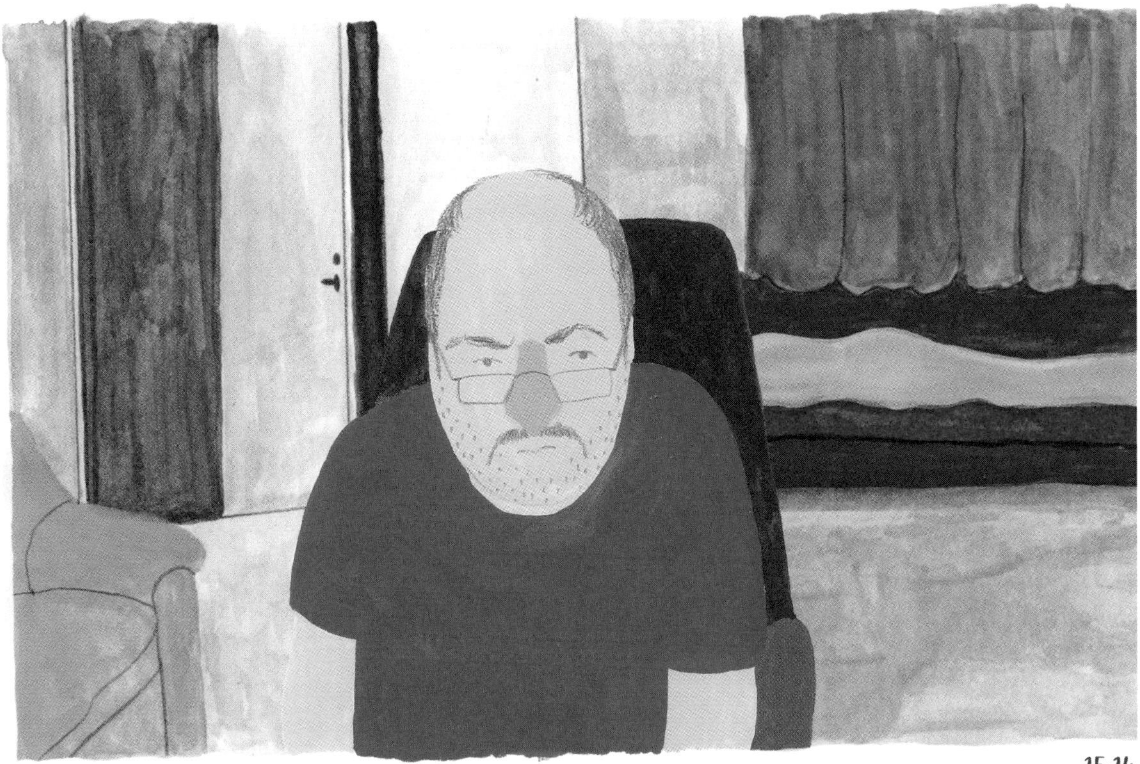

15:14

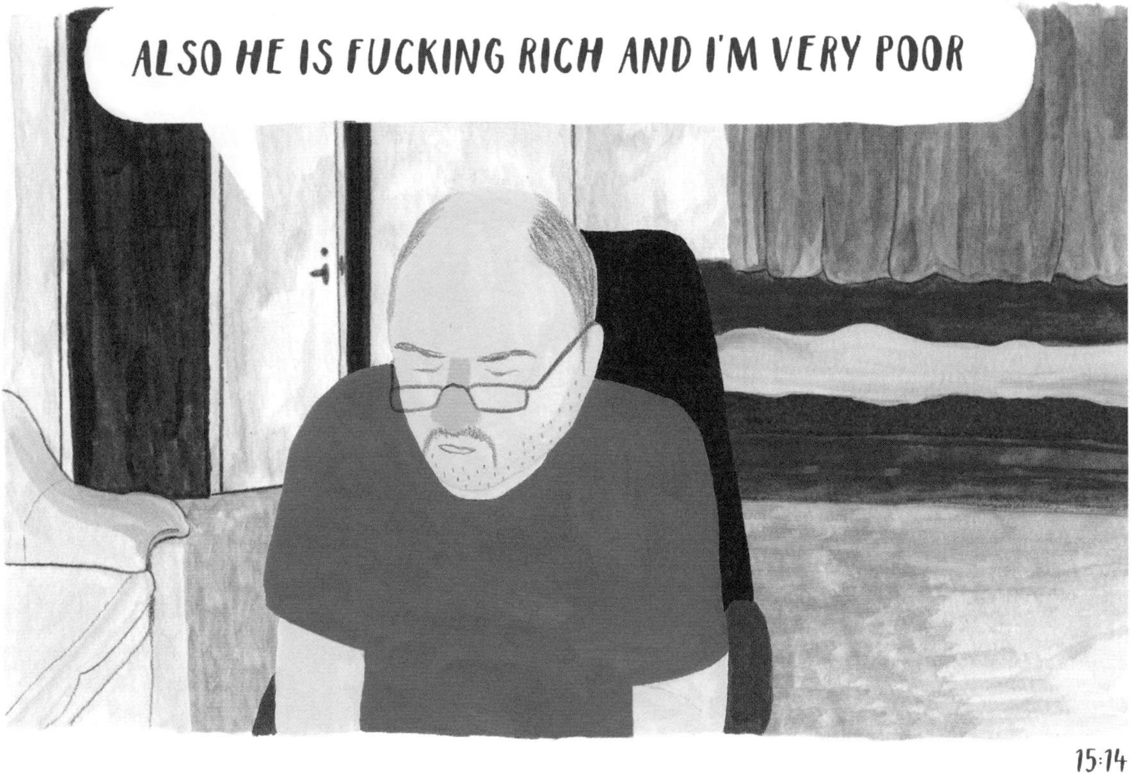
ALSO HE IS FUCKING RICH AND I'M VERY POOR

15:14

27.07.2016

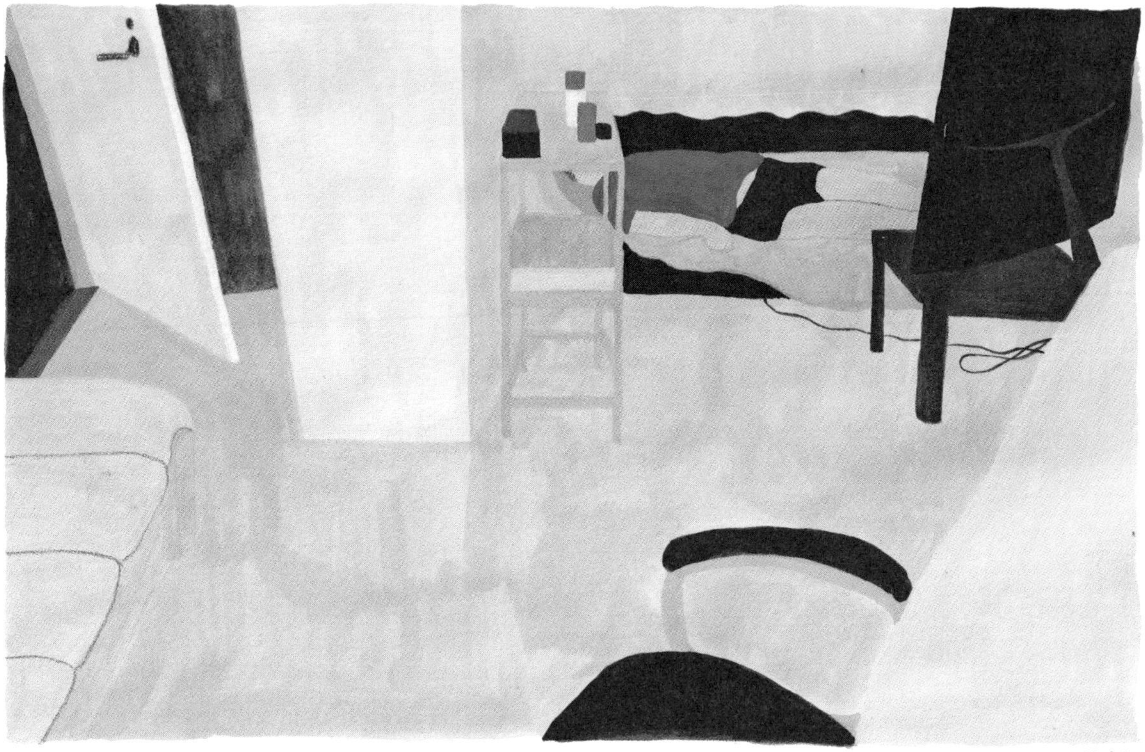

10:39

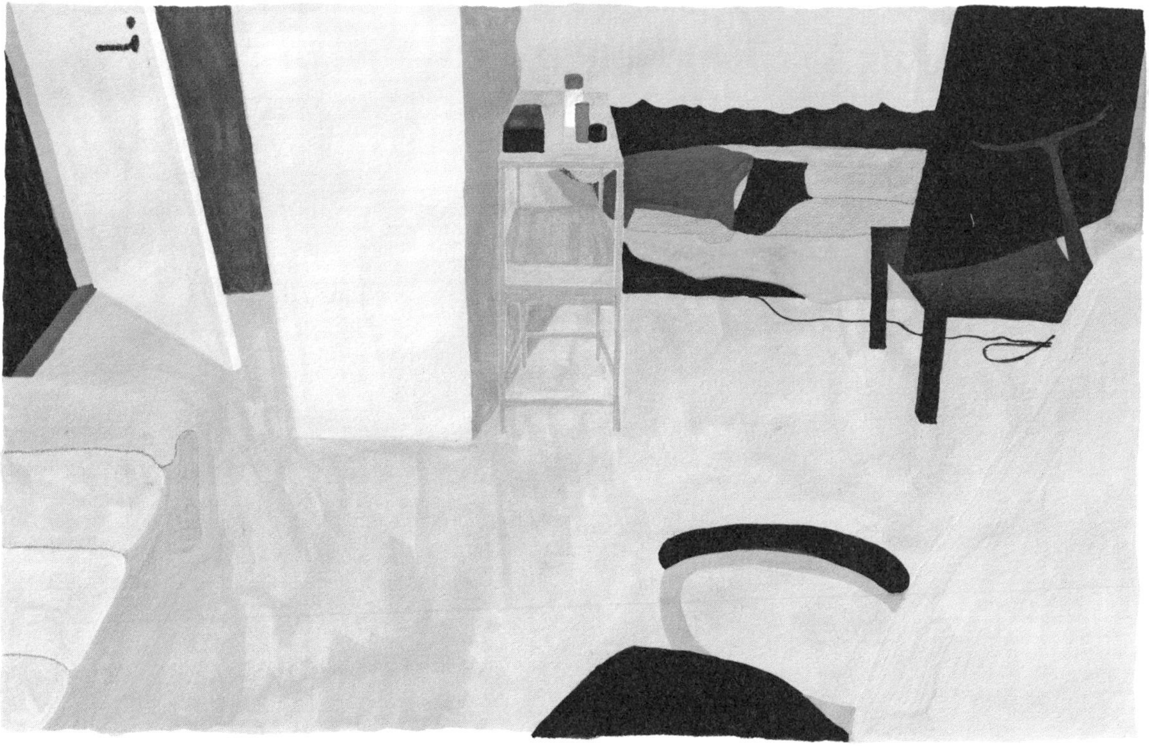

10:39

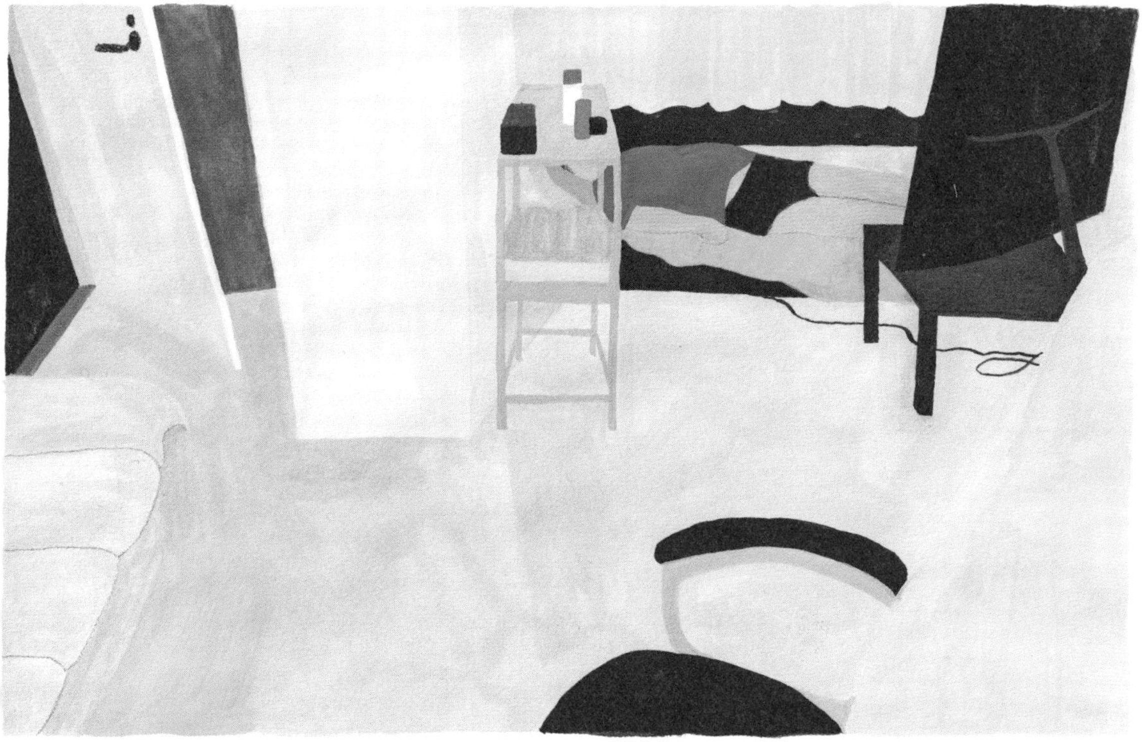

10:54

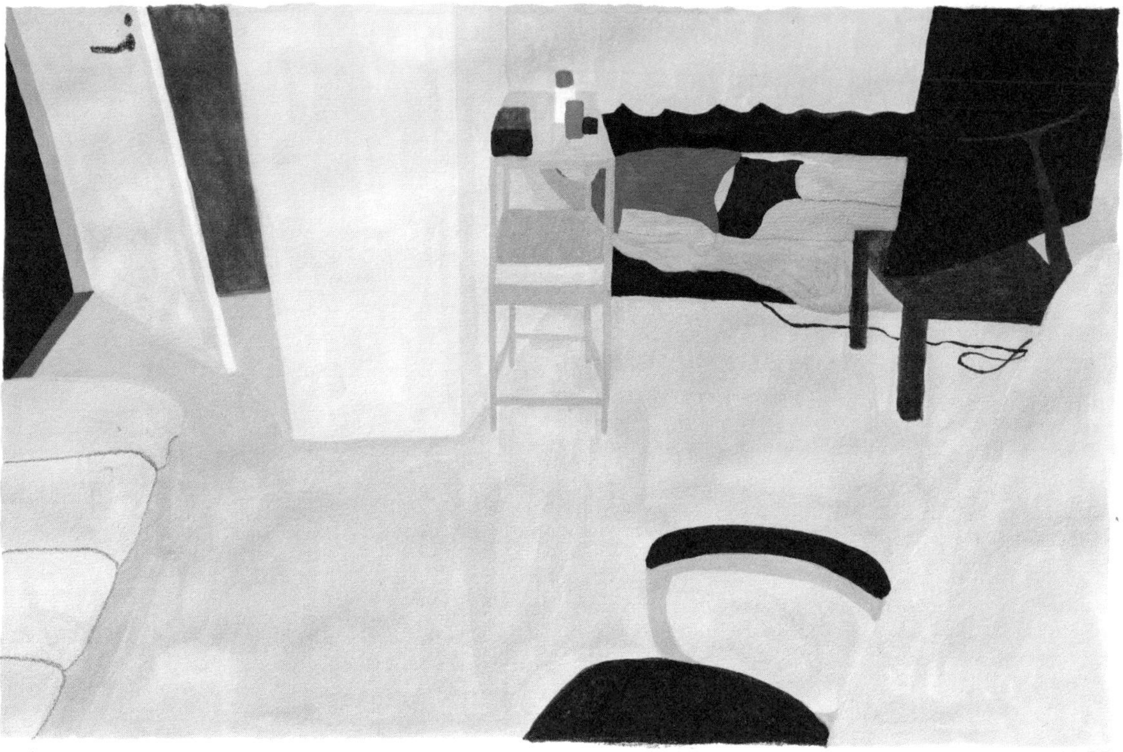

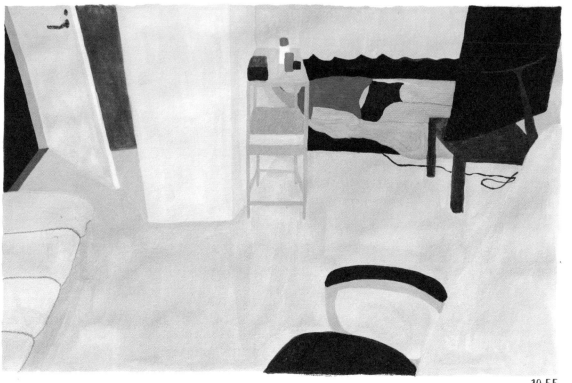

10:55

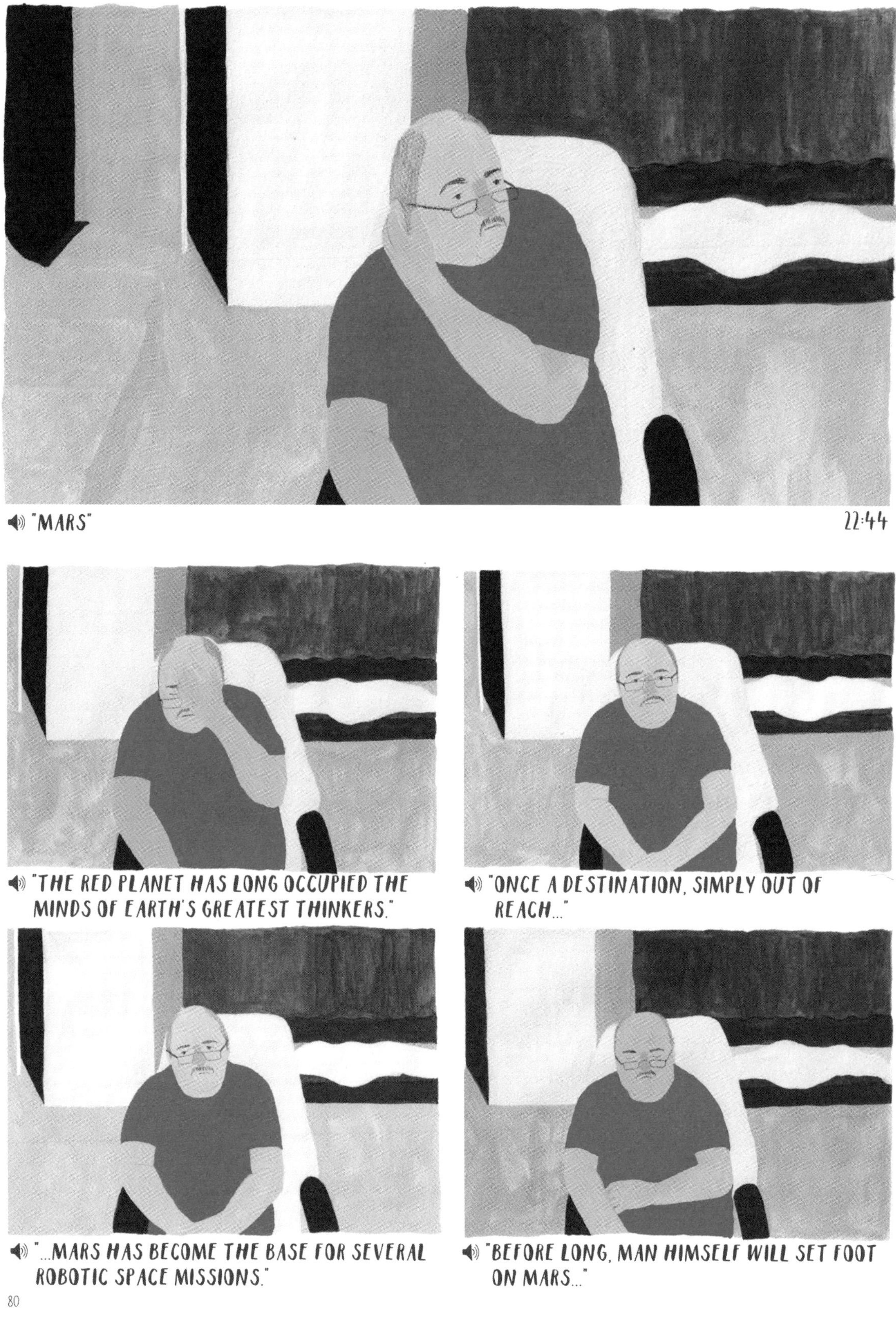
"MARS"
22:44
"THE RED PLANET HAS LONG OCCUPIED THE MINDS OF EARTH'S GREATEST THINKERS."
"ONCE A DESTINATION, SIMPLY OUT OF REACH..."
"...MARS HAS BECOME THE BASE FOR SEVERAL ROBOTIC SPACE MISSIONS."
"BEFORE LONG, MAN HIMSELF WILL SET FOOT ON MARS..."

🔊 "...AND THIS WILL ONLY BE THE BEGINNING."

🔊 "THE ULTIMATE GOAL IS A LOT BIGGER."

🔊 "A COLONY ON MARS."

22:45

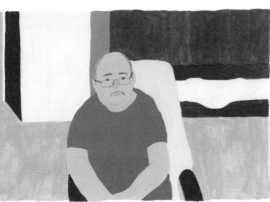

🔊 "STAY TUNED FOR A JOURNEY OTHERWORLDLY."

🔊 "AS WE LIFT OFF INTO THE AS YET UNKNOWN AND EXPLORE WHAT IT WILL TAKE TO..."

◀)) ".._LIVE_.."

◀)) ".._IN_.."

) "...SPACE."

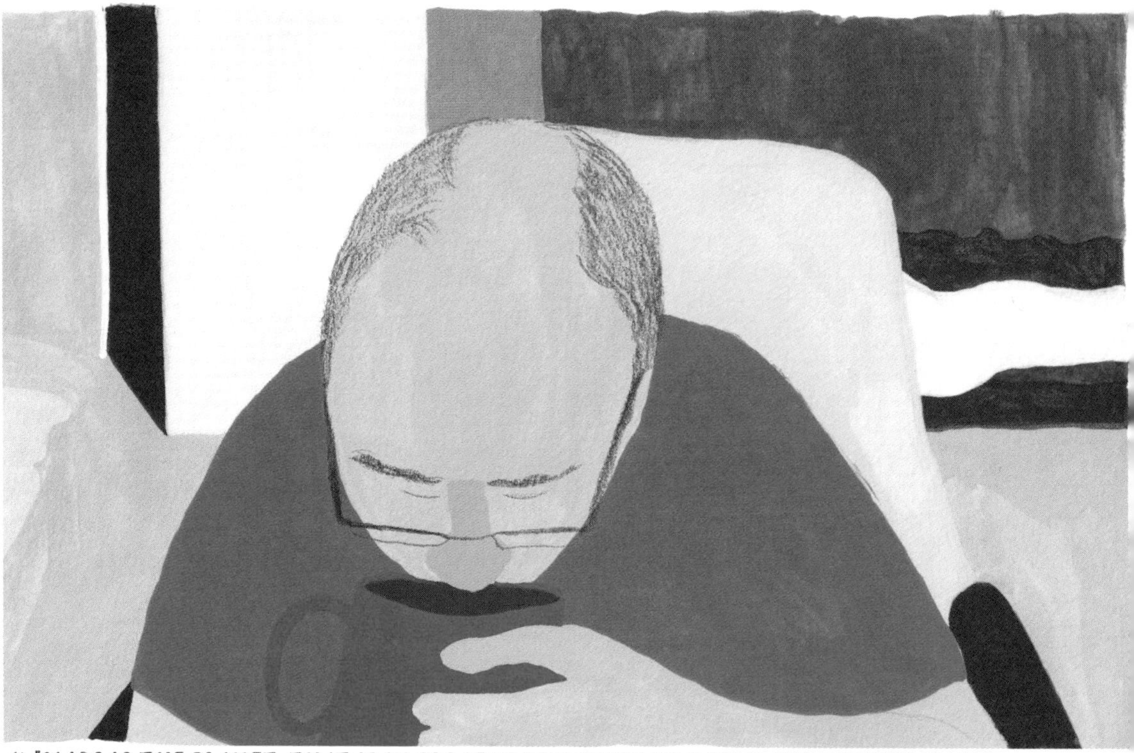

"MARS IS THE PLANET, THAT IS IN CLOSEST PROXIMITY TO EARTH AND DESPITE MAJOR DIFFERENCES, SHARES MANY COMMON ATTRIBUTES WITH OUR HOME PLANET." 22:45

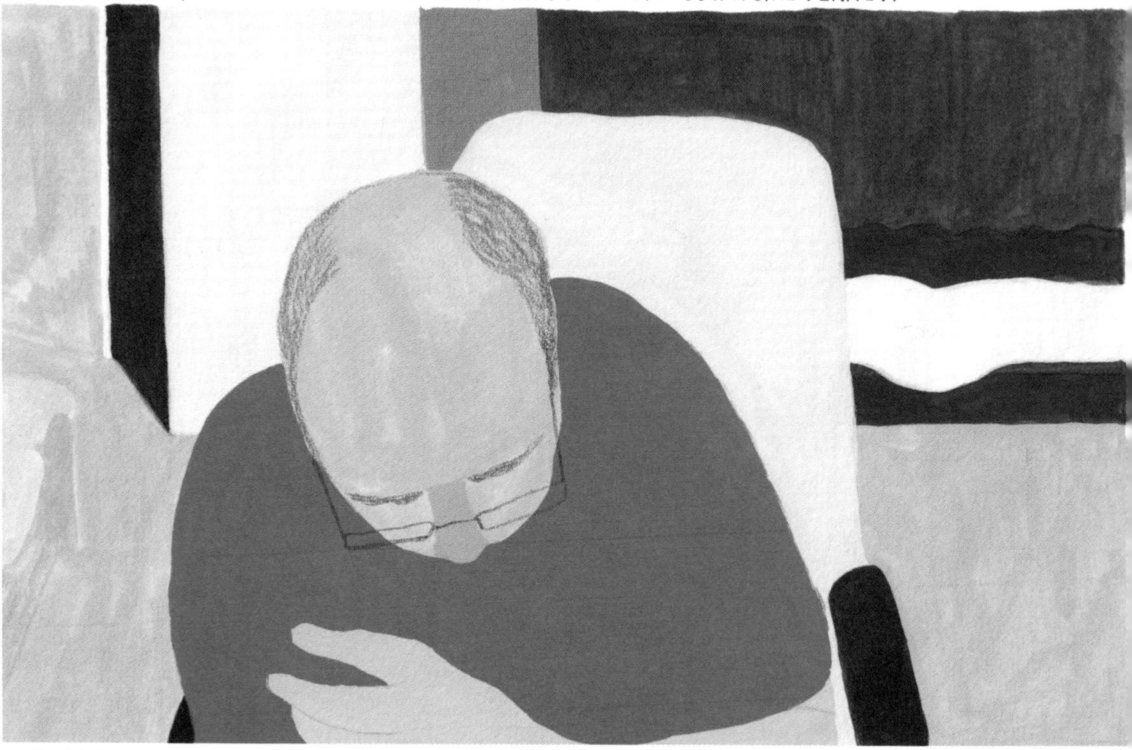

"BUT LIFE ON MARS WILL NOT BE EASY." 22:45

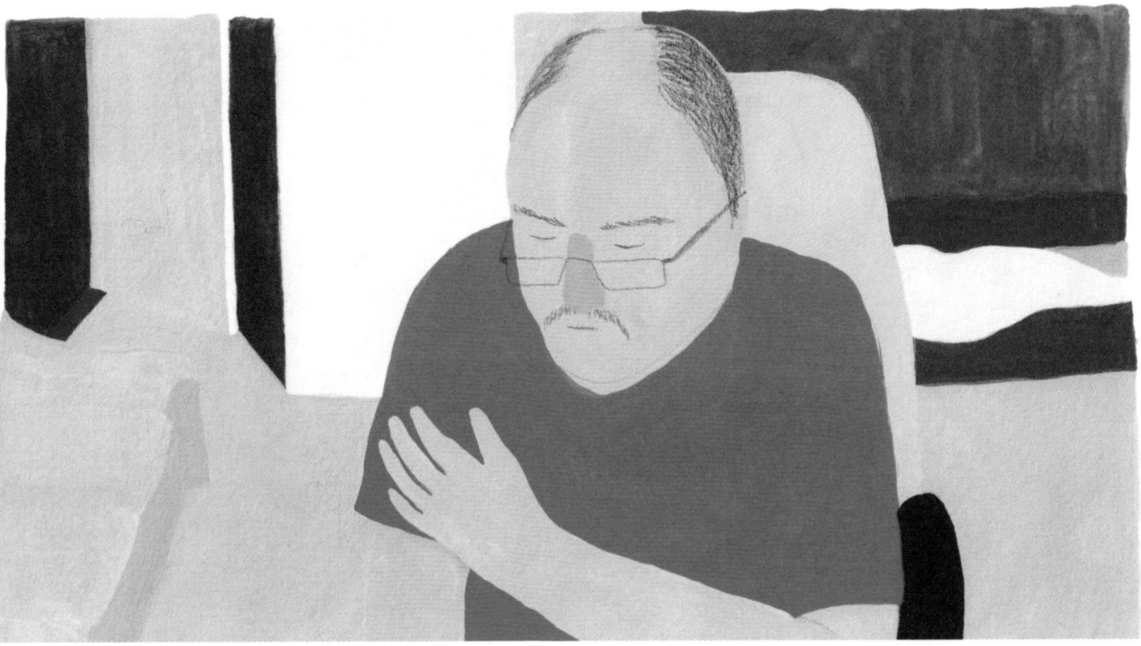

🔊 "IT IS NOT WITHOUT REASON THAT THE PLANET WAS NAMED AFTER THE ANCIENT ROMAN'S GOD OF WAR." 22:45

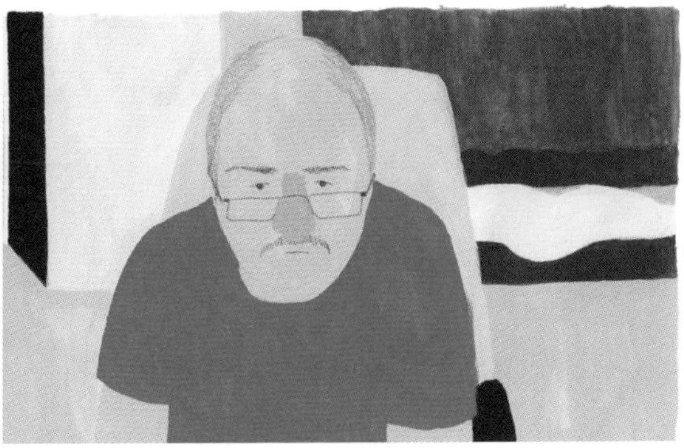

🔊 "THE MARTIAN CIVILISATION WILL HAVE TO FIND A WAY TO EXIST UNDER MOST STRAINING CONDITIONS"

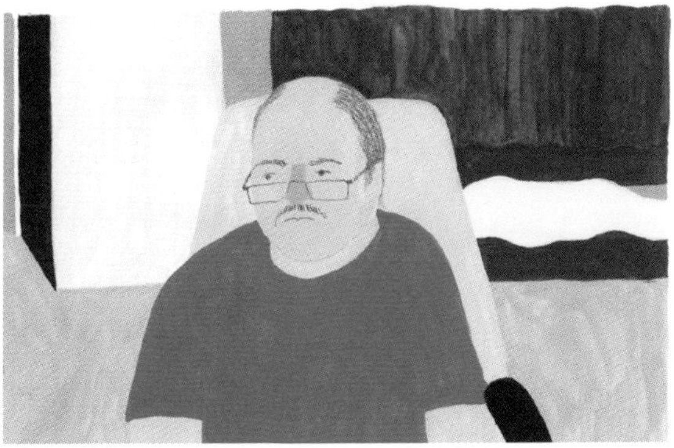

🔊 "WHERE HIGH RADIATION AND SAVAGING SANDSTORMS ARE PART OF THE DAILY AGENDA"

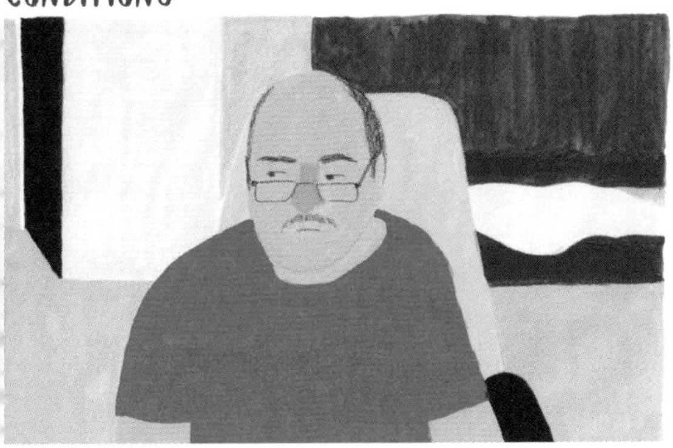

🔊 "ESPECIALLY, THE DRASTICALLY FLUCTUATING TEMPERATURES WILL MAKE A MARTIAN HABITAT MOST CHALLENGING."

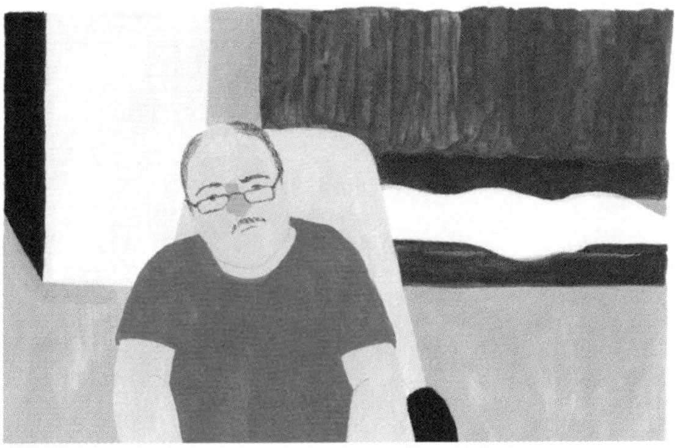

🔊 "ONE MIGHT WONDER WHY TO COLONIZE THE PLANET AT ALL?"

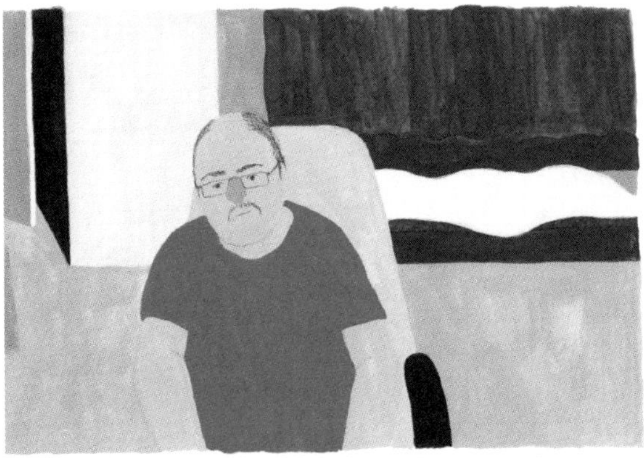

"WHY NOT JUST SETTLE FOR WHAT WE KNOW AND STAY ON OUR OWN PLANET EARTH?"

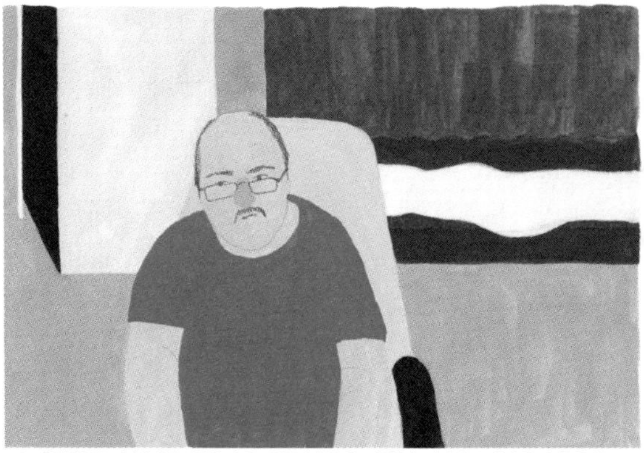

"THE ANSWER IS SIMPLE: IT'S ALWAYS GOOD TO HAVE A PLAN B AT HAND."

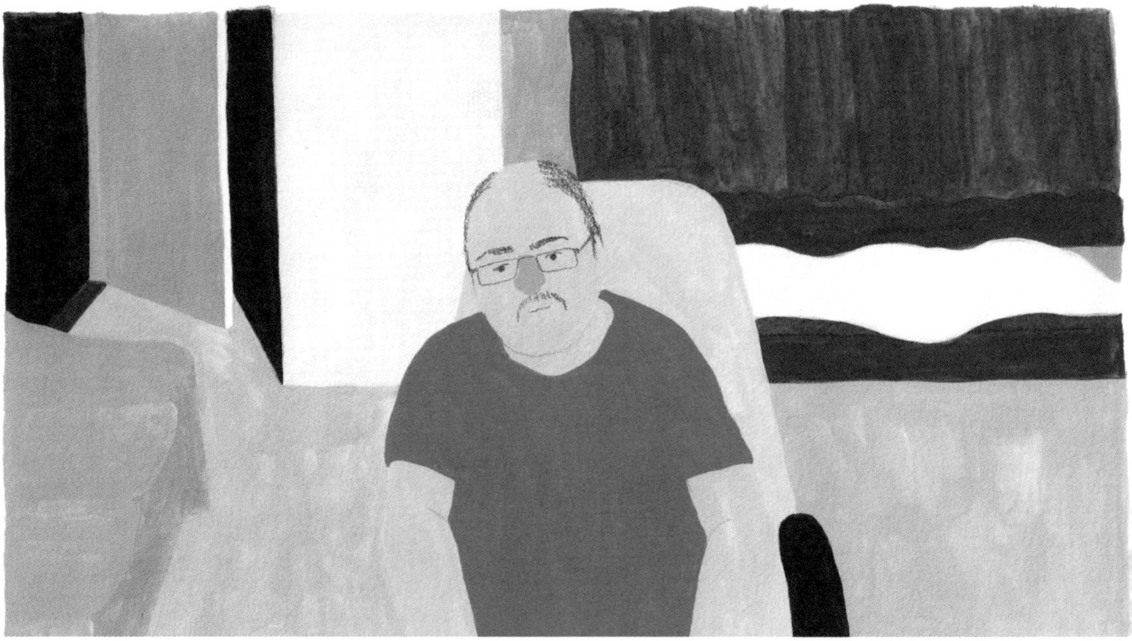

"MARS IS THE IDEAL SOURCE FOR A SECOND HABITAT IN THE UNIVERSE, AS BOTH EARTH AND MARS ARE TERRESTRIAL PLANETS AND SHARE MANY PHYSICAL LAND FEATURES. 22:46

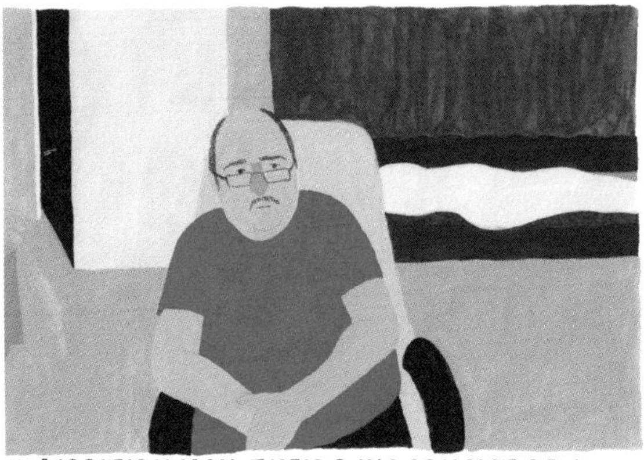

"ADDITIONALLY, THEIR DAYS CONSIST OF A SIMILAR AMOUNT OF HOURS."

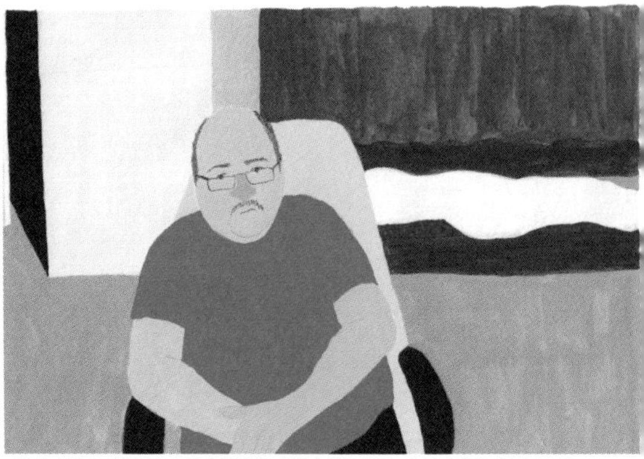

"AND EVEN THEIR SEASONS SHARE HOMOGENOUS PATTERNS DUE TO THEIR AXIAL TILTS."

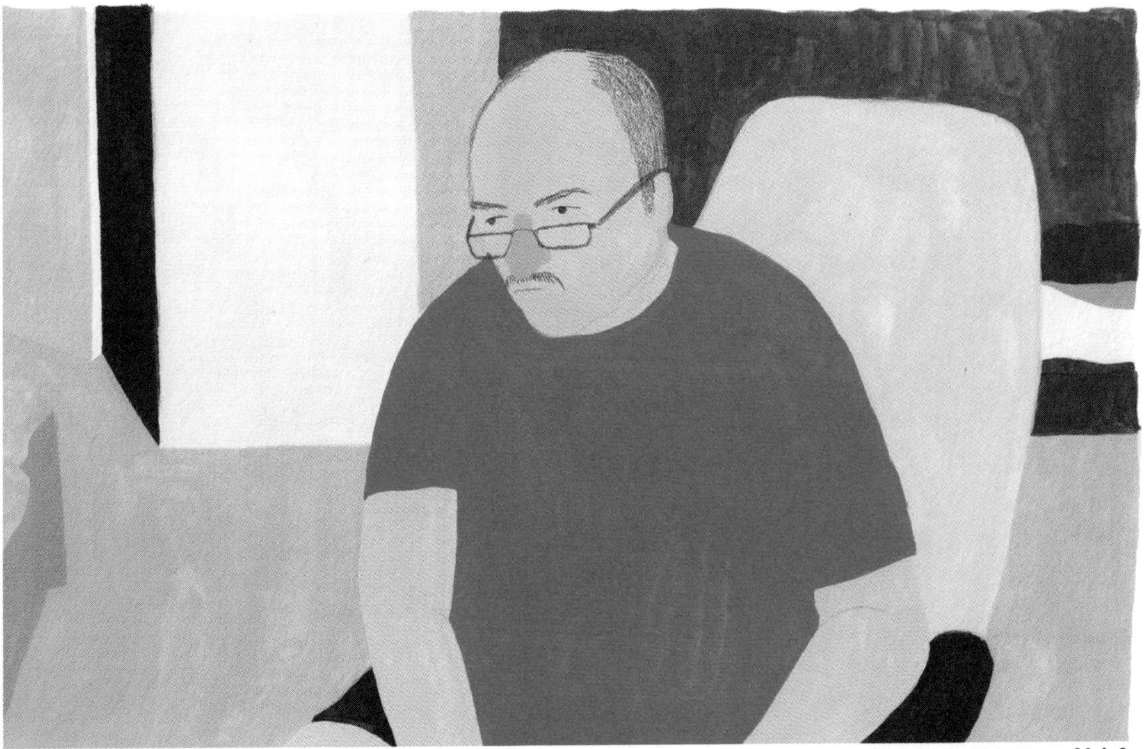

"BUT MOST IMPORTANT IS THE RESOURCE, THAT IS VITAL FOR ALL LIVING SPECIES KNOWN TO MANKIND AND IT EXISTS RIGHT THERE ON MARS." 22:46

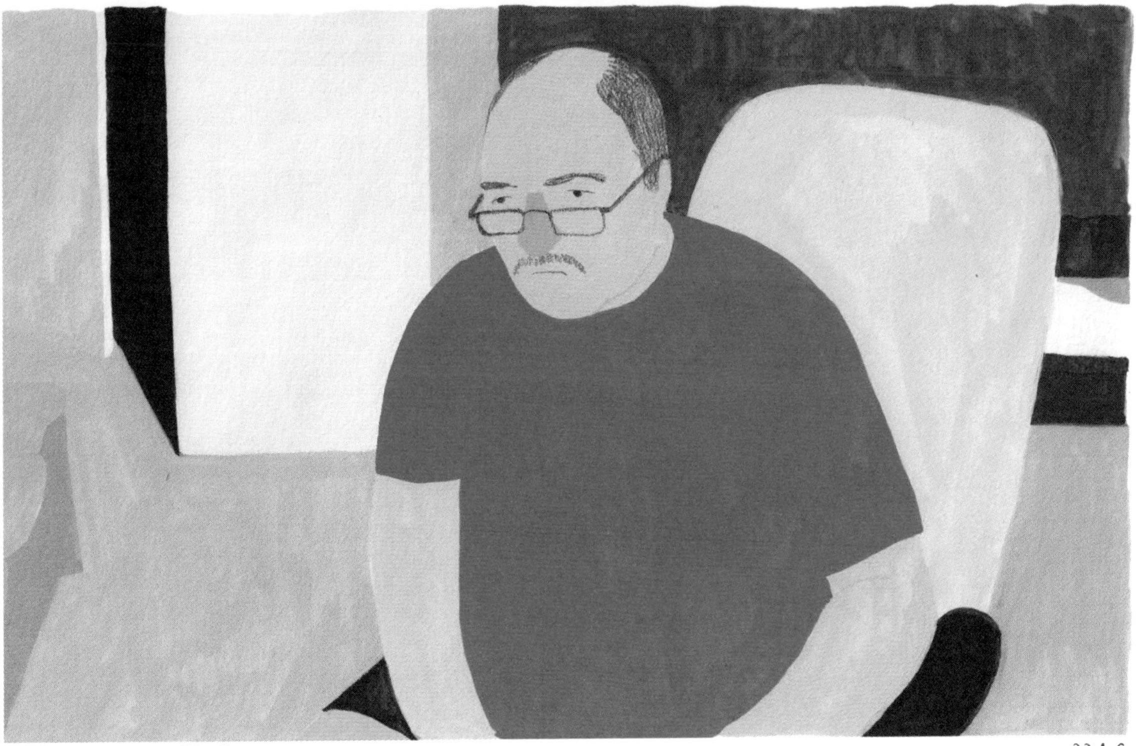

"FROZEN WATER." 22:46

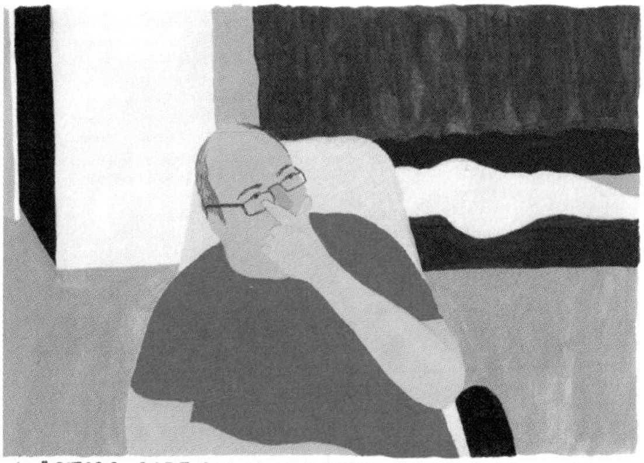

"STILL, LIFE ON MARS WILL POSE A CONSTANT STRUGGLE."

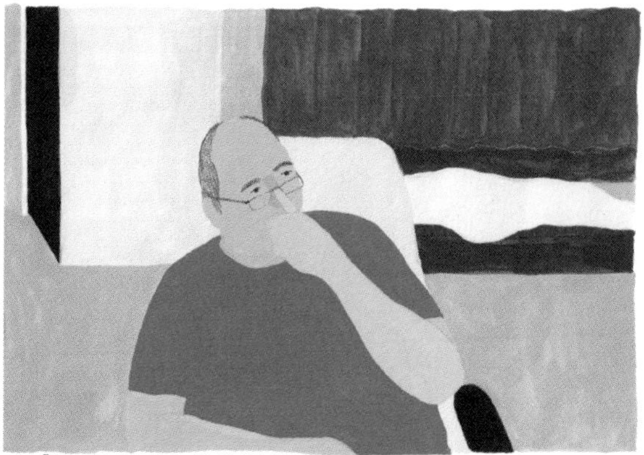

"MAN WILL HAVE TO ADAPT TO TINY LIVING QUARTERS,"

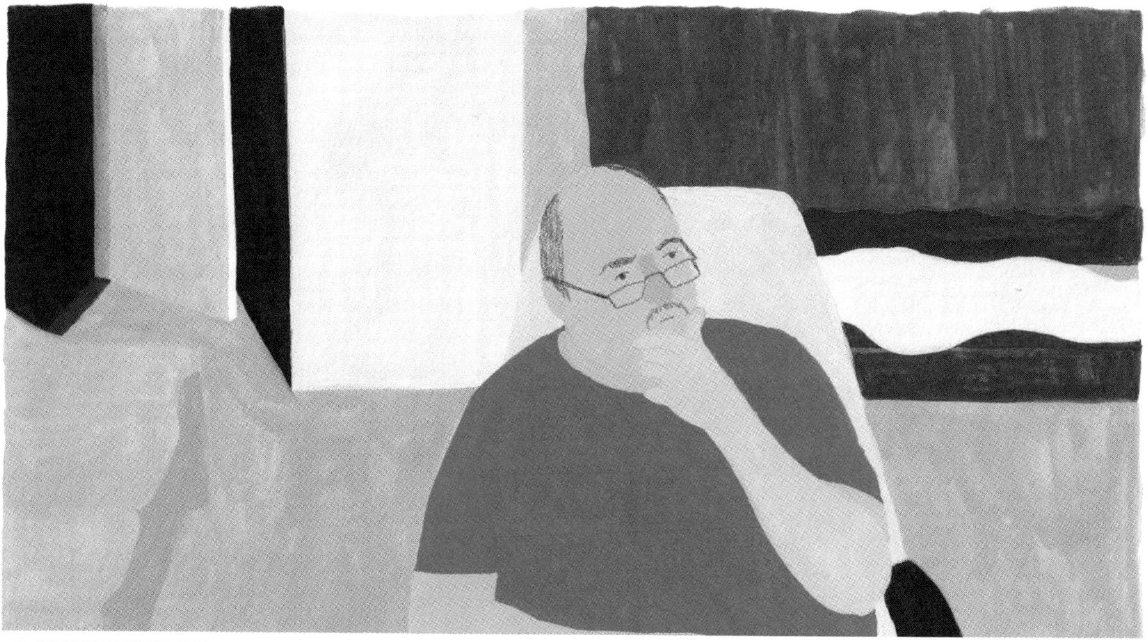

"SHELTERED FROM THE LETHAL ATMOSPHERE OUTSIDE."

22:47

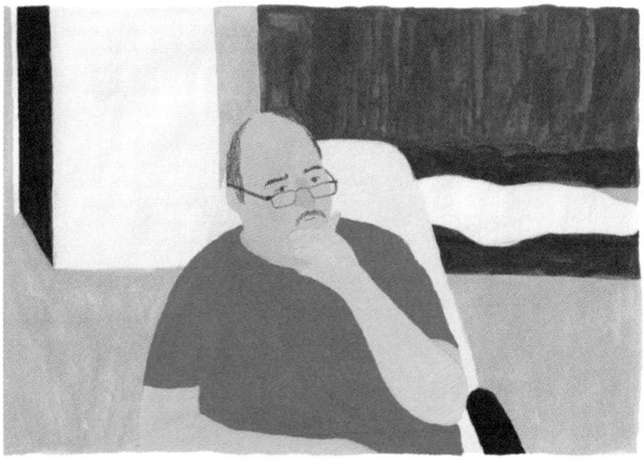

"LIFE WILL BE NOTHING LIKE IT WAS ON PLANET EARTH."

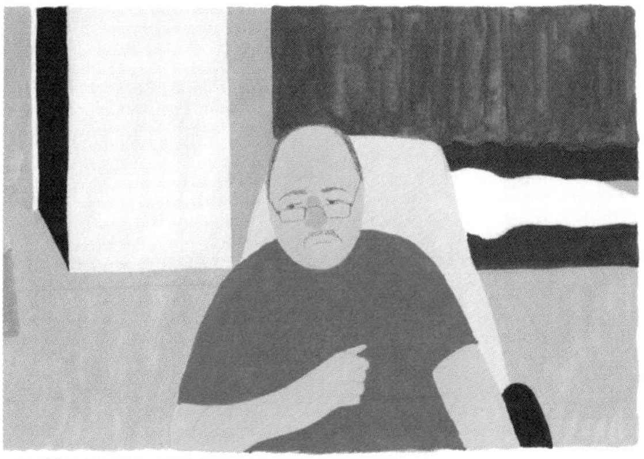

"IT WILL BE MONOTONOUS."

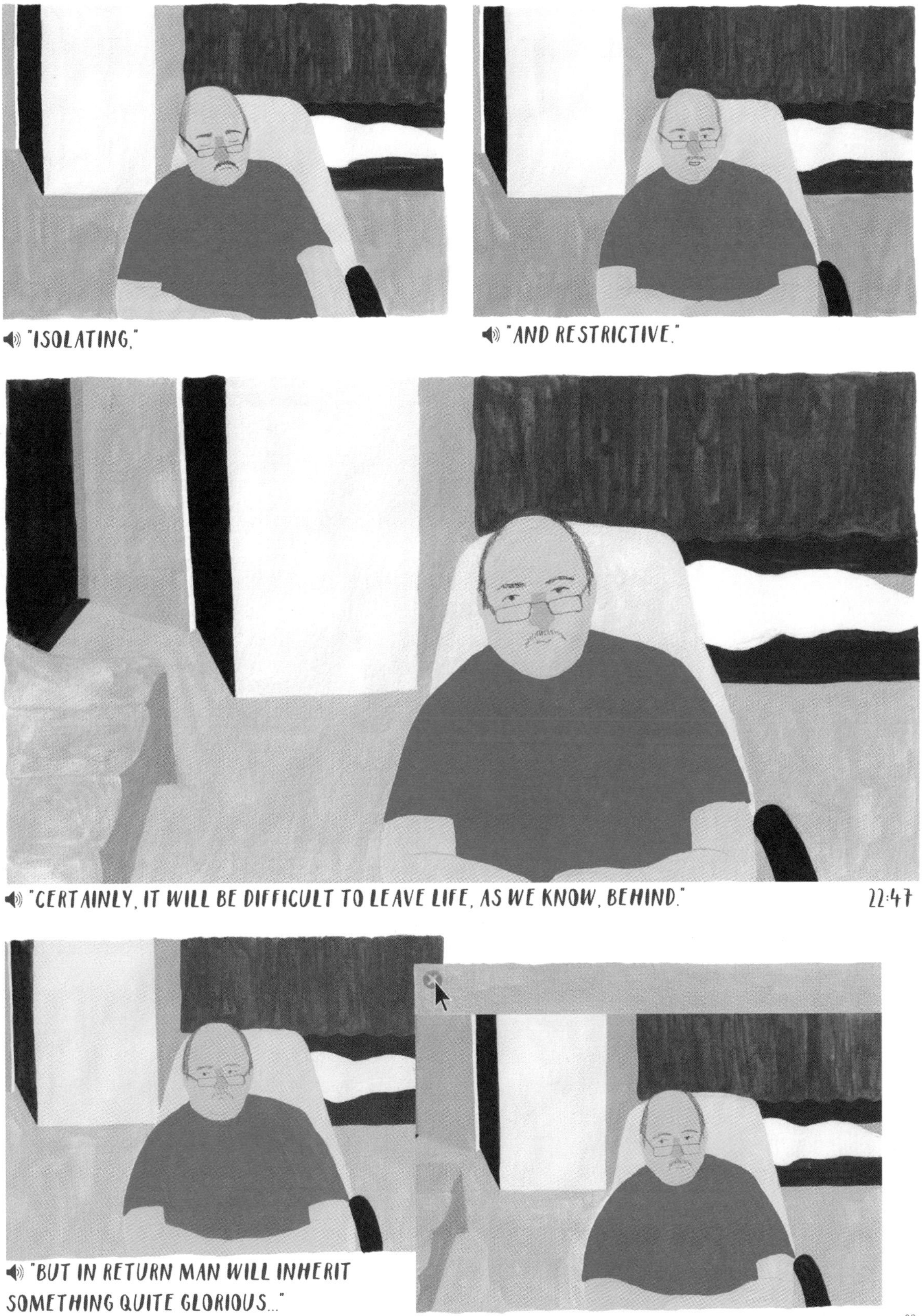
"ISOLATING."
"AND RESTRICTIVE."
"CERTAINLY, IT WILL BE DIFFICULT TO LEAVE LIFE, AS WE KNOW, BEHIND."
22:47
"BUT IN RETURN MAN WILL INHERIT SOMETHING QUITE GLORIOUS..."

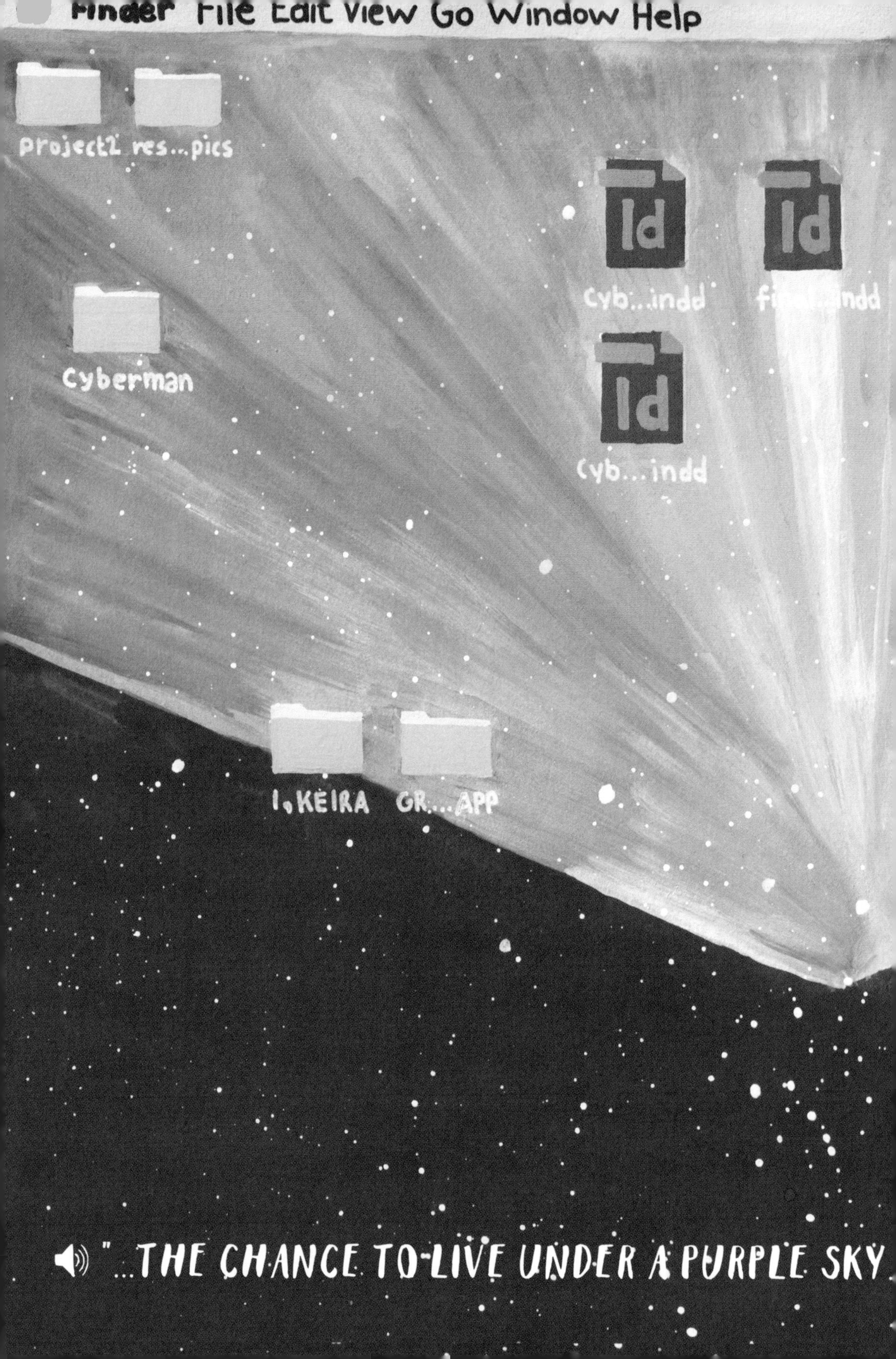
Finder File Edit View Go Window Help
project2
res...pics
Cyberman
cyb...indd
cyb...indd
I,KEIRA
GR...APP
"...THE CHANCE TO LIVE UNDER A PURPLE SKY

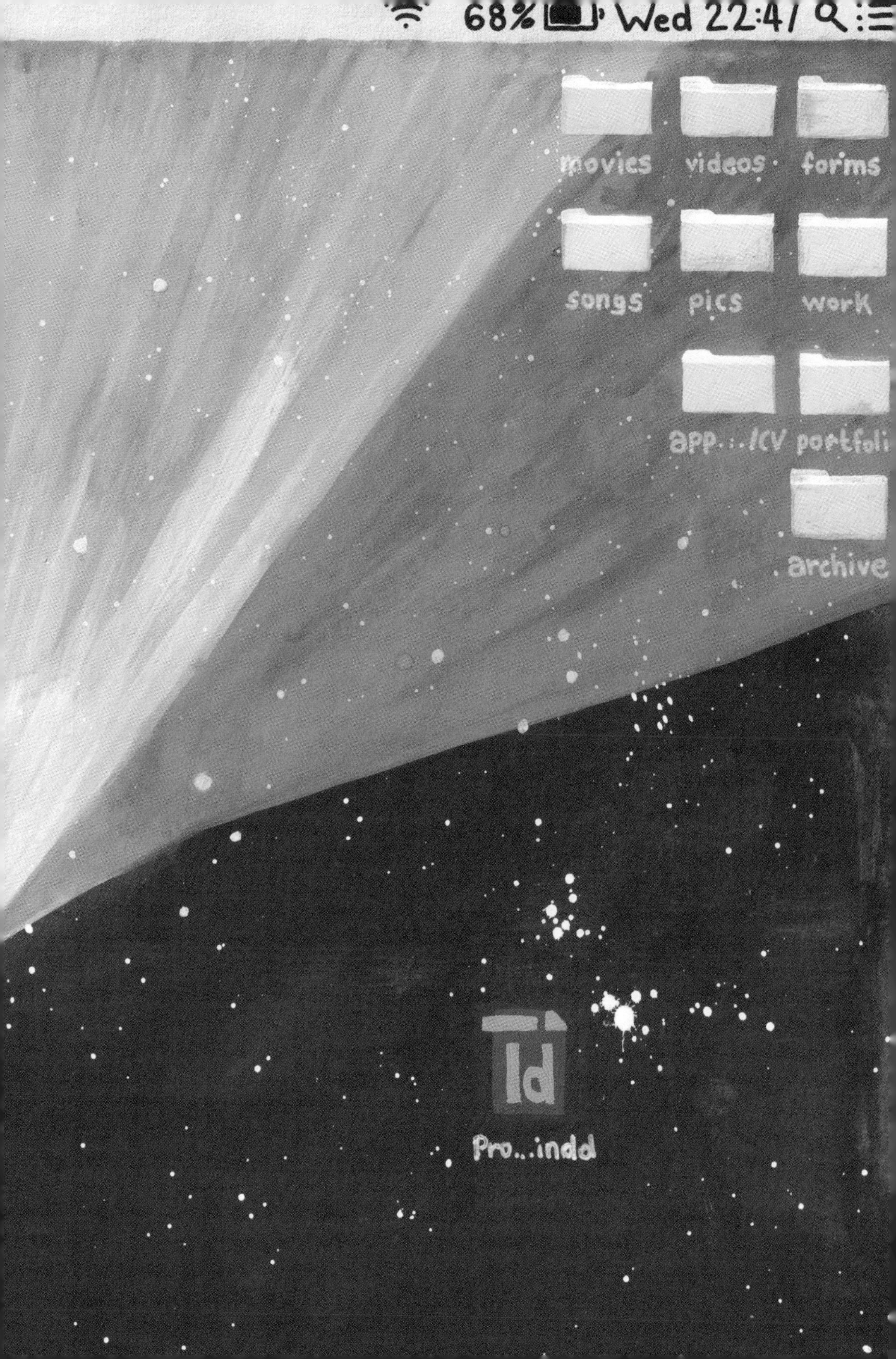
68% Wed 22:47
movies
videos
forms
songs
pics
work
app...CV
portfoli
archive
Id
Pro...indd

01.09.2016

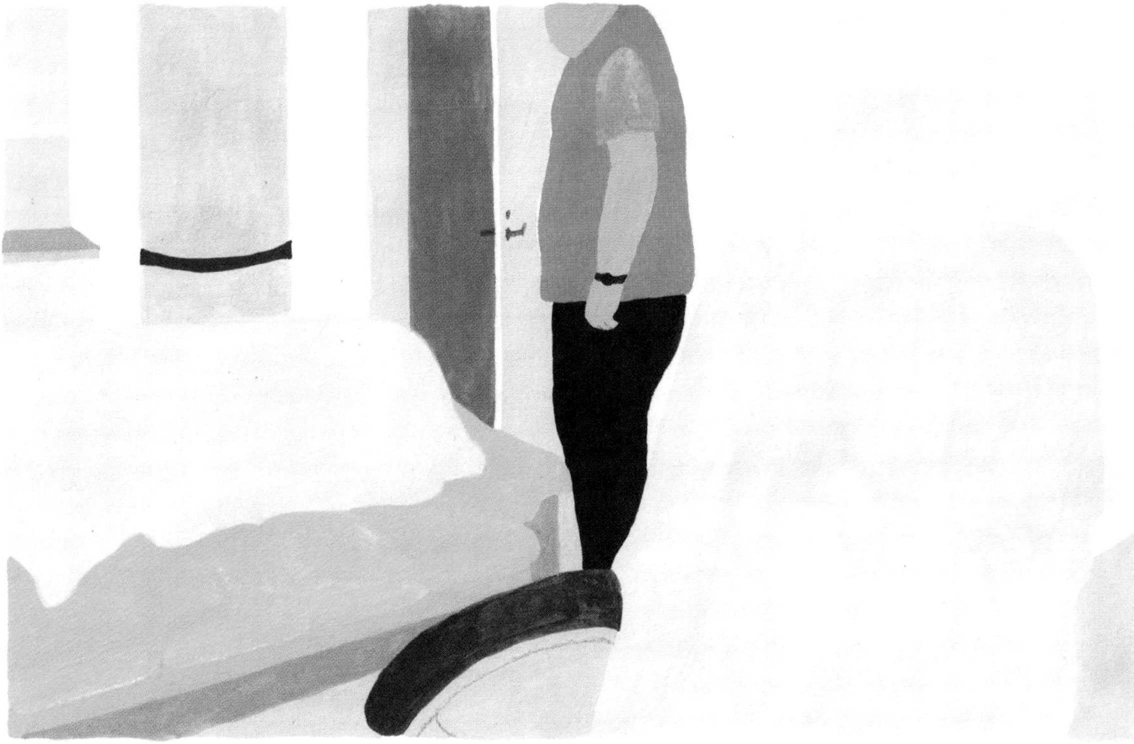

12:04

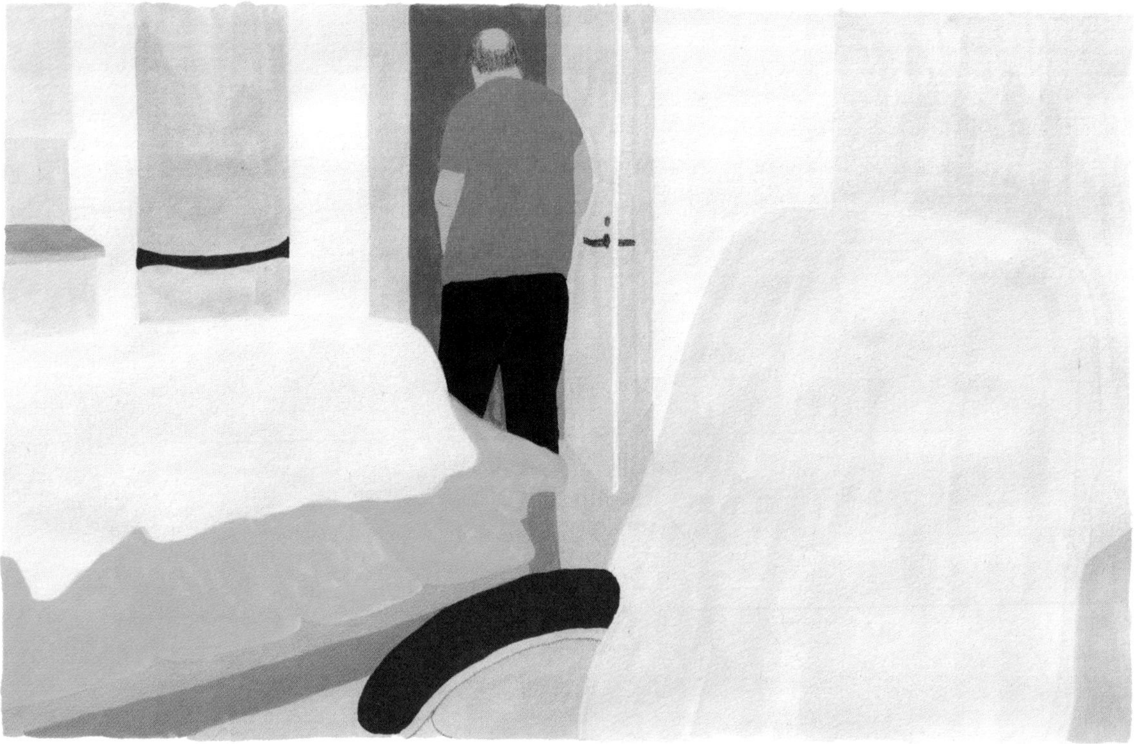

12:05

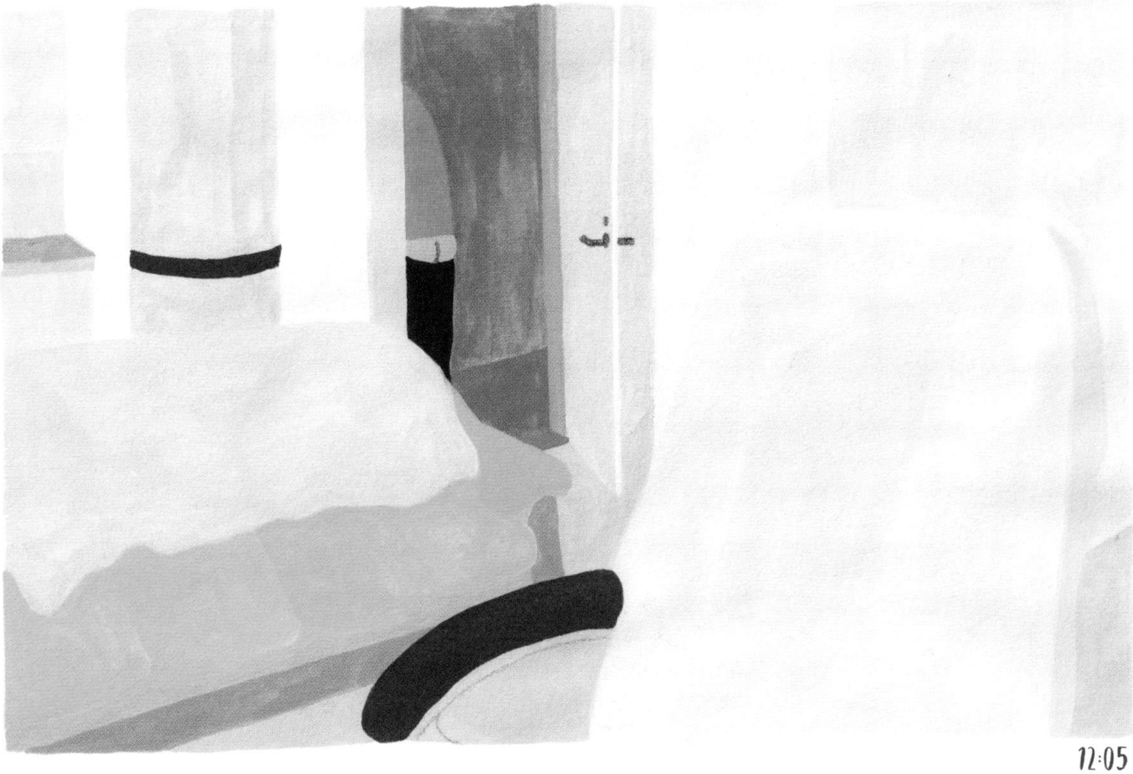

12:05

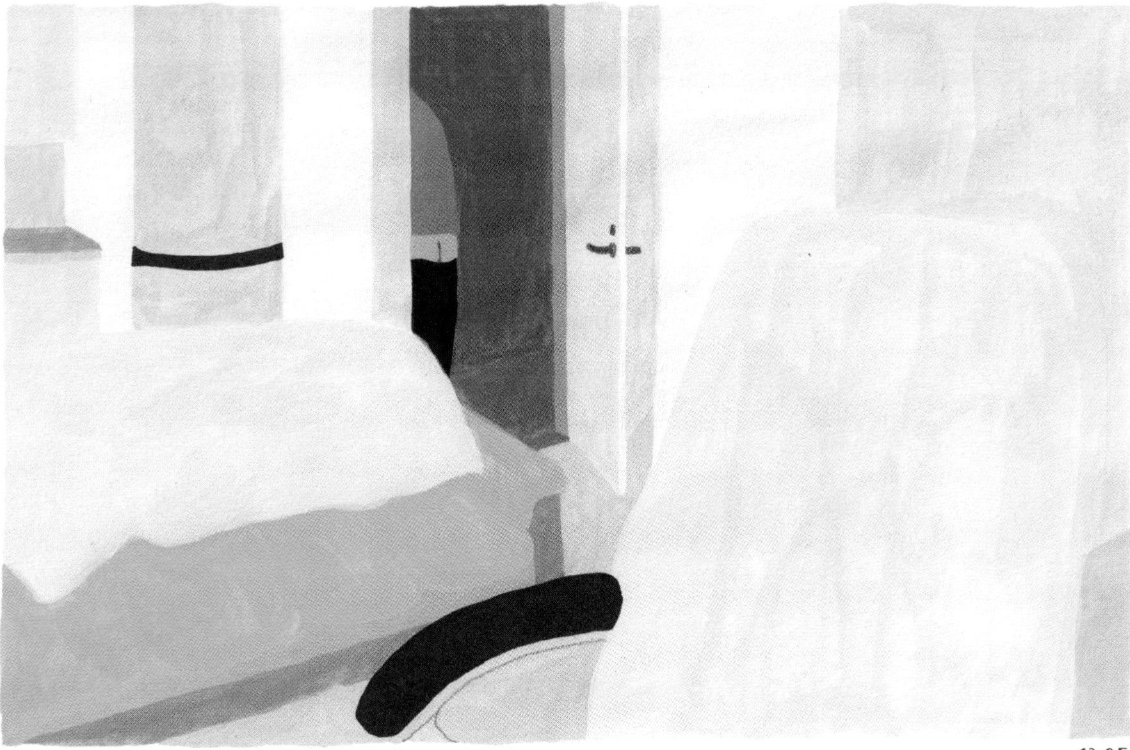

12:05

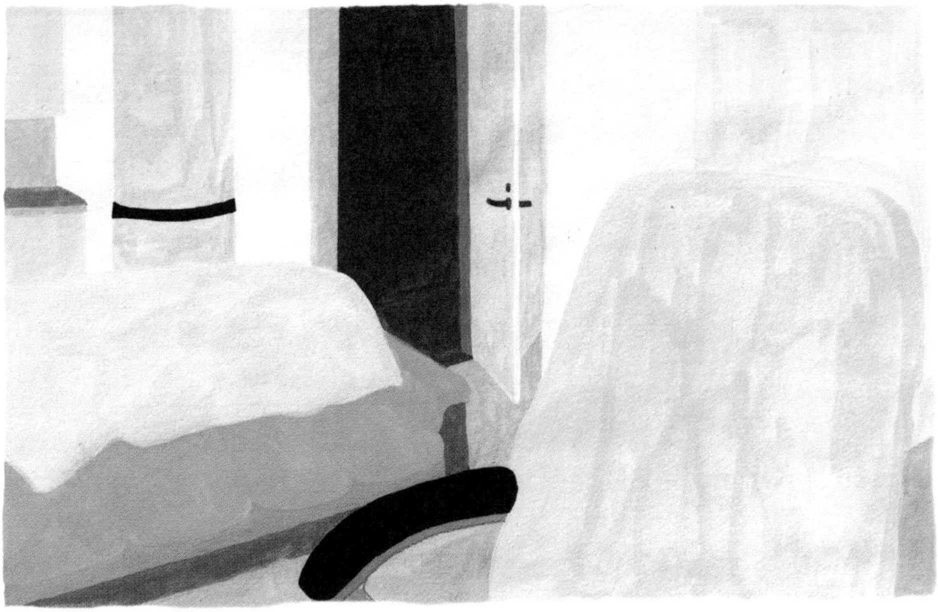

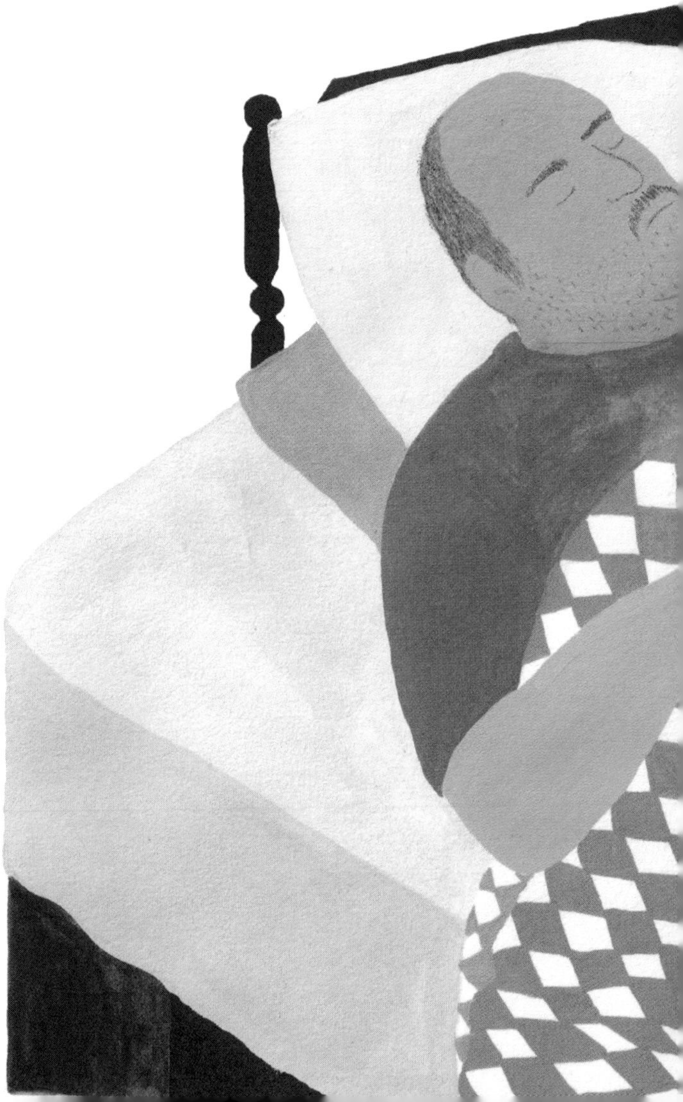

15:38

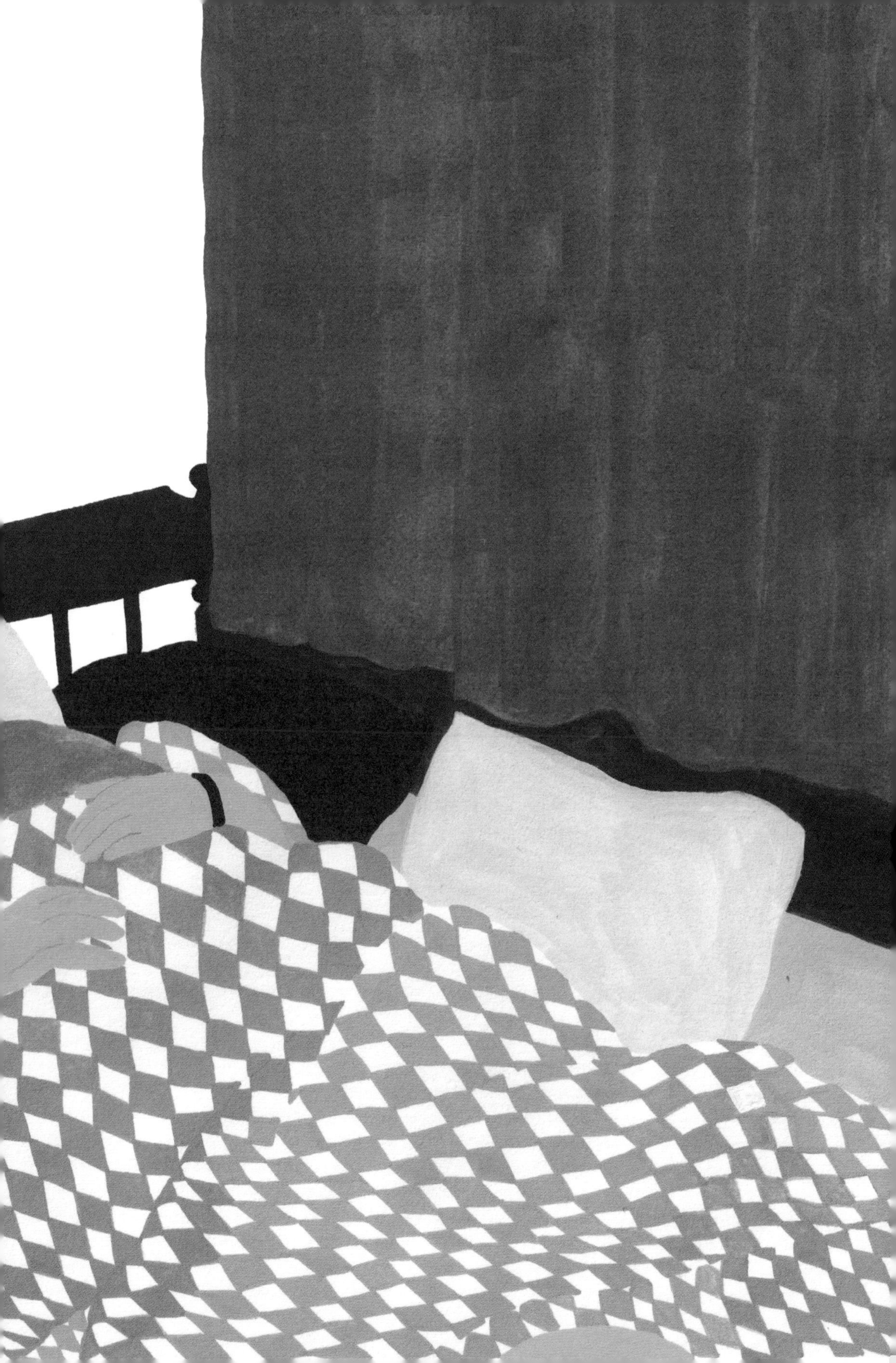

14.09.2016

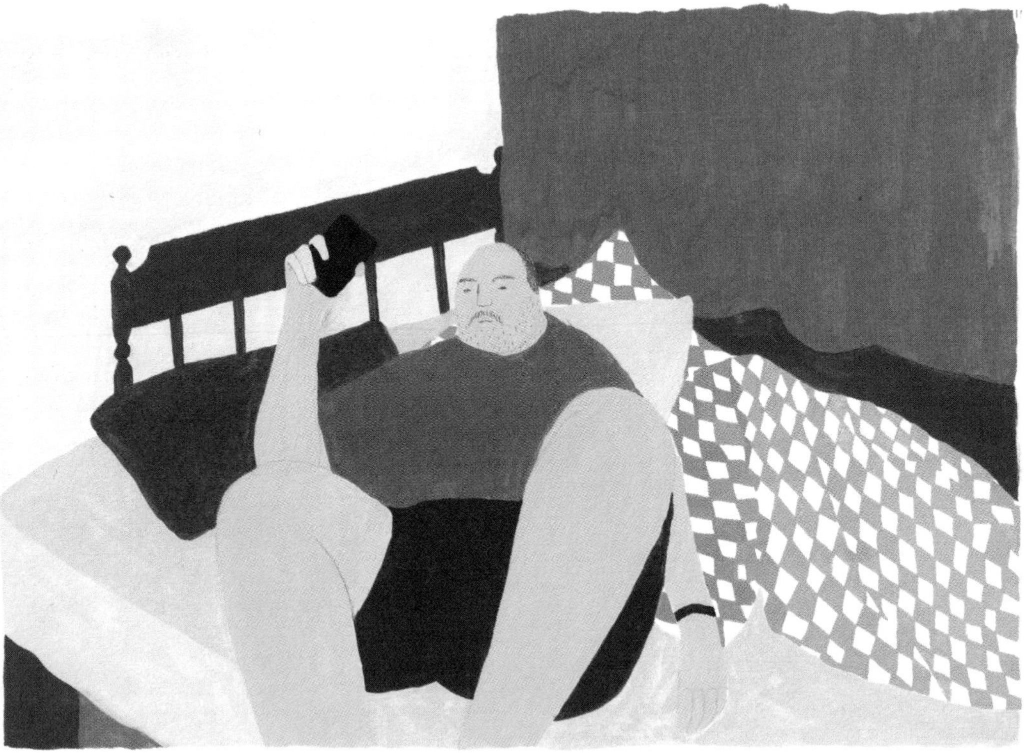

15:48

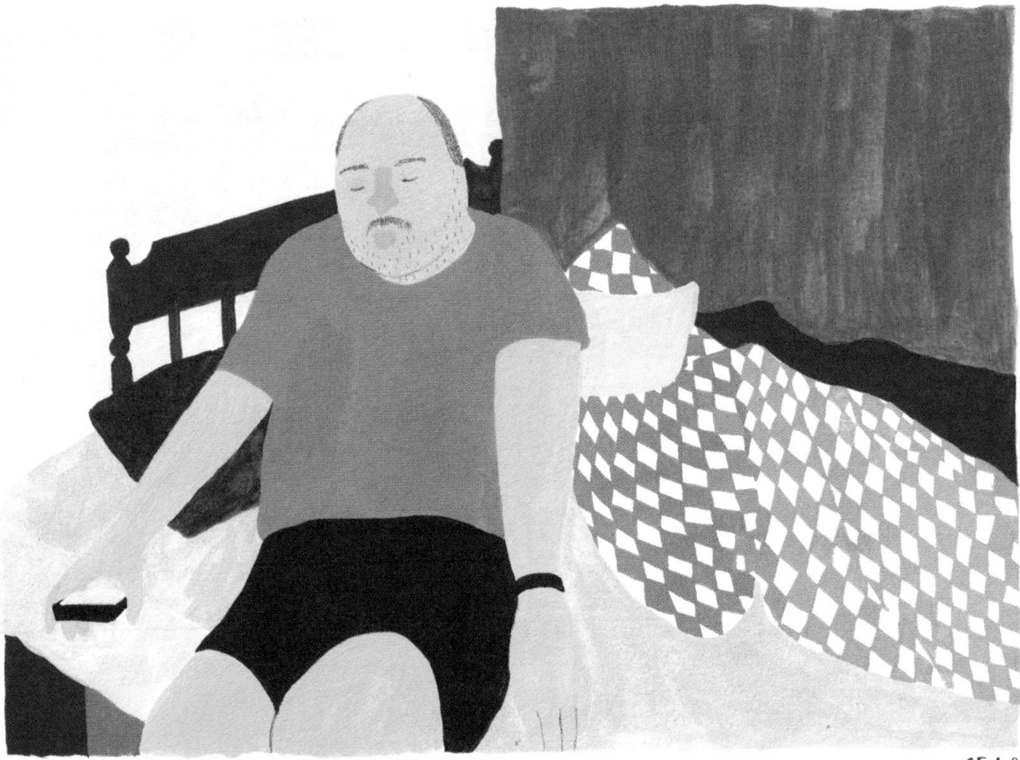

15:48

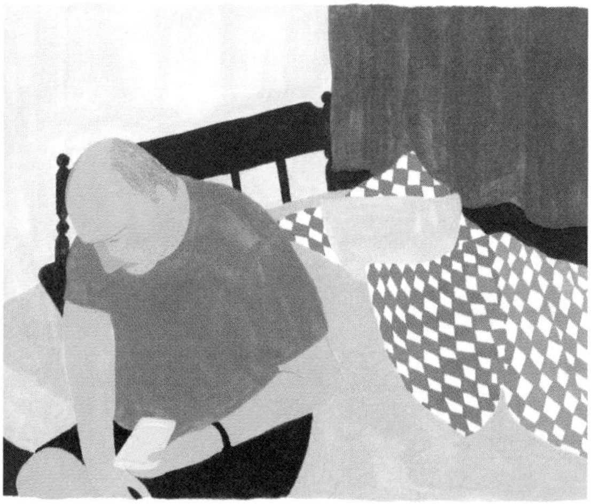

15:48

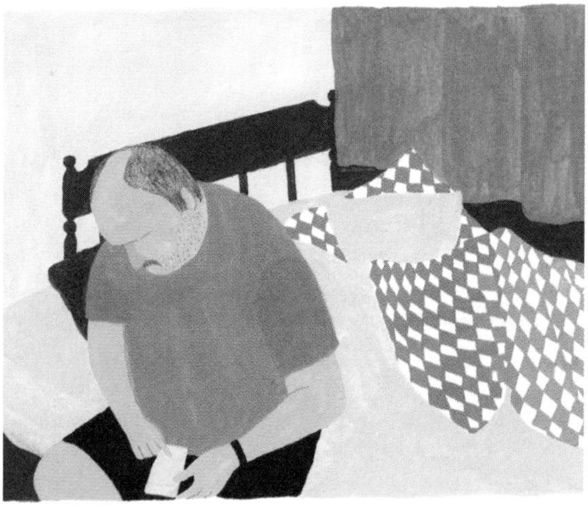

15:48

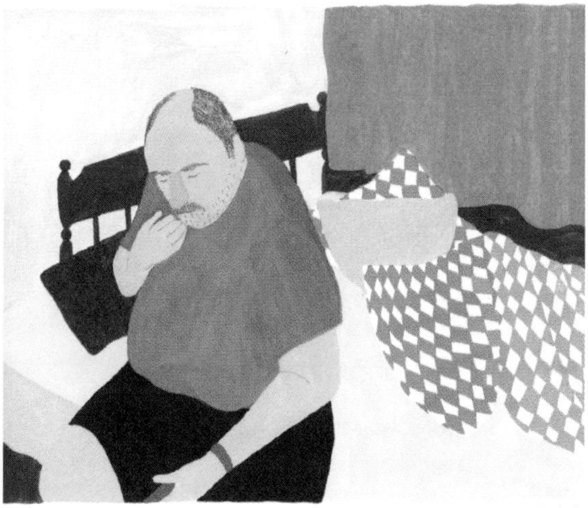

15:49

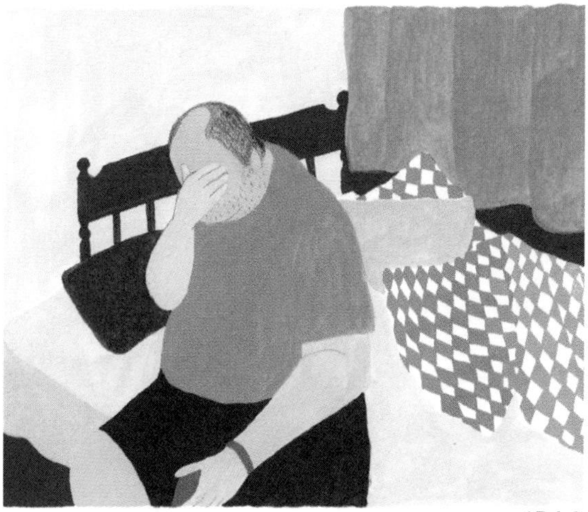

15:49

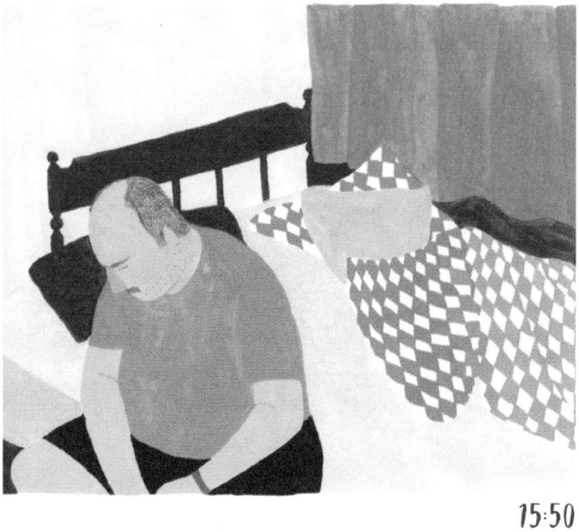

15:50

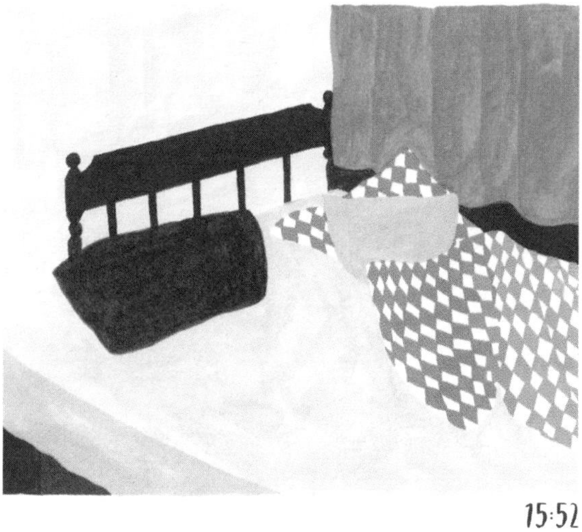

15:52

21.09.2016

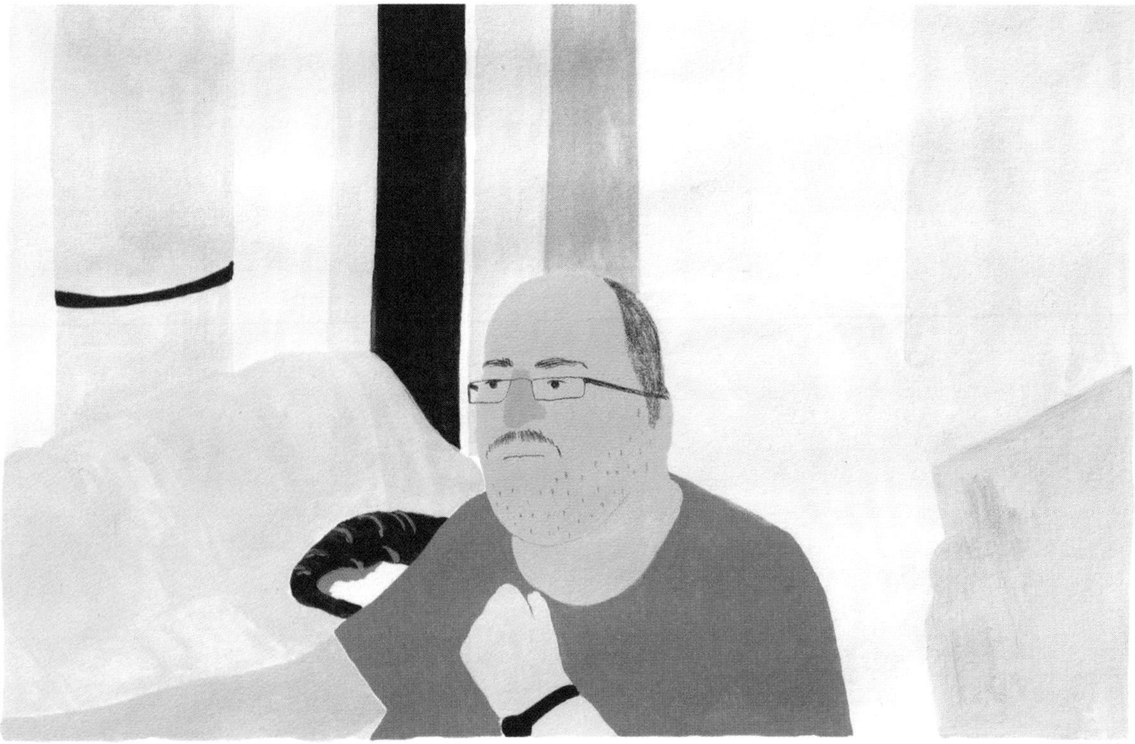

13:04

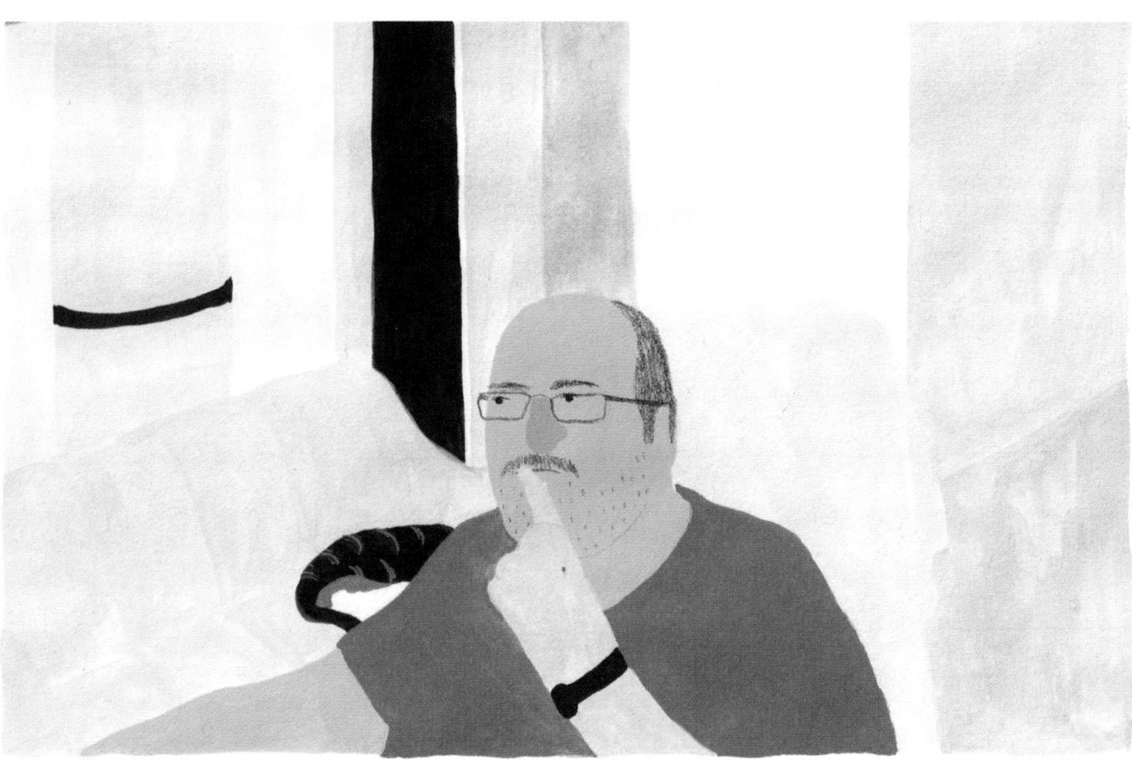

13:14

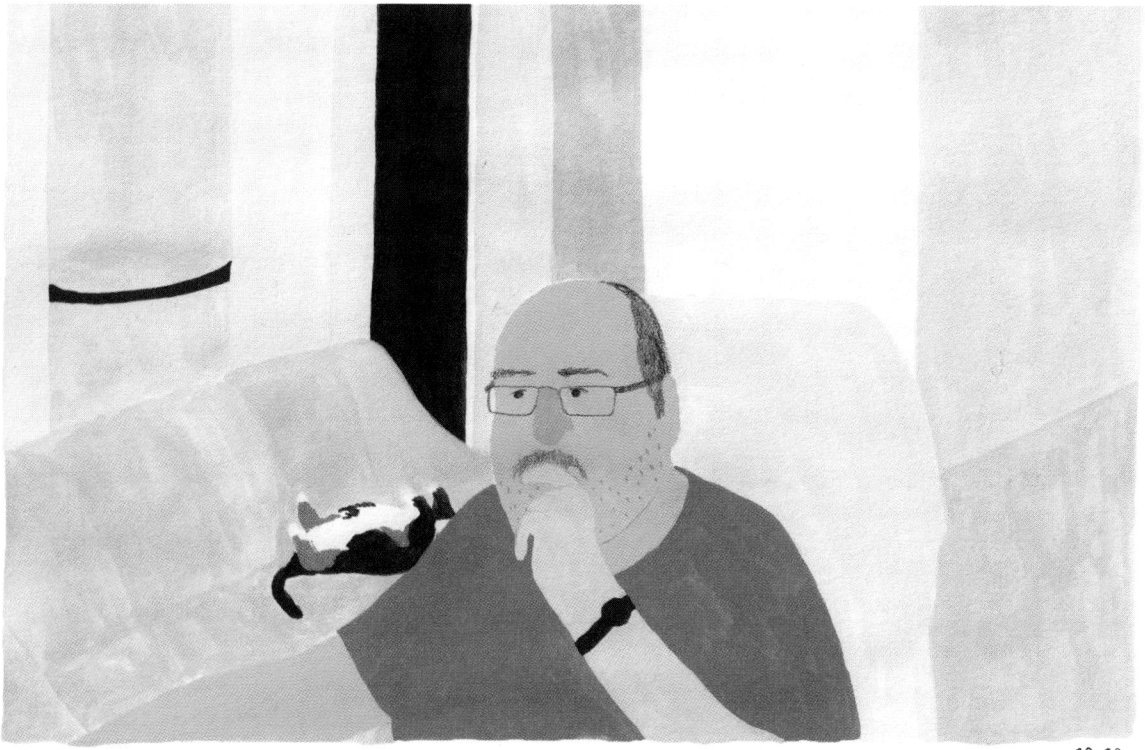

13:18

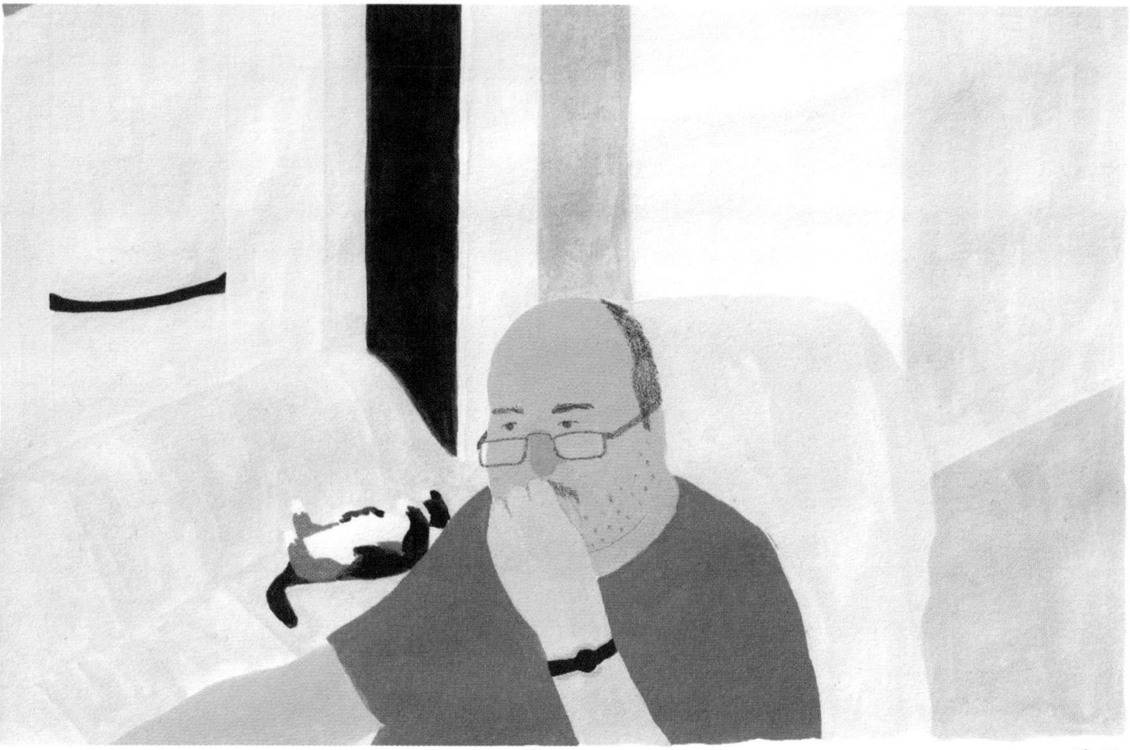

13:18

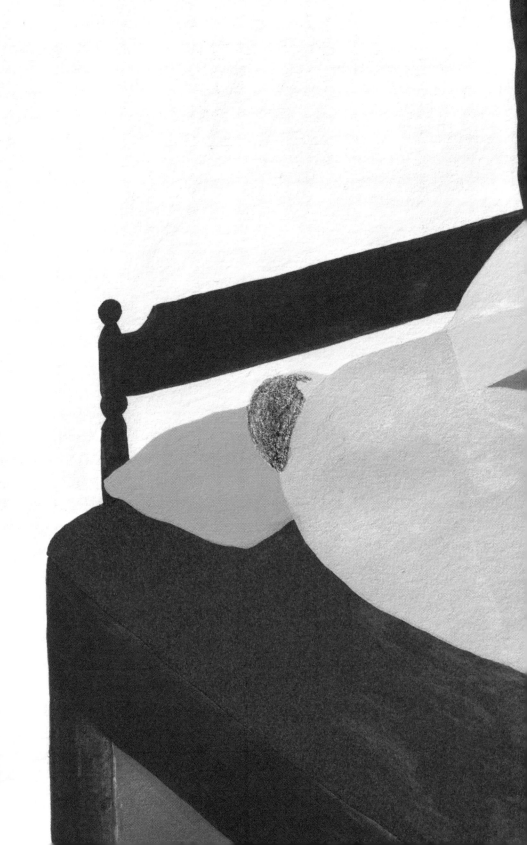

15:49

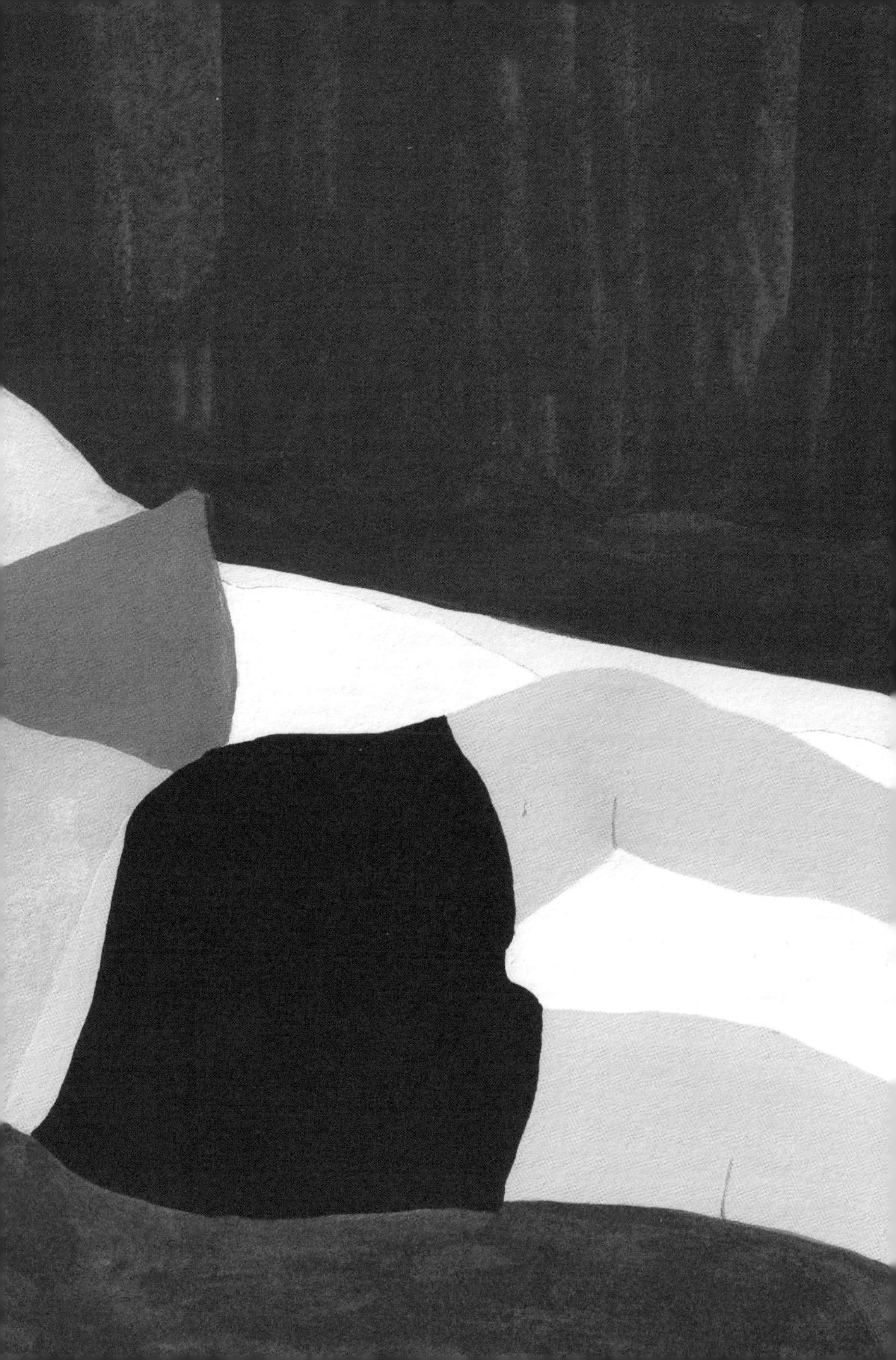

22.09.2016

status | #cyberman

#cyberman: welcome to cyberman

[16:03] == lb_jefferies [webchat@host-95-195-138-143.mobileonline.telia.com] has joined #cyberman
[16:03] <lb_jefferies> hi cyberman, I saw you had a new cat. how is she doing?
[16:03] <Kyrpaman> näänkö somasesta sun striimiä?

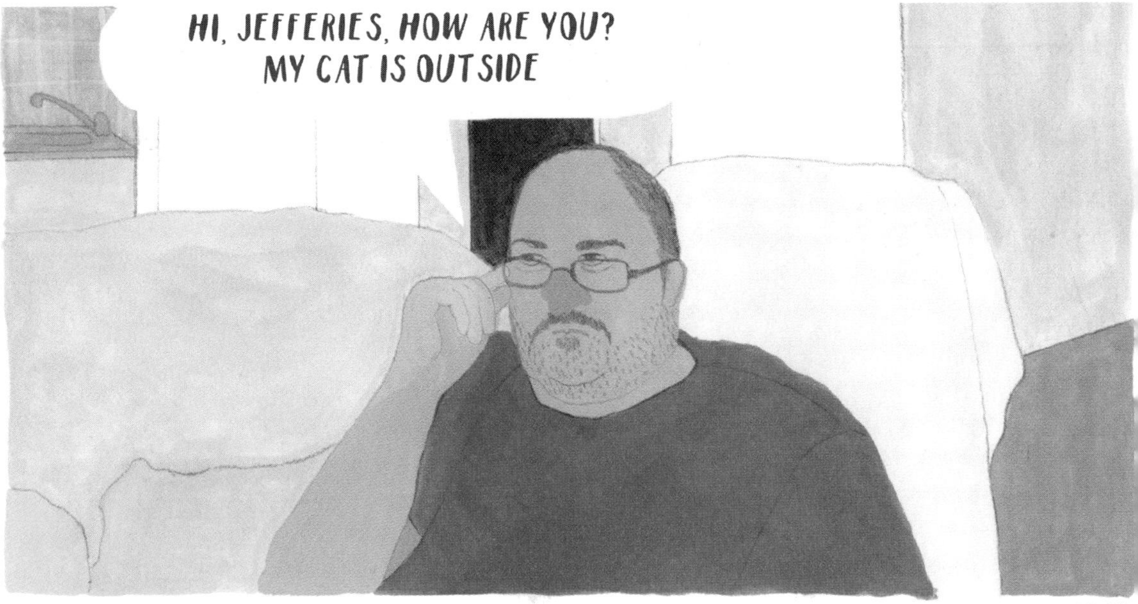
HI, JEFFERIES, HOW ARE YOU?
MY CAT IS OUTSIDE

16:04

status | #cyberman

[16:04] <Kyrpaman> viheraho kävi somasen toimistolla oulussa viime viikolla.
[16:04] <lb_jefferies> I'm good thank you! did you have a good nap?
[16:04] <ihemies> ahaaa jooo : D

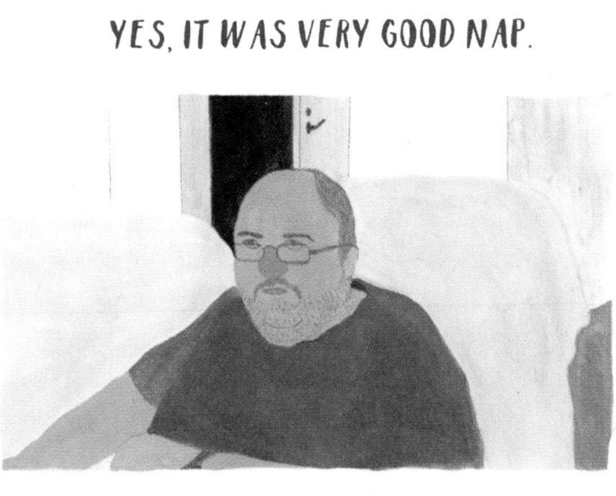
YES, IT WAS VERY GOOD NAP.

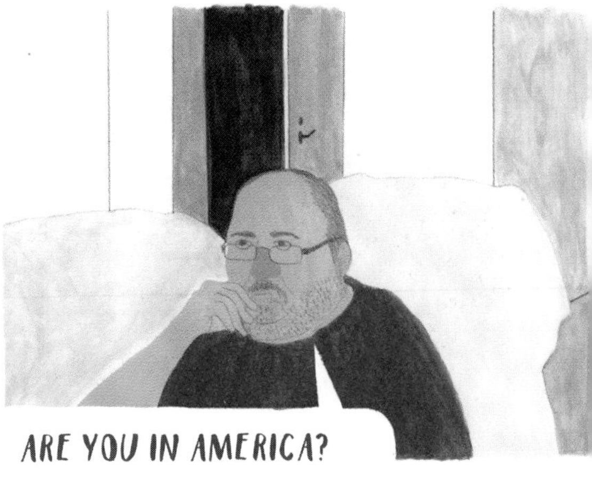
ARE YOU IN AMERICA?

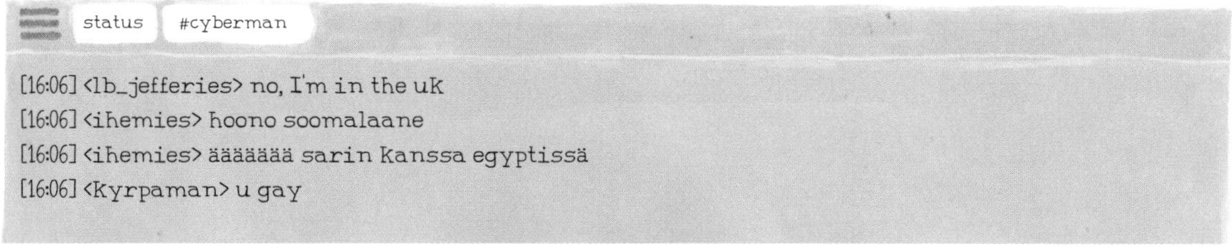
status
#cyberman
[16:06] <lb_jefferies> no, I'm in the uK
[16:06] <ihemies> hoono soomalaane
[16:06] <ihemies> äääääää sarin Kanssa egyptissä
[16:06] <Kyrpaman> u gay

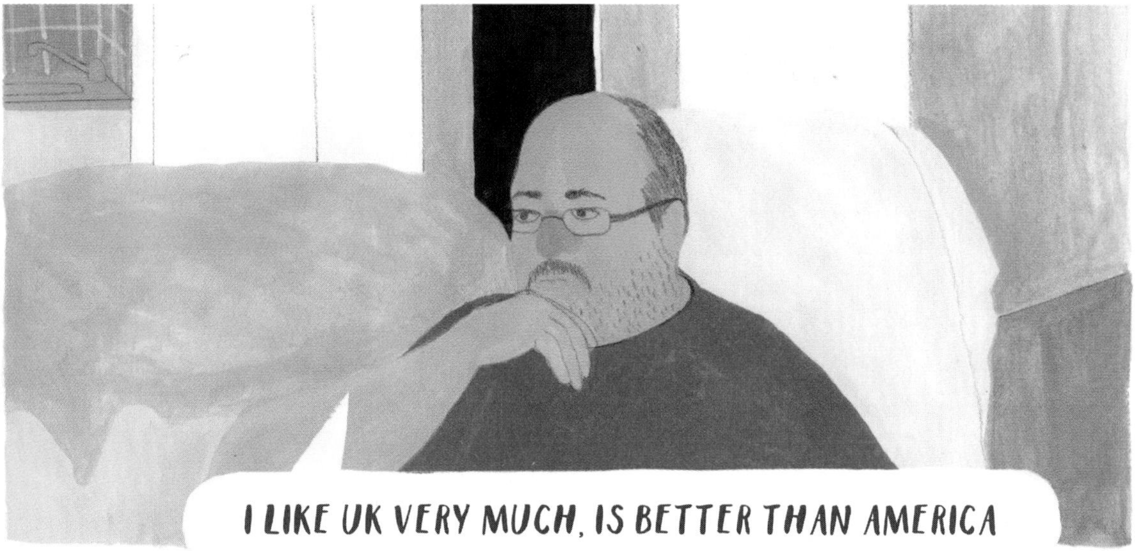
I LIKE UK VERY MUCH, IS BETTER THAN AMERICA

16:06

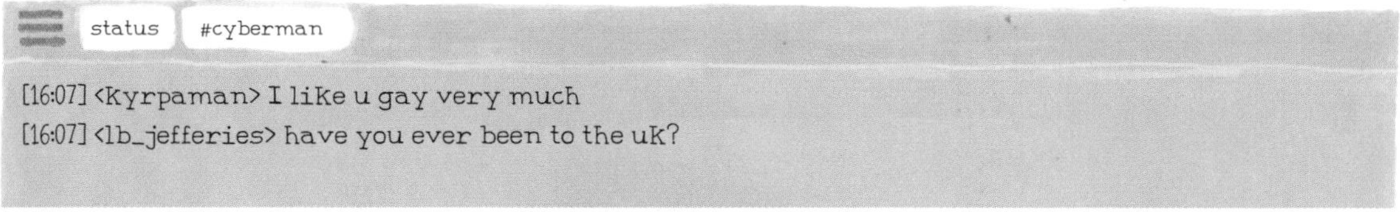
status
#cyberman
[16:07] <Kyrpaman> I liKe u gay very much
[16:07] <lb_jefferies> have you ever been to the uK?

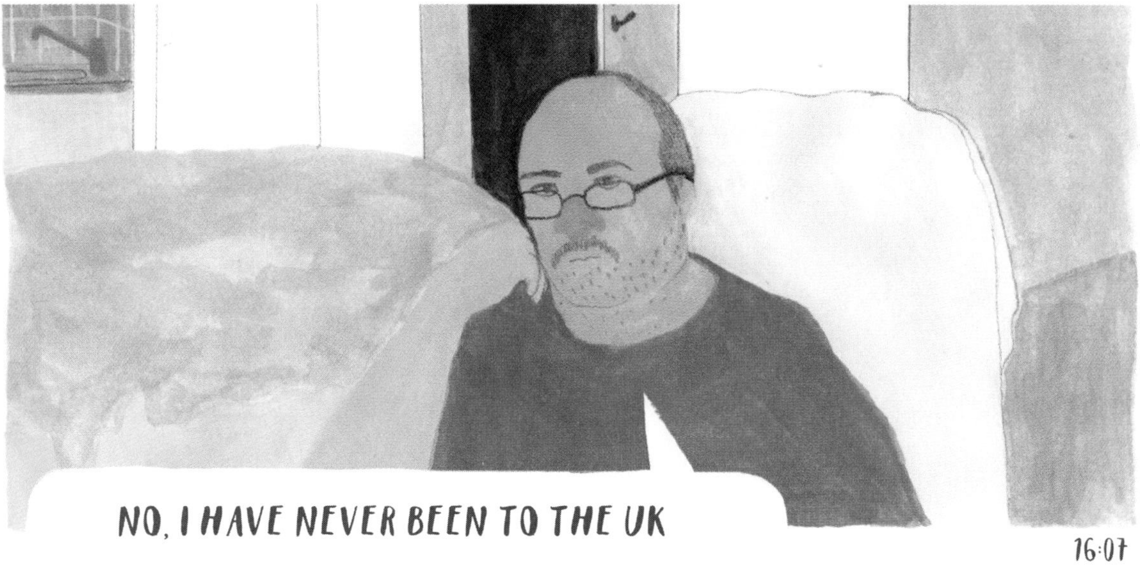
NO, I HAVE NEVER BEEN TO THE UK

16:07

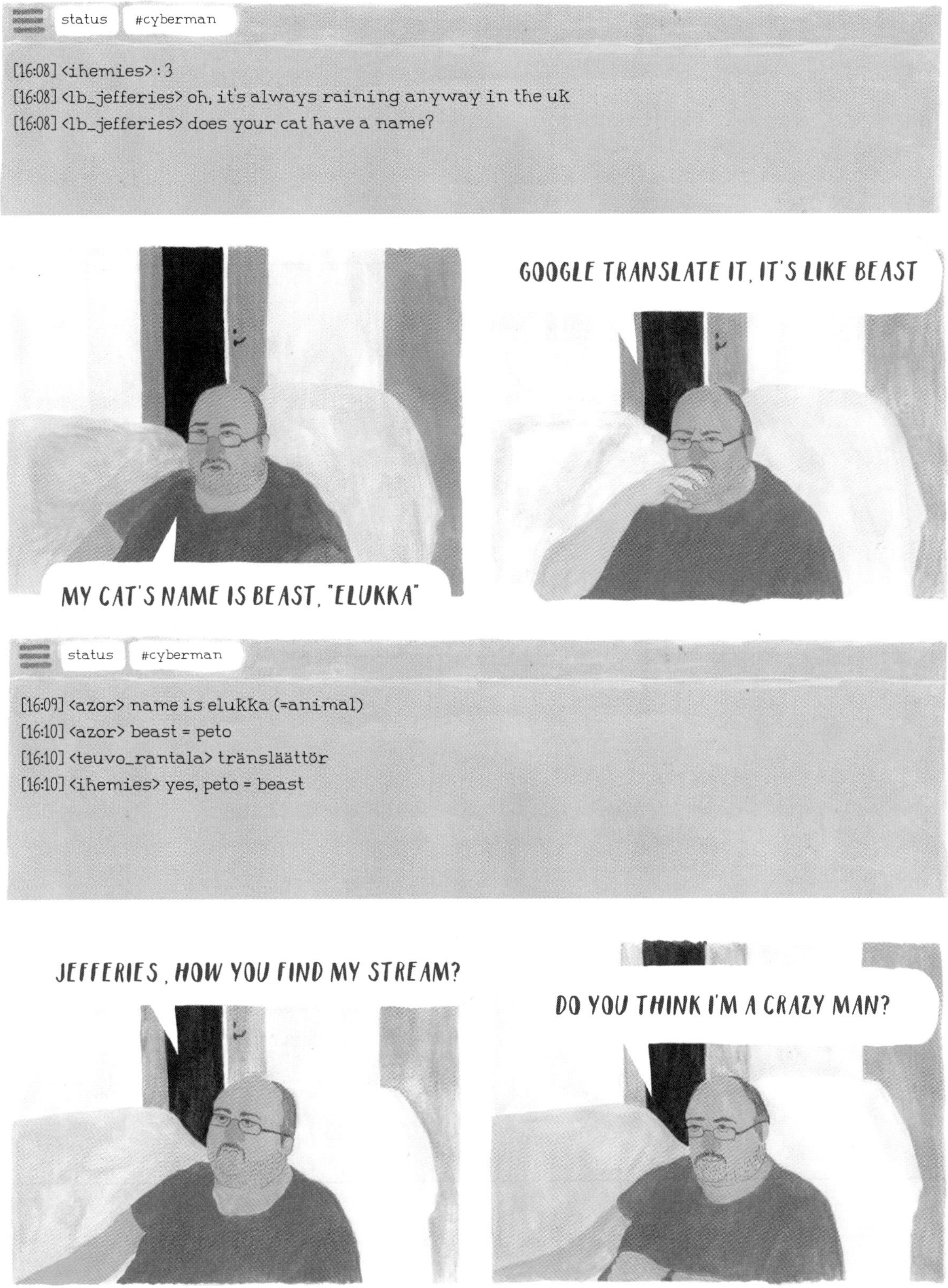
status #cyberman
[16:08] <ihemies> :3
[16:08] <lb_jefferies> oh, it's always raining anyway in the uK
[16:08] <lb_jefferies> does your cat have a name?
MY CAT'S NAME IS BEAST, "ELUKKA"
GOOGLE TRANSLATE IT, IT'S LIKE BEAST
status #cyberman
[16:09] <azor> name is eluKKa (=animal)
[16:10] <azor> beast = peto
[16:10] <teuvo_rantala> tränsläättör
[16:10] <ihemies> yes, peto = beast
JEFFERIES, HOW YOU FIND MY STREAM?
DO YOU THINK I'M A CRAZY MAN?

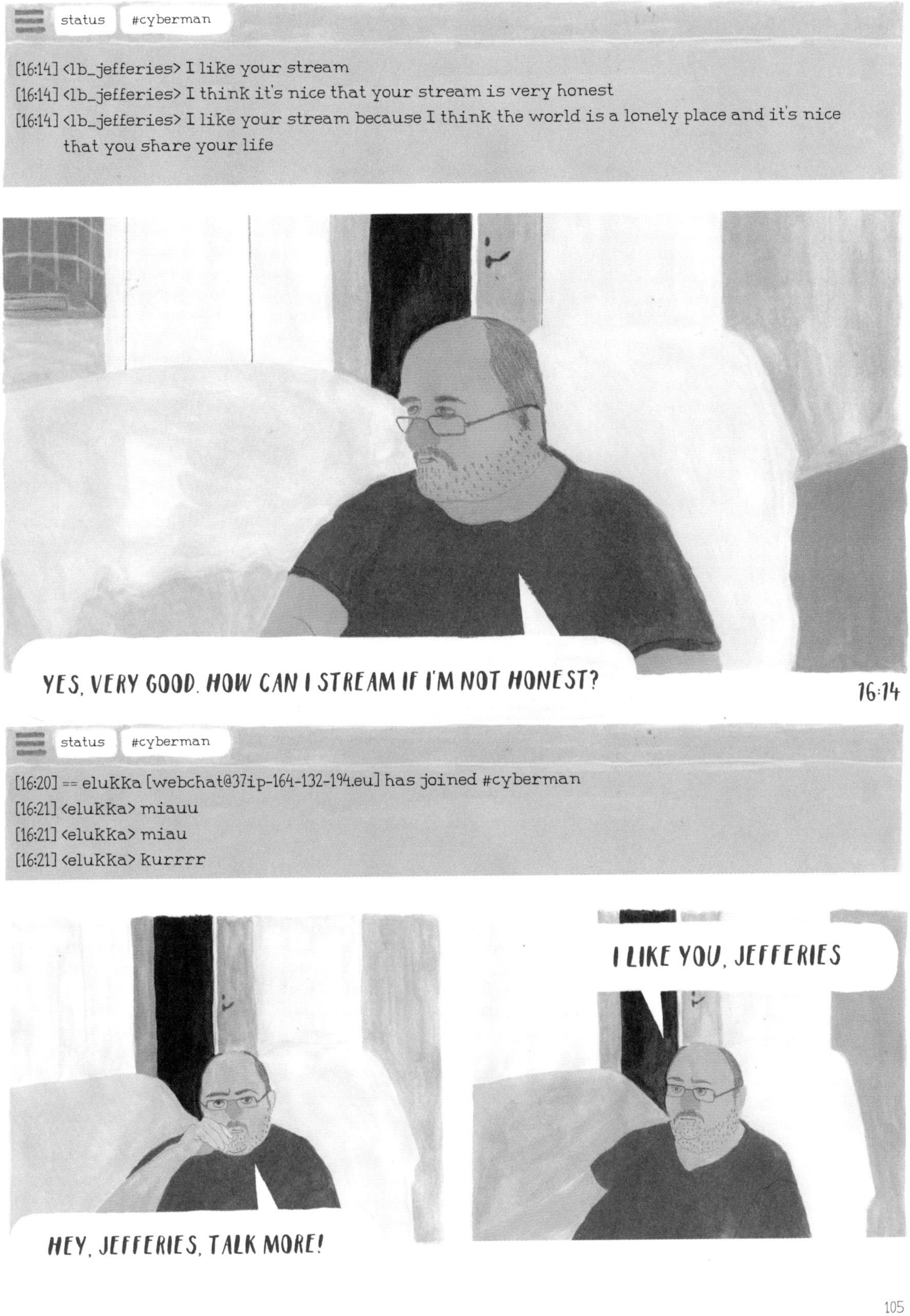
status #cyberman
[16:14] <lb_jefferies> I like your stream
[16:14] <lb_jefferies> I think it's nice that your stream is very honest
[16:14] <lb_jefferies> I like your stream because I think the world is a lonely place and it's nice that you share your life
YES, VERY GOOD. HOW CAN I STREAM IF I'M NOT HONEST?
16:14
status #cyberman
[16:20] == eluKka [webchat@37ip-164-132-194.eu] has joined #cyberman
[16:21] <eluKka> miauu
[16:21] <eluKka> miau
[16:21] <eluKka> Kurrrr
HEY, JEFFERIES, TALK MORE!
I LIKE YOU, JEFFERIES

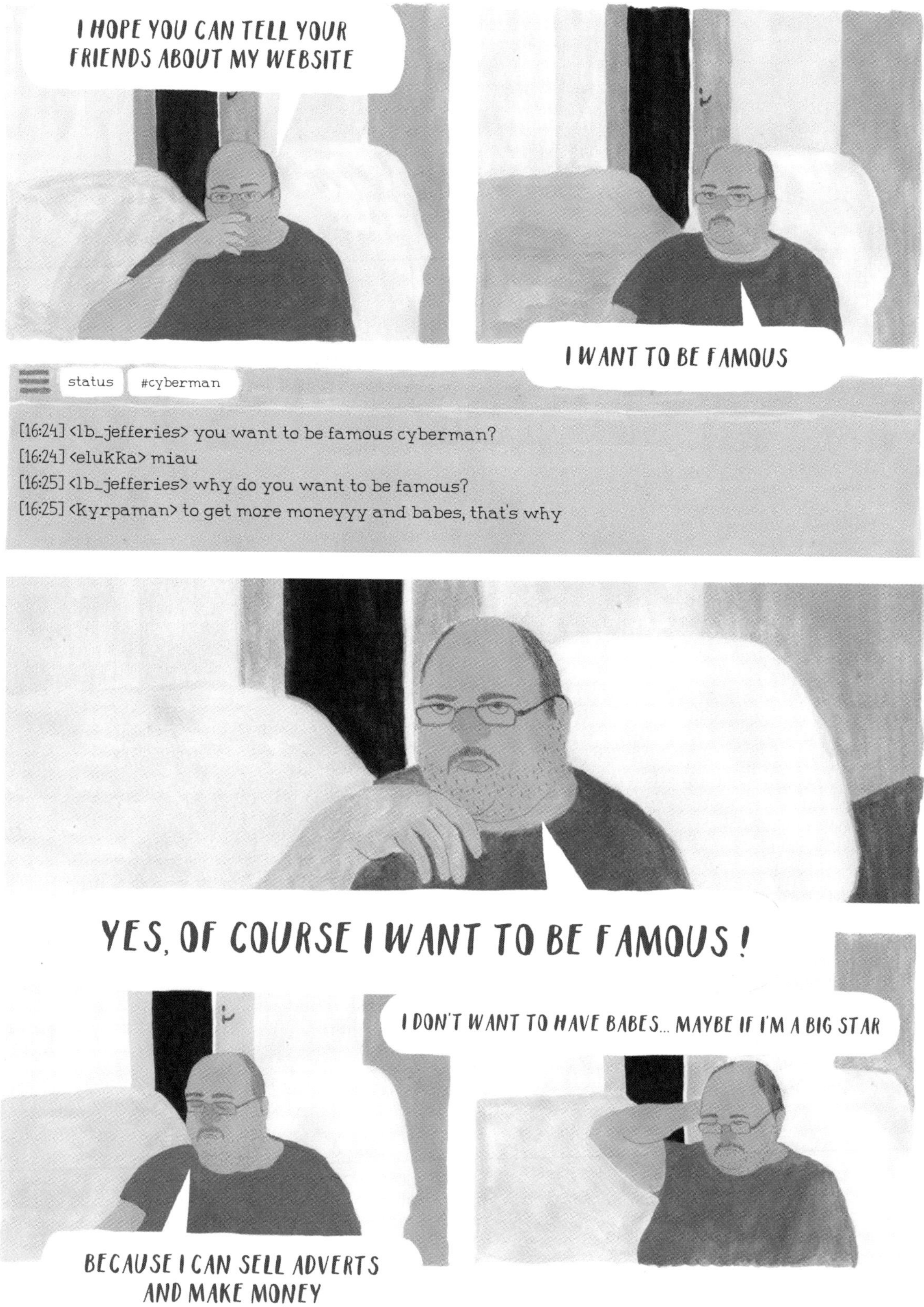
I HOPE YOU CAN TELL YOUR FRIENDS ABOUT MY WEBSITE
I WANT TO BE FAMOUS
status
#cyberman
[16:24] <lb_jefferies> you want to be famous cyberman?
[16:24] <eluKKa> miau
[16:25] <lb_jefferies> why do you want to be famous?
[16:25] <Kyrpaman> to get more moneyyy and babes, that's why
YES, OF COURSE I WANT TO BE FAMOUS!
BECAUSE I CAN SELL ADVERTS AND MAKE MONEY
I DON'T WANT TO HAVE BABES... MAYBE IF I'M A BIG STAR

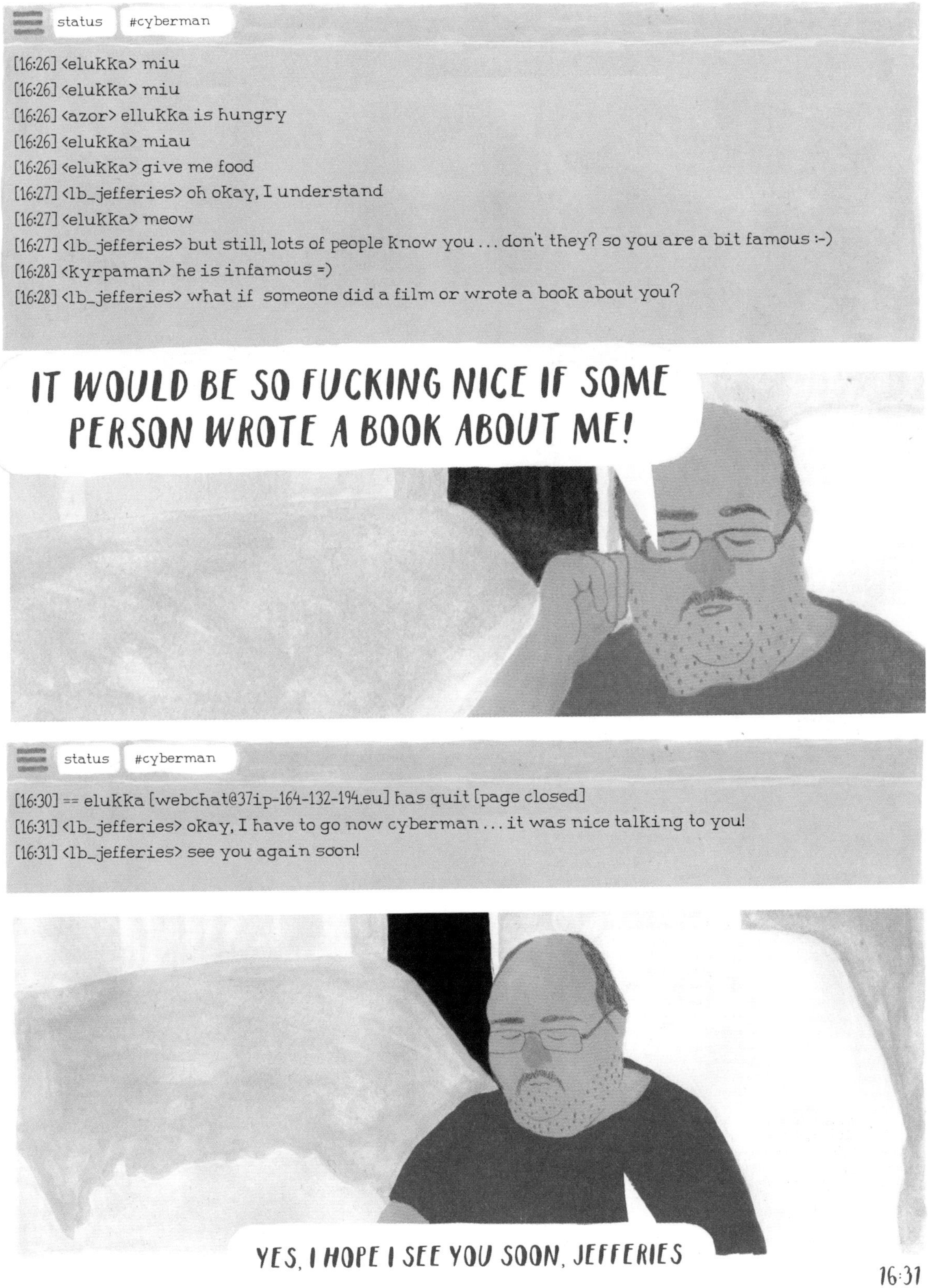
status #cyberman
[16:26] <elukKa> miu
[16:26] <elukKa> miu
[16:26] <azor> ellukKa is hungry
[16:26] <elukKa> miau
[16:26] <elukKa> give me food
[16:27] <lb_jefferies> oh oKay, I understand
[16:27] <elukKa> meow
[16:27] <lb_jefferies> but still, lots of people Know you . . . don't they? so you are a bit famous :-)
[16:28] <Kyrpaman> he is infamous =)
[16:28] <lb_jefferies> what if someone did a film or wrote a booK about you?
IT WOULD BE SO FUCKING NICE IF SOME PERSON WROTE A BOOK ABOUT ME!
status #cyberman
[16:30] == eluKka [webchat@37ip-164-132-194.eu] has quit [page closed]
[16:31] <lb_jefferies> oKay, I have to go now cyberman . . . it was nice talKing to you!
[16:31] <lb_jefferies> see you again soon!
YES, I HOPE I SEE YOU SOON, JEFFERIES
16:31

24.09.2016

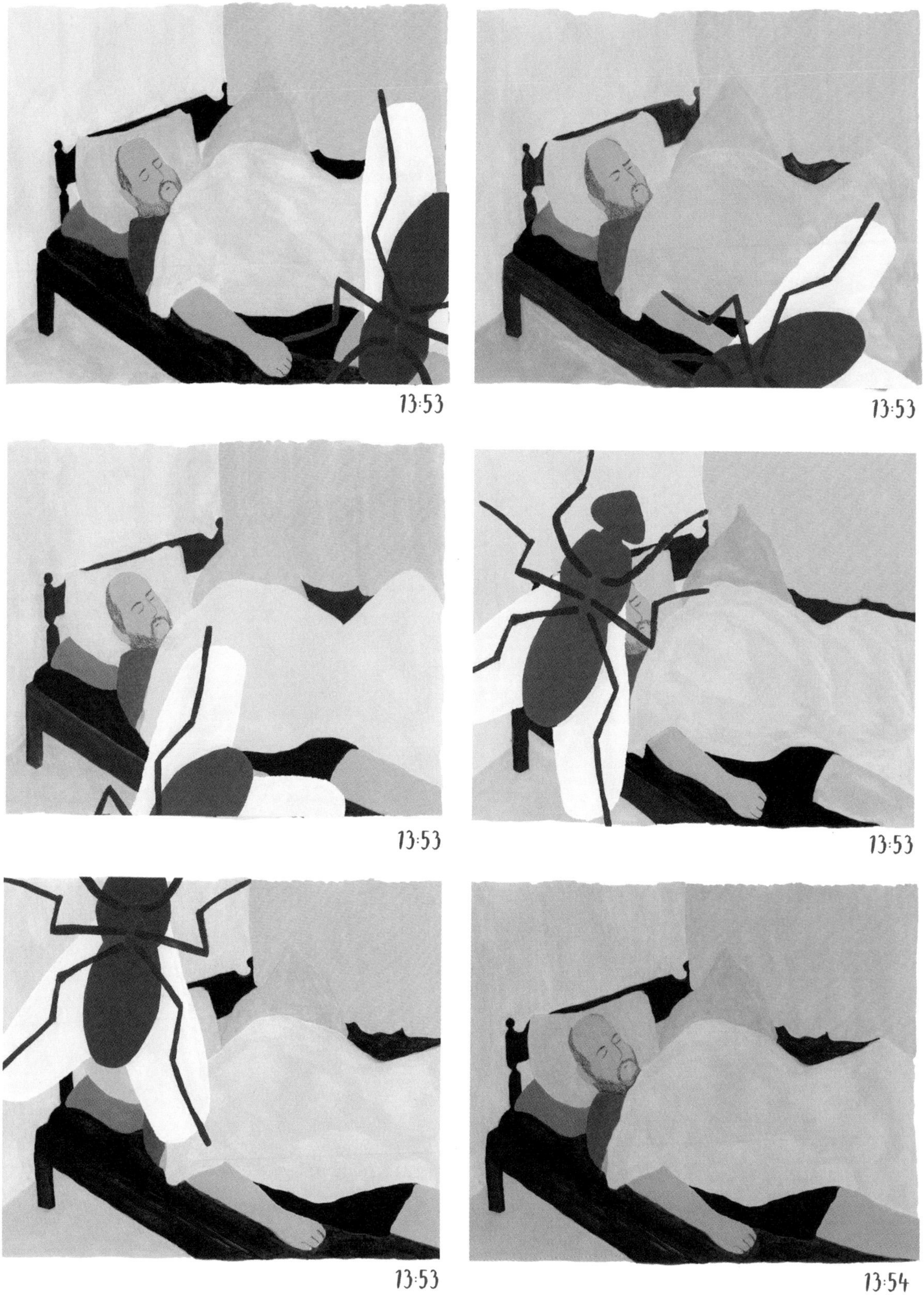
13:53
13:53
13:53
13:53
13:53
13:54

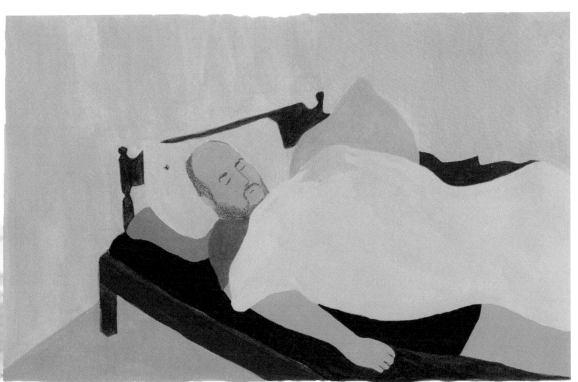

13:54

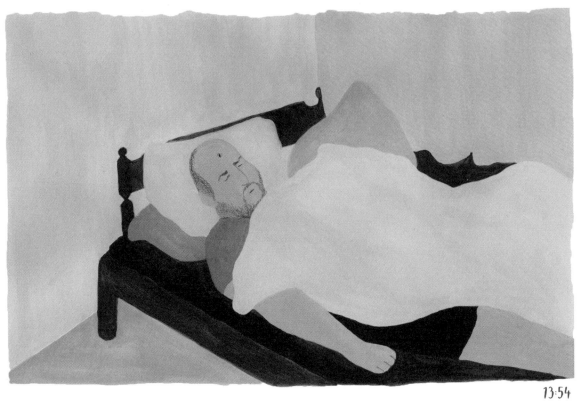

13:54

03.10.2016

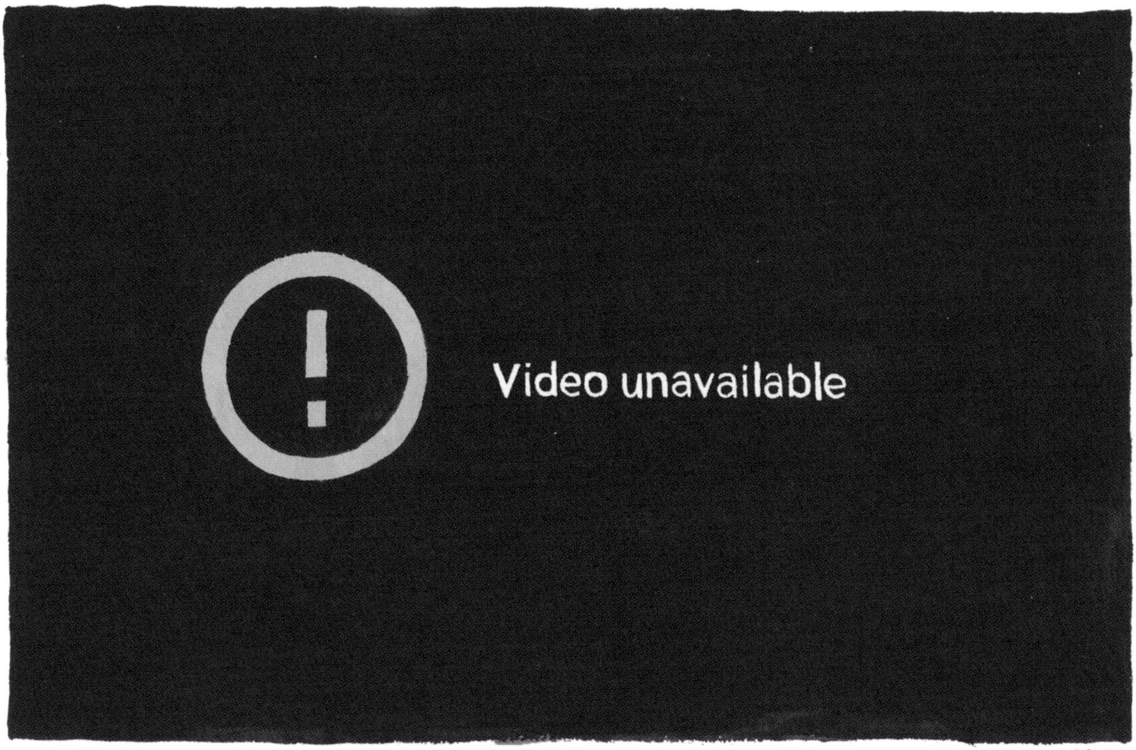
Video unavailable

23:04

05.10.2016

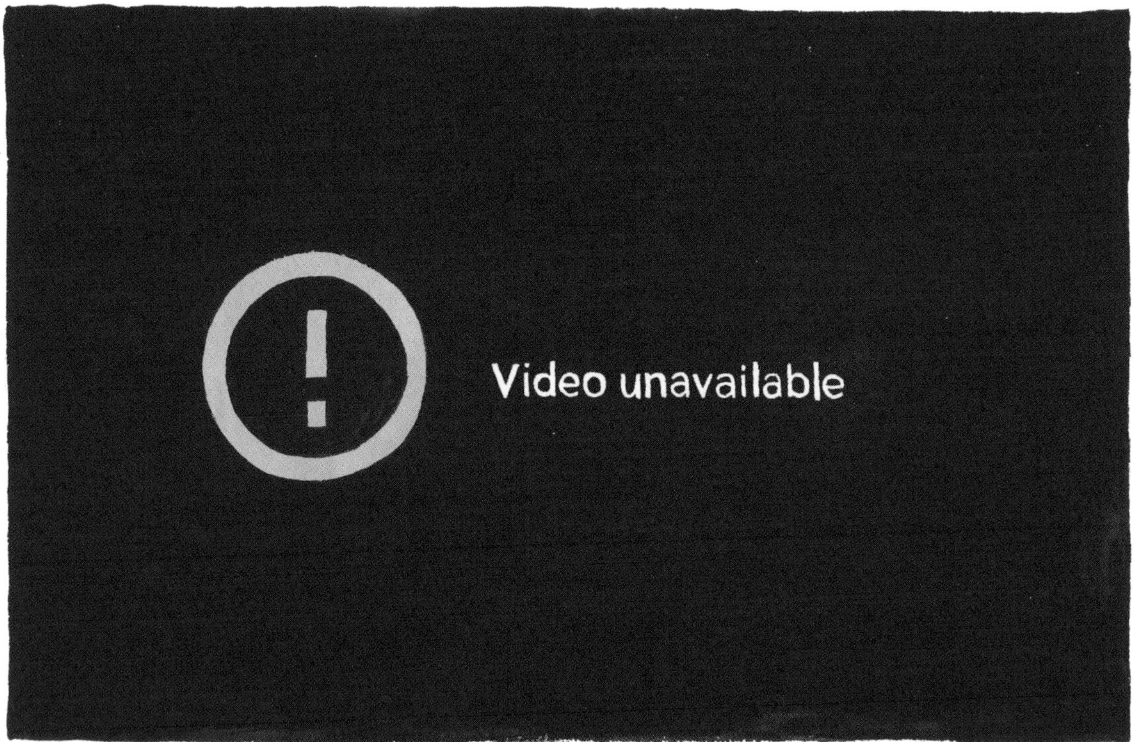
Video unavailable

14:19

30.10.2016

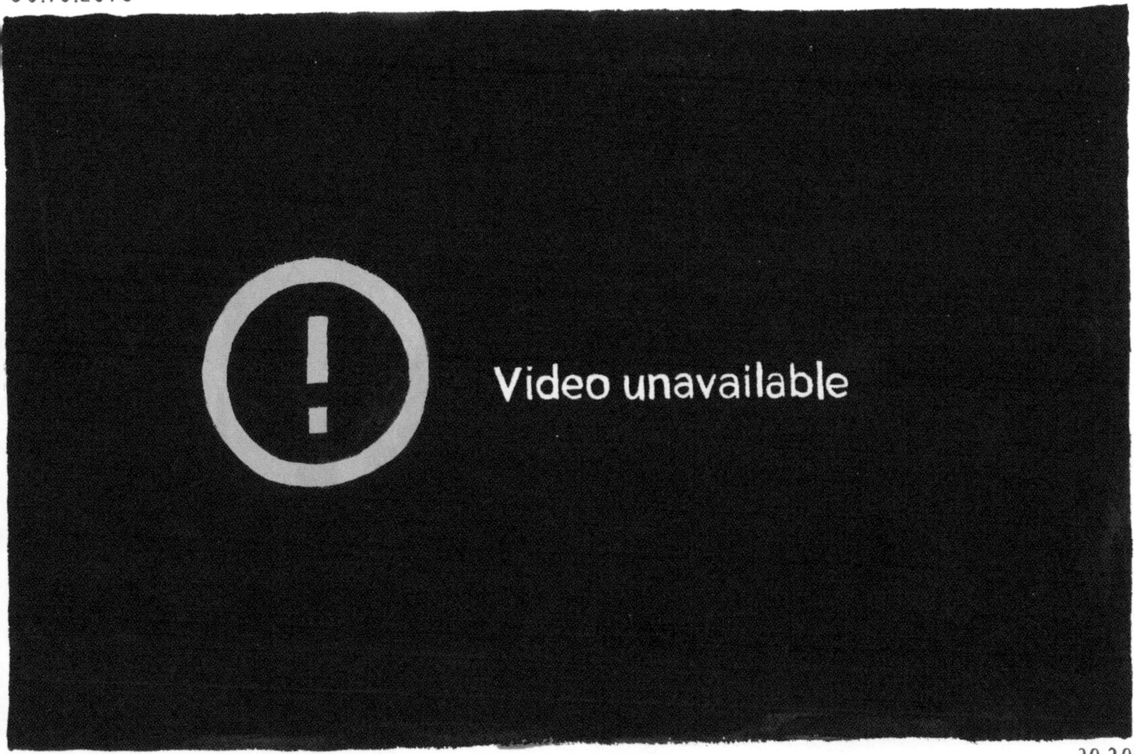
Video unavailable

20:30

23.11.2016

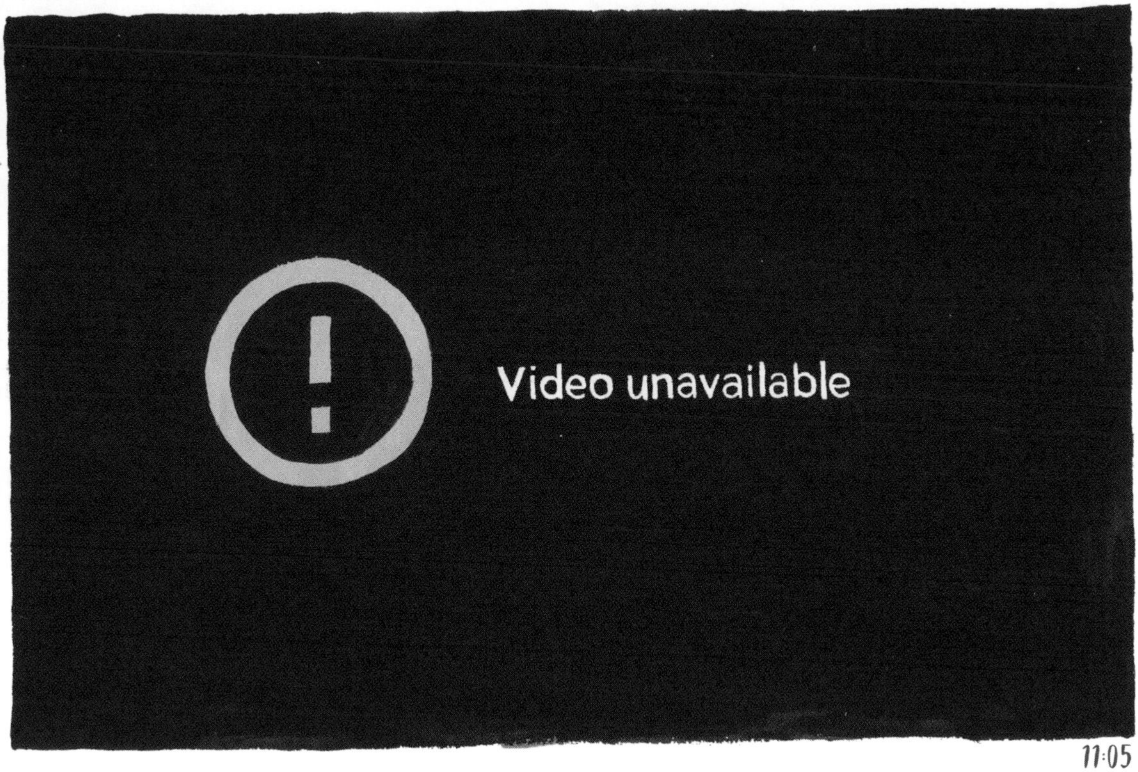
Video unavailable

11:05

09.12.2016

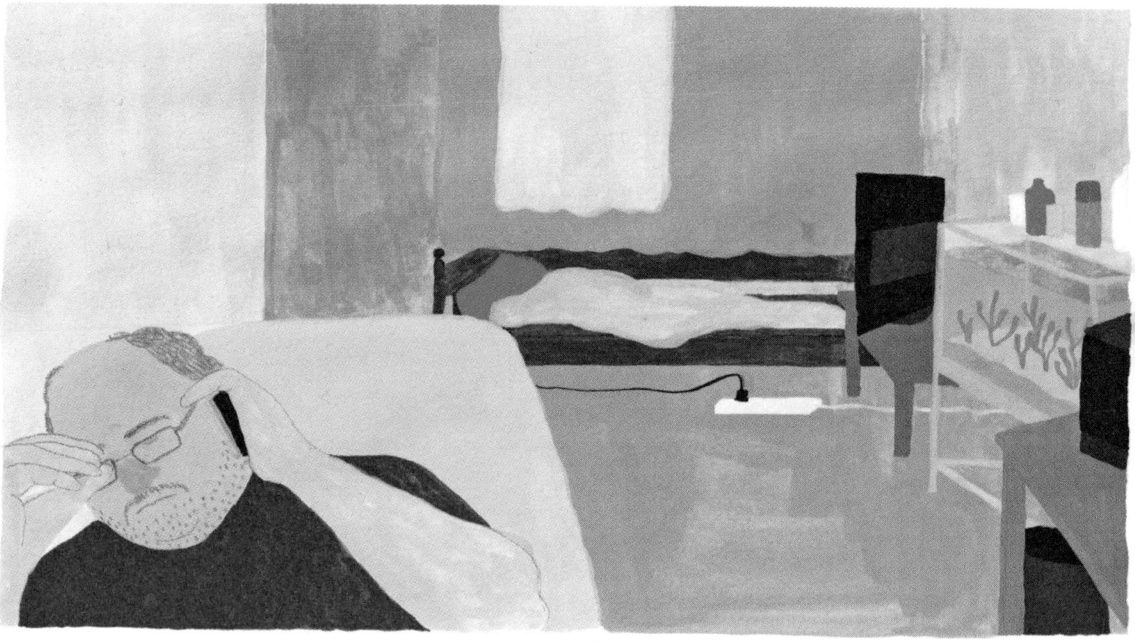

17:53

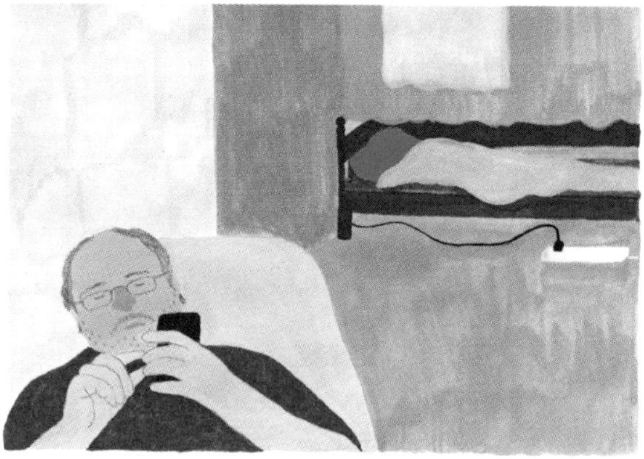

17:53

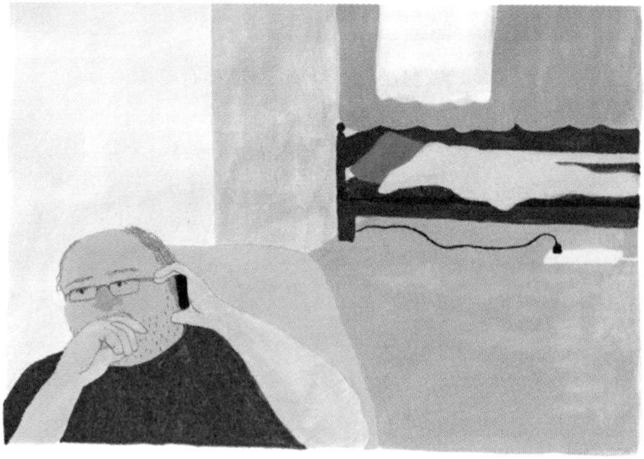

17:54

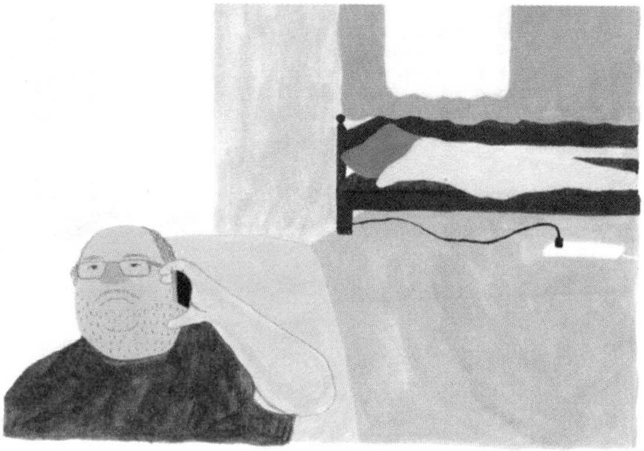

17:54

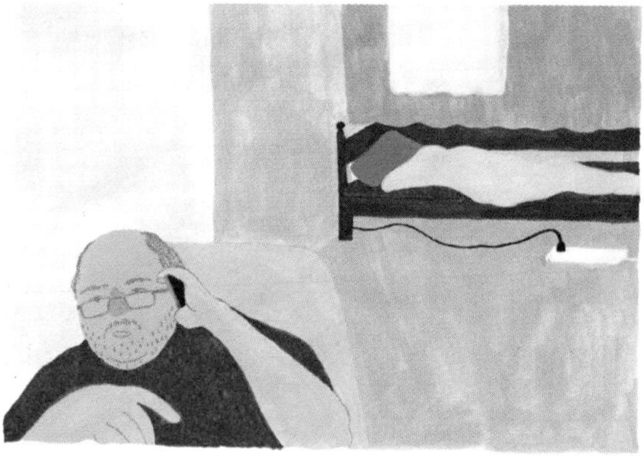

18:00

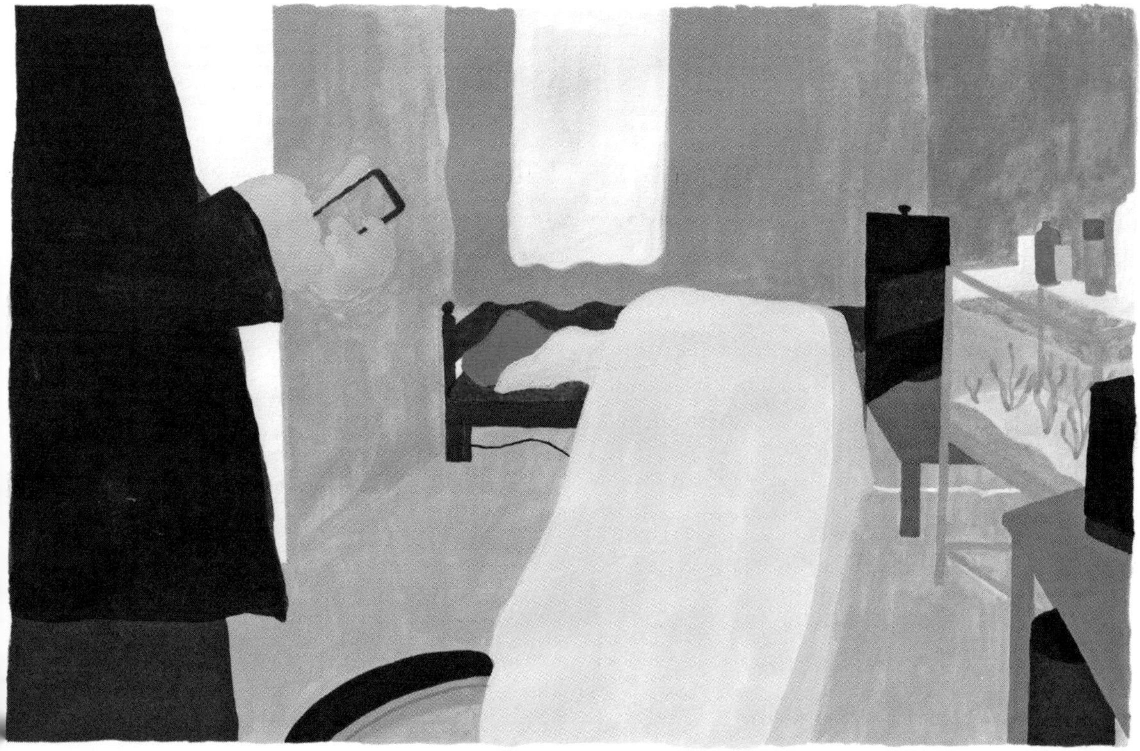

18:02

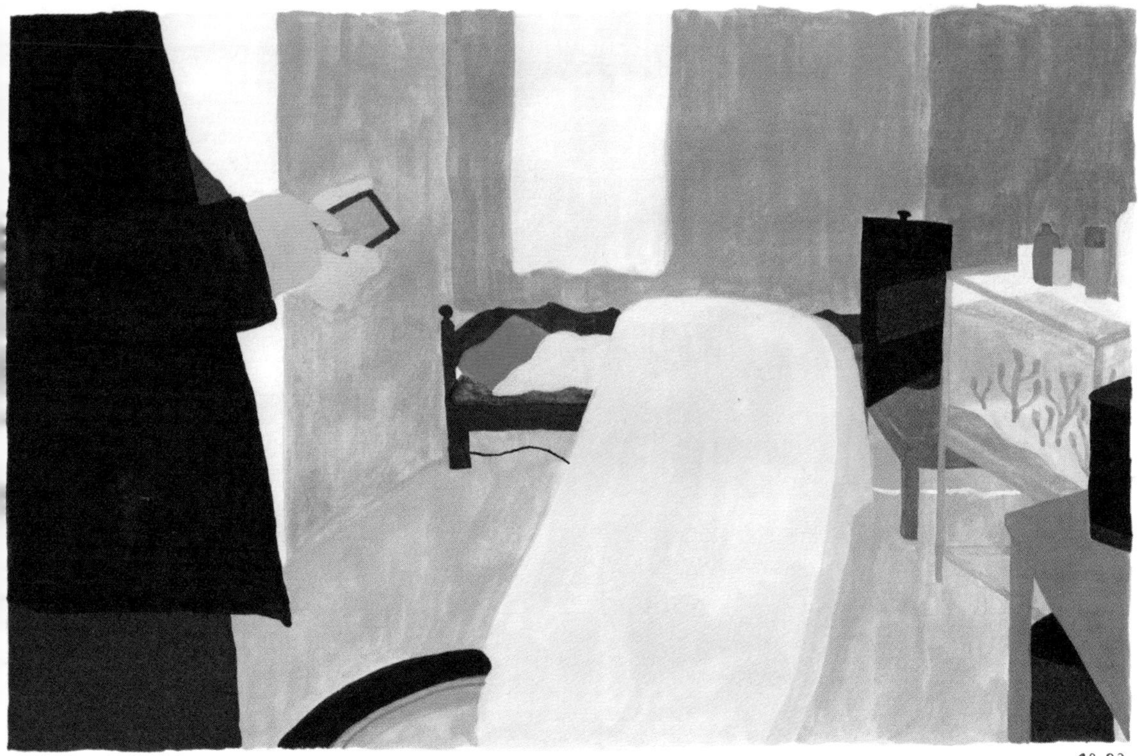

18:02

11:58

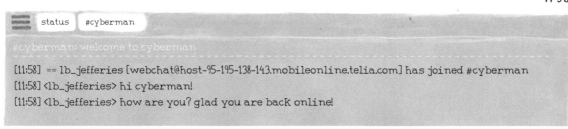

| ≡ | status | #cyberman |

#cyberman: welcome to cyberman

[11:58] == lb_jefferies [webchat@host-95-195-138-143.mobileonline.telia.com] has joined #cyberman
[11:58] <lb_jefferies> hi cyberman!
[11:58] <lb_jefferies> how are you? glad you are back online!

11:58

11:58

11:58

11:58

11:59   11:59

status   #cyberman

[12:00] <dydermani> Kypermani
[12:01] <ihemies> he is cooking something
[12:01] <ihemies> he is a wonderful cook

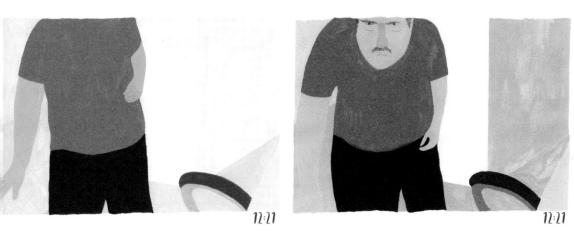

12:21   12:21

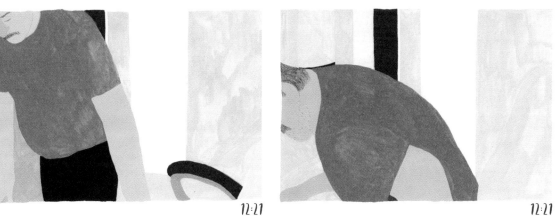

12:21   12:21

115

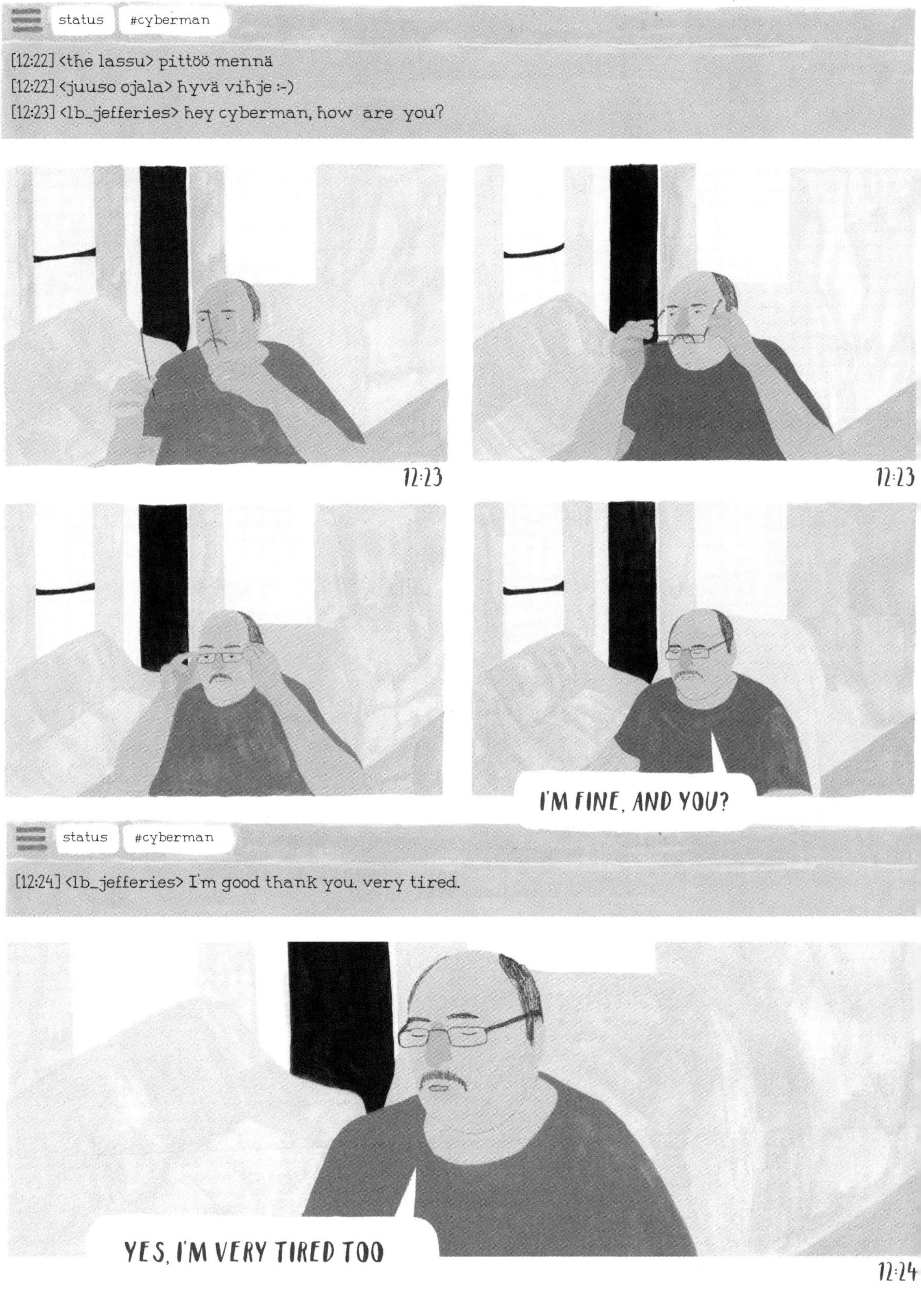
status
#cyberman
[12:22] <the lassu> pittöö mennä
[12:22] <juuso ojala> hyvä vihje :-)
[12:23] <lb_jefferies> hey cyberman, how are you?
12:23
12:23
I'M FINE, AND YOU?
status
#cyberman
[12:24] <lb_jefferies> I'm good thank you. very tired.
YES, I'M VERY TIRED TOO
12:24

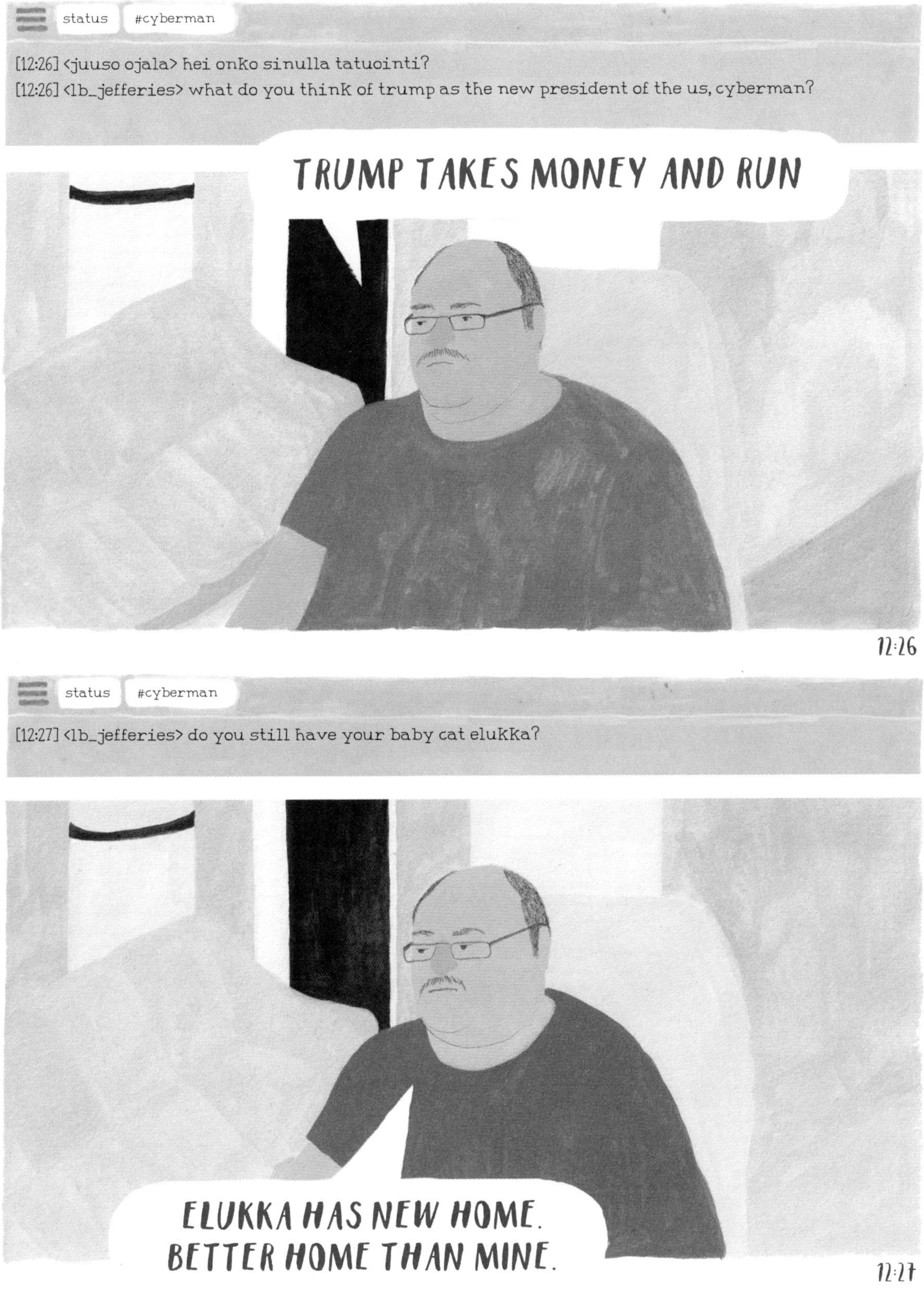
status
#cyberman
[12:26] <juuso ojala> hei onko sinulla tatuointi?
[12:26] <lb_jefferies> what do you think of trump as the new president of the us, cyberman?
TRUMP TAKES MONEY AND RUN
12:26
status
#cyberman
[12:27] <lb_jefferies> do you still have your baby cat elukka?
ELUKKA HAS NEW HOME.
BETTER HOME THAN MINE.
12:27

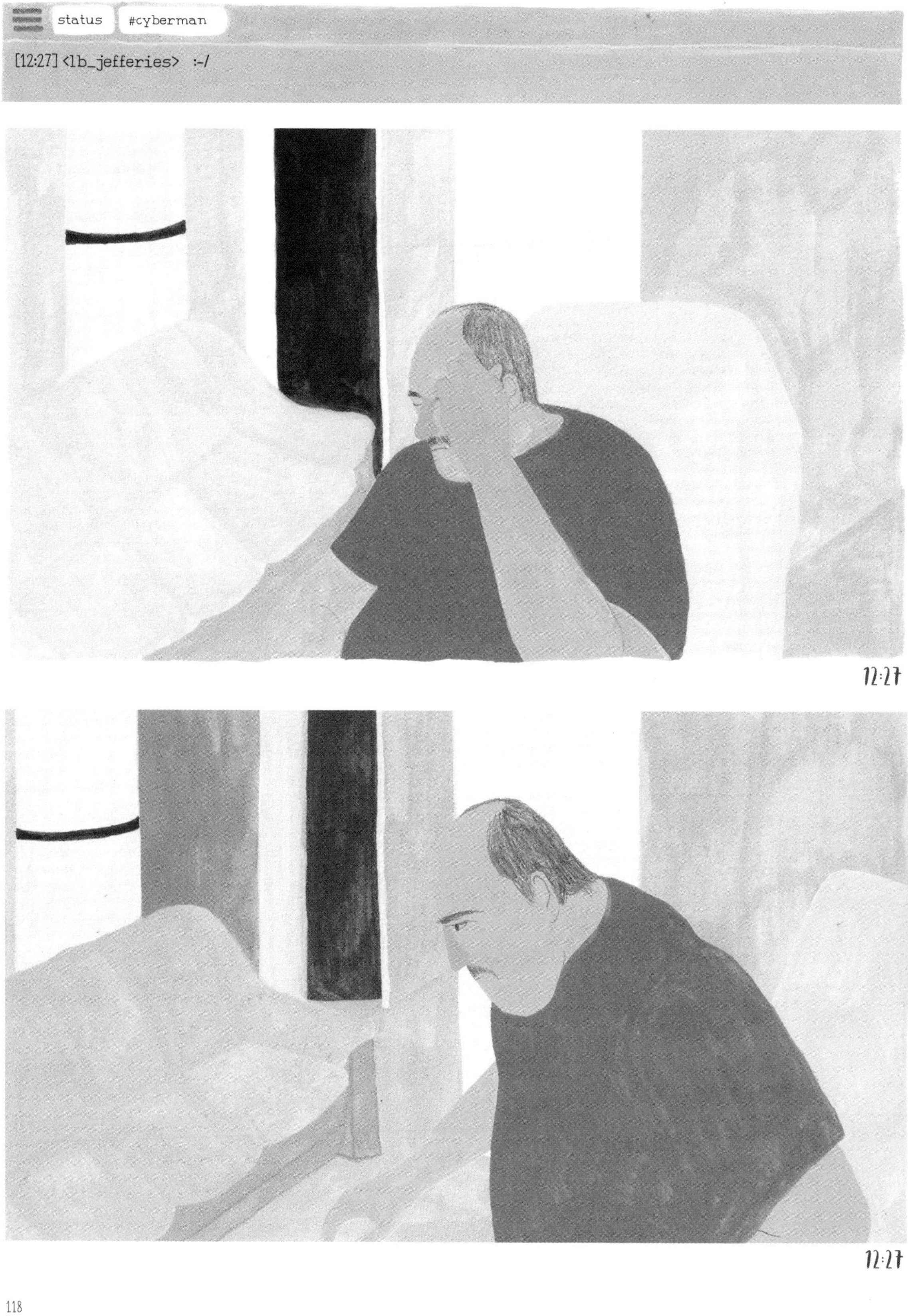
status
#cyberman
[12:27] <lb_jefferies> :-/
12:27
12:27

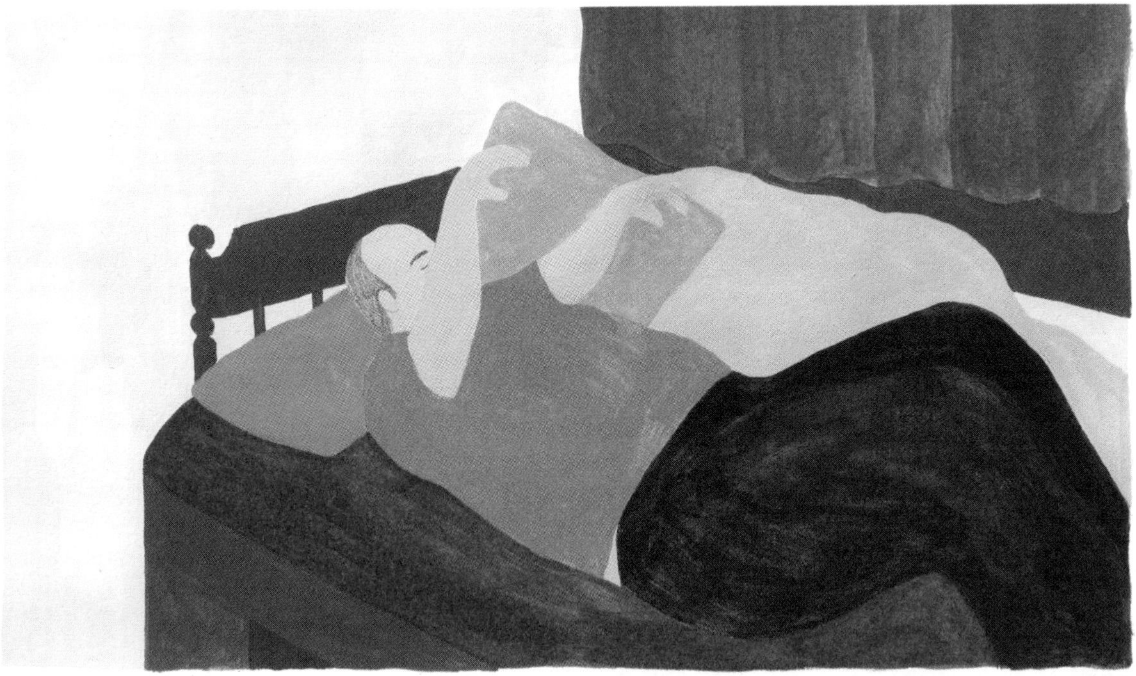

12:27

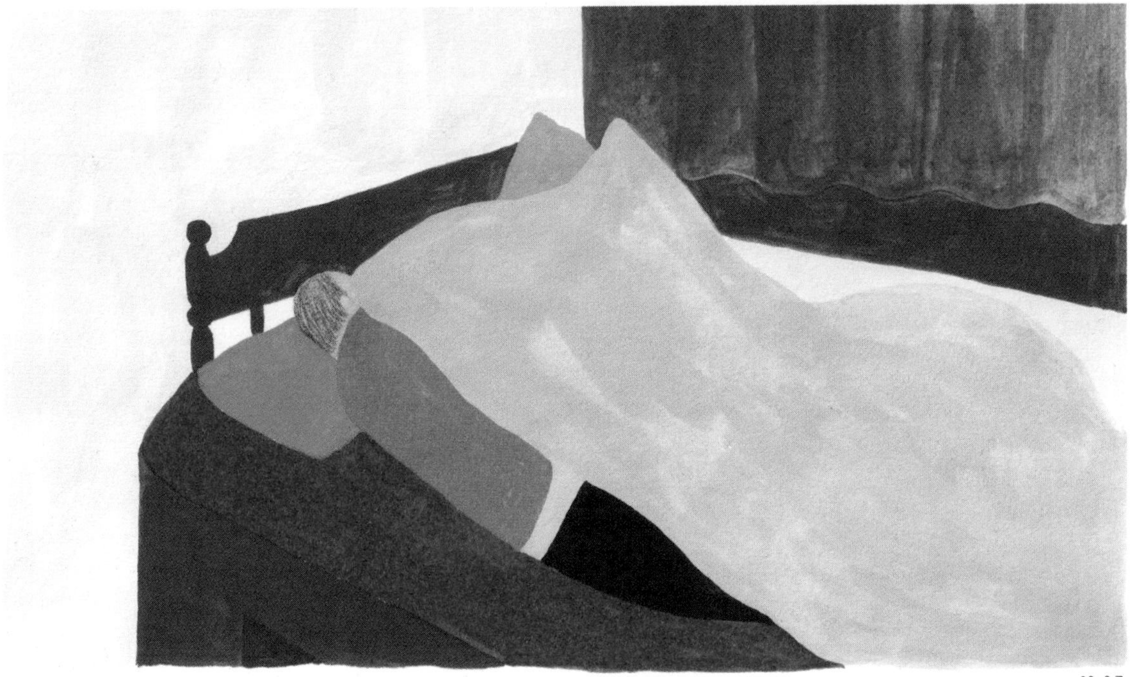

12:27

status #cyberman

[12:27] <lb_jefferies> have a good nap cyberman

21:43

17:16

17:41

17:42

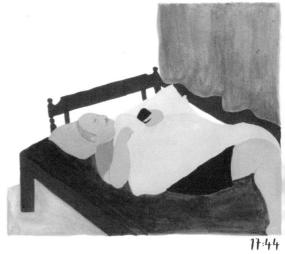

17:44

17:44

17:44

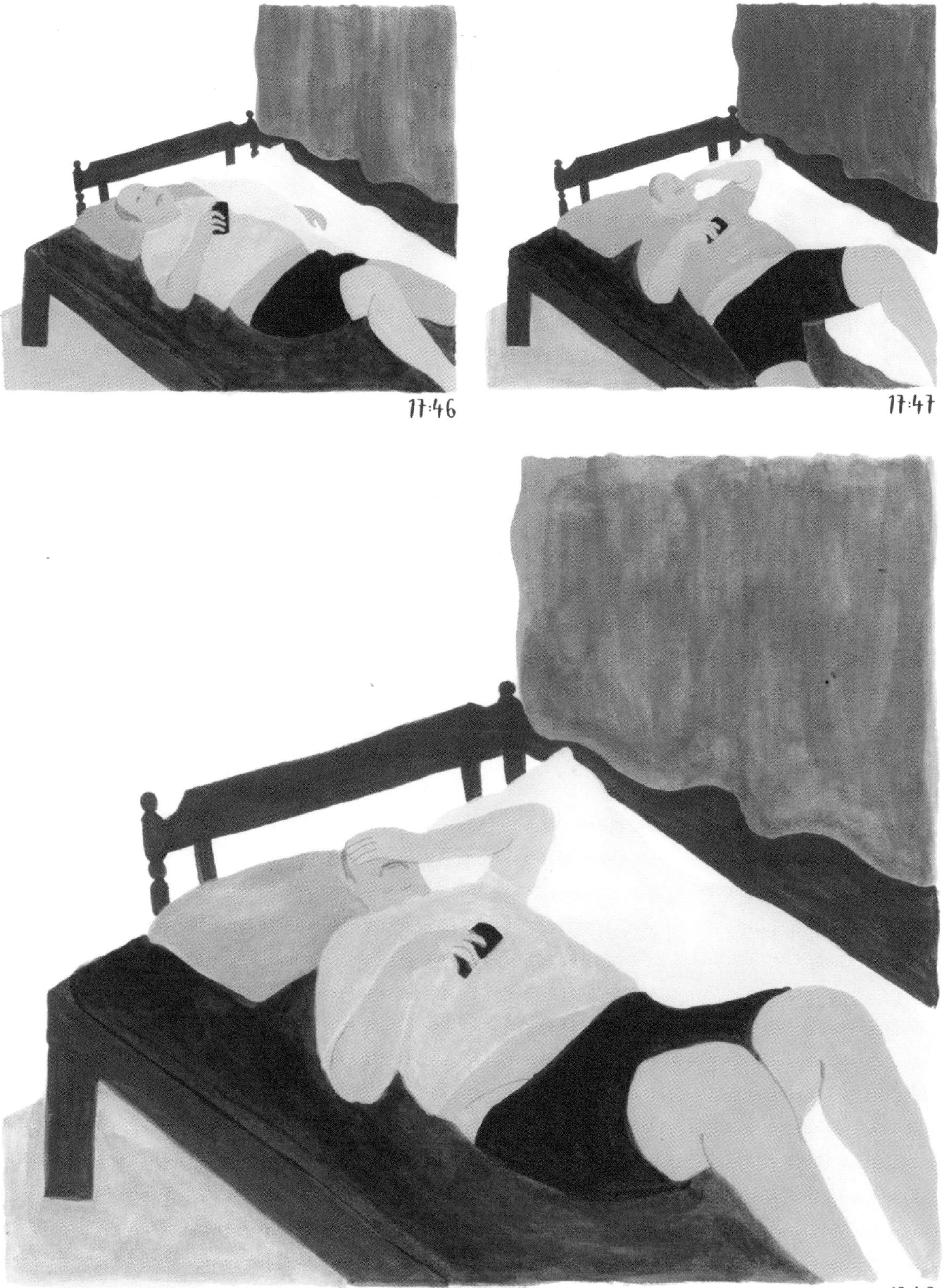
17:46
17:47
17:47

08.07.2017

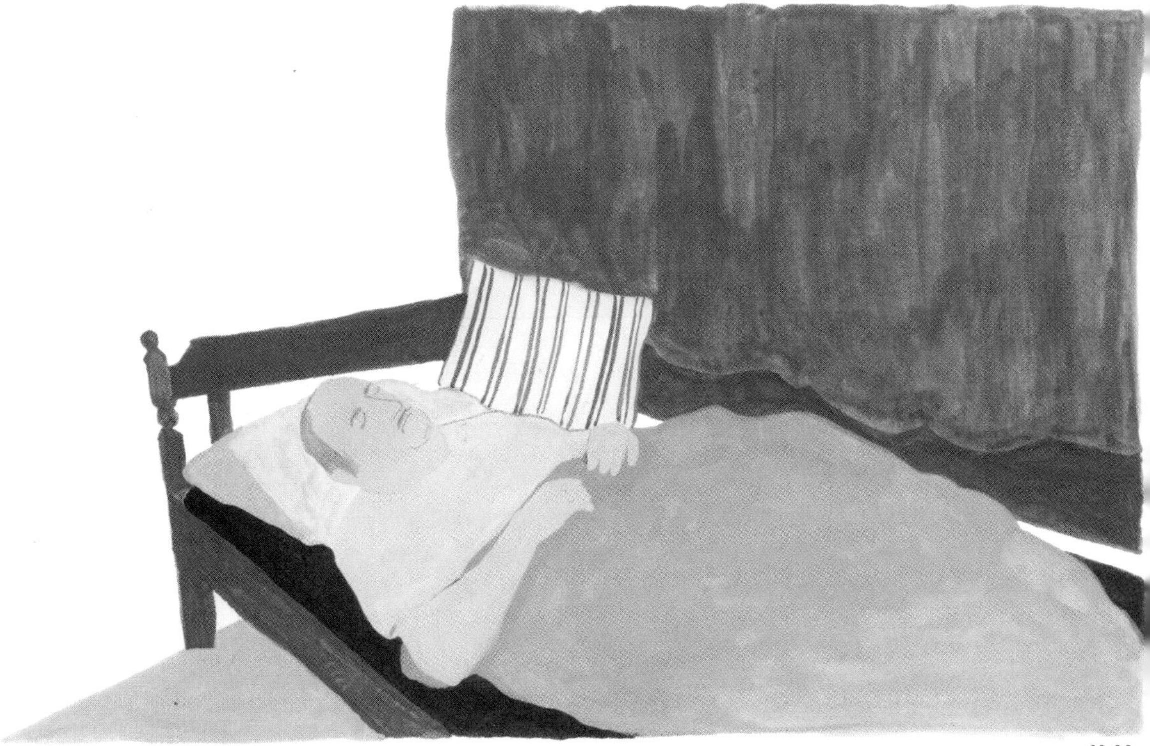

"DO YOU KNOW THE SONG 'HEY THERE DELILAH'?" 18:22

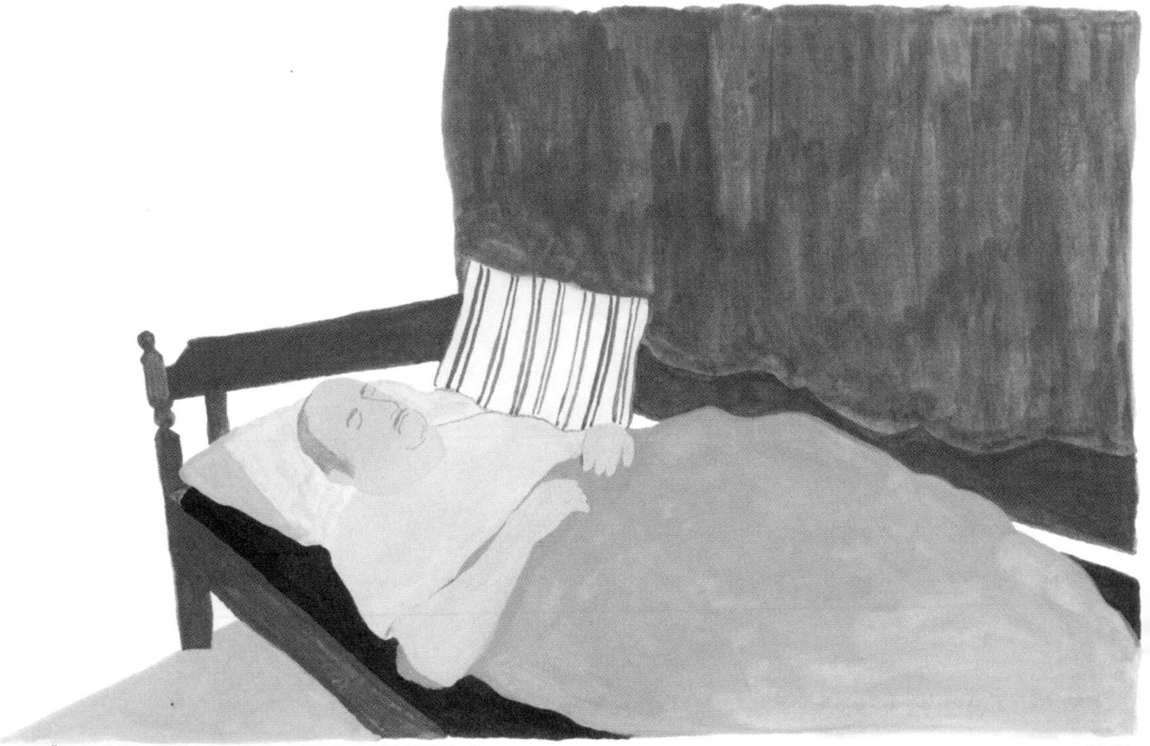

"YEAH, IT'S BY OASIS I THINK." 18:22

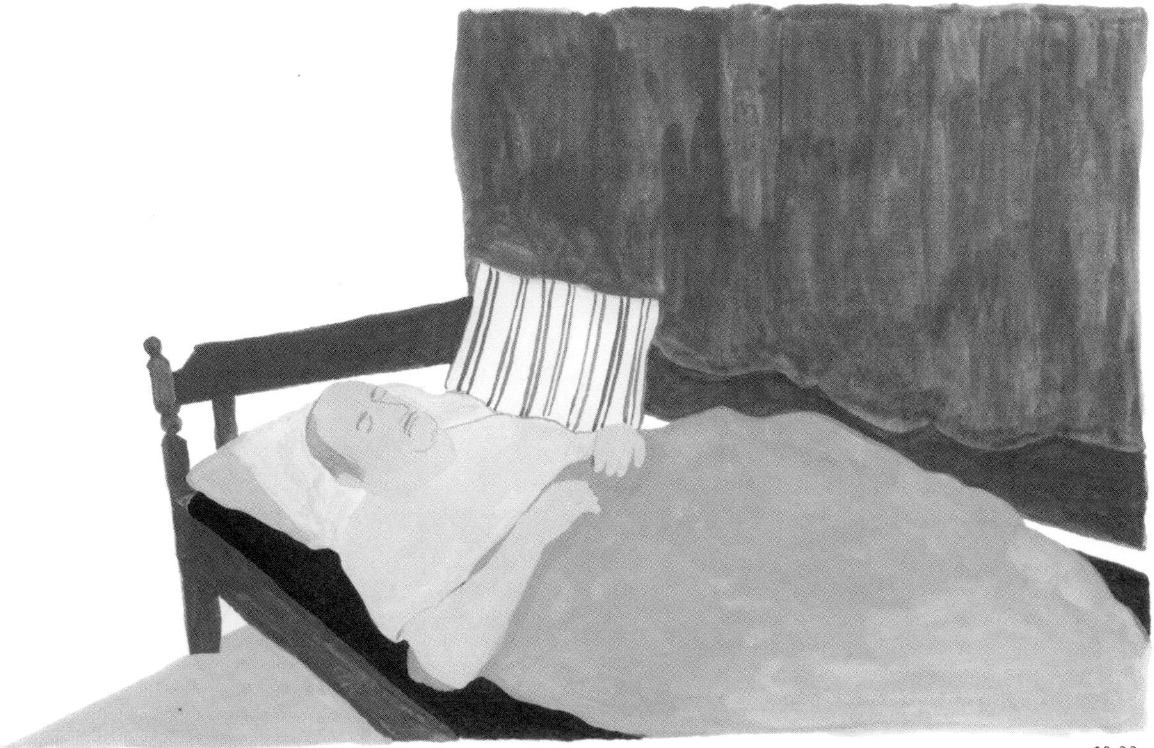

🔊 "SOUNDS LIKE 'HEY THERE DIARRHOEA, HAHAHA" 18:22

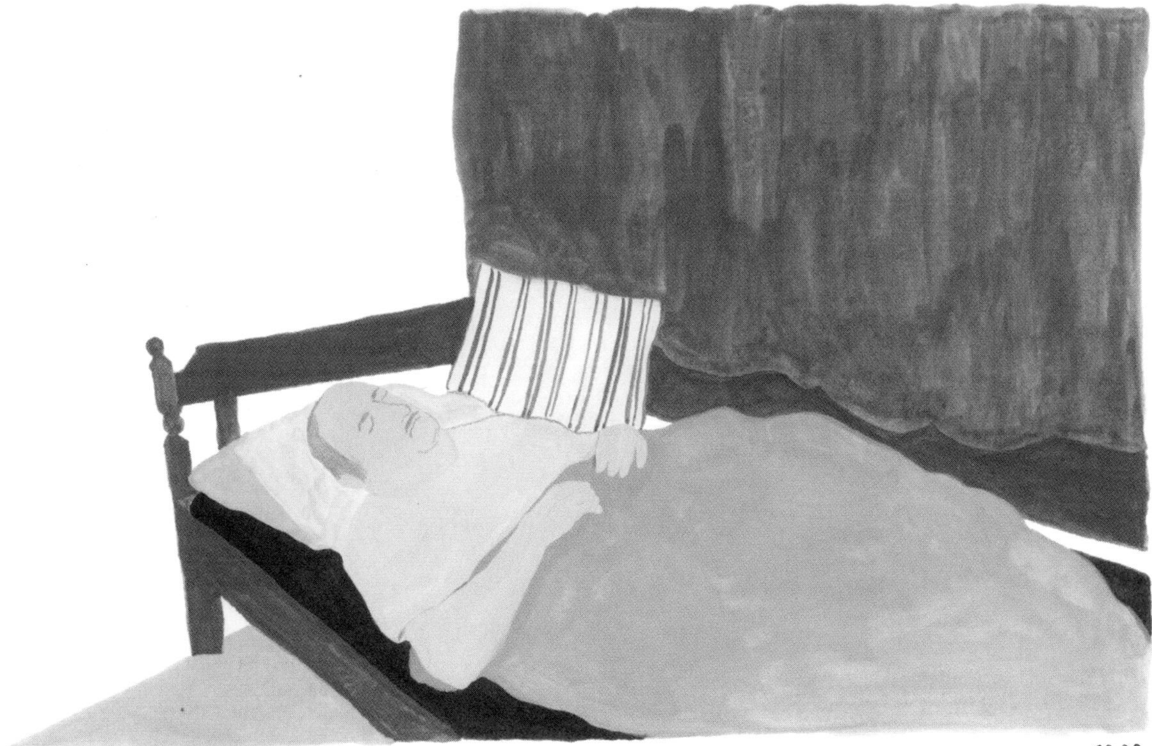

🔊 "HAHAHAHA" 18:23

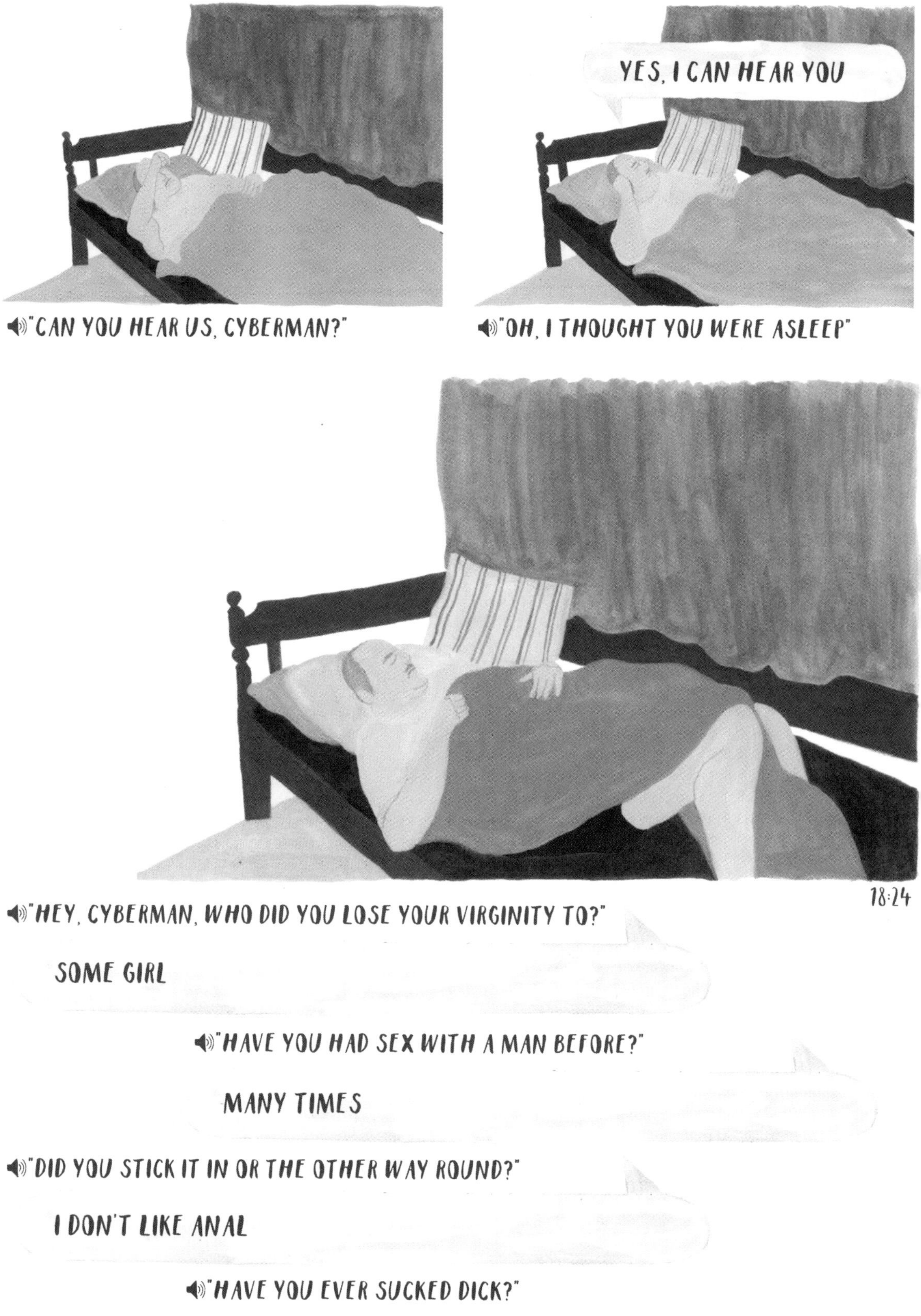
"CAN YOU HEAR US, CYBERMAN?"
YES, I CAN HEAR YOU
"OH, I THOUGHT YOU WERE ASLEEP"
18:24
"HEY, CYBERMAN, WHO DID YOU LOSE YOUR VIRGINITY TO?"
SOME GIRL
"HAVE YOU HAD SEX WITH A MAN BEFORE?"
MANY TIMES
"DID YOU STICK IT IN OR THE OTHER WAY ROUND?"
I DON'T LIKE ANAL
"HAVE YOU EVER SUCKED DICK?"

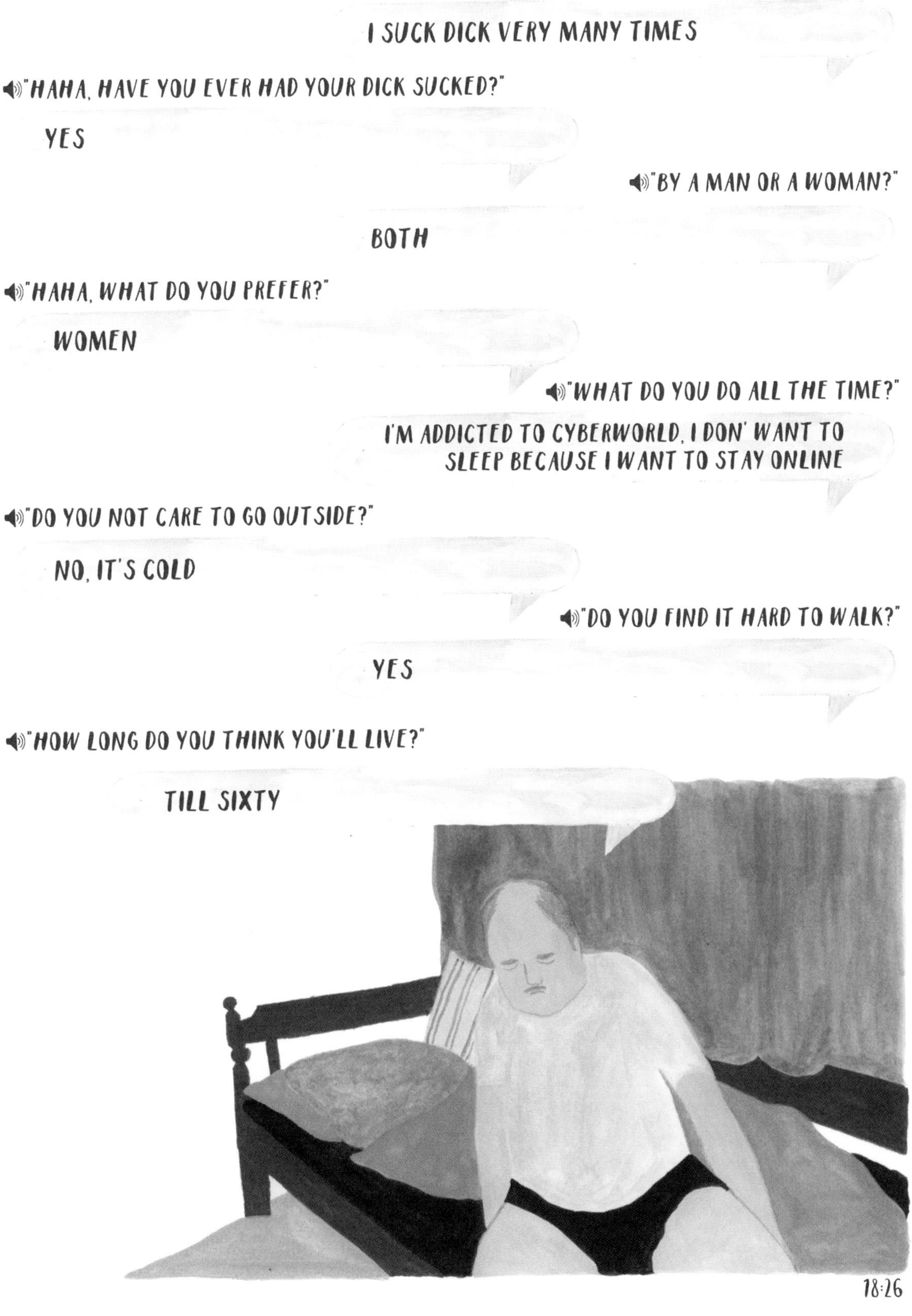
I SUCK DICK VERY MANY TIMES
"HAHA, HAVE YOU EVER HAD YOUR DICK SUCKED?"
YES
"BY A MAN OR A WOMAN?"
BOTH
"HAHA, WHAT DO YOU PREFER?"
WOMEN
"WHAT DO YOU DO ALL THE TIME?"
I'M ADDICTED TO CYBERWORLD, I DON' WANT TO SLEEP BECAUSE I WANT TO STAY ONLINE
"DO YOU NOT CARE TO GO OUTSIDE?"
NO, IT'S COLD
"DO YOU FIND IT HARD TO WALK?"
YES
"HOW LONG DO YOU THINK YOU'LL LIVE?"
TILL SIXTY
18:26

"YEAH, YOU DON'T MOVE AT ALL, DO YOU? YOU DON'T DO ANY EXERCISE?"
"LOOK AT HIM, HE MOVES LIKE A SLOTH, HE MOVES LIKE A SLUG"
"HOW DO YOU FINANCE YOURSELF, CYBERMAN?"

I TOOK AN EIGHTEEN THOUSAND EURO LOAN JUST FOR FUN.
I'M IN MUCH DEBT NOW

"HAHA, WHAT DID YOU USE IT FOR?"

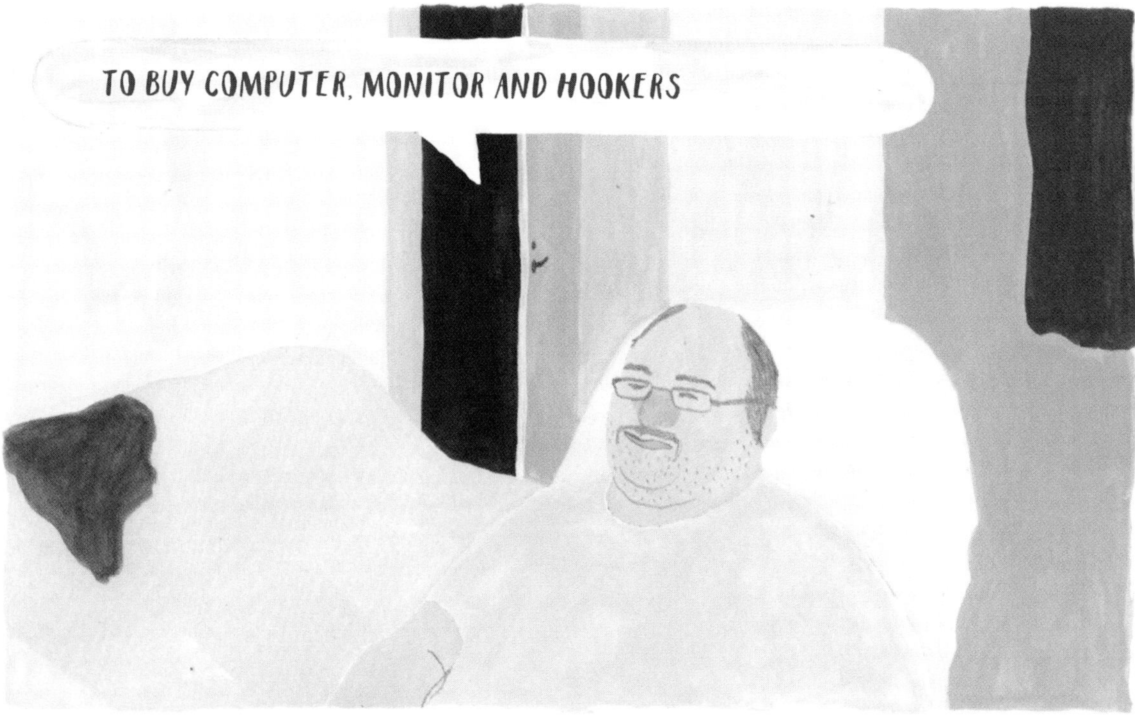
TO BUY COMPUTER, MONITOR AND HOOKERS

"HOOKERS, MONITORS AND COMPUTERS? HAHAHA! DO YOU HAVE ANY MONEY LEFT? WHAT ARE YOU GOING TO DO ABOUT YOUR DEBT?" 18:28

NO, I SPENT IT ALL... I CAN'T PAY IT.

"WHAT WOULD YOU DO IF YOU GET HOMELESS?"

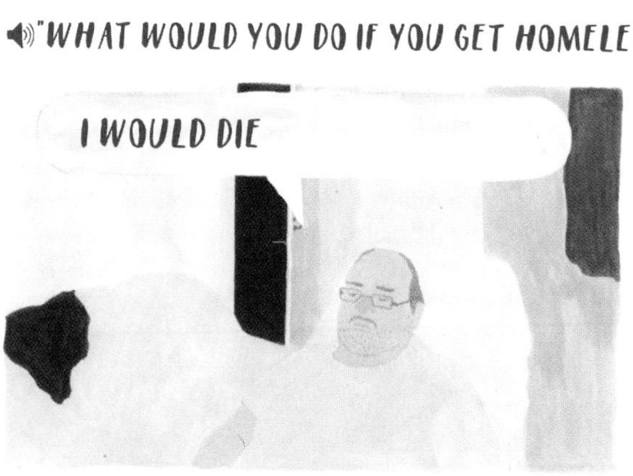
I WOULD DIE

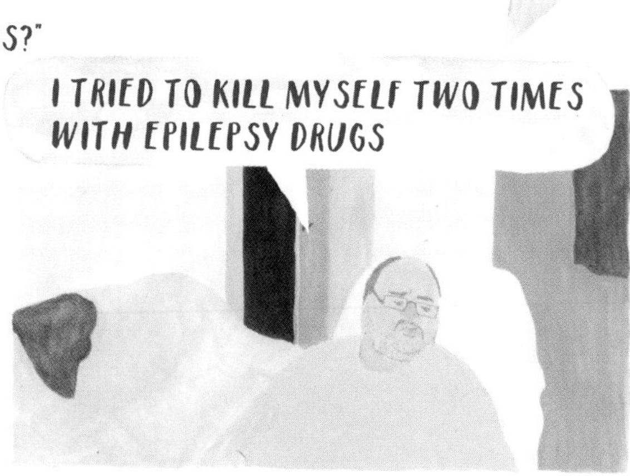
I TRIED TO KILL MYSELF TWO TIMES WITH EPILEPSY DRUGS

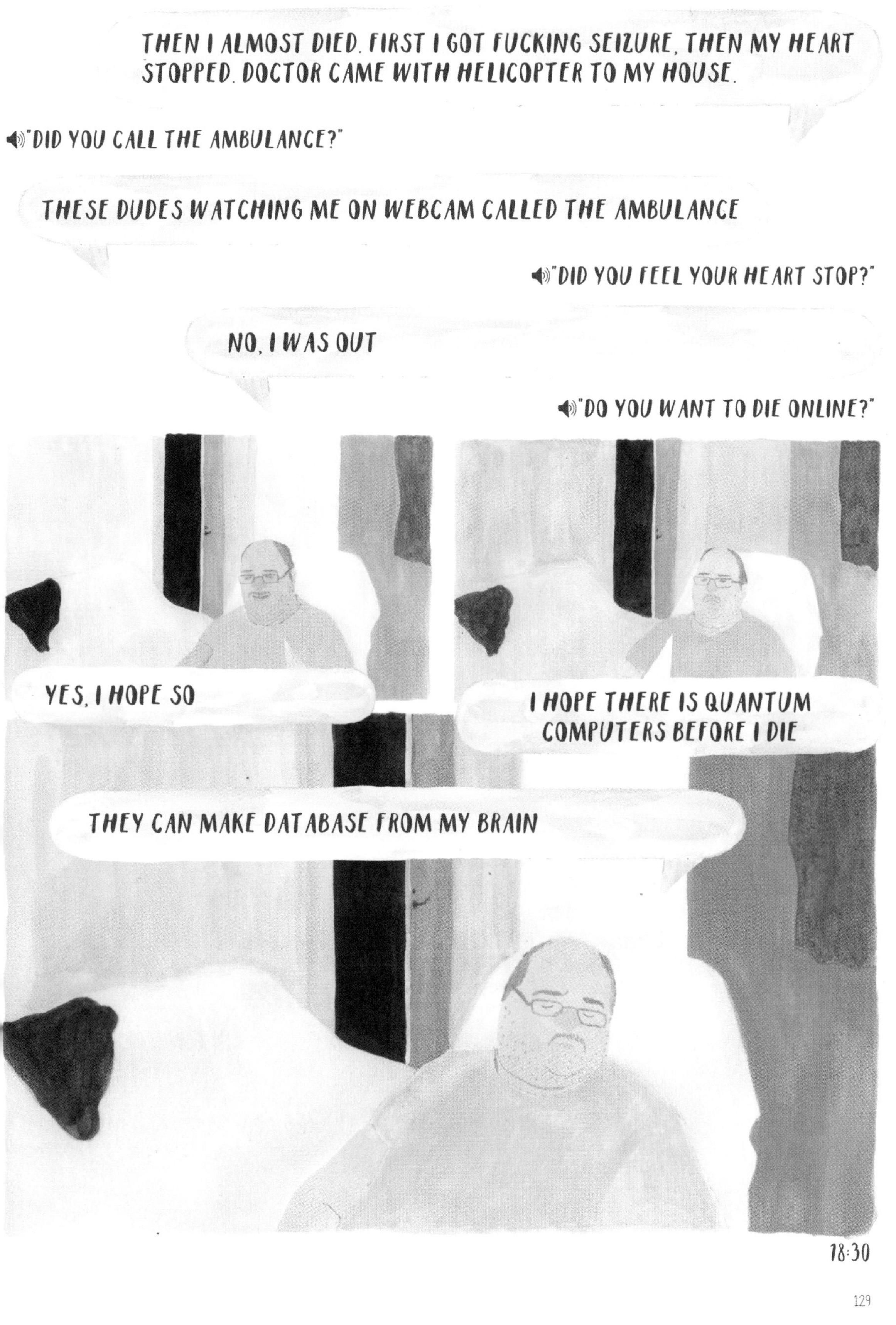
THEN I ALMOST DIED. FIRST I GOT FUCKING SEIZURE, THEN MY HEART STOPPED. DOCTOR CAME WITH HELICOPTER TO MY HOUSE.
"DID YOU CALL THE AMBULANCE?"
THESE DUDES WATCHING ME ON WEBCAM CALLED THE AMBULANCE
"DID YOU FEEL YOUR HEART STOP?"
NO, I WAS OUT
"DO YOU WANT TO DIE ONLINE?"
YES, I HOPE SO
I HOPE THERE IS QUANTUM COMPUTERS BEFORE I DIE
THEY CAN MAKE DATABASE FROM MY BRAIN
18:30

🔊 "HOW OFTEN DO YOU SHOWER, CYBERMAN?"

LIKE ONCE A WEEK

🔊 "HAHA THAT'S THE SAME AS ME.
THIS GUY I KNOW IS THE SEVENTEEN-YEAR-OLD VERSION OF YOU, CYBERMAN,
HE DOESN'T DO ANYTHING. HE IS STUCK IN THE SAME GRADE FOR LIKE THREE YEARS NOW.
I'VE BEEN LIKE HIM TOO, I HARDLY LEFT THE HOUSE. I NEVER FINISHED HIGH SCHOOL BUT
I'VE BEEN WORKING FOR THE PAST FIVE MONTHS. I'M GOING TO TURN NINETEEN SOON."

18:36

🔊 "HAHA, SOMEONE IN THE CHAT JUST WROTE:
'CYBERMAN IS EXACTLY HOW I IMAGINE GOD TO BE LIKE'
SO, CYBERMAN, IF YOU HAD THE CHOICE TO BE A COMPLETELY DIFFERENT
PERSON, WOULD YOU BE SOMEONE ELSE?"

I DON'T KNOW WHAT THE OTHER CHOICE WOULD BE

🔊 "OH, OKAY WAIT, I GIVE YOU A CHOICE... HOW ABOUT A RICH BILLIONAIRE IN ITALY?
LIKE THIS GUY, I'LL SEND YOU A PICTURE..."

NO WAY, I THINK HE'S NOT HAPPY

"ARE YOU HAPPY, CYBERMAN?"

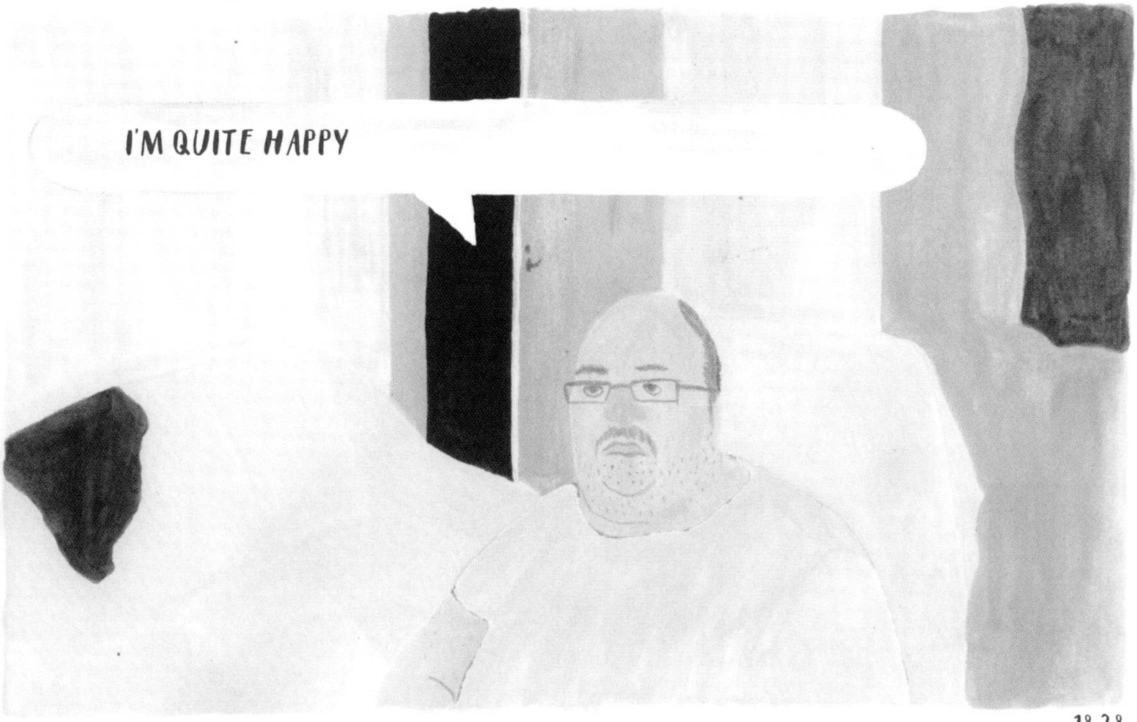
I'M QUITE HAPPY

18:38

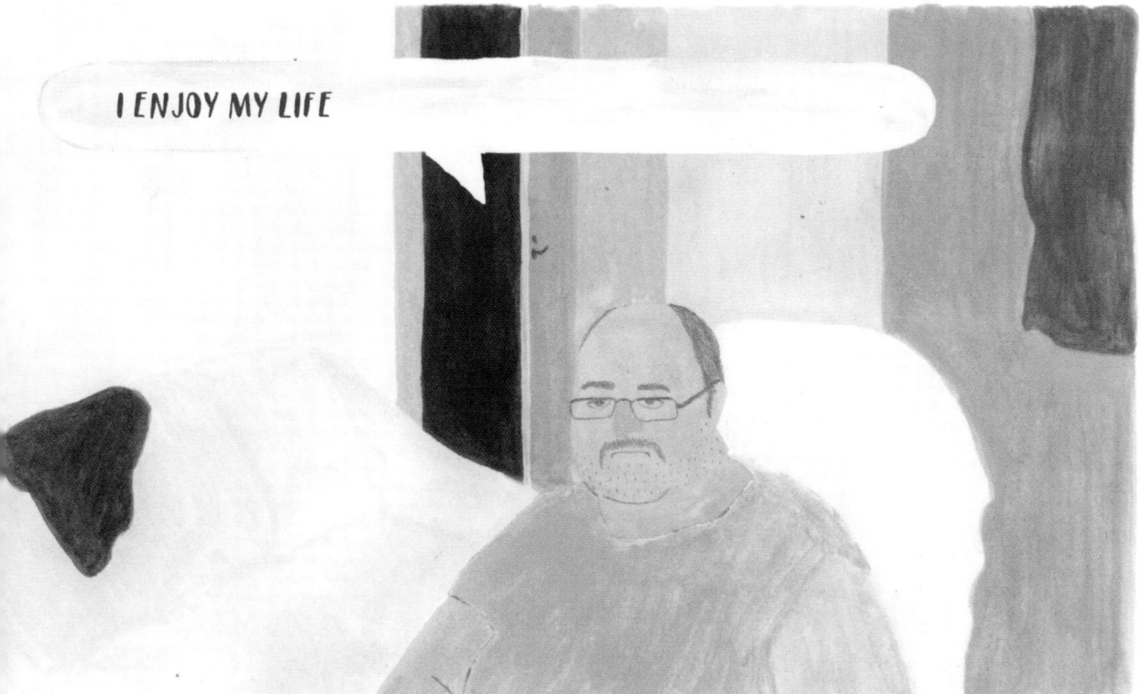
I ENJOY MY LIFE

18:38

"THAT'S INTERESTING, YOU KNOW LIKE FOR EXAMPLE CHRISTIANITY SAYS YOU NEED JESUS TO BE HAPPY BUT CYBERMAN DOESN'T NEED LIFE TO HAVE MEANING TO BE CONTENT. MAYBE WE SHOULD ALL BE LIKE CYBERMAN."

16:57

16:57

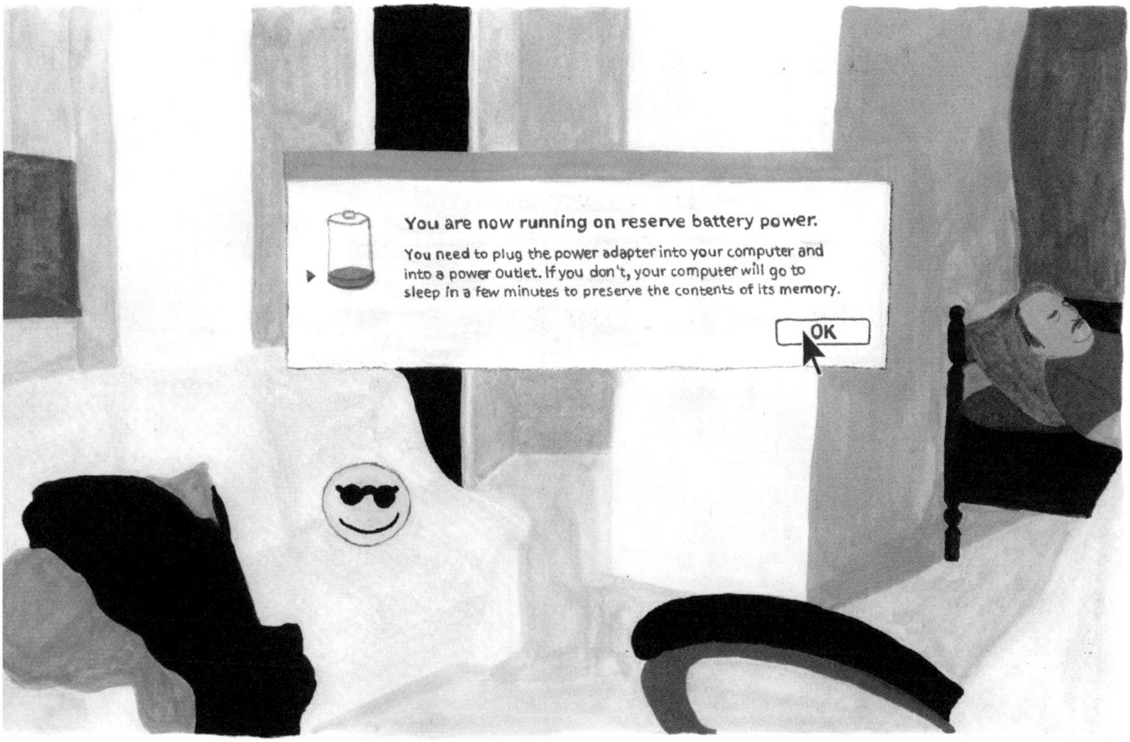
You are now running on reserve battery power.
You need to plug the power adapter into your computer and into a power outlet. If you don't, your computer will go to sleep in a few minutes to preserve the contents of its memory.
OK

16:57

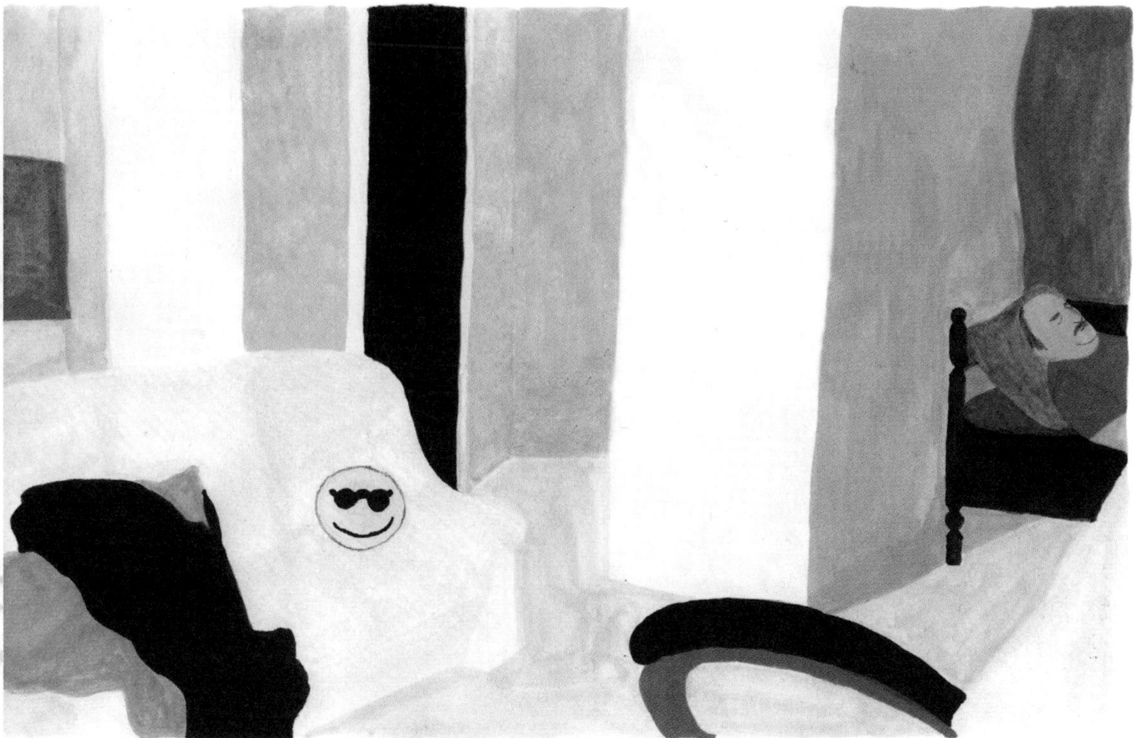

16:57

08.02.2017

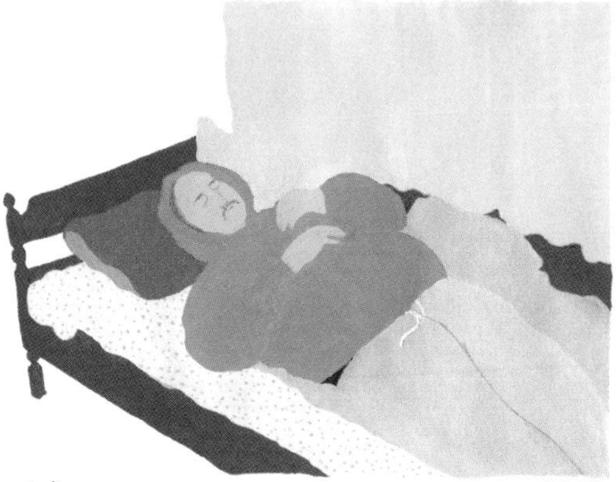

🔊... ♫♪ 13:14

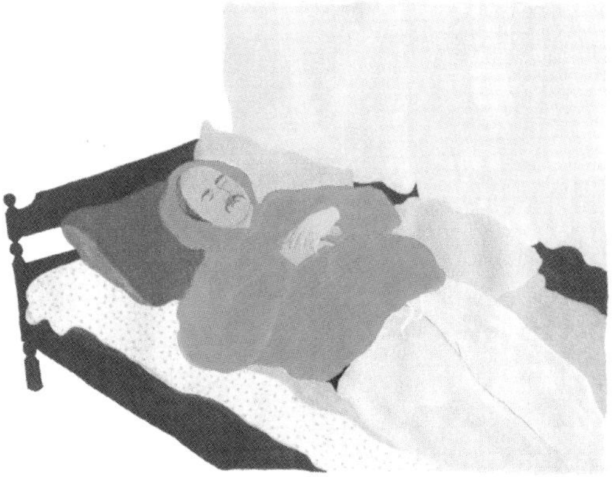

🔊... ♫♪ 13:14

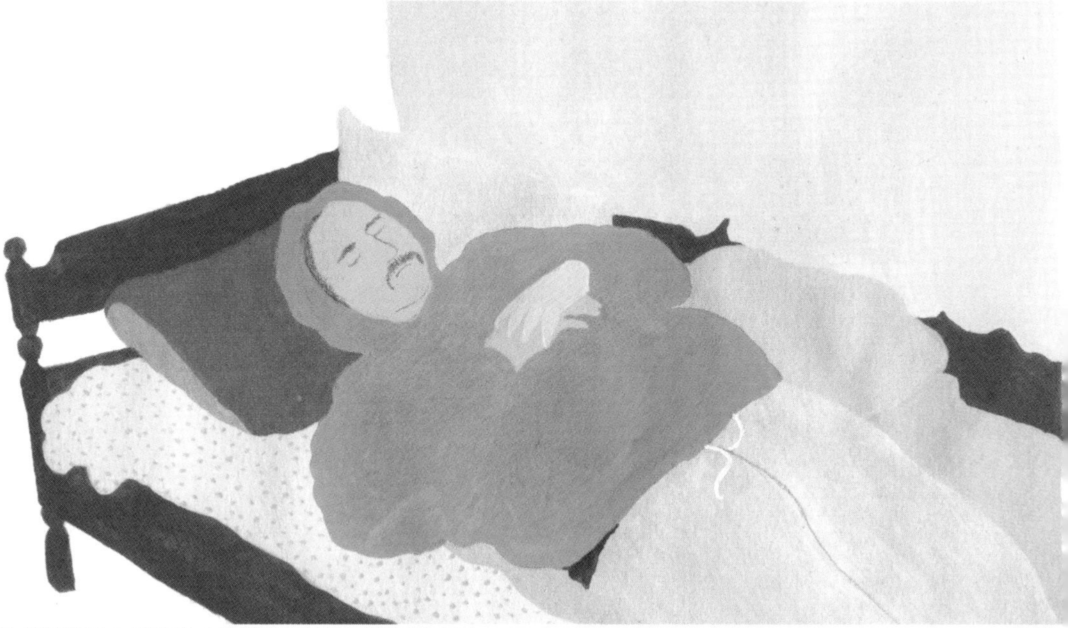

🔊 "I'M SITTING HERE ALONE UP IN MY ROOM...
AND THINK ABOUT THE TIMES THAT WE'VE BEEN THROUGH" ♫♪ 13:14

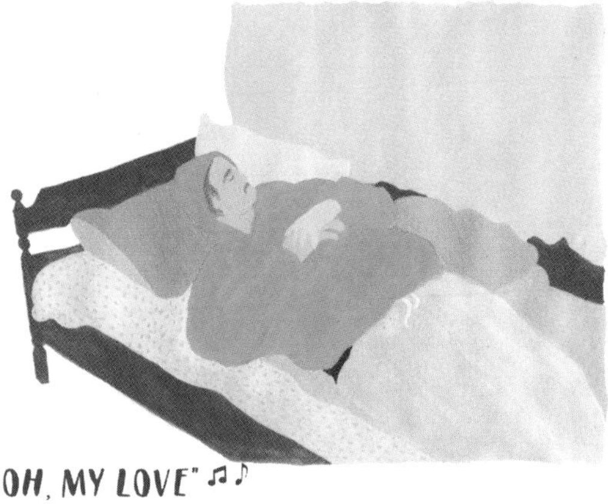

🔊 "OH, MY LOVE" ♫♪

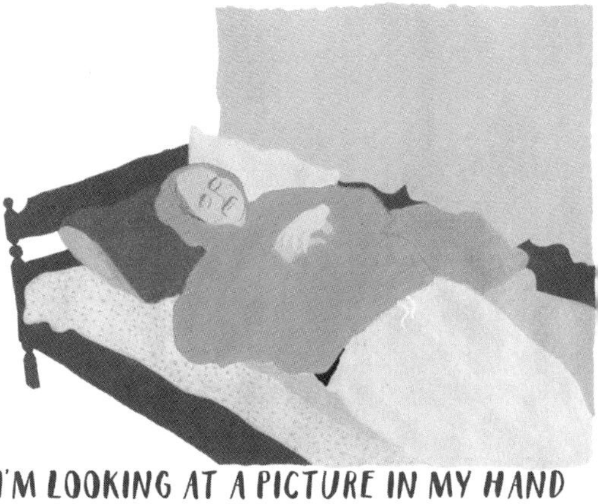

🔊 "I'M LOOKING AT A PICTURE IN MY HAND
TRYING MY BEST TO UNDERSTAND" ♫♪

🔊 "I REALLY WANT TO KNOW WHAT WE DID ♫♪
WRONG WITH THE LOVE THAT FELT SO STRONG"

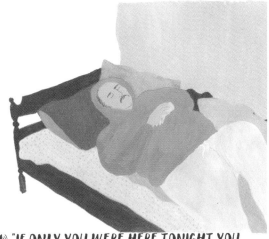

🔊 "IF ONLY YOU WERE HERE TONIGHT YOU
KNOW THAT WE COULD MAKE IT RIGHT" ♫♪

🔊 "I DON'T KNOW HOW TO LIVE WITHOUT
YOUR LOVE LOVE" ♫♪

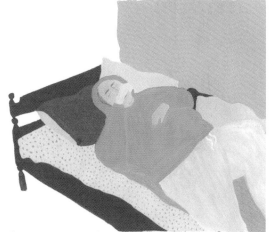

🔊 "I WAS BORN TO MAKE YOU HAPPY" ♫♪

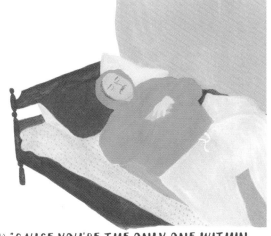

🔊 "CAUSE YOU'RE THE ONLY ONE WITHIN
MY HEART" ♫♪

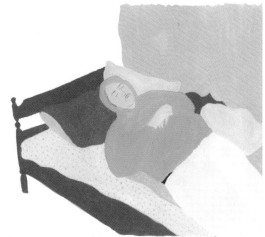

🔊 "I WAS BORN TO MAKE YOU HAPPY" ♫♪

135

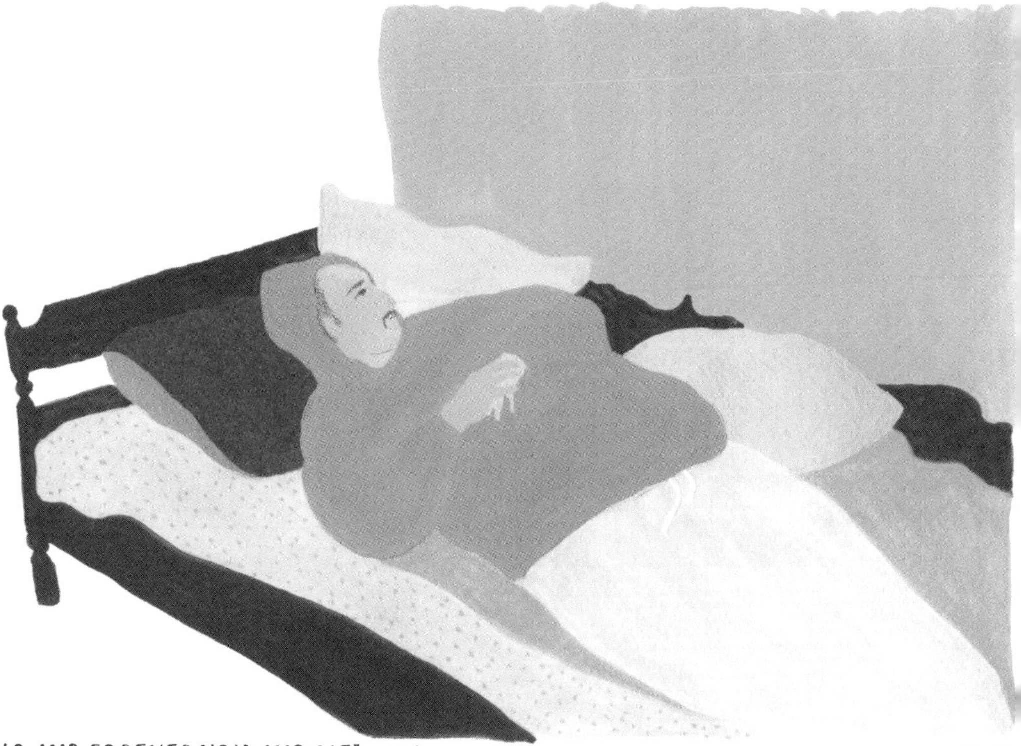

🔊 "ALWAYS AND FOREVER YOU AND ME" ♫♪ 13:15

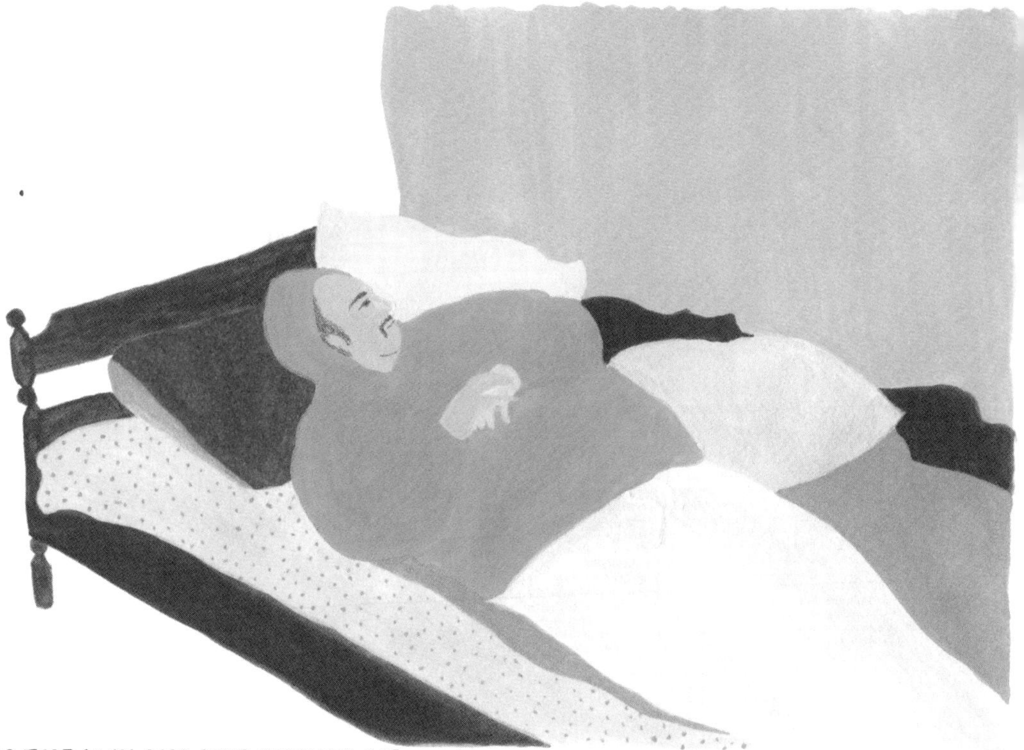

🔊 "THAT'S THE WAY OUR LIFE SHOULD BE" ♫♪ 13:15

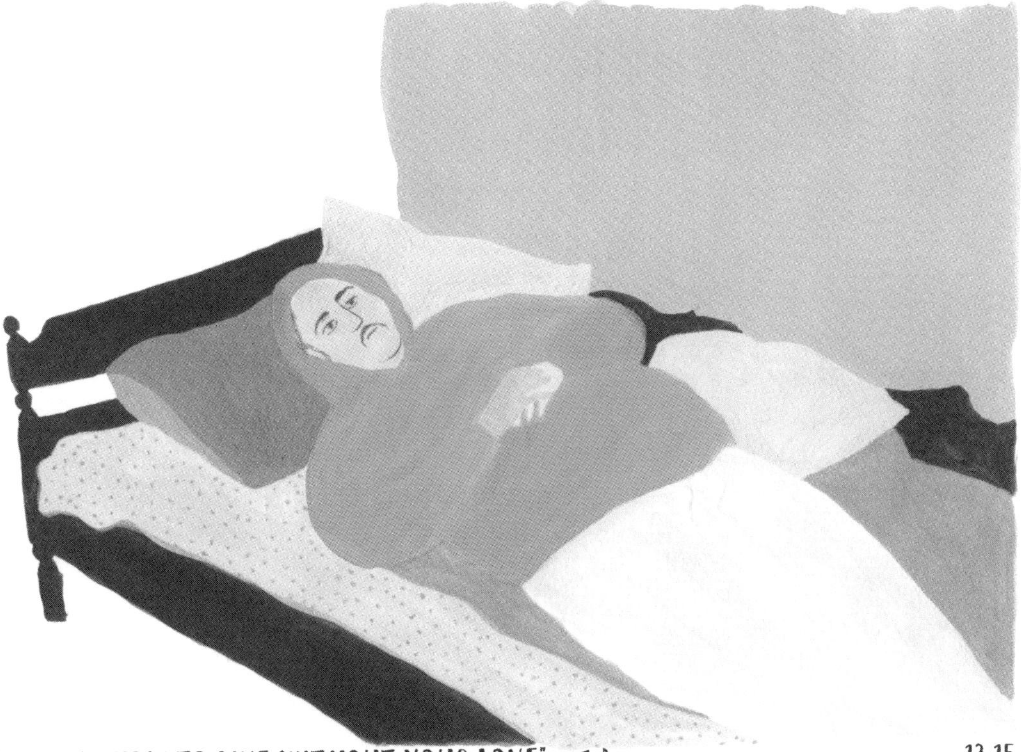
"I DON'T KNOW HOW TO LIVE WITHOUT YOUR LOVE"
13:15

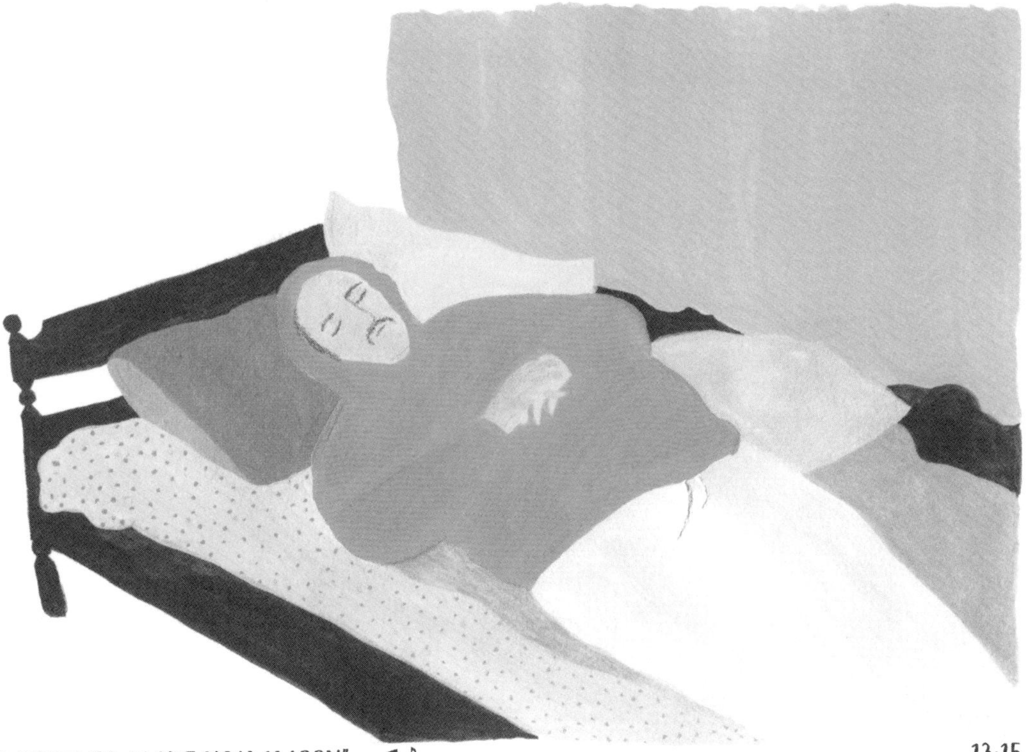
"I WAS BORN TO MAKE YOU HAPPY"
13:15

14.02.2017

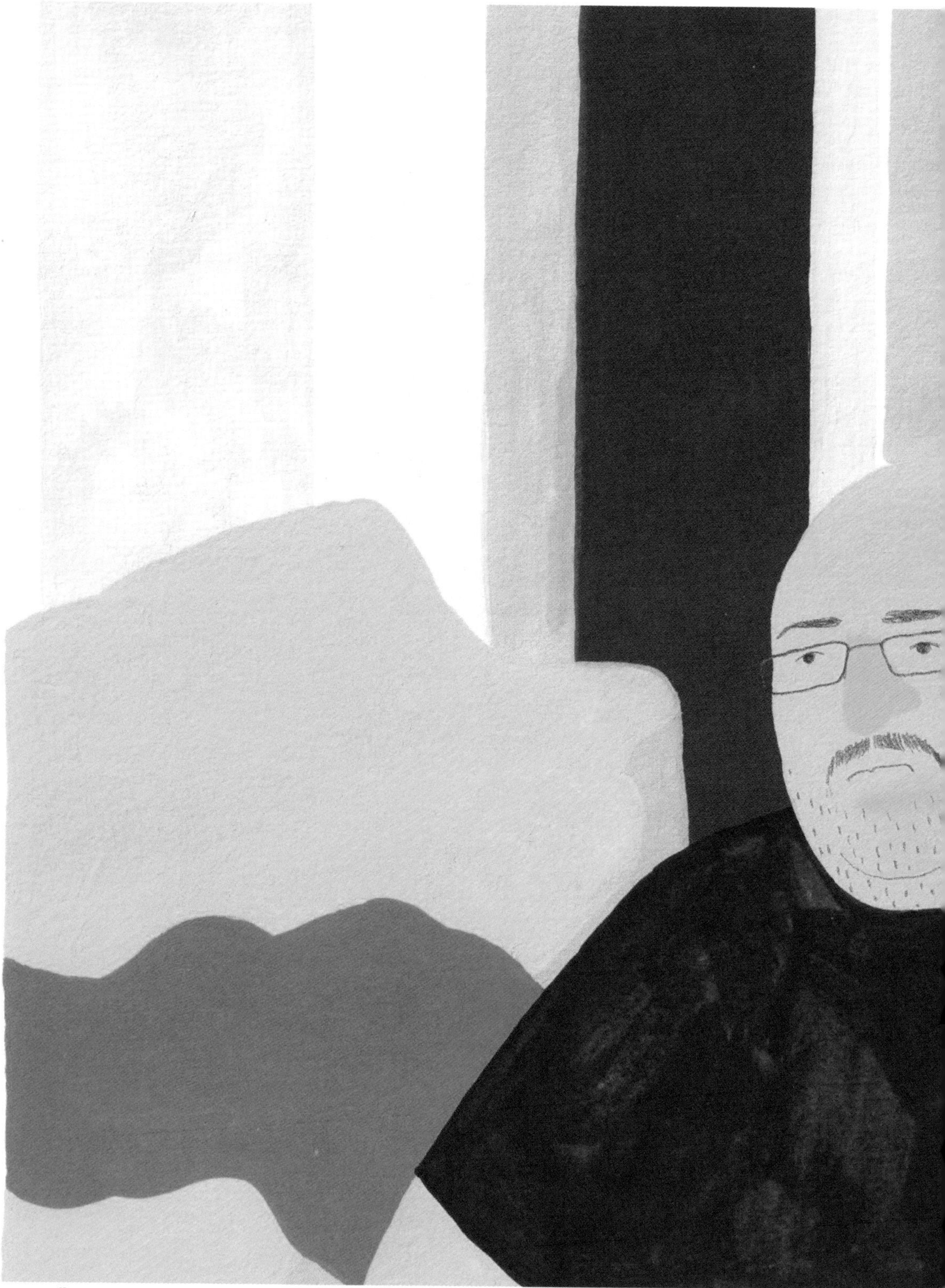

🔊 "IN ORDER TO INTENTIONALLY INFLUENCE REALITY

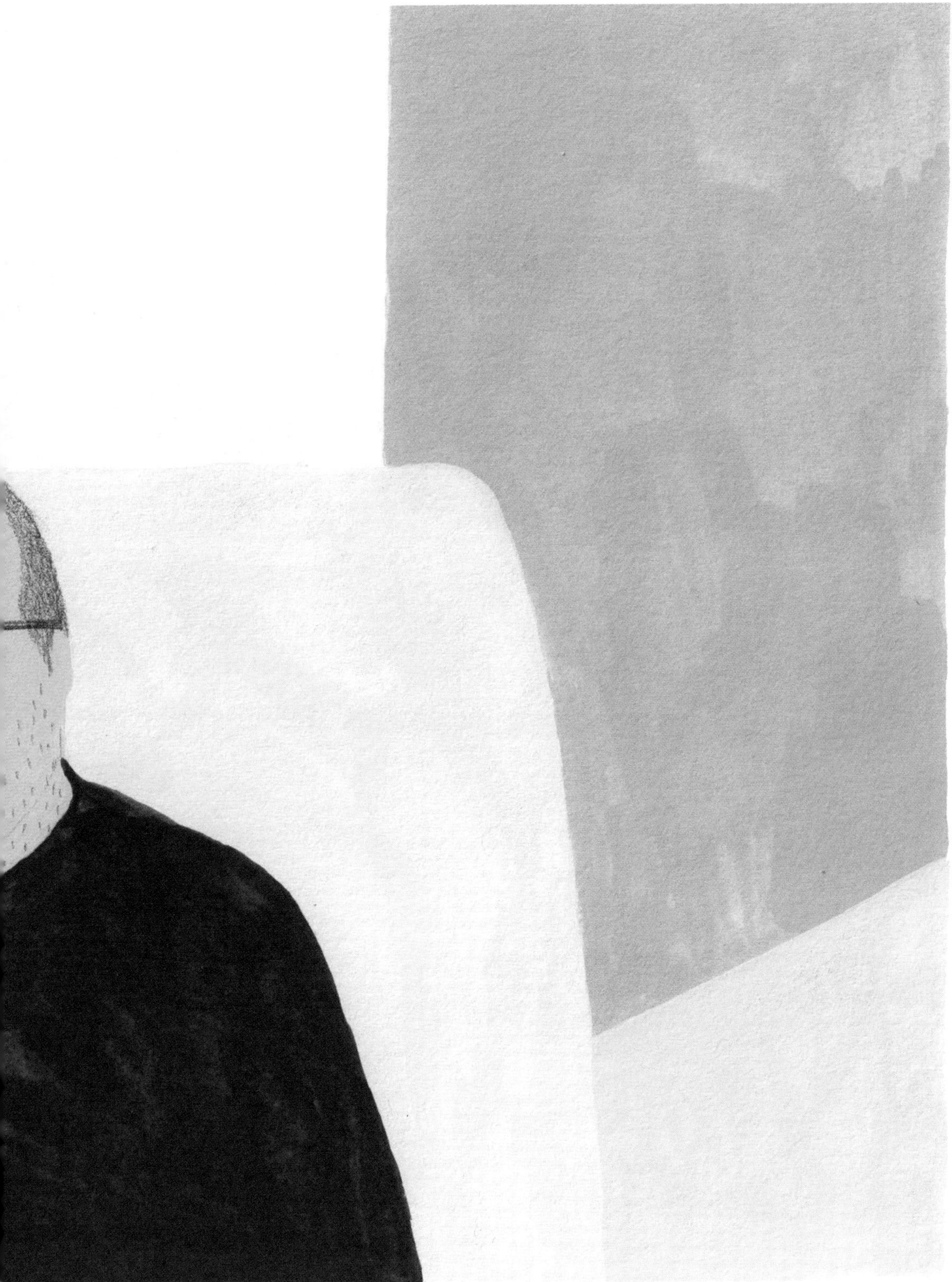

AND CONSCIOUSLY CREATE YOUR LIFE"

14:54

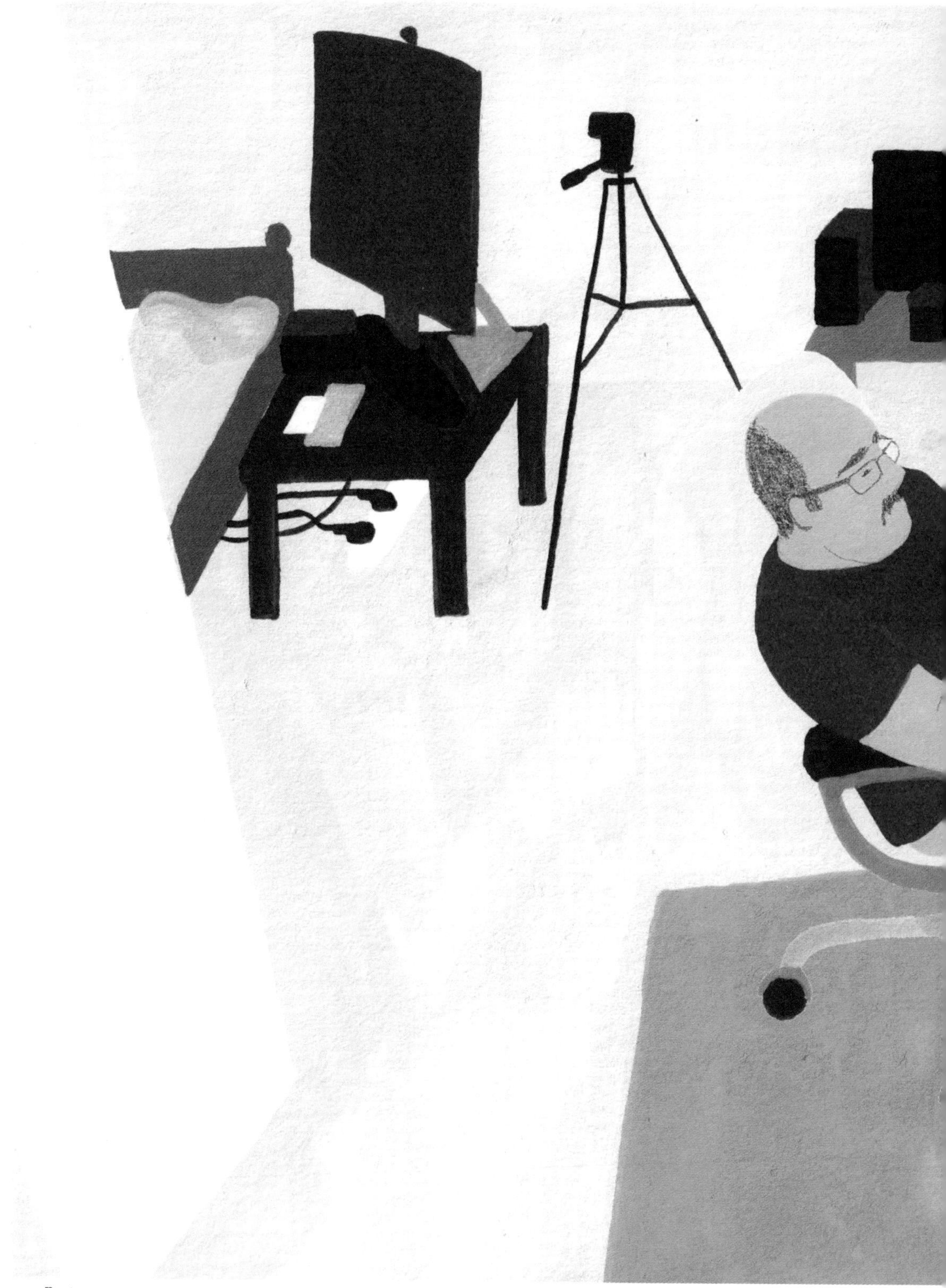

🔈 "YOU MUST OVERWRITE SUBCONSCIOUS PROGRAMMING

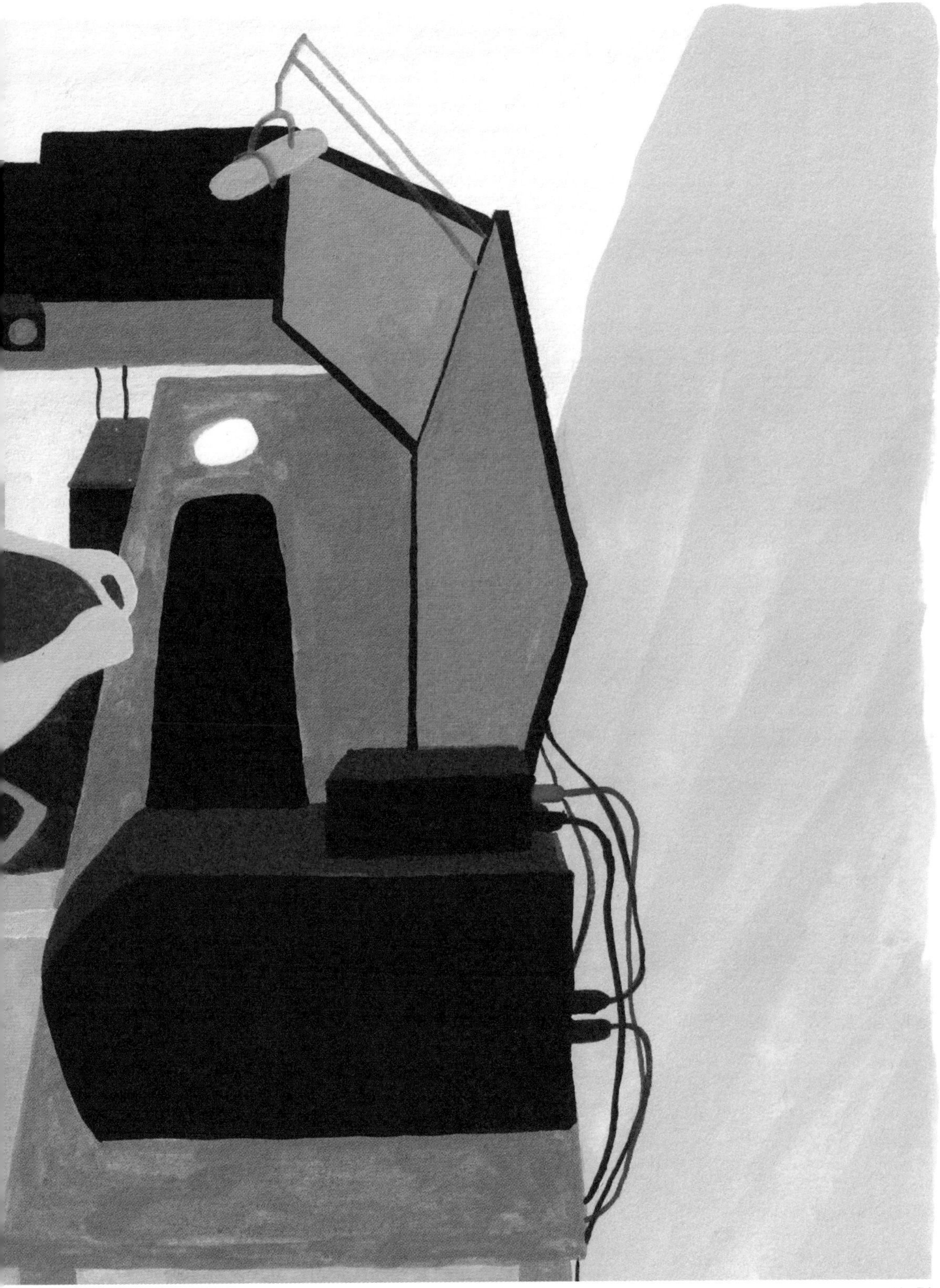

AND MAKE CONSCIOUS CHOICES" 14:54

◀)) "BUT IN ORDER TO DO SO"   14:54

🔊 "YOU MUST PLAY THE GAME OF LIFE AS YOUR HIGHER SELF"   14:55

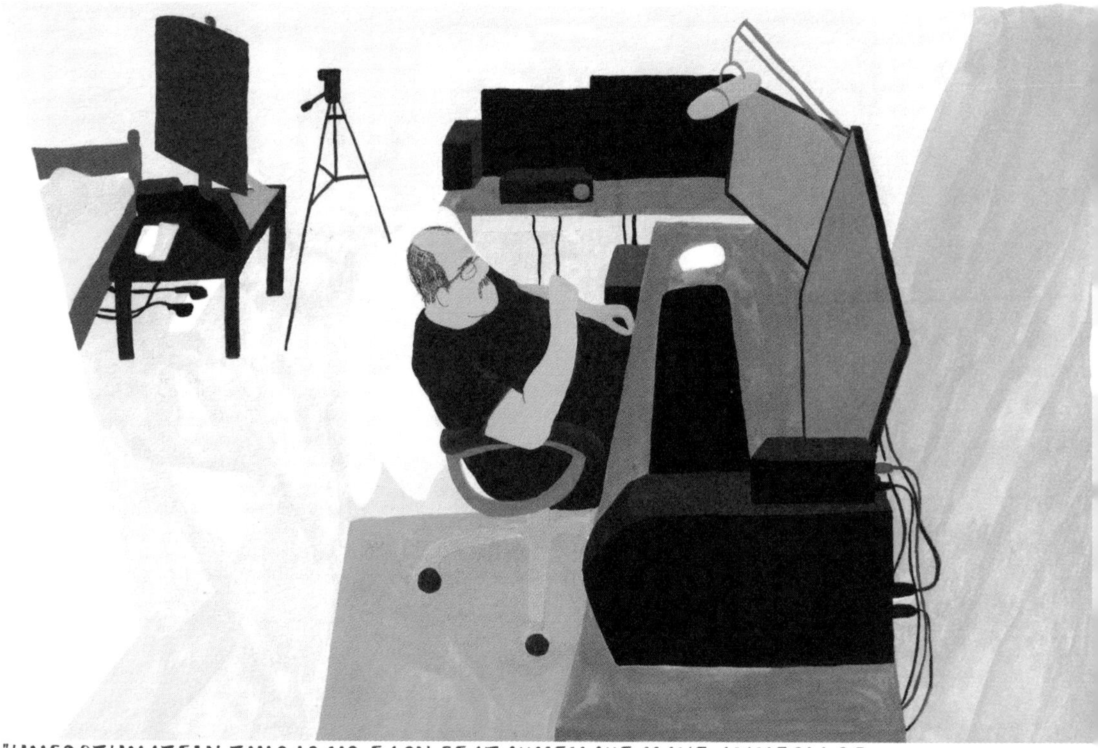

🔊 "UNFORTUNATELY THIS IS NO EASY FEAT WHEN WE HAVE AMNESIA OF OUR HIGHER SELVES" 14:55

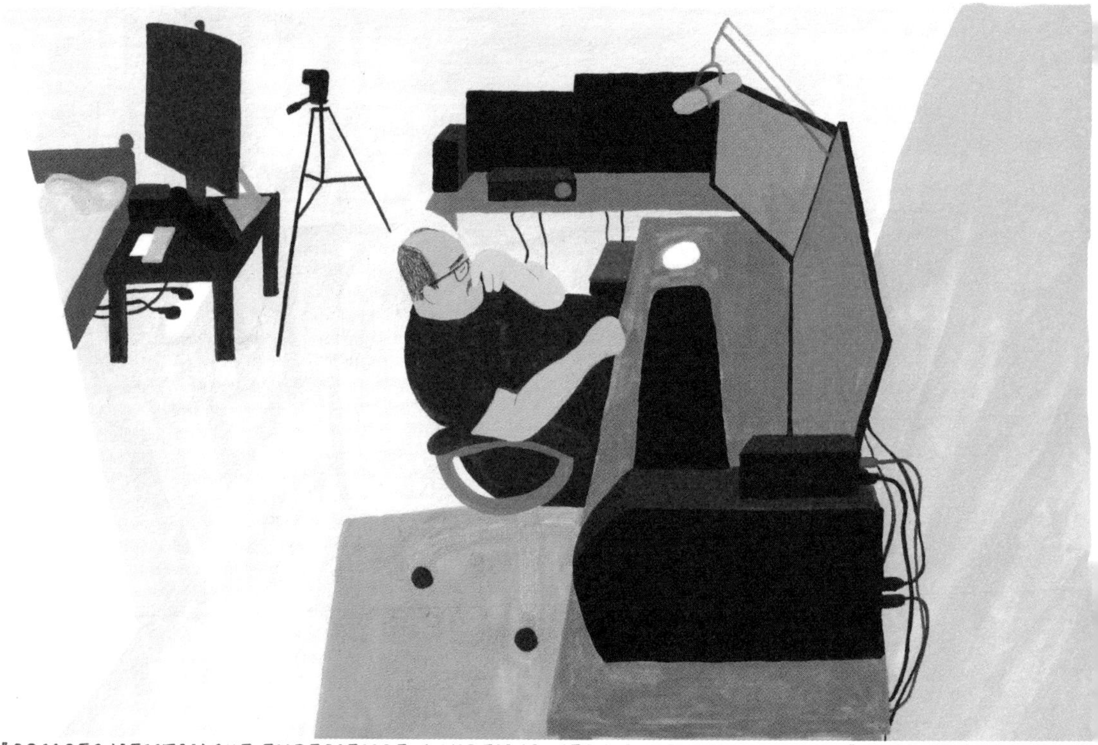

🔊 "CONSEQUENTLY WE EXPERIENCE A VIRTUAL VERSION OF OURSELVES." 14:55

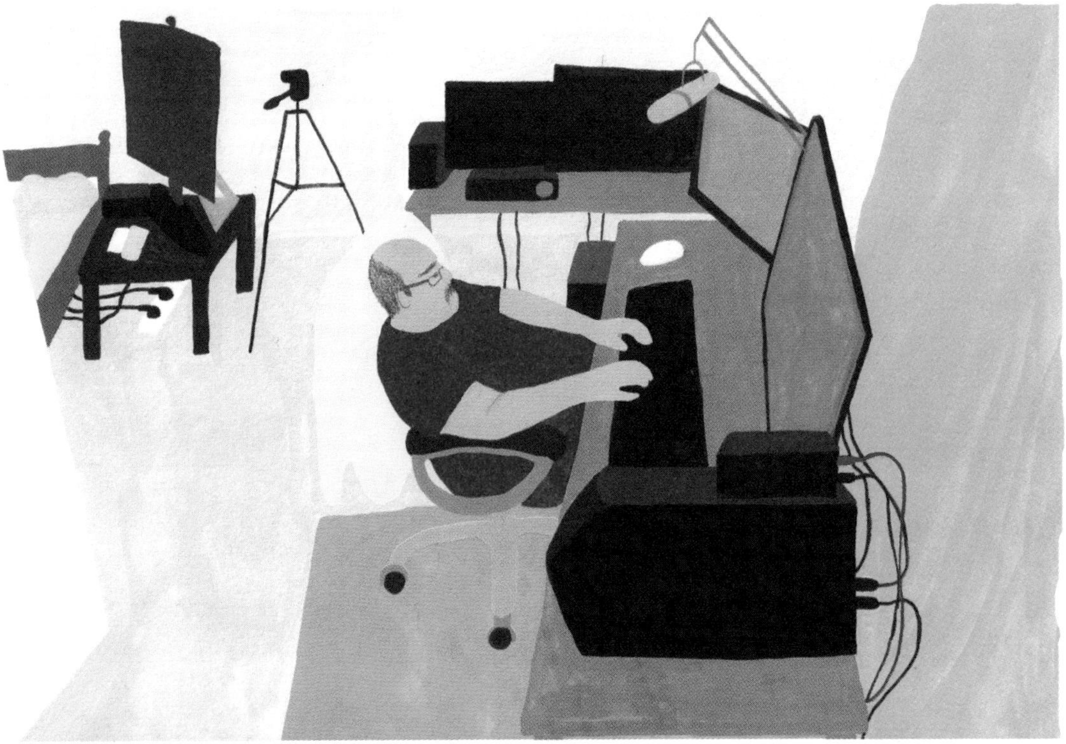

"TRAPPED WITHIN THE CONFINES OF A SIMULATED WORLD" 14:55

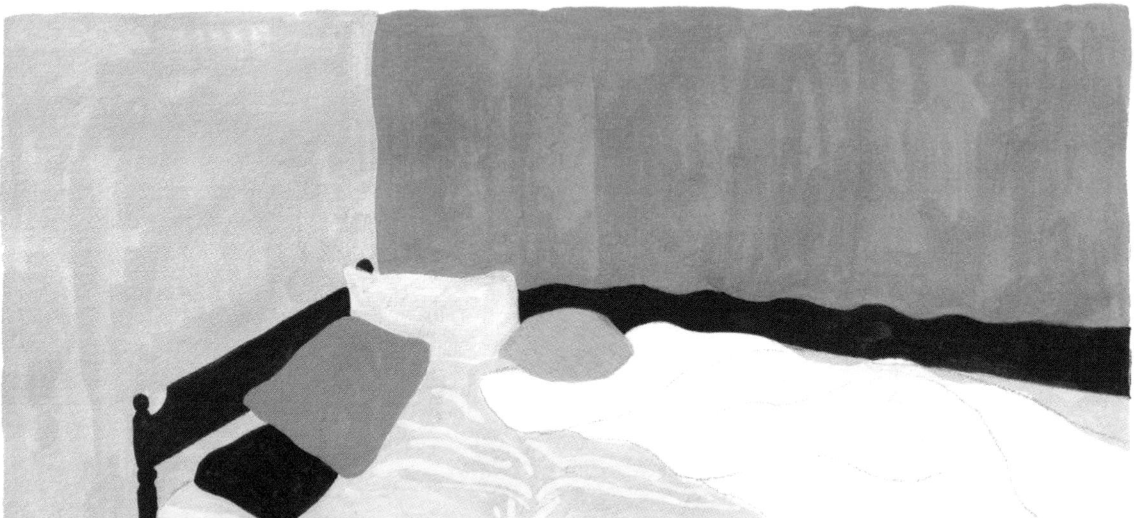

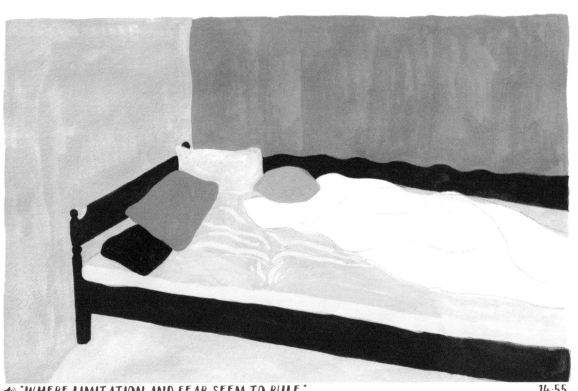

"WHERE LIMITATION AND FEAR SEEM TO RULE." 14:55

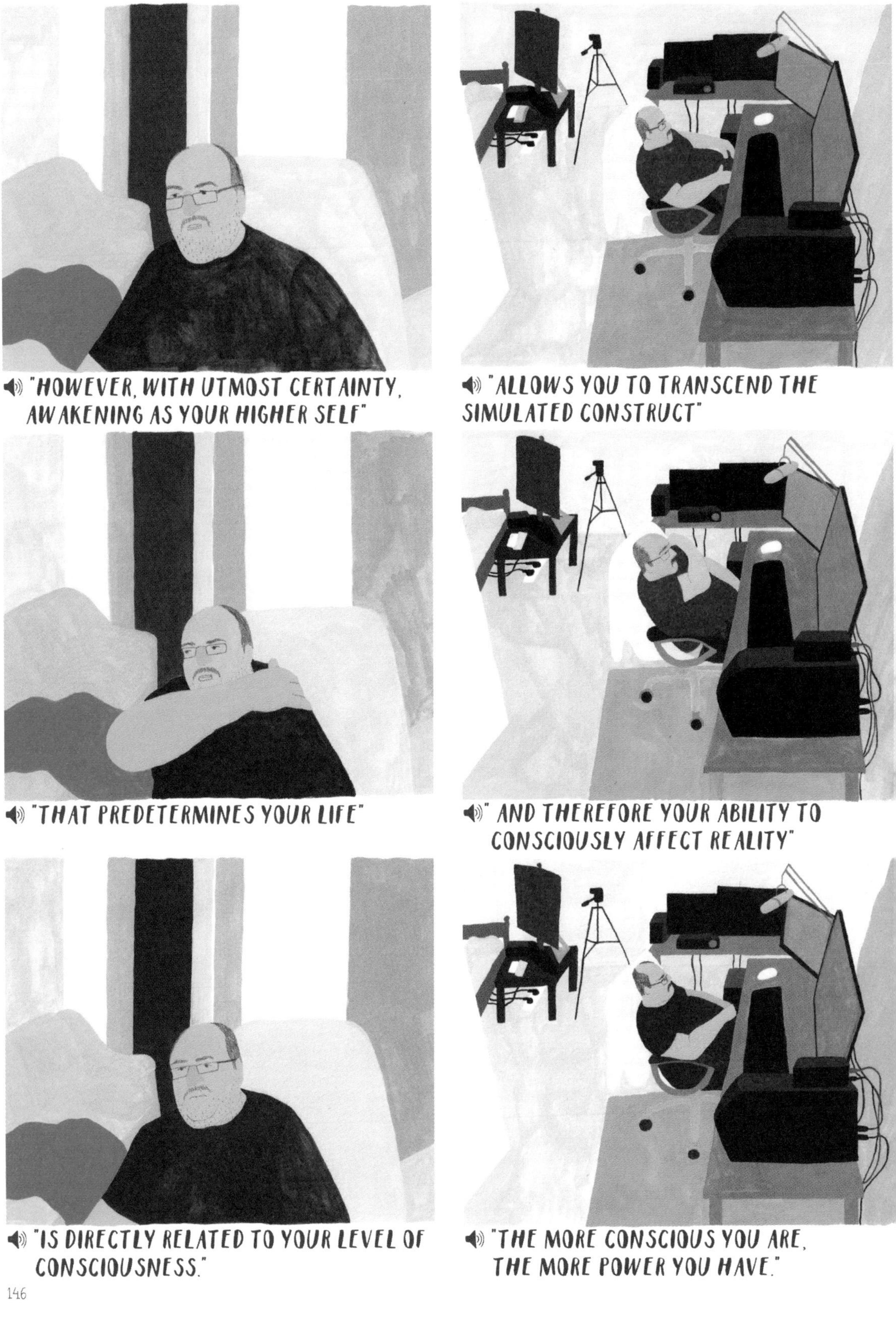
"HOWEVER, WITH UTMOST CERTAINTY, AWAKENING AS YOUR HIGHER SELF"
"ALLOWS YOU TO TRANSCEND THE SIMULATED CONSTRUCT"
"THAT PREDETERMINES YOUR LIFE"
" AND THEREFORE YOUR ABILITY TO CONSCIOUSLY AFFECT REALITY"
"IS DIRECTLY RELATED TO YOUR LEVEL OF CONSCIOUSNESS."
"THE MORE CONSCIOUS YOU ARE, THE MORE POWER YOU HAVE."

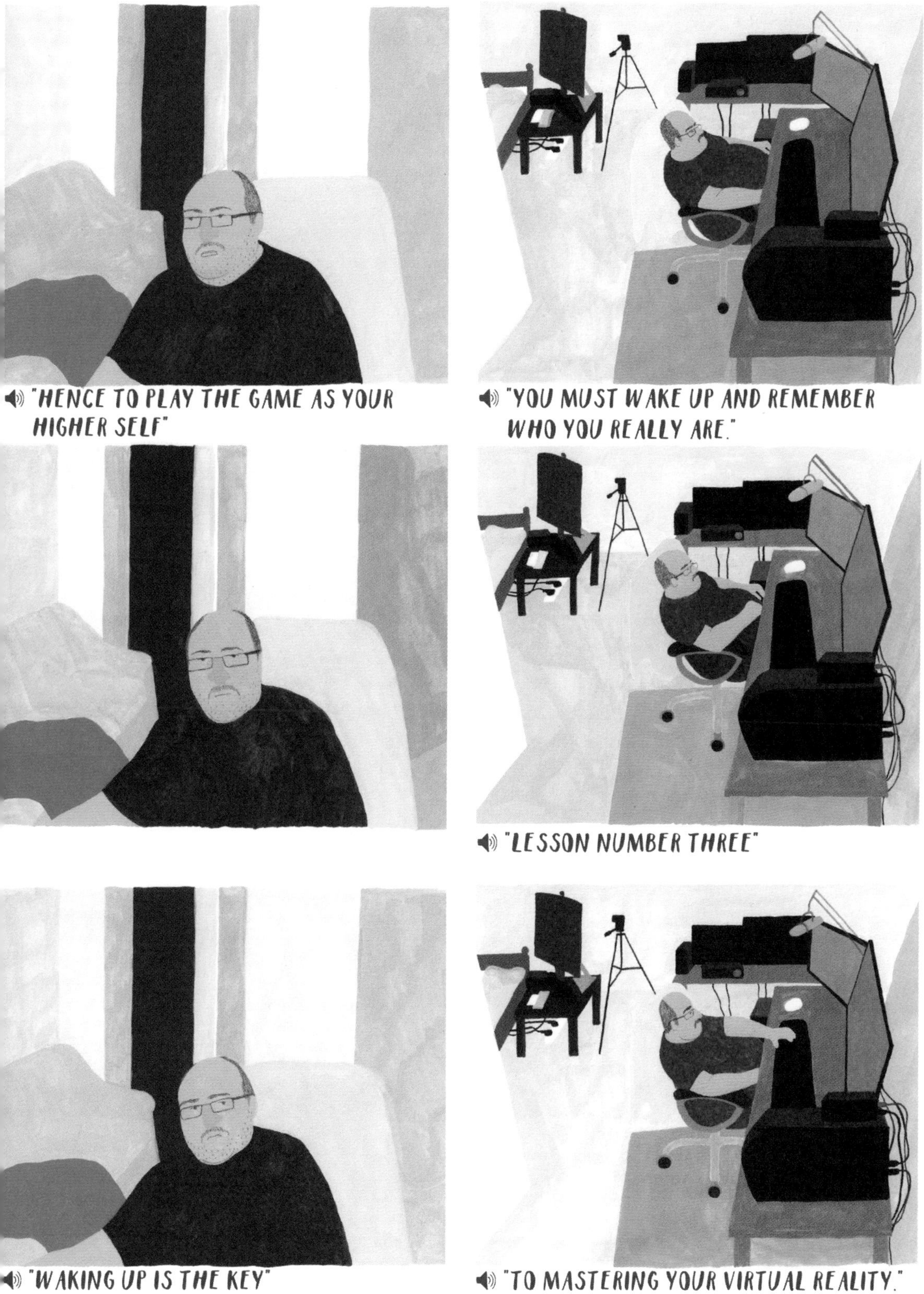
"HENCE TO PLAY THE GAME AS YOUR HIGHER SELF"
"YOU MUST WAKE UP AND REMEMBER WHO YOU REALLY ARE."
"LESSON NUMBER THREE"
"WAKING UP IS THE KEY"
"TO MASTERING YOUR VIRTUAL REALITY."

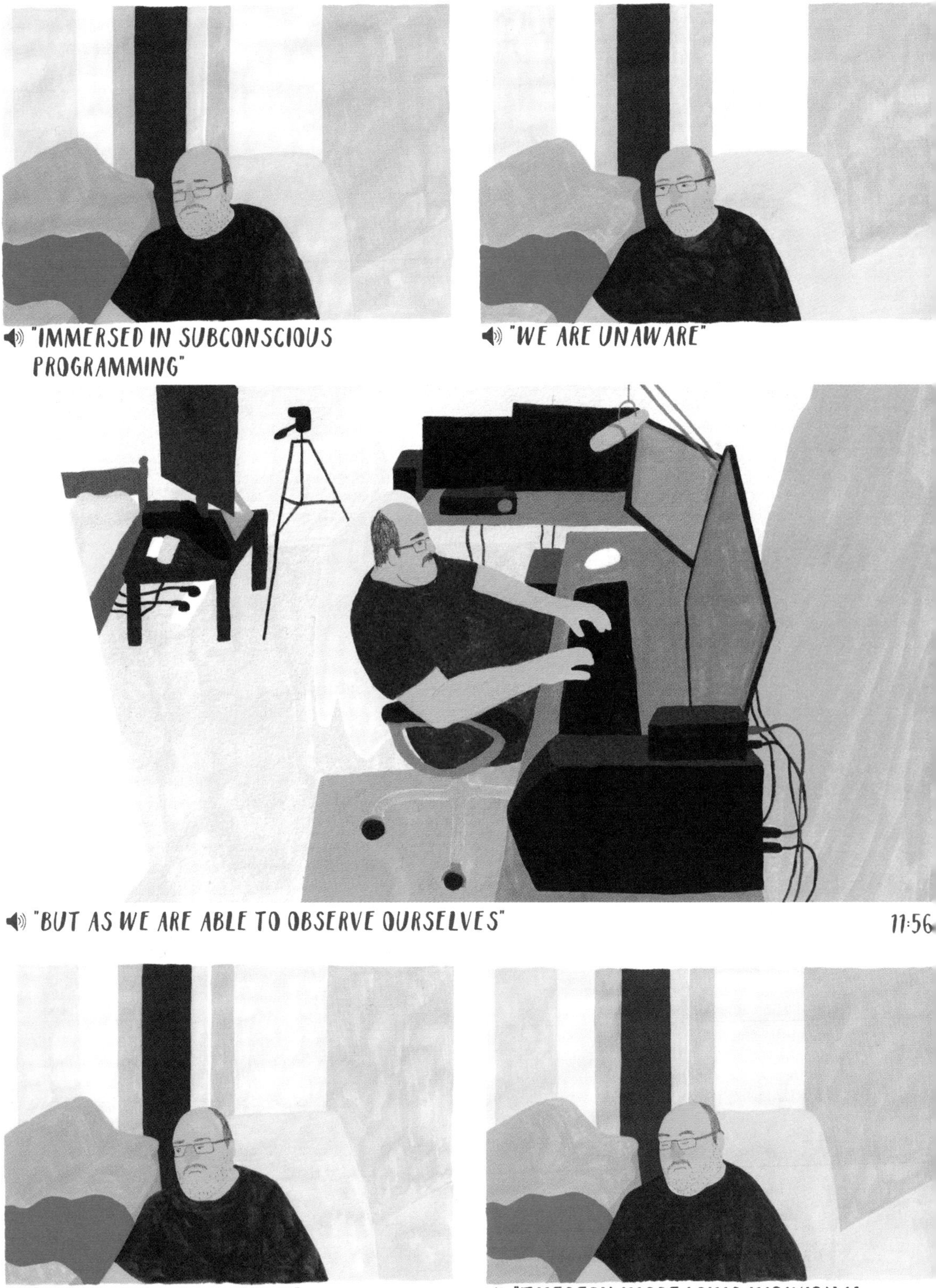
"IMMERSED IN SUBCONSCIOUS PROGRAMMING"
"WE ARE UNAWARE"
"BUT AS WE ARE ABLE TO OBSERVE OURSELVES"
11:56
"WE BECOME SELF-AWARE"
"THEREBY INCREASING INDIVIDUAL CONSCIOUSNESS"

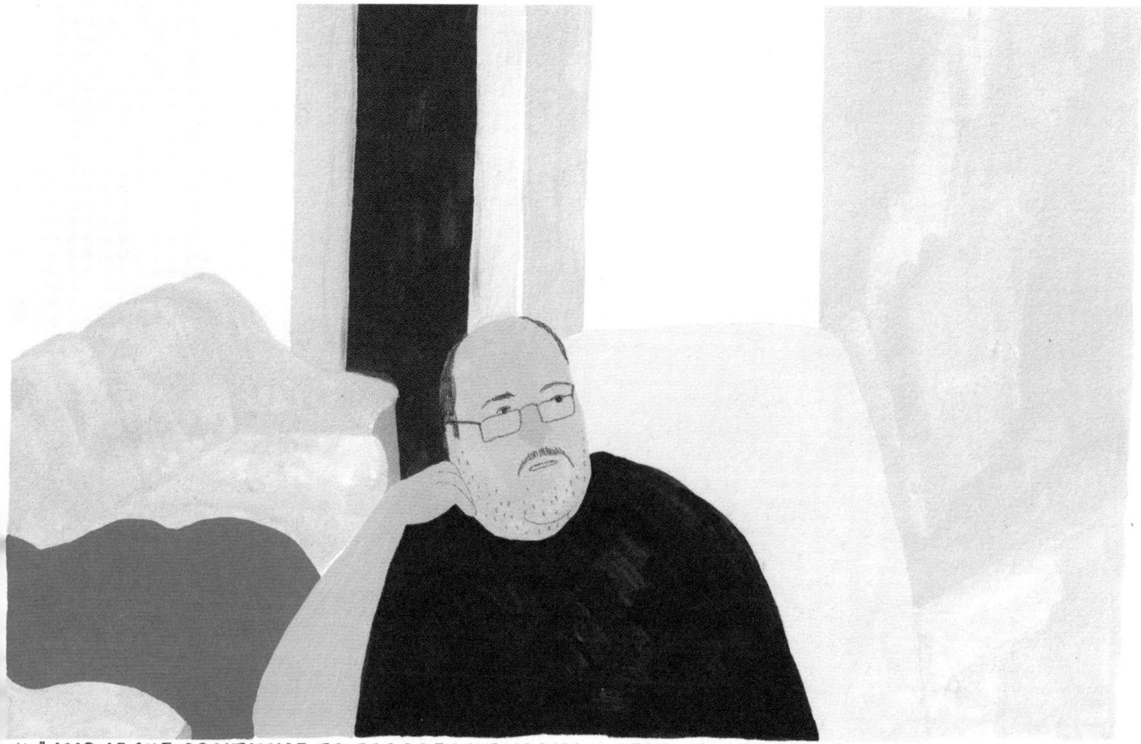

"AND IF WE CONTINUE TO PROGRESS THROUGH SELF-AWARENESS" 11:56

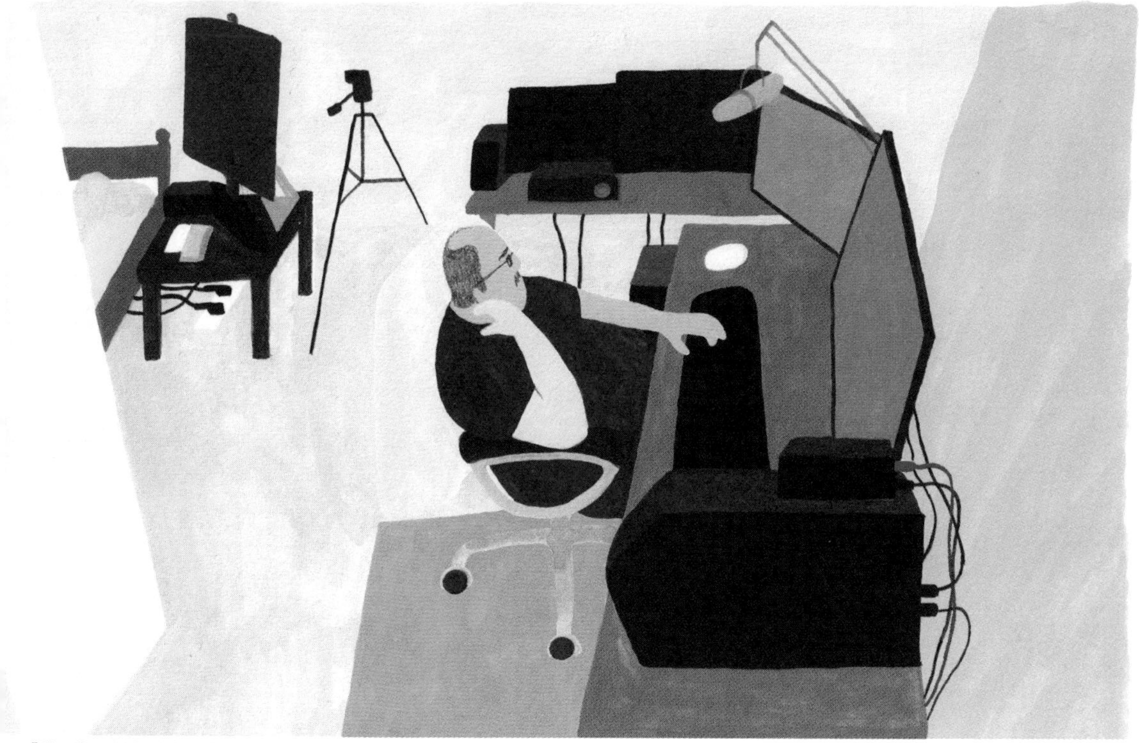

"EVENTUALLY WE AWAKE AS THE OBSERVER, WHICH IS ANOTHER WORD FOR HIGHER SELF." 11:56

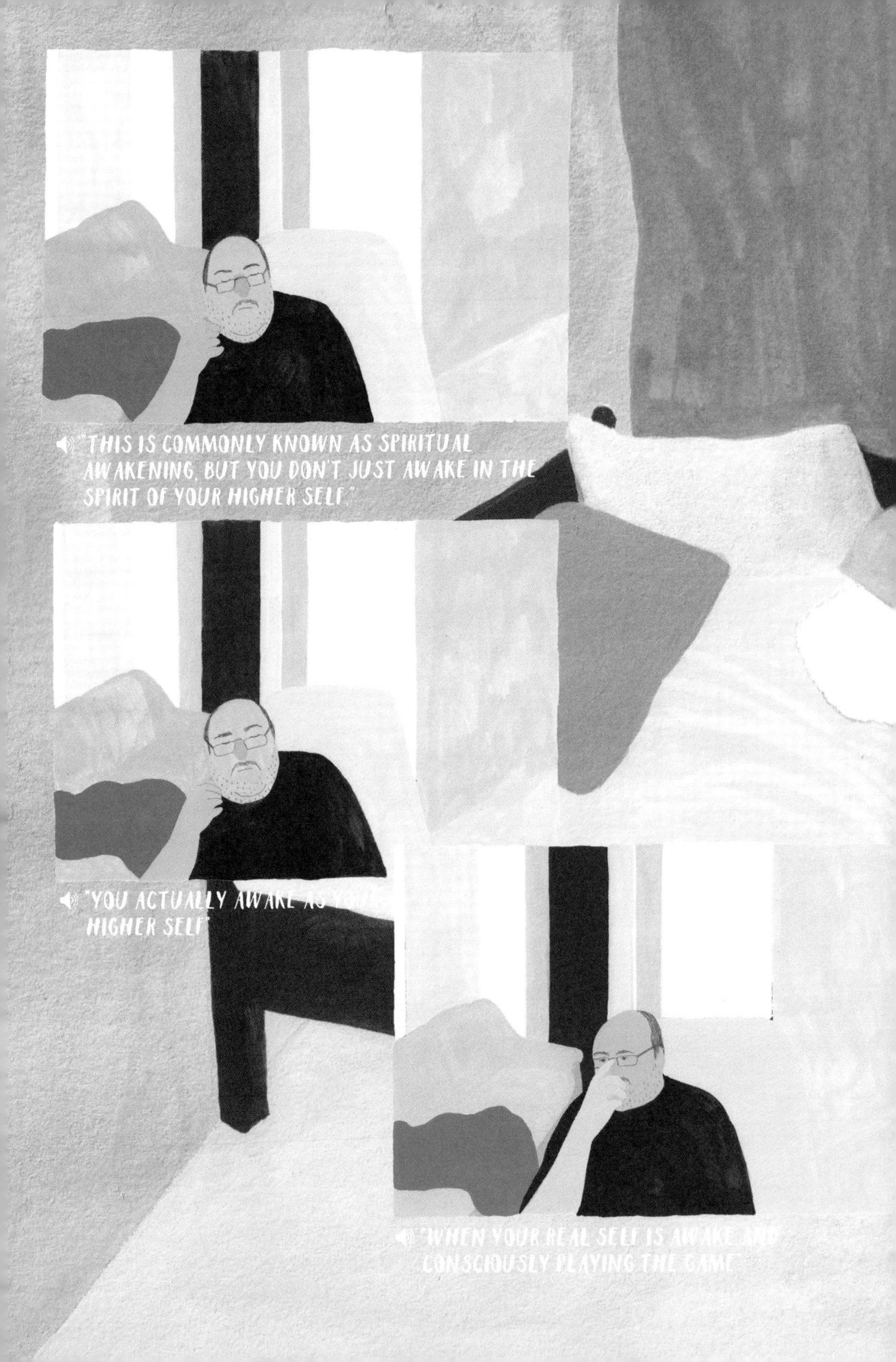
"THIS IS COMMONLY KNOWN AS SPIRITUAL AWAKENING, BUT YOU DON'T JUST AWAKE IN THE SPIRIT OF YOUR HIGHER SELF."
"YOU ACTUALLY AWAKE AS
HIGHER SELF"
"WHEN YOUR REAL SELF IS AWAKE AND CONSCIOUSLY PLAYING THE GAME"

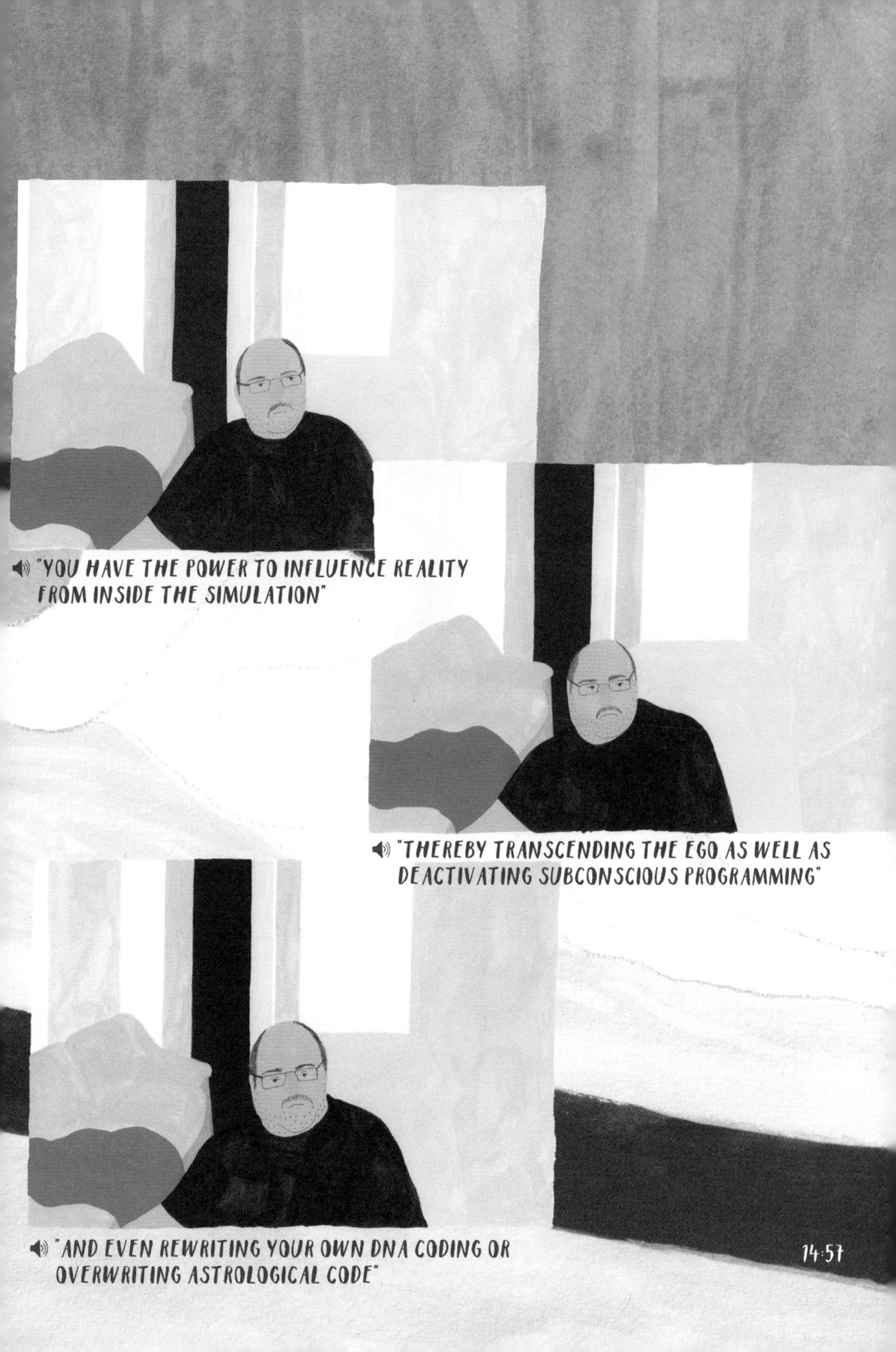
"YOU HAVE THE POWER TO INFLUENCE REALITY FROM INSIDE THE SIMULATION"
"THEREBY TRANSCENDING THE EGO AS WELL AS DEACTIVATING SUBCONSCIOUS PROGRAMMING"
"AND EVEN REWRITING YOUR OWN DNA CODING OR OVERWRITING ASTROLOGICAL CODE"
14:57

◀)) "IF YOU SO CHOOSE."

14:58

🔊 "SPIRITUAL AWAKENING IS NOT A DESTINATION AS MUCH AS IT IS A"

14:58

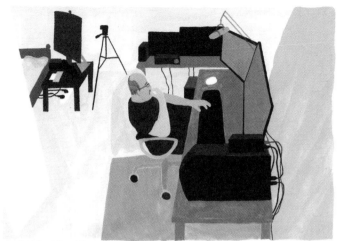

🔊 "MOMENT"

🔊 "TO"

🔊 "MOMENT"

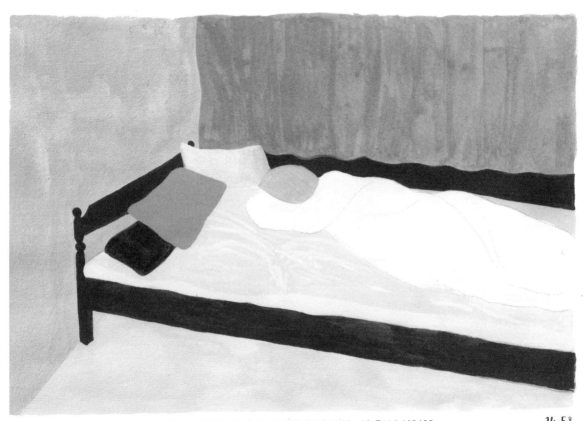

🔊 "CHOICE AND SIMPLY BEING PRESENT IN THE NOW AWAKENS YOUR
HIGHER SELF FOR AS LONG AS YOU ARE CONSCIOUS."

14:58

16.02.2017

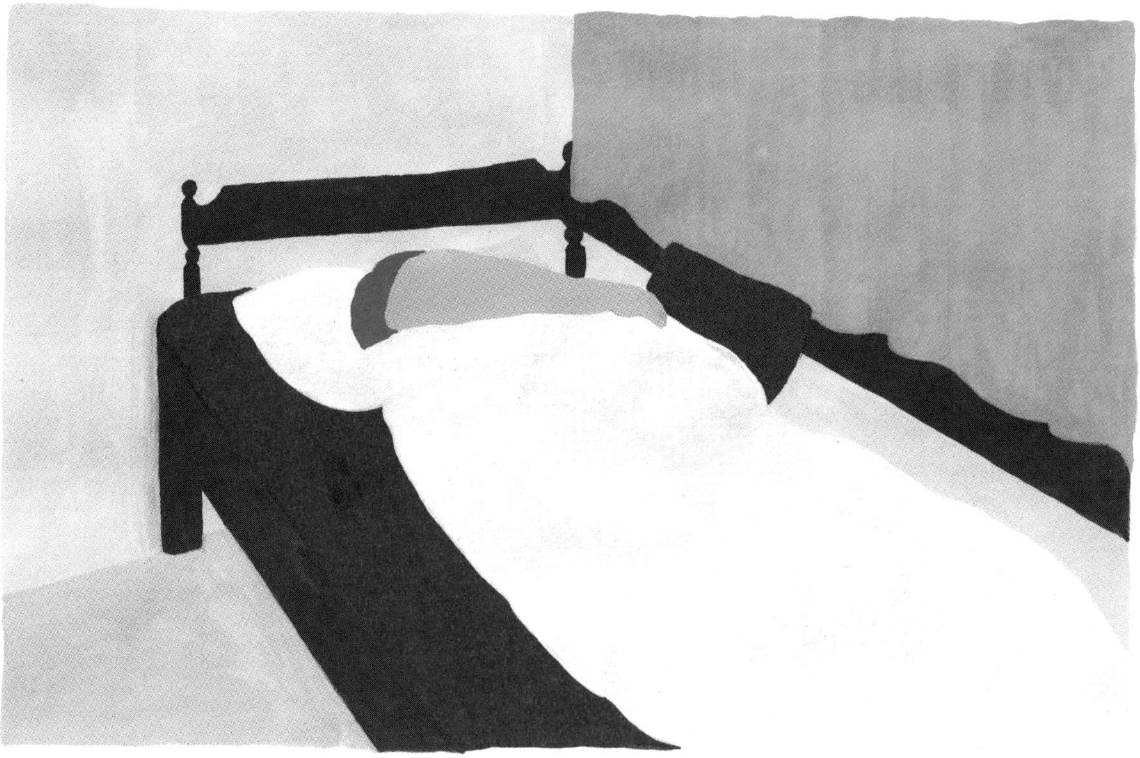

12:02

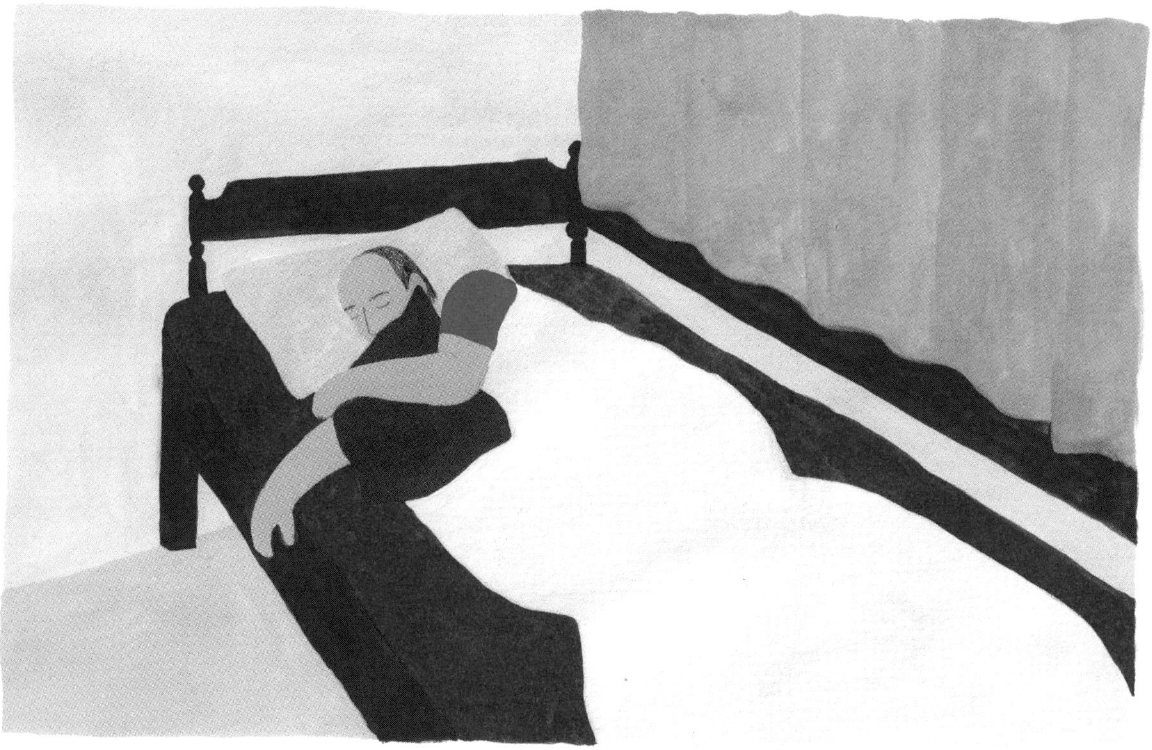

12:14

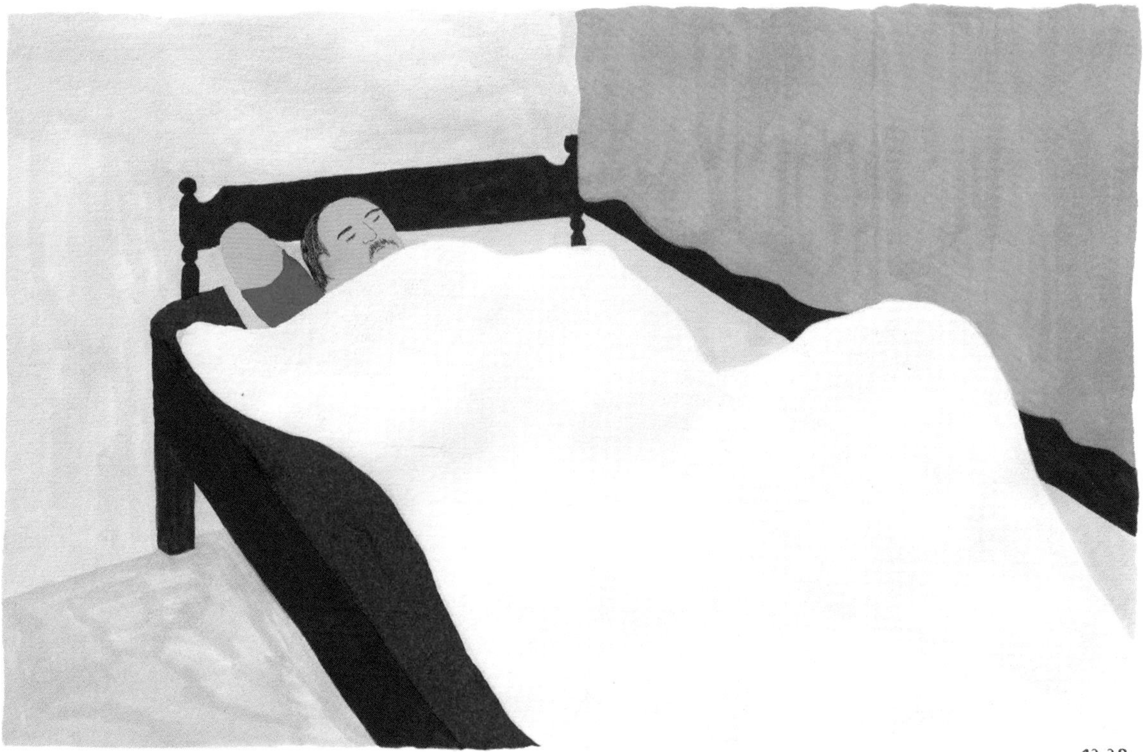

12:29

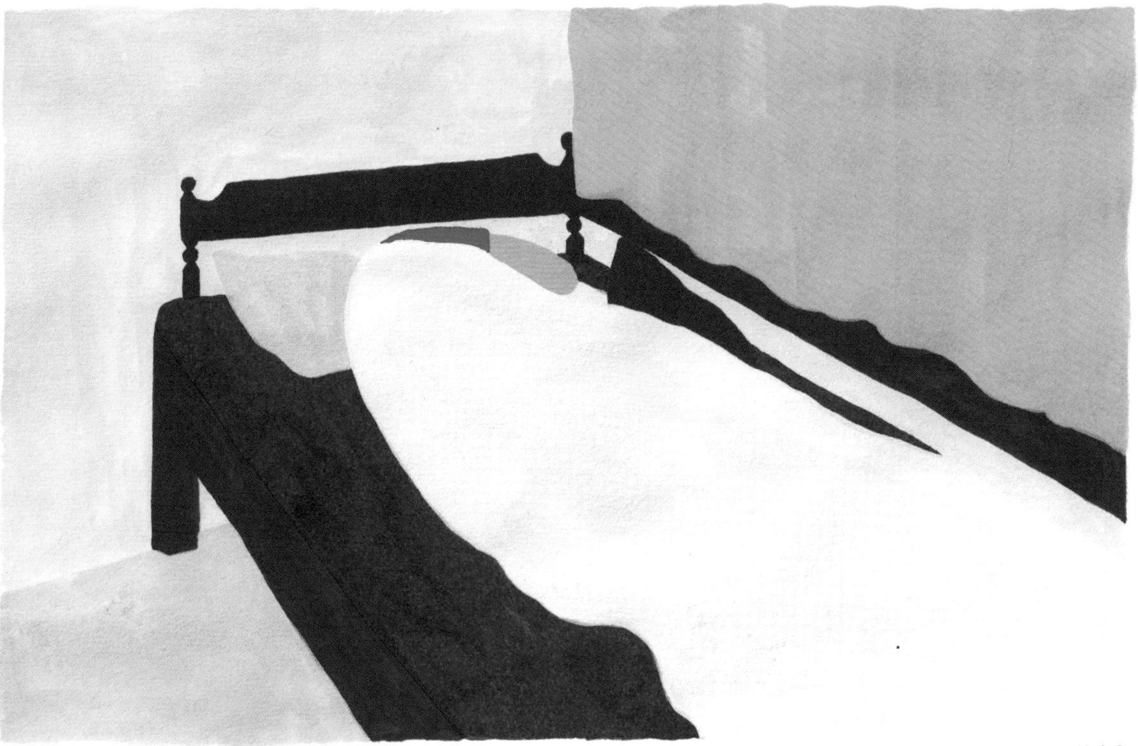

12:49

22.02.2017

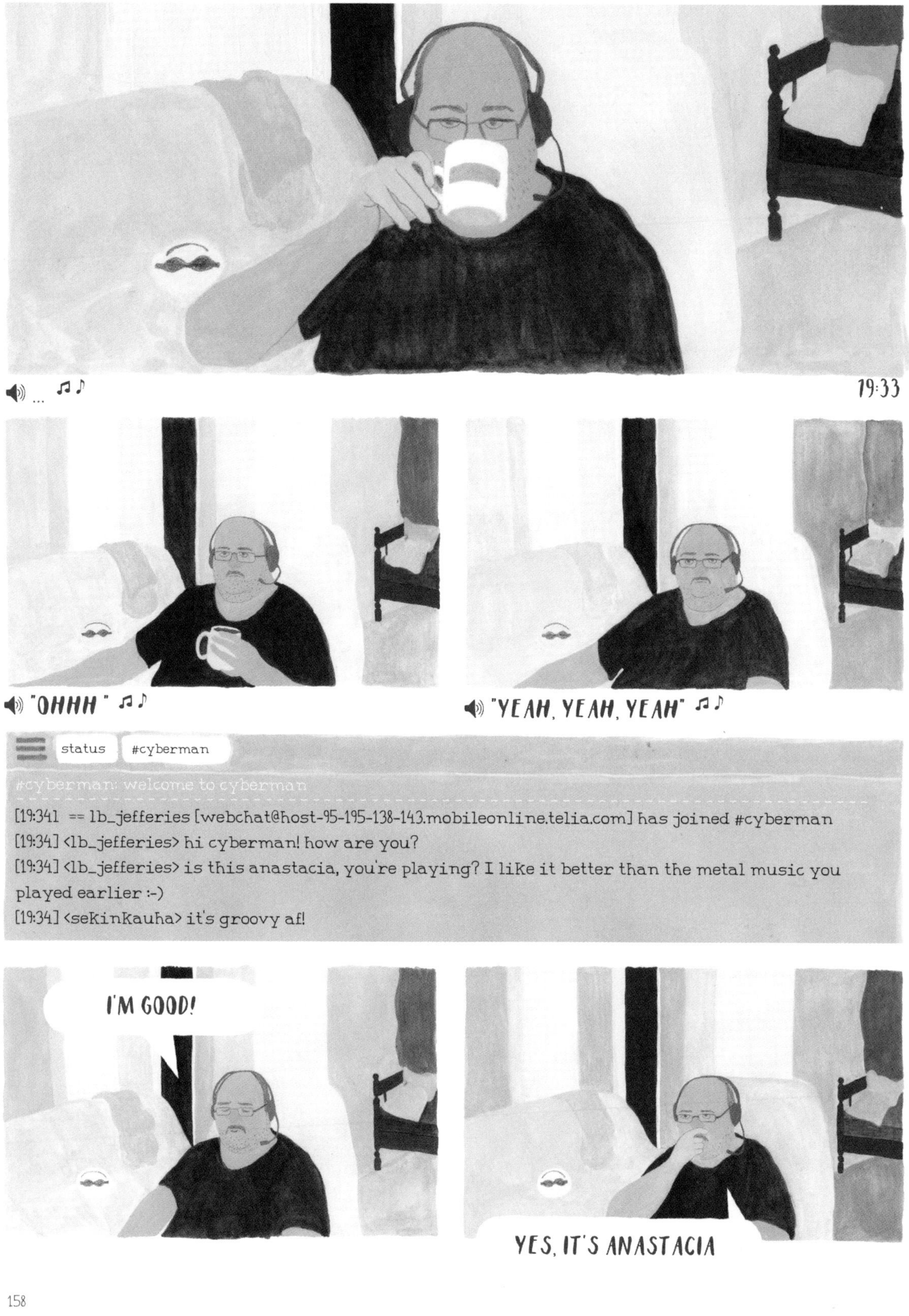
... ♫♪
19:33
"OHHH" ♫♪
"YEAH, YEAH, YEAH" ♫♪
status
#cyberman
#cyberman: welcome to cyberman
[19:34] == lb_jefferies [webchat@host-95-195-138-143.mobileonline.telia.com] has joined #cyberman
[19:34] <lb_jefferies> hi cyberman! how are you?
[19:34] <lb_jefferies> is this anastacia, you're playing? I like it better than the metal music you played earlier :-)
[19:34] <seKinKauha> it's groovy af!
I'M GOOD!
YES, IT'S ANASTACIA

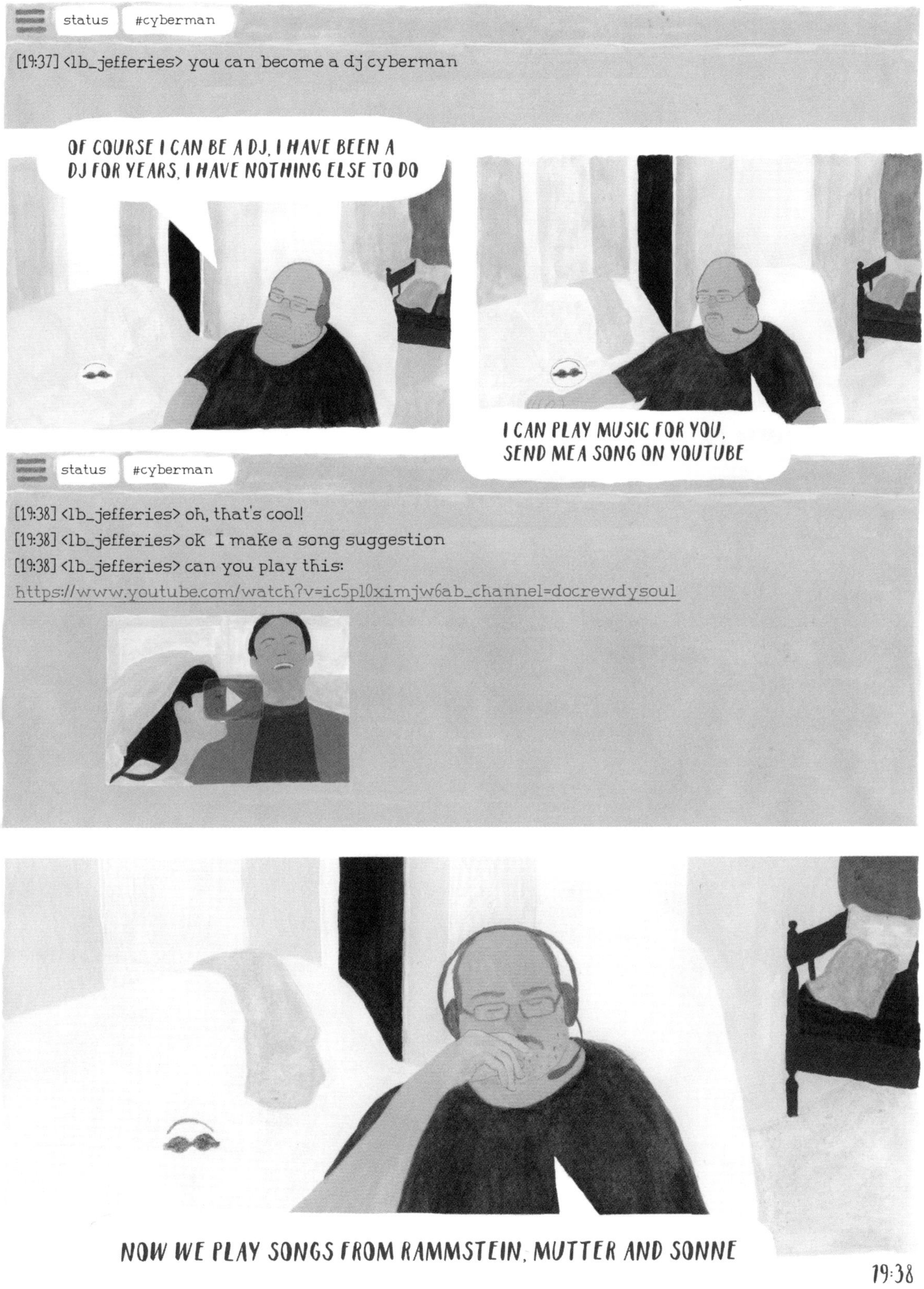
status
#cyberman
[19:37] <lb_jefferies> you can become a dj cyberman
OF COURSE I CAN BE A DJ, I HAVE BEEN A DJ FOR YEARS, I HAVE NOTHING ELSE TO DO
I CAN PLAY MUSIC FOR YOU, SEND ME A SONG ON YOUTUBE
status
#cyberman
[19:38] <lb_jefferies> oh, that's cool!
[19:38] <lb_jefferies> ok I make a song suggestion
[19:38] <lb_jefferies> can you play this:
https://www.youtube.com/watch?v=ic5pl0ximjw6ab_channel=docrewdysoul
NOW WE PLAY SONGS FROM RAMMSTEIN, MUTTER AND SONNE
19:38

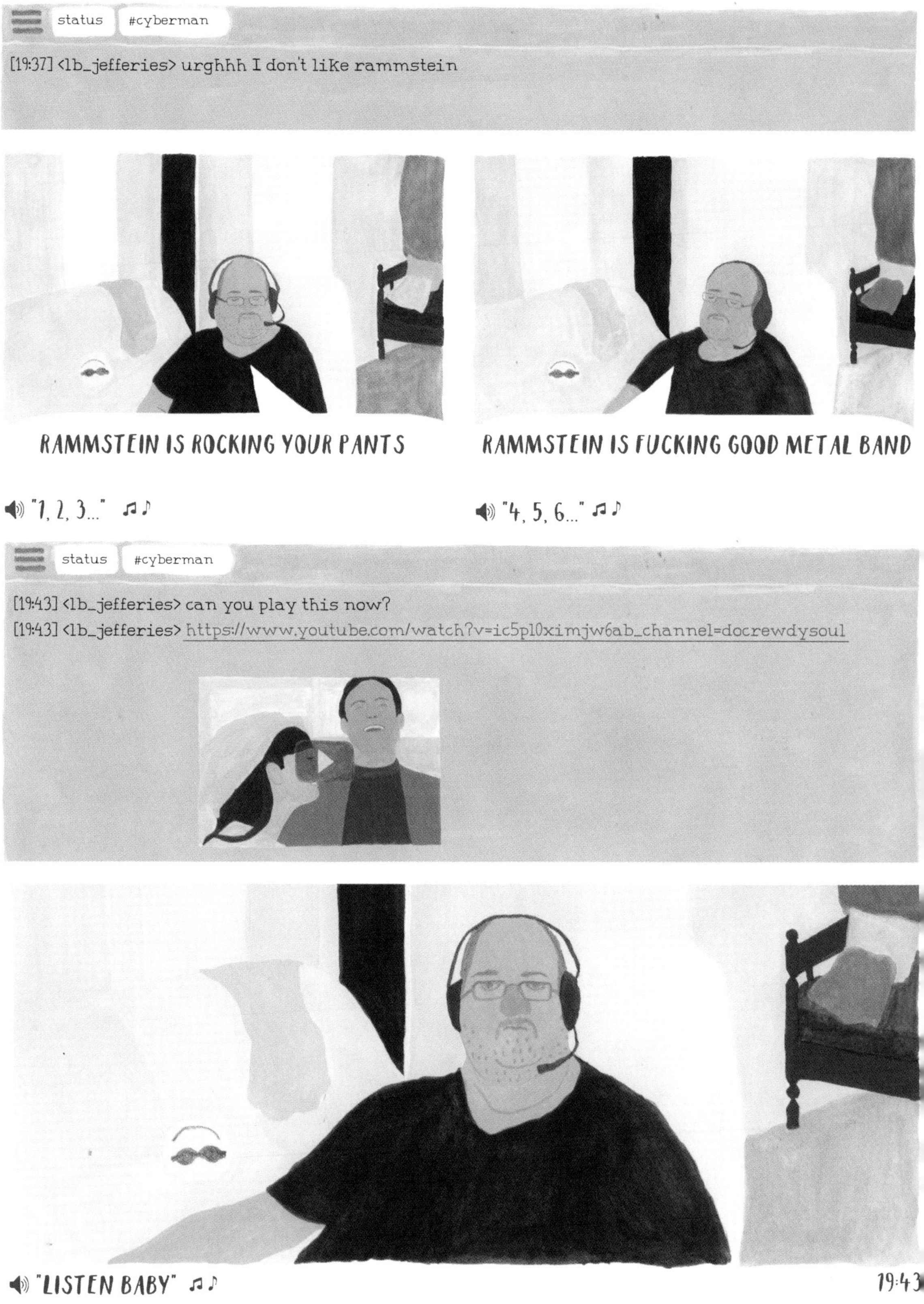
status
#cyberman
[19:37] <lb_jefferies> urghhh I don't like rammstein
RAMMSTEIN IS ROCKING YOUR PANTS
"1, 2, 3..."
RAMMSTEIN IS FUCKING GOOD METAL BAND
"4, 5, 6..."
status
#cyberman
[19:43] <lb_jefferies> can you play this now?
[19:43] <lb_jefferies> https://www.youtube.com/watch?v=ic5pl0ximjw6ab_channel=docrewdysoul
"LISTEN BABY"
19:43

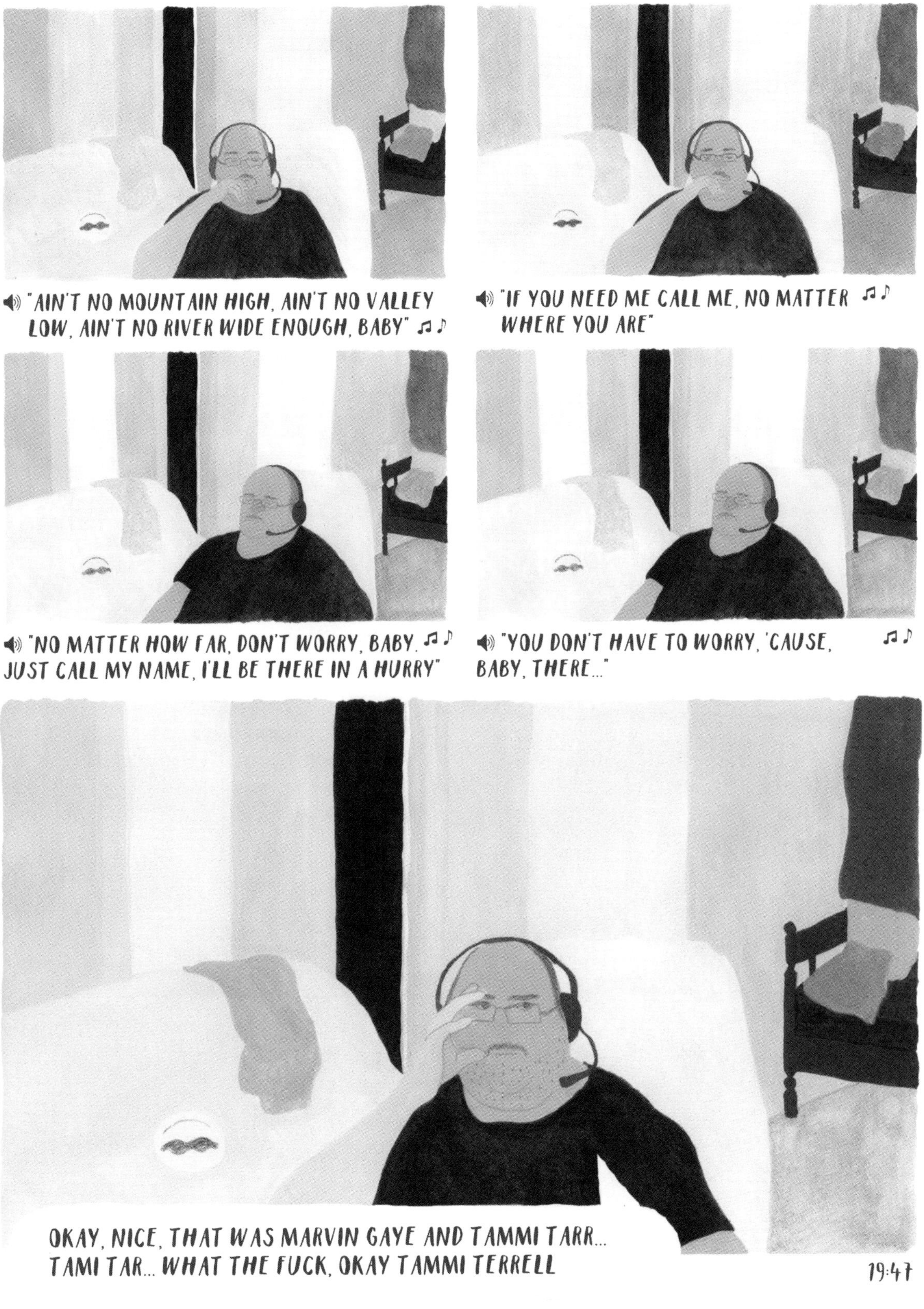
"AIN'T NO MOUNTAIN HIGH, AIN'T NO VALLEY LOW, AIN'T NO RIVER WIDE ENOUGH, BABY" ♫♪
"IF YOU NEED ME CALL ME, NO MATTER WHERE YOU ARE" ♫♪
"NO MATTER HOW FAR, DON'T WORRY, BABY. JUST CALL MY NAME, I'LL BE THERE IN A HURRY" ♫♪
"YOU DON'T HAVE TO WORRY, 'CAUSE, BABY, THERE..." ♫♪
OKAY, NICE, THAT WAS MARVIN GAYE AND TAMMI TARR... TAMI TAR... WHAT THE FUCK, OKAY TAMMI TERRELL
19:47

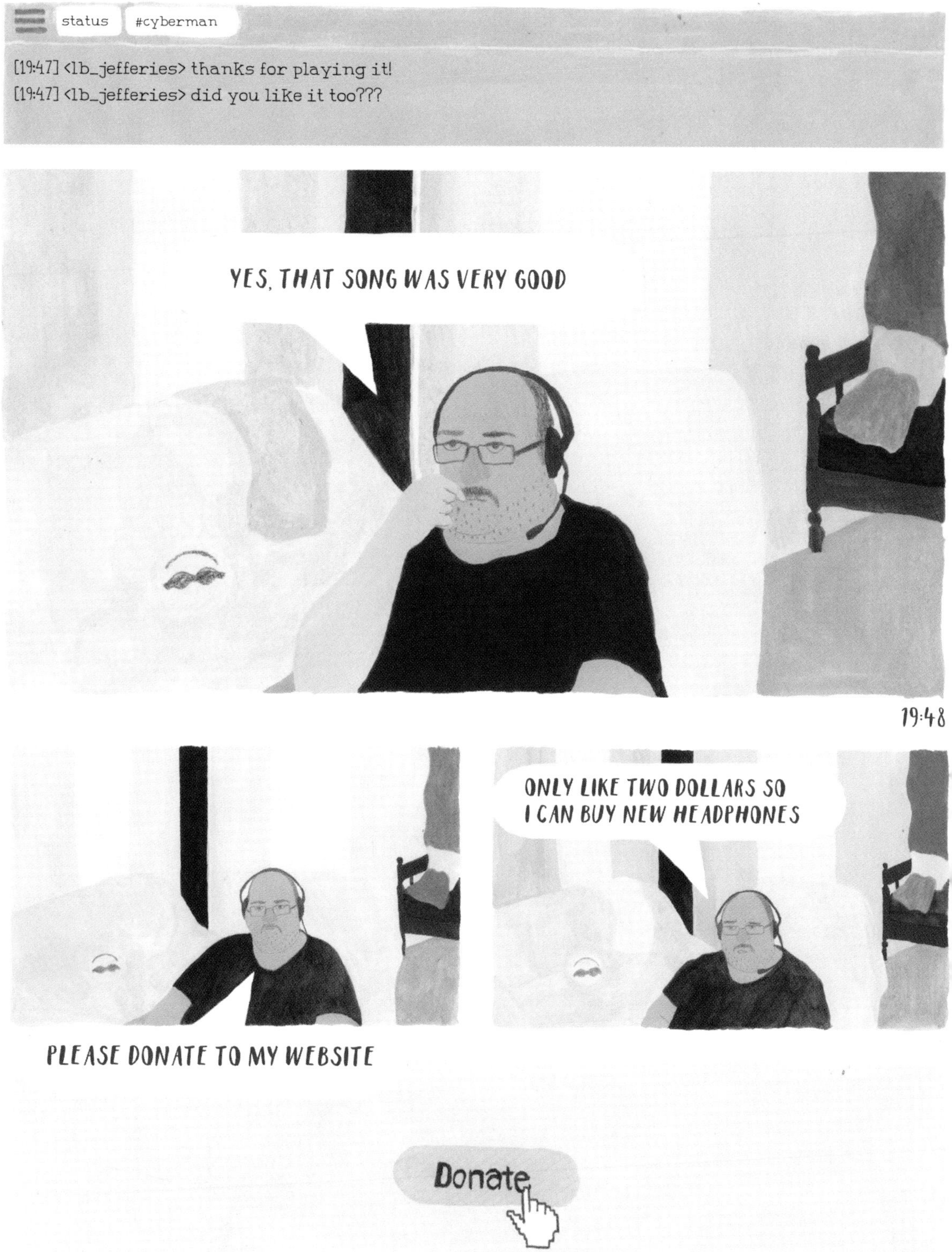
status
#cyberman
[19:47] <lb_jefferies> thanks for playing it!
[19:47] <lb_jefferies> did you like it too???
YES, THAT SONG WAS VERY GOOD
19:48
PLEASE DONATE TO MY WEBSITE
ONLY LIKE TWO DOLLARS SO
I CAN BUY NEW HEADPHONES
Donate

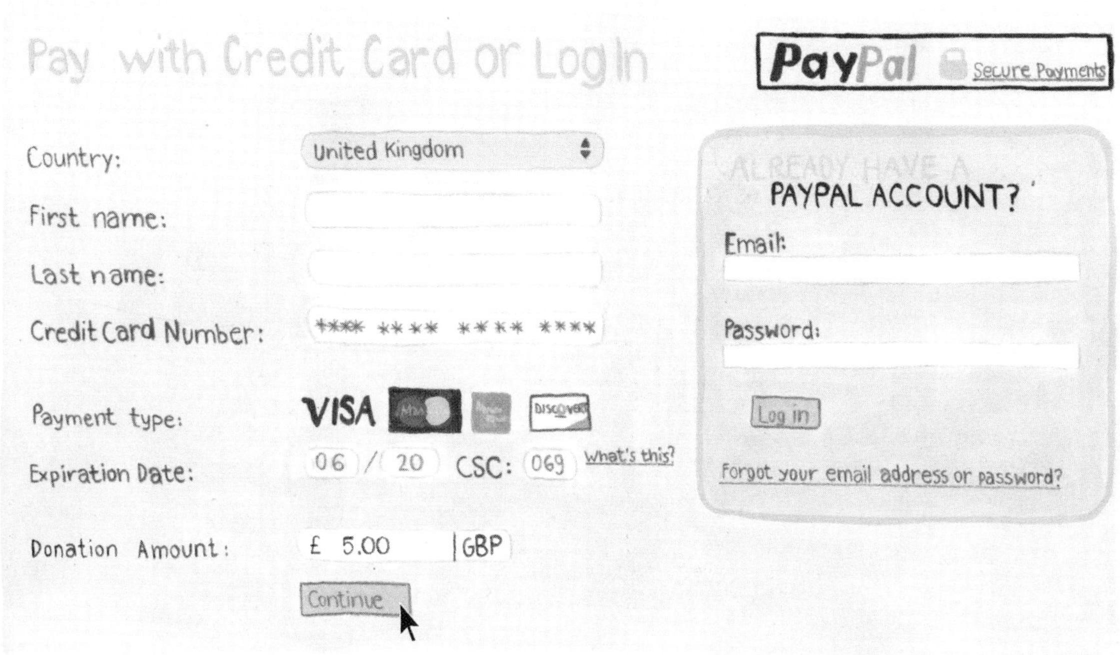

Pay with Credit Card or Log In

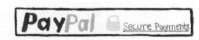
PayPal 🔒 Secure Payments

Country:	United Kingdom ⬍
First name:	
Last name:	
Credit Card Number:	**** **** **** ****
Payment type:	VISA 💳 💳 DISCOVER
Expiration Date:	06 / 20 CSC: 069 What's this?
Donation Amount:	£ 5.00 GBP

Continue 🖱

ALREADY HAVE A PAYPAL ACCOUNT?

Email:

Password:

Log in

Forgot your email address or password?

Pay with Credit Card or Log In

PayPal 🔒 Secure Payments

Country:	United Kingdom ⬍
First name: *Empty fields must be filled out	Veronika
Last name: *Empty fields must be filled out	Muchitsch
Credit Card Number:	**** **** **** ****
Payment type:	VISA 💳 💳 DISCOVER
Expiration Date:	06 / 20 CSC: 069 What's this?
Donation Amount:	£ 5.00 GBP

Continue   🖱

ALREADY HAVE A PAYPAL ACCOUNT?

Email:

Password:

Log in

Forgot your email address or password?

Thank you for your donation!

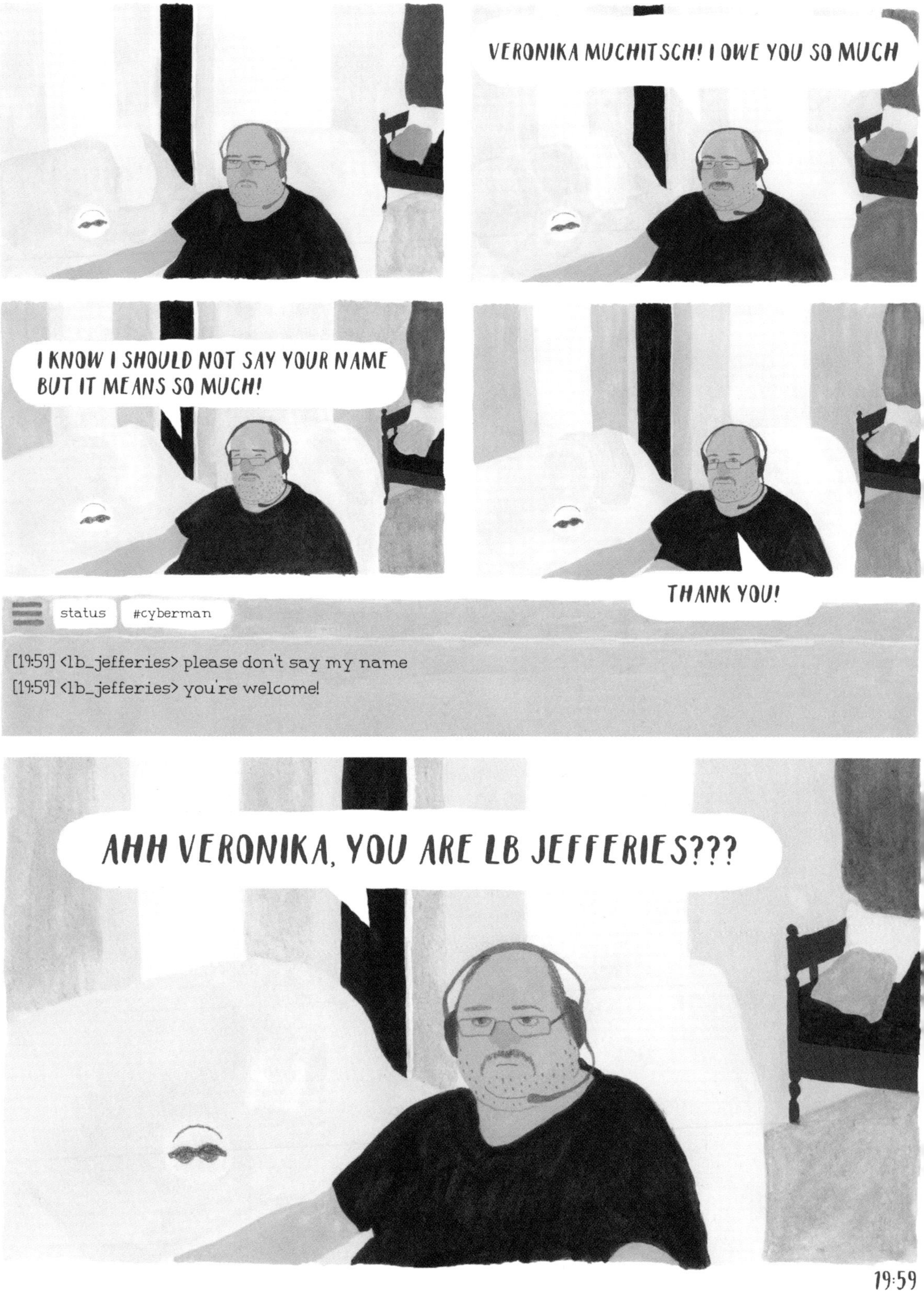
VERONIKA MUCHITSCH! I OWE YOU SO MUCH
I KNOW I SHOULD NOT SAY YOUR NAME BUT IT MEANS SO MUCH!
THANK YOU!
status
#cyberman
[19:59] <lb_jefferies> please don't say my name
[19:59] <lb_jefferies> you're welcome!
AHH VERONIKA, YOU ARE LB JEFFERIES???
19:59

19:59

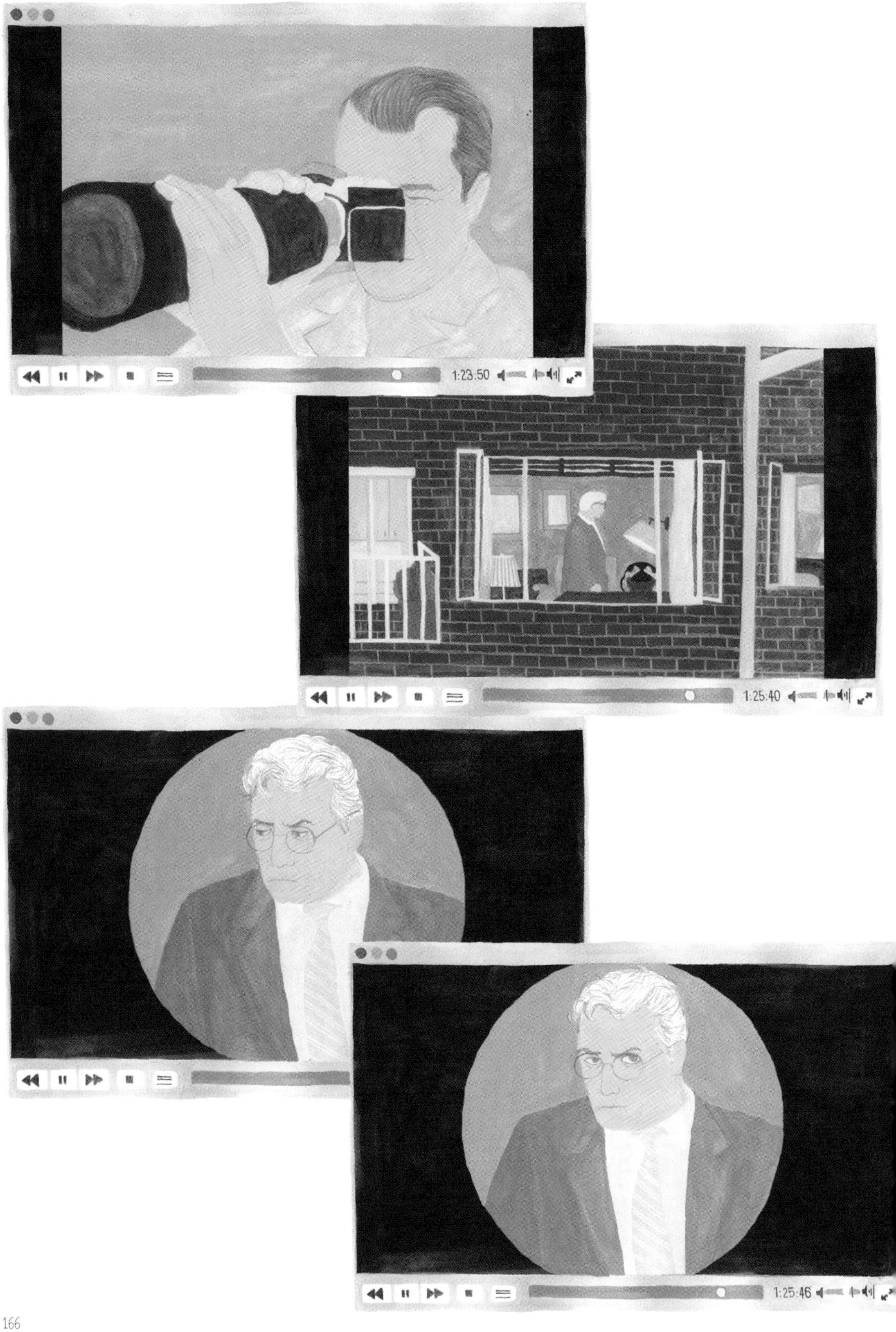
1:23:50
1:25:40
1:25:46

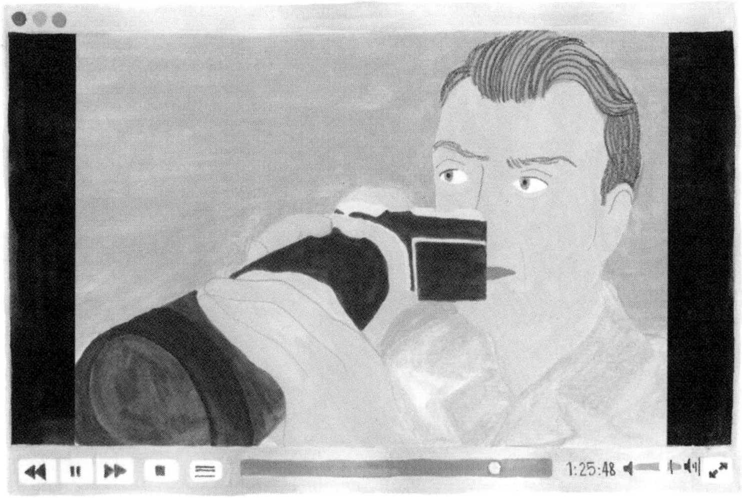
1:25:48

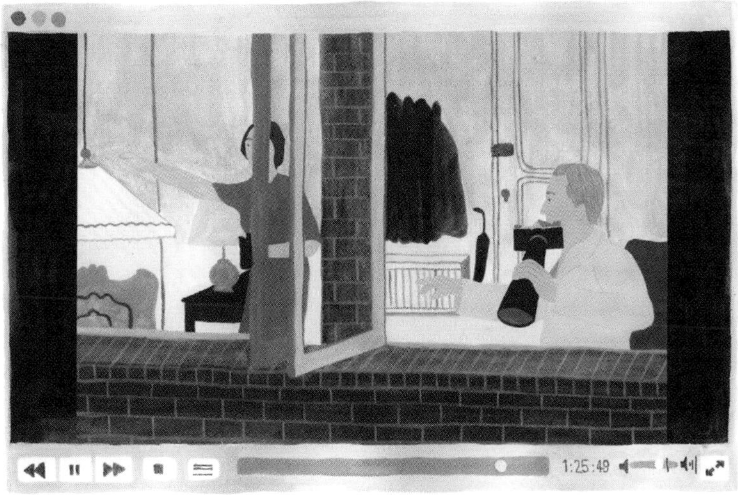
1:25:49

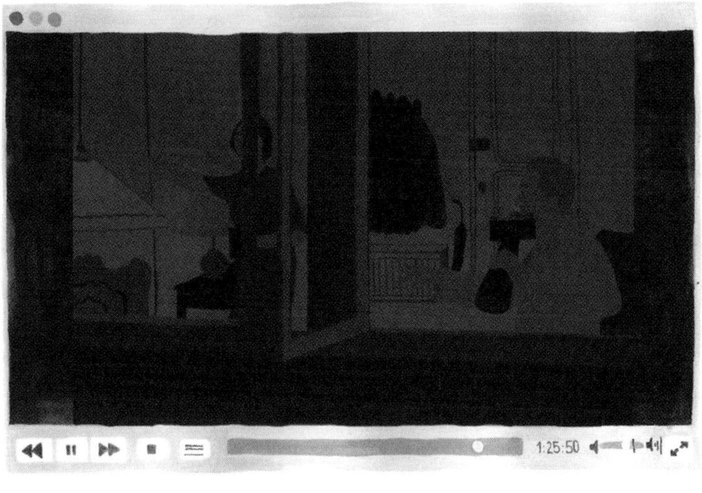
1:25:50

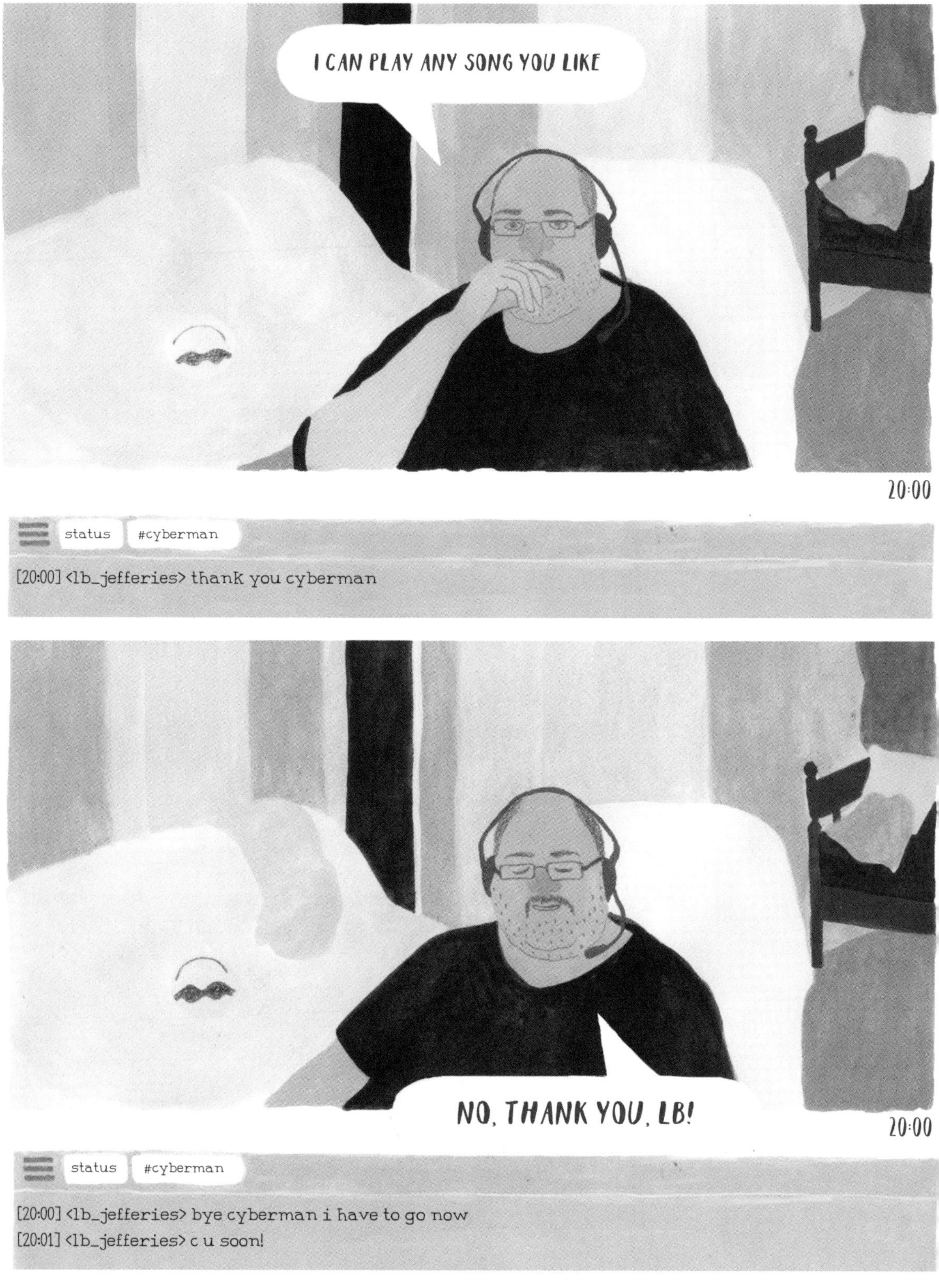
I CAN PLAY ANY SONG YOU LIKE
20:00
status
#cyberman
[20:00] <lb_jefferies> thank you cyberman
NO, THANK YOU, LB!
20:00
status
#cyberman
[20:00] <lb_jefferies> bye cyberman i have to go now
[20:01] <lb_jefferies> c u soon!

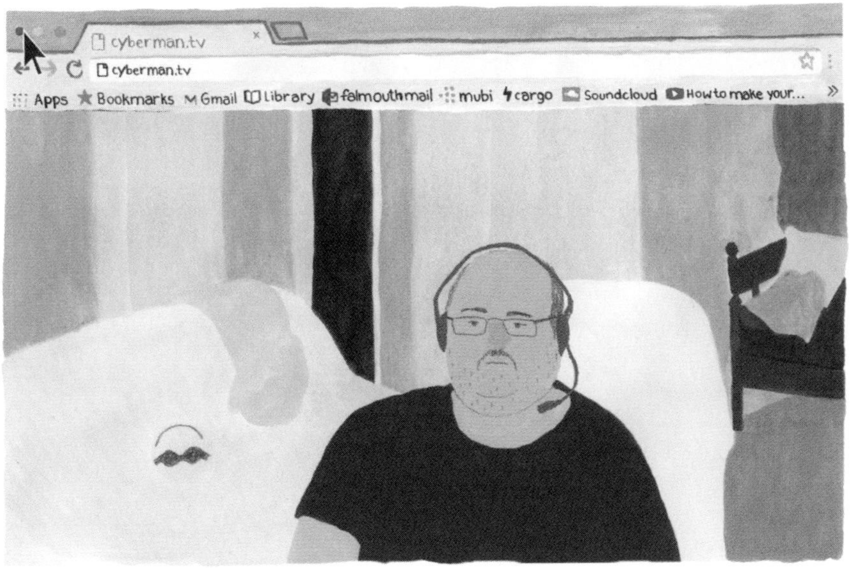
cyberman.tv
cyberman.tv
Apps
Bookmarks
Gmail
Library
falmouthmail
mubi
cargo
Soundcloud
How to make your...

16.03.2017

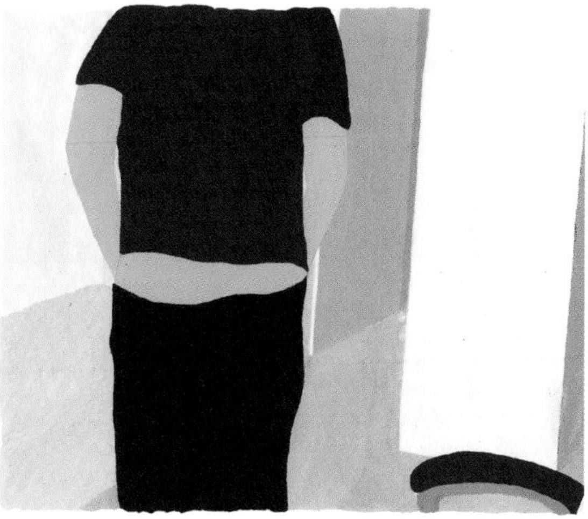

16:33

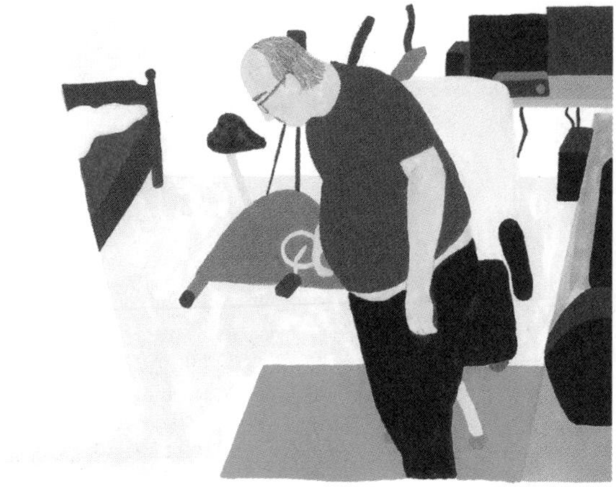

16:33

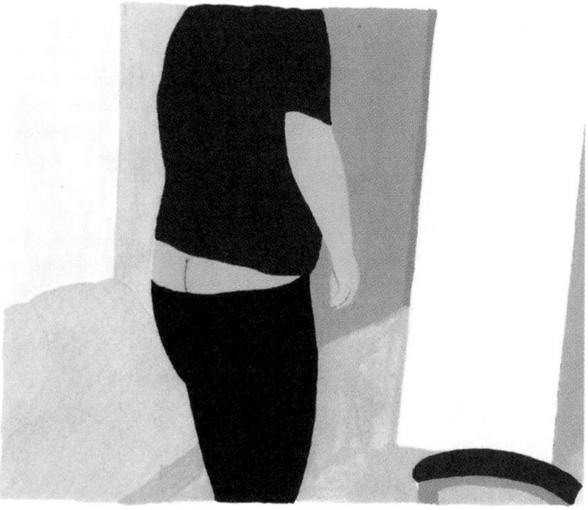

16:33

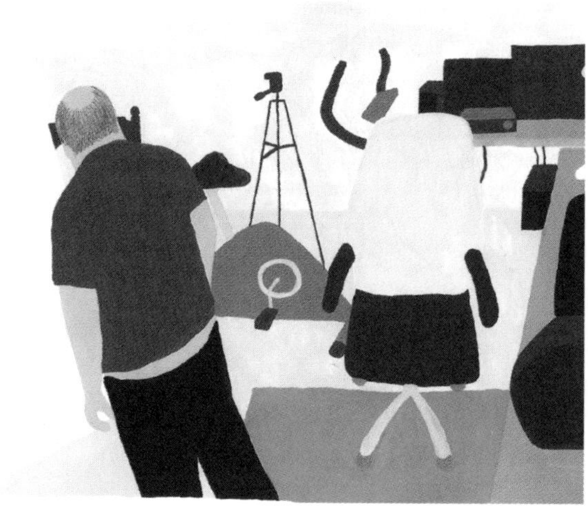

16:33

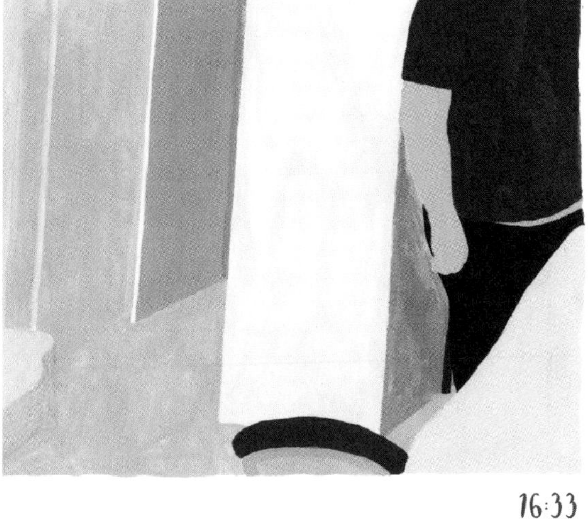

16:33

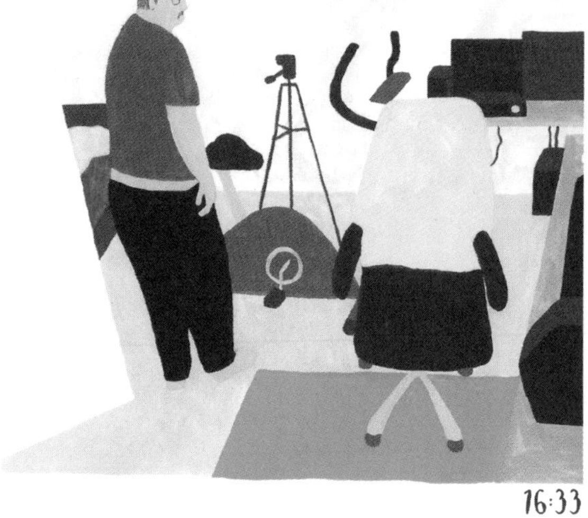

16:33

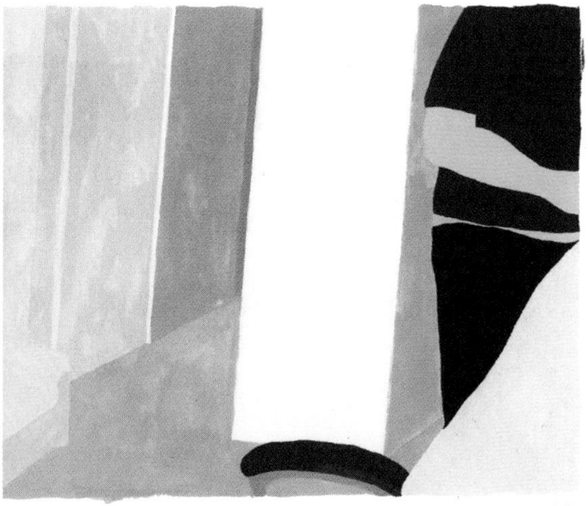
16:33

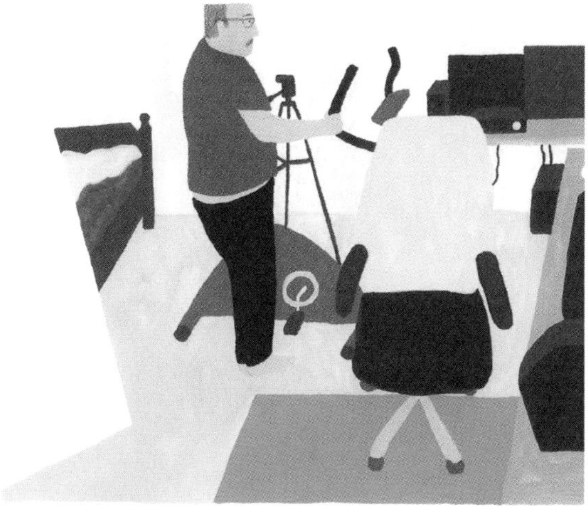
16:33

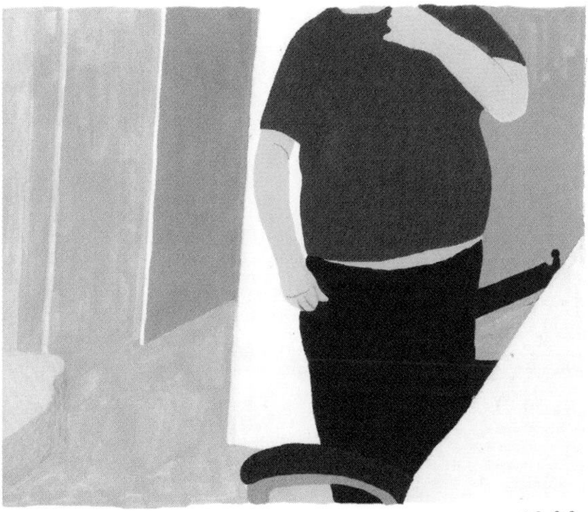
16:33

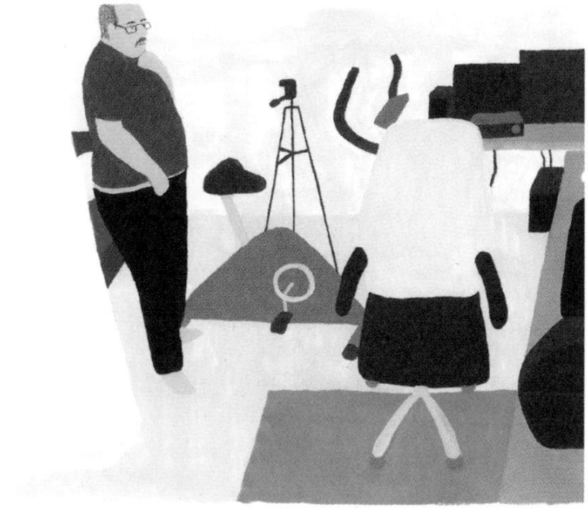
16:33

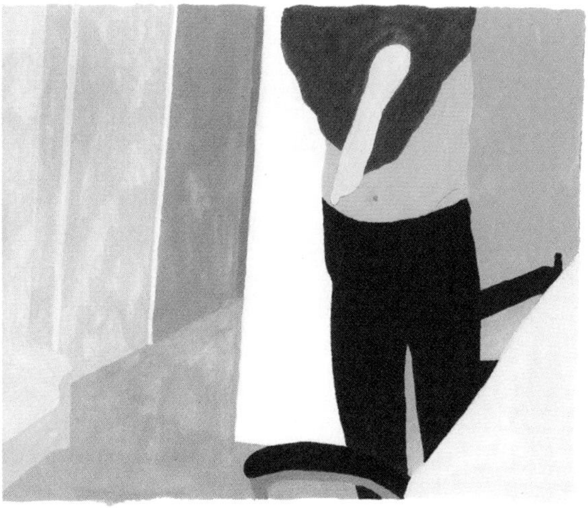
16:33

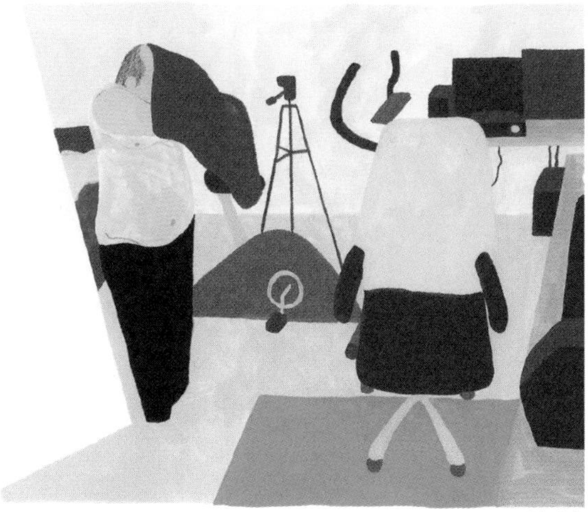
16:33

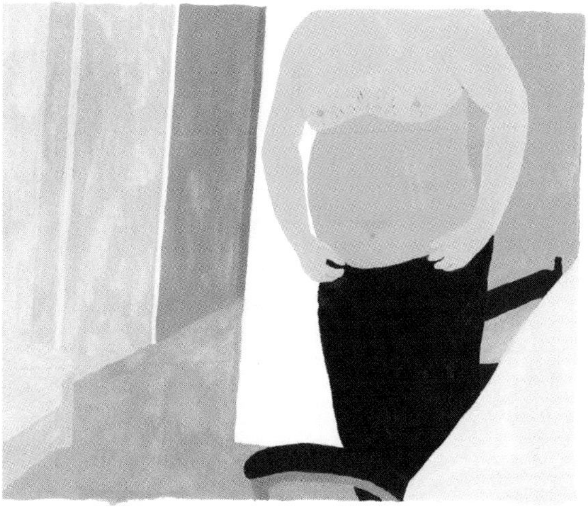

16:33

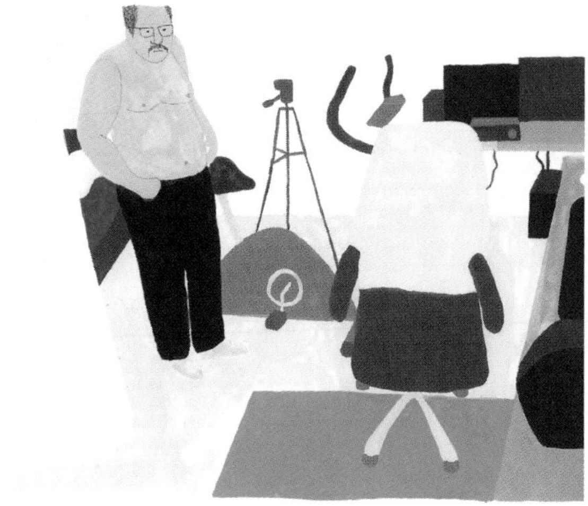

16:33

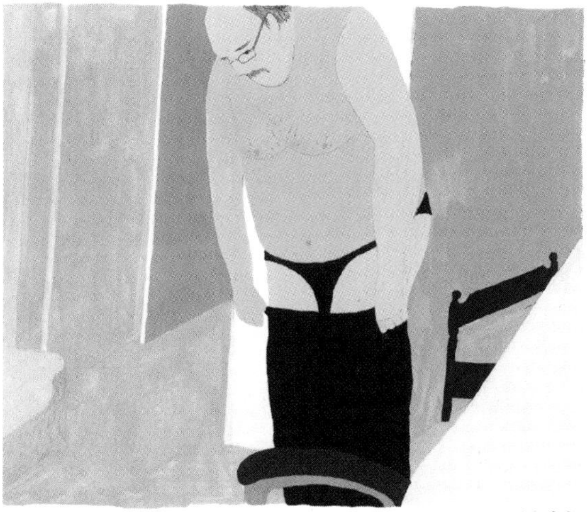

16:33

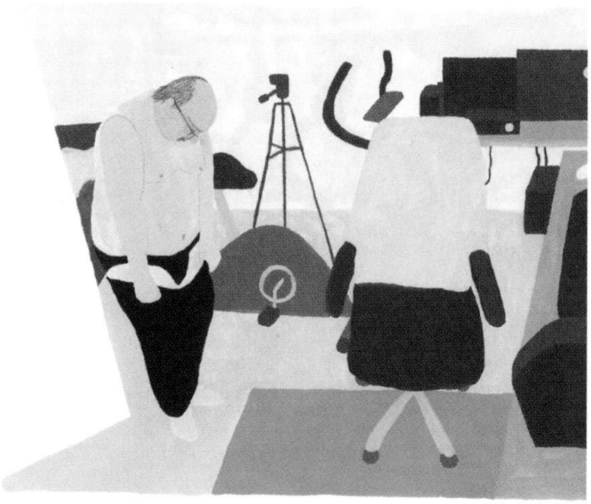

16:33

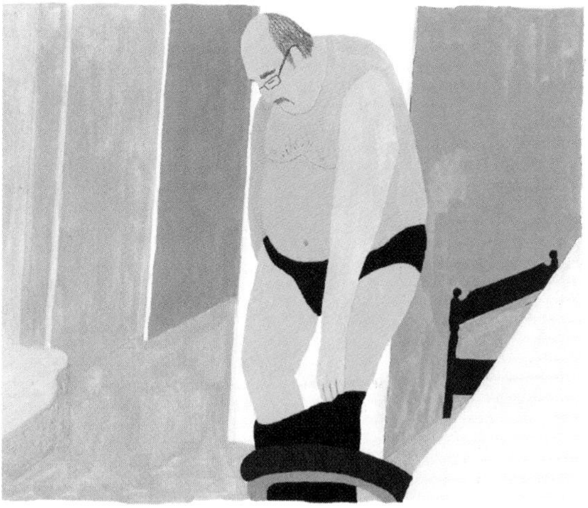

16:34

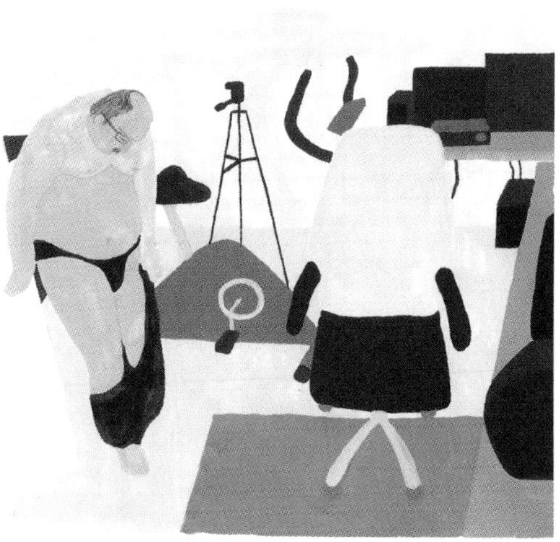

16:34

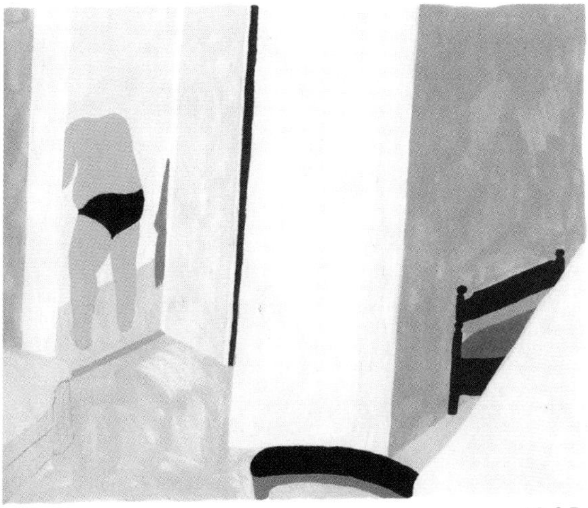

16:35

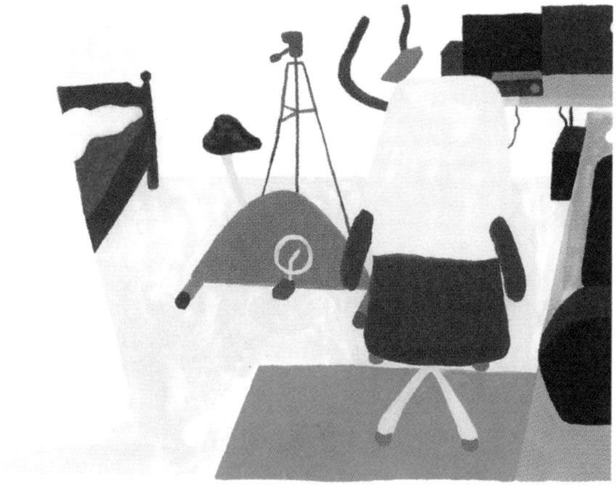

16:35

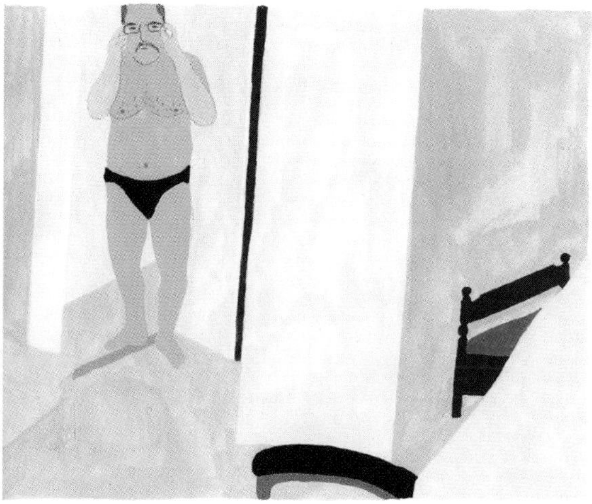

16:35

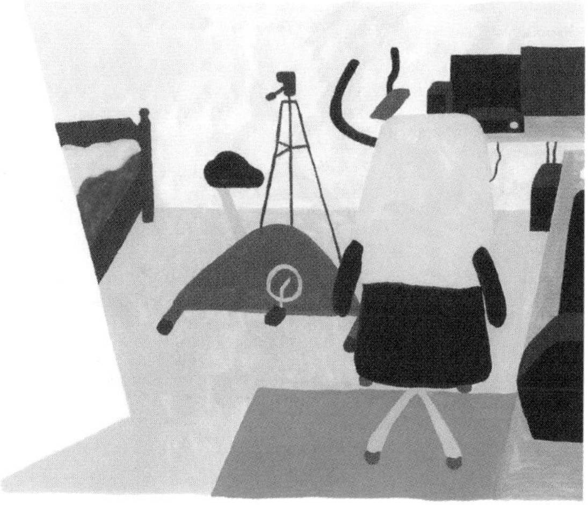

16:35

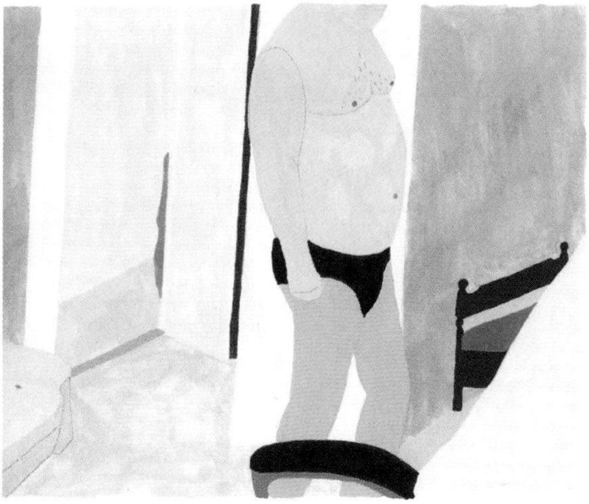

16:36

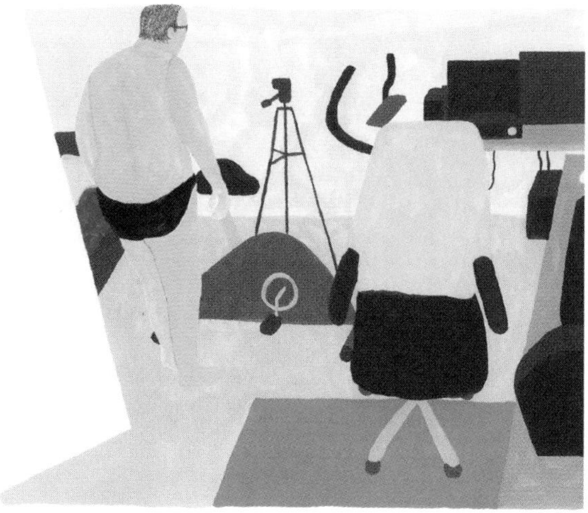

16:36

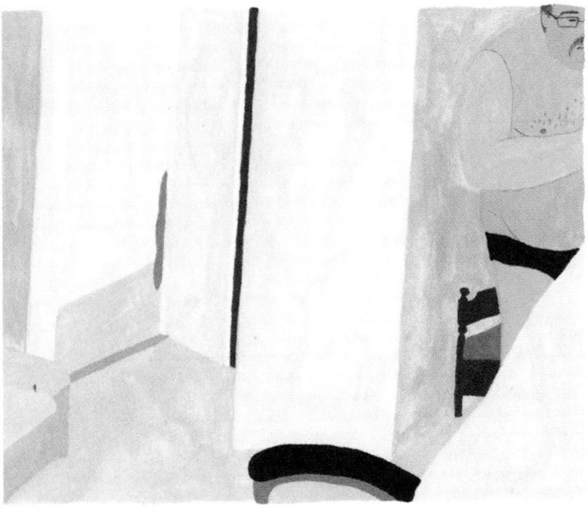

16:36

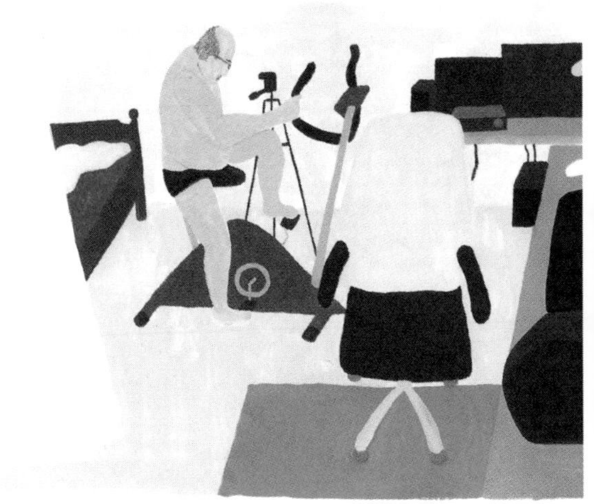

16:36

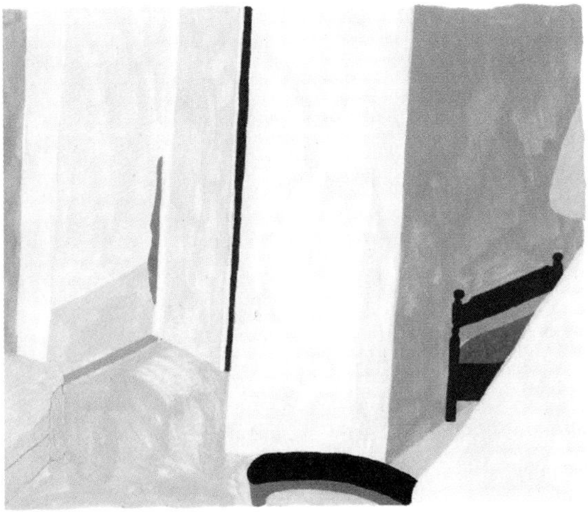

16:36

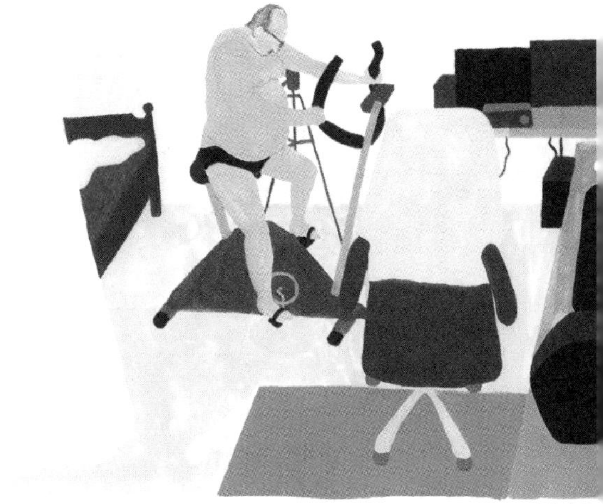

16:36

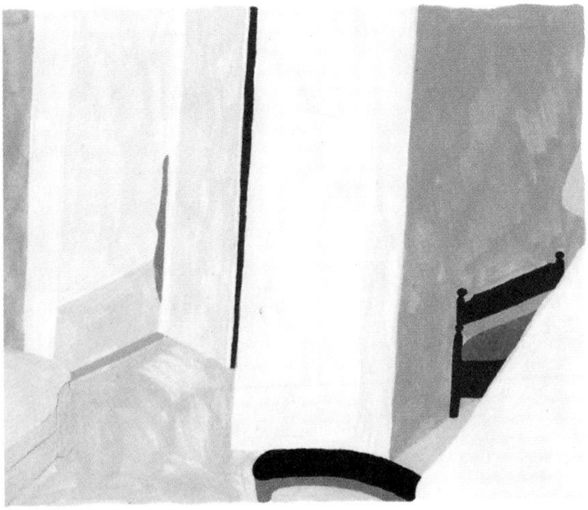

16:36

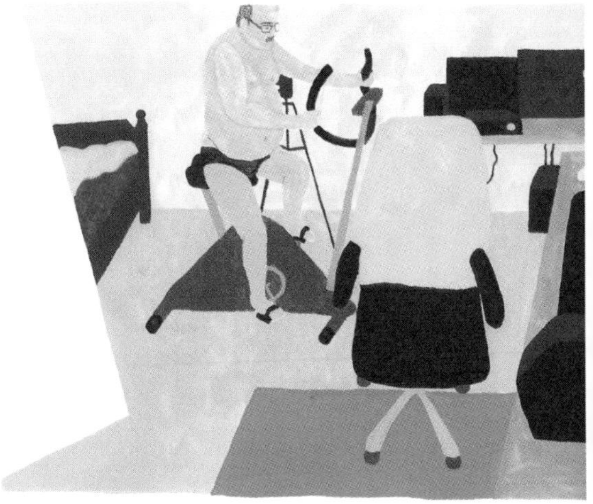

16:36

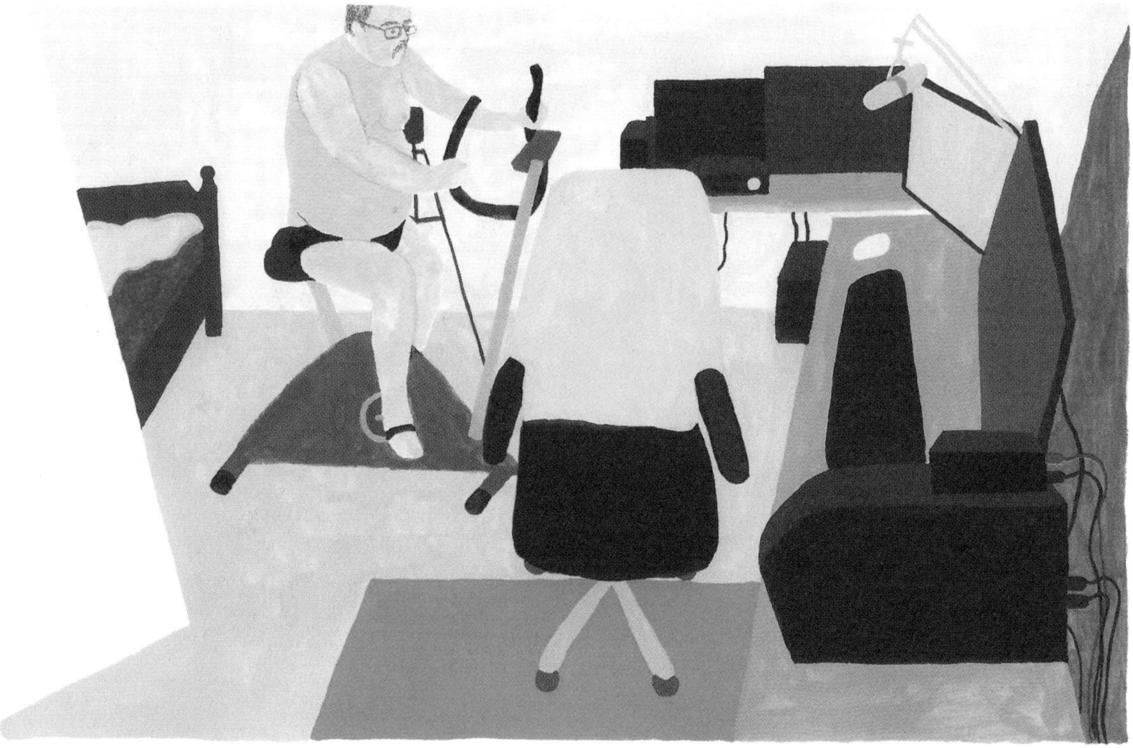

16:37

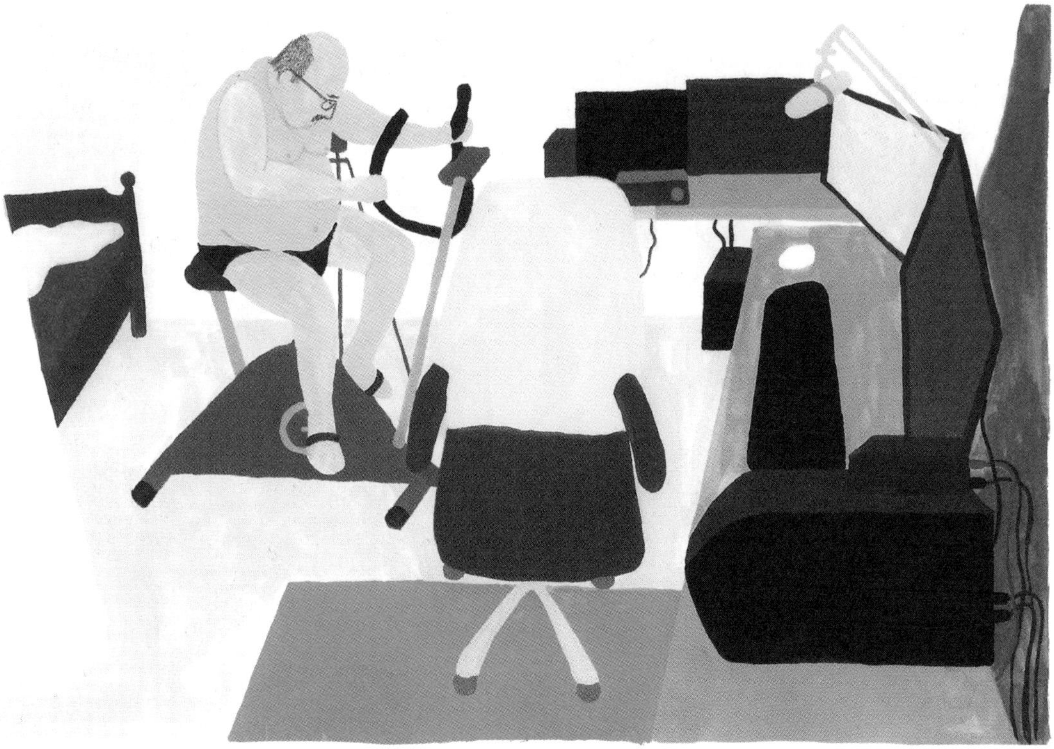

16:40

EPILOGUE

HI ARI!
HOW ARE YOU? I'M VERONIKA - I'M A PAINTER
AND COMIC BOOK ARTIST LIVING IN THE UK.
SORRY THIS LETTER IS PROBABLY VERY OUT OF
THE BLUE, BUT I WANTED TO (FINALLY) TELL YOU
THAT FOR THE PAST YEAR I'VE BEEN WORKING ON
A COMIC BOOK, WHICH IS ABOUT YOU AND YOUR
STREAM. I'VE SENT YOU THE VERY FIRST COPY OF
MY BOOK - I REALLY REALLY HOPE YOU LIKE IT!
I'VE LOVED WATCHING YOUR STREAM BECAUSE I
ADMIRE HOW HONEST YOU ARE AND THAT YOU
ARE NOT AFRAID OF SHARING YOUR LIFE WITH
OTHER PEOPLE. THANK YOU FOR THAT! SO FAR I
HAVE NOT SHOWN THE BOOK TO ANYONE, BUT
I'D LOVE TO SEND IT TO A PUBLISHER VERY SOON,
HOW DO YOU FEEL ABOUT THAT? I'D REALLY LIKE
TO HEAR YOUR OPINION ABOUT THE BOOK.
MAYBE YOU COULD SEND ME AN EMAIL AT:
L.B.JEFFERIES2@GMAIL.COM

I HOPE YOU ARE DOING WELL.
ALL MY VERY BEST WISHES TO YOU,

VERONIKA, AKA L.B. JEFFERIES

CYBERMAN

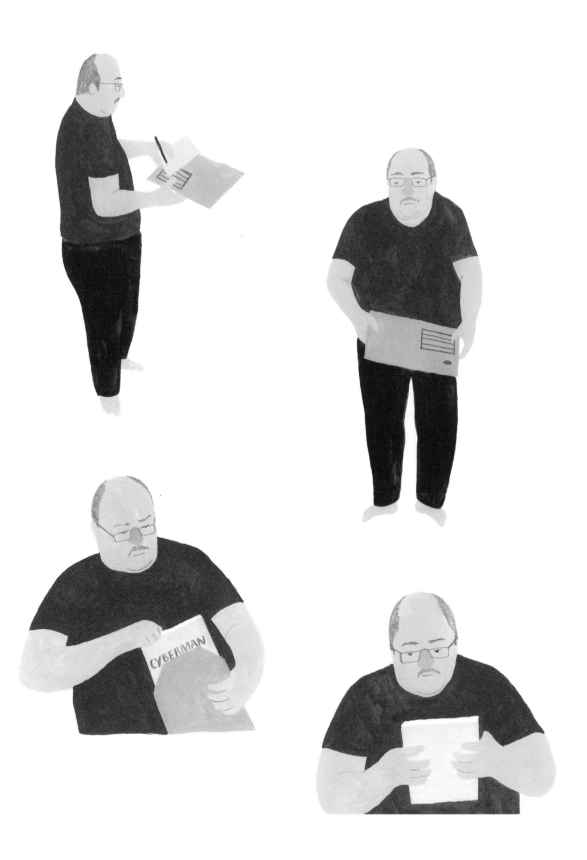

[20:25] <lb_jefferies>

My contributions to social media are fairly infrequent, and their main use is to promote my work. Despite this, whenever I create a post, it leaves me feeling anxious about how I'm being perceived. Admittedly, I mostly enjoy snooping around other people's accounts, being the invisible eye. This leads to an underlying feeling of guilt, which is dominated, however, by my obsessive curiosity.

When I first came across Ari's website, I was struck by his unfiltered presentation of self. It was unsettling to watch someone so closely and in real time, all the more because he gave a downbeat impression. Despite his deliberate self-exposure, I felt like a voyeur and it seemed intrusive to watch. Although irrational, I was petrified that somehow, by watching him, he and his viewers could see me too. Instead of following an impulse to close the window, I decided to examine these sentiments, to try and personalise this act of surveillance.

Coincidentally, I had just re-watched Alfred Hitchcock's *Rear Window* and I began to recognise parallels to my own experience. It was particularly the lead character, L B Jefferies, whom I identified with. In the movie, Jefferies, played by James Stewart, is bound to his apartment due to an injury and passes his time by watching his neighbours across the courtyard. He prefers not to engage with his own problems, but rather to focus his attention on the dramas that are unfolding in the miniature movie-screen-like windows across from his apartment. Just as the reader of *CYBERMAN* is limited to my documentation of events - as I get to decide what is important for my version of the story - *Rear Window* is also channelled through L B's perspective.

Stuart's character represents the traditional image of the voyeur, often depicted in popular culture as detective, spy, reporter or pervert. In Jefferies' case, his voyeuristic act is legitimised, as he eventually becomes the hero of the story by solving a murder. The role of the observer contains something quite powerful, especially from a female perspective, as voyeurism through film and literature is highly appropriated by men and often turns the woman into the object that is being spied on. It therefore felt satisfying and important to reclaim the patriarchal space of watching and to put it in reverse.

Rear Window expresses a sense for the isolation of people in our society. Everyone is confined to their own world; in *Rear Window* people are figuratively and literally separated from each other through window frames. The graphic novel is also a suitable medium to visualise this solitude, as the story is told through panels. Ari, for instance, is secluded within the frame of his live-stream as well as within my squared paintings, floating on the page. At the same time, I sit alone, watching and documenting him through the frame of my computer screen.

From his point of solitude, Jefferies finds himself identifying with the neighbours he's watching, relating their stories to his own life and troubles. It is the lethargy and loneliness that Ari radiates in which I saw myself reflected. However intrusive it might feel to observe a stranger so intimately, there is something soothing about being able to tune in and out of someone's life at any given time - and I found comfort, when lying awake unable to sleep in the middle of the night, through checking on what Cyberman was doing in that moment. This might be the most seductive attribute of social media, that we have a portal through which we are constantly connected.

To me painting is an affectionate process. I spent hours and hours hovering over my desk, stroking the paper with my brush until Ari's face would appear. As unfortunately is very common in anonymous online forums, Ari was exposed to a lot of cyber-bullying. Some of the conversations I witnessed were really quite bleak. This made me want to put as much warmth into the book as I could, to create a product of 'anti-trolling'.

After anonymously documenting Ari for so long, it was a particularly nerve-wracking moment when I sent him the first handmade draft of *CYBERMAN*. However, I was over the moon when I got a most enthusiastic response from him. We stayed email friends and I updated him regularly regarding the book's progress. About a year later he emailed me with the very sad news that he'd been diagnosed with cancer and had to have an operation. He kept streaming for a while, until he grew very quiet. I learned of his passing a few months after he died in 2019. It's sad that he will never see the book in its entirety, but I like to look at it as a tribute to his life.

I truly miss visiting Ari on his stream, getting to see him. Somehow, by finishing this book and by painting him almost every day, it felt like my time with him was extended. There's a moment when a project has to be concluded, even if it's very hard for me to put this one down. Not least because there has never been anything that I love to draw and paint as much as I do Cyberman.

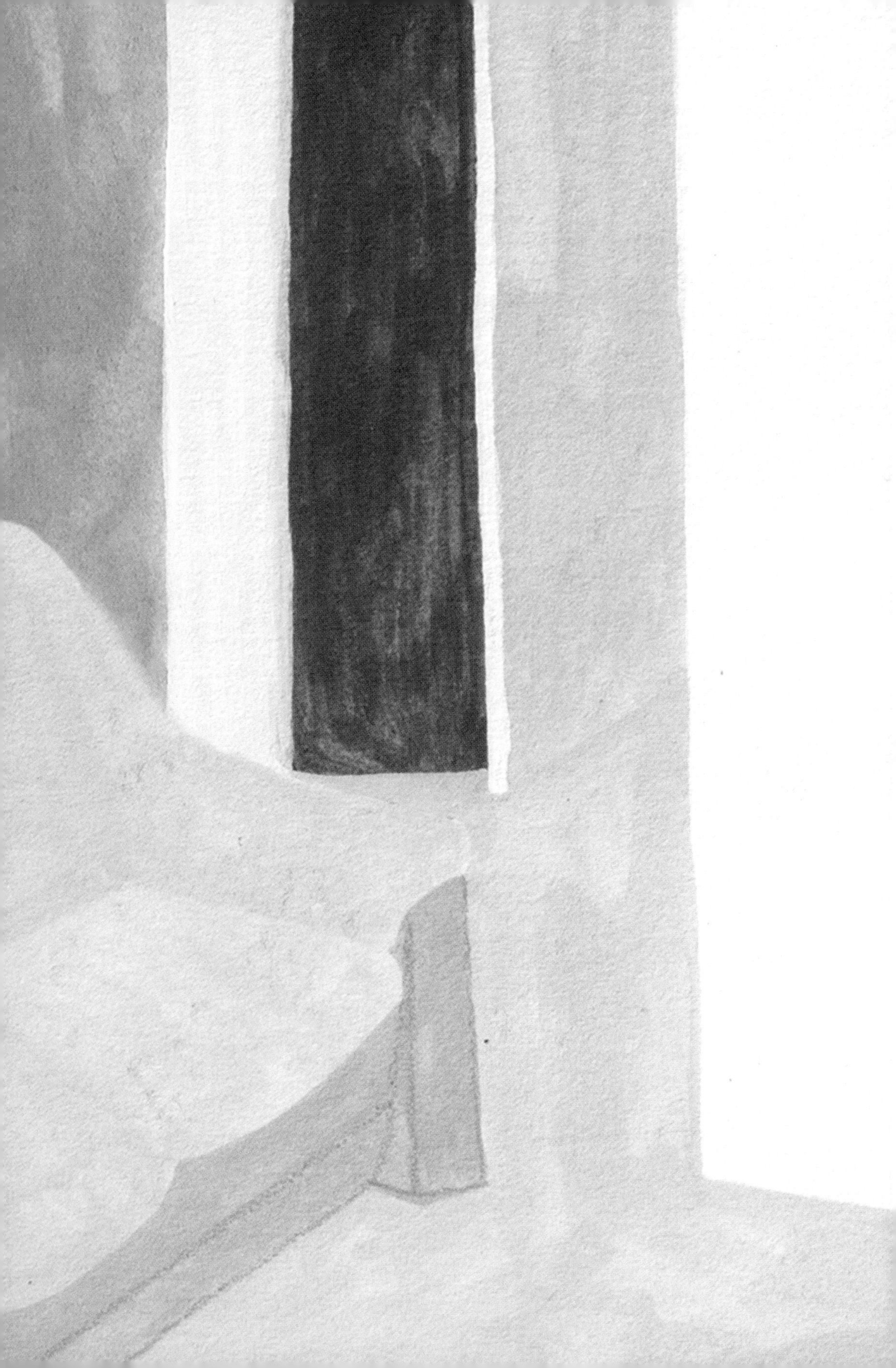

ACKNOWLEDGEMENTS

PAGE 42-43:

IN THE END
WORDS AND MUSIC BY ROB BOURDON, BRAD
DELSON, JOE HAHN, MIKE SHINODA AND
CHARLES BENNINGTON
COPYRIGHT © 2000 UNIVERSAL MUSIC - Z SONGS,
ROB BOURDON MUSIC, NONDISCLOSURE
AGREEMENT MUSIC,
BIG BAD MR. HAHN MUSIC, KENJI KOBAYASHI
MUSIC AND UNIVERSAL MUSIC - Z TUNES LLC
ALL RIGHTS ADMINISTERED BY CONCORD MUSIC
PUBLISHING
INTERNATIONAL COPYRIGHT SECURED
ALL RIGHTS RESERVED
REPRINTED BY PERMISSION OF HAL LEONARD
EUROPE LTD

HTTPS://WWW.YOUTUBE.COM/WATCH?V=EVTX-
PUF4OZ4&AB_CHANNEL=LINKINPARK

PAGE 134-137:

BORN TO MAKE YOU HAPPY
WORDS AND MUSIC BY KRISTIAN LUNDIN AND
ANDREAS CARLSSON
COPYRIGHT © 1999 GV MARATONE
ALL RIGHTS ADMINISTERED BY KOBALT MUSIC
GROUP LTD.
INTERNATIONAL COPYRIGHT SECURED
ALL RIGHTS RESERVED
REPRINTED BY PERMISSION OF HAL LEONARD
EUROPE LTD.

HTTPS://WWW.YOUTUBE.COM/WATCH?V=YY-
5CKX4JBKQ&AB_CHANNEL=BRITNEYSPEARSVEVO

PAGE 138-155:

SUBCONSCIOUS PROGRAMMING
QUOTES WRITTEN BY NANICE ELLIS
BASED ON HER WORK
"ARE WE LIVING IN A SIMULATED REALITY?"
COPYRIGHT © NANICE ELLIS 2019.
ALL RIGHTS RESERVED / WWW.NANICE.COM

HTTPS://WWW.YOUTUBE.COM/WATCH?-
V=PW9E8UPJ6RM&T=170S&AB_CHANNEL=HIG-
HERSELF

PAGE 160-161:

AIN'T NO MOUNTAIN HIGH ENOUGH
WORDS AND MUSIC BY NICKOLAS ASHFORD AND
VALERIE SIMPSON
COPYRIGHT © 1967 JOBETE MUSIC CO., INC.
COPYRIGHT RENEWED
ALL RIGHTS ADMINISTERED BY SONY MUSIC
PUBLISHING (US) LLC, 424 CHURCH STREET,
SUITE 1200, NASHVILLE, TN 37219
INTERNATIONAL COPYRIGHT SECURED
ALL RIGHTS RESERVED
REPRINTED BY PERMISSION OF HAL LEONARD
EUROPE LTD.

HTTPS://WWW.YOUTUBE.COM/WATCH?V=IC-
5PLOXIMJW&AB_CHANNEL=DOCREWDYSOUL

PAGES 16-21, 166-167:

IMAGES BASED ON A VIEWING OF REAR WINDOW,
DIRECTED BY ALFRED HITCHCOCK. COPYRIGHT ©
PARAMOUNT PICTURES, 1954.

EVERY EFFORT HAS BEEN MADE TO OBTAIN THE
NECESSARY PERMISSIONS FOR USE OF COPYRIGHT
MATERIAL. IF ANY OMISSION HAS BEEN MADE,
DO CONTACT US WITH FURTHER INFORMATION:
FUTURE EDITIONS WILL INCLUDE APPROPRIATE
ACKNOWLEDGEMENT.

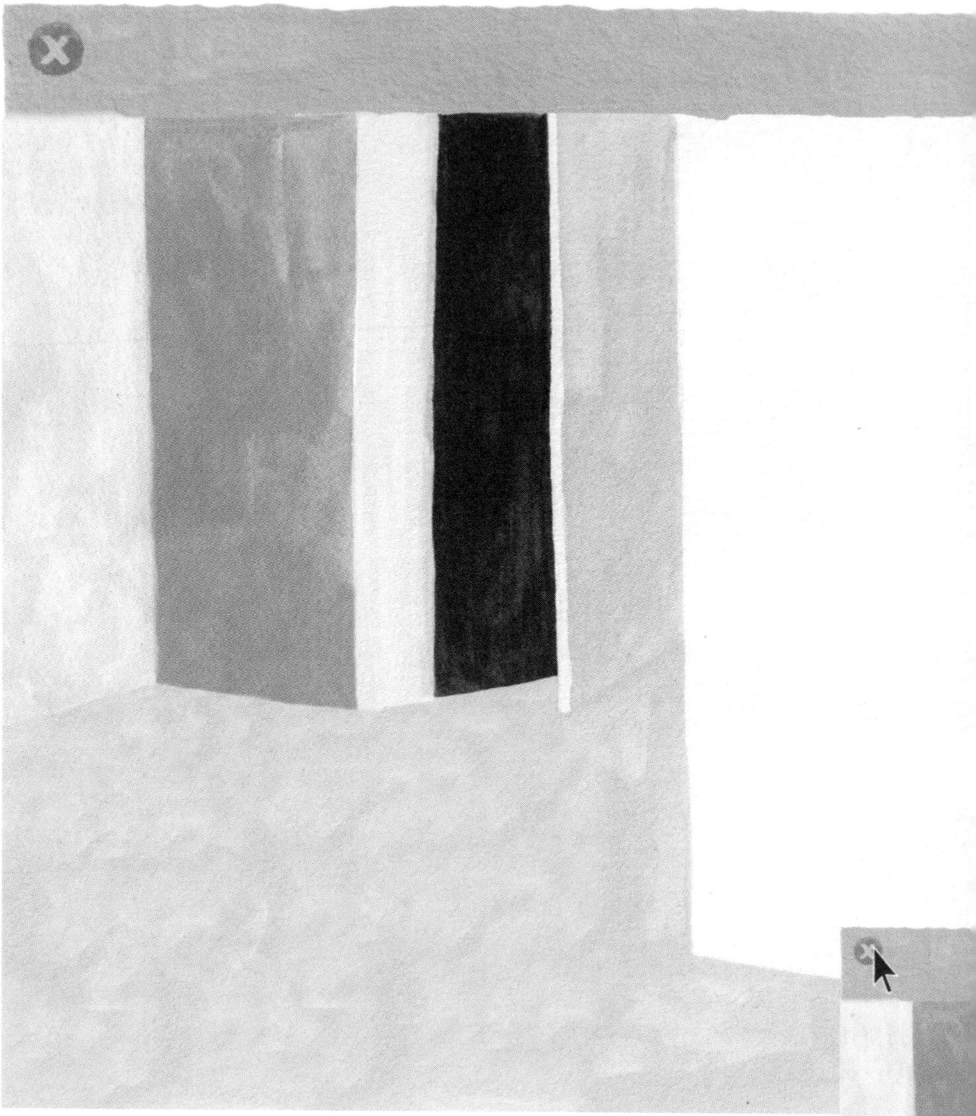

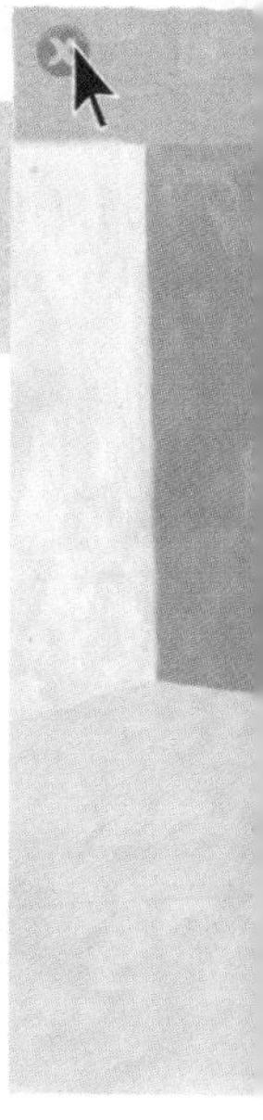

THIS BOOK IS DEDICATED TO ARI KIVIKANGAS
1965 - 2019

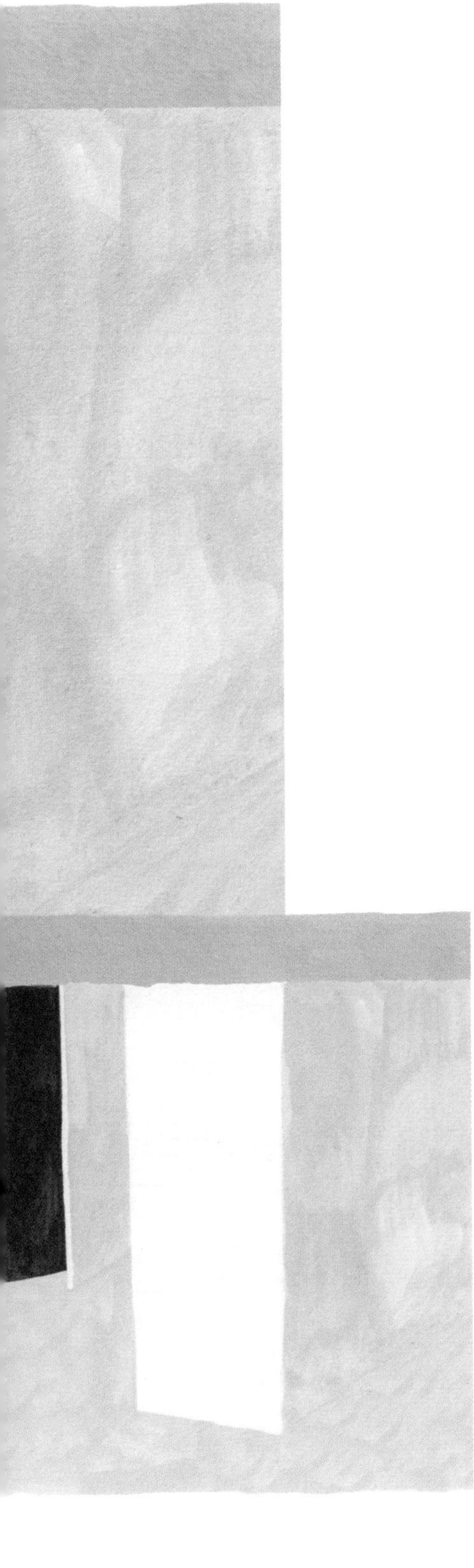

THANKS TO CHARLIE FAIRBAIRN,
IRENE VIDAL CAL AND LEE MCINTYRE AT
RUBICUND STUDIOS, CORINNE PEARLMAN
AND VICKI HEATH-SILK AT MYRIAD
EDITIONS, STEVE BRAUND, CATRIN MORGAN,
MATT OSMOND AND EVERYONE ON MA
AUTHORIAL ILLUSTRATION IN FALMOUTH,
MAREI SCHWEIZER, POPPY ROBINSON,
CHARLIE MURPHY, JOSH TURNER,
RYAN CLEAVE, ALICE LAWRENCE, SARAH
PODBELSEK, ASHLEY POTTER, NANICE ALICE
AND HAL LEONARD. THANKS, TOO, TO THE
JUDGES OF MYRIAD'S FIRST GRAPHIC NOVEL
COMPETITION 2020: ZOE ADJONYOH, SACHA
CRADDOCK, CORINNE PEARLMAN, JULIE TAIT
AND IAN WILLIAMS, AND TO THE LAKES
INTERNATIONAL COMIC ART FESTIVAL.

SPECIAL THANKS TO MY FAMILY,
MICHAELA, WOLFGANG, AND KATHARINA.

MOST OF ALL THANKS TO ARI KIVIKANGAS
FOR GENEROUSLY LETTING ME, AND THE
REST OF THE WORLD-WIDE-WEB, INTO HIS
LIFE. MAY THERE BE A QUANTUM COMPUTER
INVENTED TO MAKE A DATABASE FROM
HIS BRAIN.

PHOTO: CHARLIE FAIRBAIRN

VERONIKA MUCHITSCH WAS BORN IN
GRAZ, AUSTRIA, AND NOW LIVES IN
FALMOUTH, CORNWALL.
SHE RECEIVED AN MA IN AUTHORIAL
ILLUSTRATION WITH DISTINCTION AT
FALMOUTH UNIVERSITY IN 2017. HER
STORIES HAVE BEEN PUBLISHED BY
FANTAGRAPHICS IN THE ANTHOLOGY
NOW AND SHE WAS WINNER OF THE
2017 ATLANTIC PRESS GRAPHIC
LITERATURE PRIZE.

WITH AN INTEREST IN OBSERVING
SOLITUDE AND THE WAY WE INHABIT
AND EXPERIENCE THE WORLD, HER
COMICS ARE A DECLARATION OF LOVE
TO PEOPLE WHO CREATE THEIR OWN
WORLDS IN THE DIGITAL AGE.

This site can't be reached

Check if there is a typo in cyberman.tv.

DNS_PROBE_FINISHED_NXDOMAIN

Reload

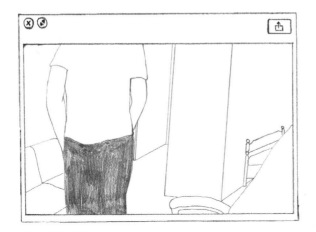

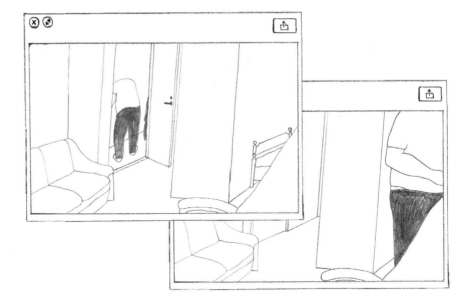